Truisms

Other Books by Alexander Theroux

NOVELS
Three Wogs
Darconville's Cat
An Adultery
Laura Warholic; or, The Sexual Intellectual

FABLES
The Schinocephalic Waif
The Great Wheadle Tragedy
Master Snickup's Cloak

SHORT FICTION
Early Stories
Fables
Later Stories

POETRY
The Lollipop Trollops and Other Poems
Collected Poems

NONFICTION
The Primary Colors
The Secondary Colors
The Enigma of Al Capp
The Strange Case of Edward Gorey
Estonia: A Ramble Through the Periphery
The Grammar of Rock: Art and Artlessness in 20th Century Pop Lyrics
Einstein's Beets: An Examination of Food Phobias

Alexander Theroux

§

Truisms

TOUGH POETS PRESS
ARLINGTON, MASSACHUSETTS

Copyright © 2022 by Alexander Theroux.

Cover artwork by Edward Sorel.

ISBN 979-8-218-04948-5

Tough Poets Press
Arlington, Massachusetts 02476
U.S.A.

www.toughpoets.com

For Sarah
and our loving poppets
Shenandoah and Shiloh

"Truth is the daughter of inevitability."
—St. Theodulus of Grammont (c. 840)

"No event is truly deathless unless its monument be built in rhyme."
—Louise Saunders, *The Knave of Hearts*

"*Veritas est adaequatio rei et intellectus.*"
—St. Thomas Aquinas

"I will not live out of me
I will not see with others' eyes
My good is good, my evil ill
I would be free—I cannot be
While I take things as others please to rate them.
I dare attempt to lay out my own road
That which myself delights in shall be Good
That which I do not want—indifferent,
That which I hate is Bad. That's flat
Henceforth, please God, forever I forego
The yoke of men's opinions."
—Ralph Waldo Emerson

"My brethren, you have deserved it."
—Fr. Paneloux in Albert Camus' *The Plague*

Prologue

"It is a truth universally acknowledged . . ." So begins the famous opening of Jane Austen's novel *Pride and Prejudice*. We are, most of us, aware of, familiar with, often quote, and are occasionally beguiled by truths universally acknowledged. Still, no one could deny that many such truths, while widely accepted —agreed on, incontestably verifiable, and of course familiar— seem flat to us simply due to the fact that the time-tested ones are either too obvious or for ages have been too often tiresomely repeated, so made dull to the ear by dint of long acquaintance. The field of truisms is white for the harvest. New truths, furthermore, beg for the certitude of axioms—principles, dicta, maxims—and while it may seem redundant to state that inevitabilities are unavoidable, any astute observer, especially one with the archival drive of a memorialist, feels the need to mine them for their universal values, seeking pithily to record them and with creative insight put them into print. An apothegm is a gnome lurking in many an enchanted garden. There may be a shock of recognition upon suddenly seeing one or hearing its assertive squeak, when the mind, actuated, as Edmund Spenser so well put it, "stoppéd is with thought's astonishment."

Overall, we tend to react to truisms in the very same way that old, familiar scenes comfort us and in the manner that warm memories beckon. A solid truth, no matter how contrary or controversial, slots in our head and then drops with a clunk like the slug of machine chocolate falling into a waiting tray. A bold truth can please us but just as often may upset, shock, hurt, or even threaten us in the manner stereotypes irk or seem to undermine. A truism can also often seem subjective, arbitrary, biased, peculiar, too obvious, too odd, sometimes profound, and, in many instances, politically incorrect. One's characteristic reaction recapitulates what Alexander Pope stated in his "Essay on Criticism:" "True wit is nature to advantage dress'd/What oft was thought but ne'er so well express'd."

Stereotypes and clichés, widely held but fixed and oversimplified images or ideas of a particular type of person or thing, do not exist in a vacuum. How cruelly insensitive it is nowadays, never mind unfashionable—offensive, démodé, disrespectful, and culturally incorrect—to point out that the Irish in fact *do* like to drink, that Greeks *do* love to open restaurants, that the Chinese almost compulsively *do* start up laundries, and that Russians— even the most common of them—continuously maintain a fanatical love for and interest in playing chess and reading poetry. It is well-trod ground, those timeless paths that best lead the way. Clichés, in short, tend to be true. Do not the lyrical Welsh like to sing, Austrians love to ski, Germans have an extravagant passion for beer and wursts and exactitude? While such observations, at least in terms of any legitimate final summation or definition, may seem to many people simplistically outrageous because they state receivable facts that are also provably ungainsayable—beyond argument, obvious—old axioms are generally just that, venerable, time-tested verities tending to the bromidic, solemn, sometimes ironic, often sagaciously repeated by sententious or ministerial types, the kind of aphorisms or epigrams that can be traced back to the apophthegmata of such early thinkers as Xenophon, Aristotle, and Diogenes Laertes, and, in this young country of ours, go as far back as—and, indeed, in many ways define—those truisms we come across in those old, biscuity American chapbooks, early tracts, and grade school alphabet books from the 18th century, of the Benjamin Franklin sort. Every country, each nation, a bolus of types, provides punch lines of truisms. To the brightly alert, to the insightful, truisms constantly beckon us and are as modern as the 21st-century. During the course any given day, I find them unavoidable, beckoning truths, as common as pig tracks in wet weather.

"It is a trite but true observation, that examples work more forcibly on the mind than precepts," writes Henry Fielding at the beginning of his wonderful novel, *Joseph Andrews*. And I can say I fondly hope that the compilation of truisms that follow here reach to a definition of both, examples and precepts.

Truisms to the constant and perspicacious reader can be found like shells along any given strand: "Dead trees love the fire" (Thoreau); "When one teaches, two learn" (Robert Heinlein); "Choose to be rich by making your wants few" (Emerson); "An idea that is not dangerous is unworthy of being called an idea at all" (Oscar Wilde); "A line is a dot that went for a walk" (Paul Klee). Truisms are not necessarily confined to the gnomic writer, although he is chiefly the maker of them. To a degree, truisms approximate in a minor and secular way those utterances and oracular remarks that scholars often link to and associate with those ancient writings which are called "logion." A logion—a particular saying of a religious leader made traditional—was generally written down in a devotional way, more often than not by one of his or her followers. Rhetorically, a truism or gnome tends to run along the lines of the succinct, the compact, the concise, the epigrammatical. The *logia* of Jesus Christ—truths, phrases, maxims attributed to him that were not necessarily recorded in the Bible—actually *preceded* the written Gospels and in their simple and fierce directives, strict passionate condensation and concision, reveal the rude beauty of Our Savior's universal message, unadorned and un-fussified by way of glosses or wobbly interpretation. (Still, strangely, sadly, not a single one of the Aramaic sayings of Jesus has survived.) Logia, passionately recorded, were devotedly used by the earliest Christian congregations before they possessed the Gospels, and, as scholar Guy Davenport has pointed out, are always "aphoristic, self-contained, and infinitely quotable." One can scarcely discern in them the metaphysics and eschatology that, in a larger way, the church now calls theology. By definition, they dispense with narrative—precede it, arguably, in fact, supersede it. You must intuit your own narrative. Sometimes a truism or axiom is simply an interesting fact, a pigeon for a moment becoming a raptor.

    I must say that, in one form or another, truisms in their uniqueness have been the delight of many writers, virtually constituting a genre. Charles Baudelaire's loved the punch of the gnomic, the tidiness of the philosophical squib. His "*Fusées*" (Rockets) or "Squibs," written in 1867, were published posthumously in 1887. You find them in *The Brussels Journal* and *Mon coeur mis à nu*. A squib is a small explosive device used in a wide range of industries, from special effects to military applications and resemble a tiny stick of dynamite both in appearance and construction, although having considerably less explosive power. Some fierce examples are his *"Dieu est le seul être qui, pour régner, n'ait même pas besoin d'exister."* (God is the only being who need not even exist in order to reign) and *"Ce qui est créé par l'esprit est plus vivant que la matière."* (Whatever is created by the spirit is more alive than matter). In a perverse, if thought-provoking way, Baudelaire found "matter" (nature) vile and "evil" (although clearly unpleasant to have to hear) female.

Marcel Proust enjoyed compact thought and is full of such laconic, pithy, succinct, elliptical, but always trenchant comments. So too with Mark Twain ("Few things are harder to put up with than the annoyance of a good example." "As to the adjective: when in doubt, strike it out." "A home without a cat—and a well-fed, well-petted and properly revered cat—may be a perfect home, perhaps, but how can it prove title?" "Some people bring joy wherever they go, some people when*ever* they go.") It is also the case with Joseph Conrad ("A caricature is putting the face of a joke on the body of a truth." "Words, as is well known, are the great foes of reality," and so on and so forth). Rudyard Kipling generously offered several to an editor in 1898—"Some Hints on Schoolboy Etiquette"—by way of a contribution to a text: "Never shirk a master out of bounds. Pass him with an abstracted eye, and at the same time pull out a letter and study it earnestly. He may think it is a commission for someone else." "If you have any doubts about a Latin quantity, cough. In three cases out of five, this will save you being asked to 'say it again.'" "When pursued by the native farmer, always take to the nearest ploughed land. Men stick in furrows that boys can run over."

Truisms, like aphorisms, flirt with but avoid aching banalities. They were best brought to perfection by the French of former centuries, notably by wits such as Voltaire, François La Rochefoucauld, and Pascal in his *Pensées* (1670), masters of a kind of style that, located in the most stringent economy of expression and syntactical control, formulates a wide-ranging profundity of thought. Confucius's "Analects," a compilation of conversations and discussions between the Master and 22 disciples, are gnomic, as is "The Little Red Book," or, to give its full title, *Quotations from Chairman Mao Zedong*, which contains 267 aphorisms from the Communist Chinese leader, covering subjects such as class struggle, "mistaken ideas," and the "mass line," a key tenet of Mao's, including the bone-chilling remark, "Political power grows out of the barrel of a gun." In this group surely must be numbered the satirist Georg Lichtenberg, Oscar Wilde, the Viennese satirist Karl Kraus, Ambrose Bierce, he of *The Devil's Dictionary*, the Romanian philosopher and essayist Emil Cioran, novelist and philosopher Italo Calvino, along with the rather less well-known, strange satirist Multatuli (born Eduard Douwes Dekker), arguably Holland's greatest 19th-century writer and thinker held to be the father of contemporary Dutch literature, most vividly so in his *Ideën* (1862 to 1877) and collections of fables, parables, anecdotes, and, of course, aphorisms.

The strange, self-repudiating Portuguese poet and fabulist Fernando Pessoa in his *The Book of Disquiet* may in a very real sense be described as being a collector of aphorisms. I would also list here the aphorisms—the narrative tricks—of the late mulatto orphan, Joaquim Maria Machado de Assis (1839–1908), the unique Brazilian who wrote from the dead, as I write from the received notions of custom.

"Aphoristicism [sic] is a symptom of arteriosclerosis," declared the lordly novelist Vladimir Nabokov, who of course in his own inimitable way then went on to pontificate in that form, many times, viz. "A writer should have the precision of a poet and the imagination of a scientist," "There is no science without fancy, and no art without facts," "Do not be angry with the rain. It simply does not know how to fall upward," "Curiosity is insubordination in its purest form," and, among others, "Genius is finding the invisible link between two things," which may perhaps explain, I suppose, his repeated use of axioms—pontifications—even if he dismissed the form as a sign of senility.

I would also take into consideration in this distinguished group the Flemish mystic and sublime contemplative Jan van Ruysbroeck ("The measure of your holiness is proportionate to the goodness of your will") whose masterpiece, *The Spiritual Espousals* (1340), has had great influence, as well as Thomas a Kempis, whose *De Imitatione Christi* (1418–1427), basically a handbook for monks ("Each time I go out among men, I come back less a man," "Man proposes, but God disposes," "Out of sight, out of mind. The absent are always in the wrong," "No man ruleth safely but he that is willingly ruled," etc.) has left us such a memorable legacy. There are also the journals of Marie Henri Beyle, better known by the pen name of Stendahl, the 19th-century French writer and realist of fiction, which are filled with aphorisms ("Logic is neither an art nor a science but a dodge,"

"Nothing is so hideous as an obsolete fashion," "Pleasure is often spoiled by describing it," and so forth.)

One might legitimately mention here Dag Hammarskjold's *Vägmärken* (Waymarks or Markings); the punchy truths of the Swedish poet and aphorist Vilhelm Ekelund (1880–1949); and the civilized maxims of the Chinese inventor, linguist, novelist, and philosopher Lin Yutang, a quester of the first magnitude, whose journey of faith from Christianity to Taoism and Buddhism and back to Christianity in his later life was recorded in his book *From Pagan to Christian* (1959). I would even include the American spite master Hunter S. Thompson, of Gonzo journalism: "A word to the wise is infuriating," "When the going gets weird, he weird turn pro," "Buy the ticket, take the ride," "Paranoia is just another word for ignorance,"

Jacobean tragedies—and, by the way, Shakespeare was as much a Jacobean as an Elizabethan writer, if not more so—are splendid with complicated tropes and pregnant with dark and complex aphorisms that cut like a strafing bullet into the heart of mankind. One of the Bard's contemporaries, the Spanish Jesuit writer and philosopher Baltasar Gracián y Morales (1601–1658), maybe, of all of them, my favorite aphorist, whose writings, full of the punch of paradox, unsparing in irony —"Hope has a good memory, gratitude a bad one," "Life is a warfare against the malice of others," "The things we remember best are those better forgotten." "Never compete with someone who has nothing to lose," "A beautiful woman should break her mirror early," "A single lie destroys a whole reputation of integrity," etc.—was lauded by Schopenhauer and Nietzsche. He wrote in a style generically called "conceptism," characterized by ellipsis and the concentration of a maximum of significance in a minimum of form, an approach referred to in Spanish as "*agudeza*" (wit), and which is brought to its extreme in his *Oráculo Manual y Arte de Prudencia* (literally *Manual Oracle and Art of Discretion*, commonly translated as *The Art of Worldly Wisdom*), which is composed entirely of three hundred maxims with commentary, the kind of wit in which, as scholar Brian Dillon puts it, "the maximum of meaning is compacted into the minimum of style."

Gracián in his rhetorical algebra constantly played with words, with each phrase becoming a puzzle, using the most diverse rhetorical devices. Language itself intrigued him. Among his truisms, he wrote, "There is always time to add a word, never to withdraw one." And of course, "I strive to be brief, and I become obscure. Advice is sometimes transmitted more successfully through a joke than grave teaching."

A truism provides a way of seeing by way of the compendious and concise, the summary and the succinct, a thought closed like a door with a bang. It seeks if indeed it does not demand in its presentation the kind of mind, I suggest, that hopes for, indeed virtually depends upon, an immediate corroborating accord—yes, even *concord!* The axiom or maxim bears in its assertion the sort of declaration of the kind that asks for an implicit confirmation, optimistically—expectantly—seeking to have it instantly agreed upon and confirmed, claiming truth in a sense with the force of insistence, having in its conviction something like bold Christopher Columbus immediately claiming Watling Island for Spain on August 3, 1492! "Most aphorists are addicted to assertion," Brian Dillon writes in his essay "The Sharp Force and Disgraceful State of the Modern Aphorism" (*The New Yorker*,

September 10, 2018). An aphorism is a quip with a grip, and in its compact "tightly furled autonomy," as Dillon goes on to declare, "we can find a secret anatomy." Assertion is all, the "Mannerist knife-thrust, a stylistic stiletto," as Dillon tidily puts it, describing theory of the "*acutum*" elaborated by the Jesuit poet/aesthetician, Maciej Kazimierz Sarbiewski. "It has never gone away, this pert or pointed metaphor for the action of the aphorism," writes Dillon, who explains,

> "The aphorism, then, is singular and separated—or at least separable, when discovered in the midst of other aphorisms, or embedded in some more discursive text. It is sharp, also hard: in an essay on the polished maxims of La Rochefoucauld, Barthes compares the form to the brittle casing of an insect's thorax—the aphorism not as weapon but as suit of armor. The aphorism would like us to believe in its tightly furled autonomy, but we can still discern its secret anatomy. It has a well-defined structure, which at its simplest is composed of symmetries and parallels. The aphorist imagines a rhetorical algebra; everything is structured like an equation."

"Aphorisms live because they contain human truth," Adam Gopnik points out in his essay "Brevity, Soul, Wit" (*The New Yorker*, July 22, 2019), explaining that it has in its succinctness the algebraic abbreviation "a micro-model of empirical inquiry." He states, "We don't absorb aphorisms as esoteric wisdom; we test them against our own experience. The empirical test of the aphorism takes the form of laughter and then of longevity, and its confidential tone makes it candid, not cynical." More expansive than the truism, at least as I conceive this affectionate sub-genre, the aphorism manages to convey a wider, a more capacious, a more elaborate truth. Call it extended dogma, if you will. Its immediacy ideally opts for a less compact or crisper—some will say fragmentary—form. Gopnik suggests that a "cryptic fragment vindicates soul over system."

Shortness, by its very nature, seems to boast and swagger. Exhortation seems somehow involved. Brevity, anything summary, has a blunt, dismissive arrogance about it. The boldness of any statement tidily compact, briefly assertive—short and sweet, precise and condensed—in an almost comic (and you might even say totalitarian) way reveals in its vivid display a sort of what the British call "shirtiness," a sort of cheek. Terseness in its offhand way can so easily offend. Of a truism, a Frenchman might crudely put it: "*Il péte plus haut ou sac ul*"—it is farting higher than its ass!

Truisms (let us allow them, for the nonce, the honorific of a capital letter), in their irresistible insistence and importunate entreaty to be heard, inevitably take on the aura of dogma and in their presentation alone almost always seem to register, when visiting the mind, at least in my experience, with an intransigent auditory tumble-thump—very often in gently recognizable, serviceable iambic pentameter, easy for packaging, with the same kind of replicating delight that I have also often felt with having an inspiration for a poem. It is this rhythm that suggested the method of presentation that I chose for the work here presented. I suppose any assembling device would work, one of course that remains simple and, ideally, quotable. There are truisms of the banal sort, of course—forgettable. obvious platitudes that fade away as merely sententious ("A goal without execution is meaningless," "Persistence is the foundation of success," etc.), which inevitably strikes one with the leaden note of cant, humbug, pecksniffery. Intuition plays a role here. A bold and original truism needs a neat, precise, valorous wrapping to be truly memorable—indeed to be richly comprehensible—for pithiness, for style, for force, for panache. I am certain Alexander Pope would agree.

A truism, which implicitly asks—beseeches—for recognition, depends for verification, indeed corroboration, on the good will and, I insist, education, wit, and imagination of an informed reader. That he or she is also infinitely curious and profoundly eager to know is also assumed. It is a sub-genre, communal in its conviction, that is populist in the hope and expectation that, as pithily stated, it dovetails with reality. Adages, aphorisms, principles, maxims, epigrams, dictums, saws, and precepts become, when taken altogether, a human chapbook, a kind of workable theology in which many if not most people place—or should place—faith. Declaring a particular truth in a special way is a revelation of that reality, as Wallace Stevens states in *The Necessary Angel*, a reality of one's own particulars. What is looked for is an aesthetic integration of those particulars. A truism is not abstract. It is inevitable, has rigor, is ludic, and authenticates fact. The definition of its preciseness is its accuracy. Above all, it achieves individual reality, the ring of a true poem.

What is commonly believed of any truism—and that some insist defines the mode—is that it is invariably a statement obviously true and because of that *creates* nothing new or interesting, rather simply orders and codifies it. Over time, it cements itself into unalterable fact. It is said to be a platitude, in short, a commonplace, a cliché, a stock phrase, an old chestnut, an axiom, a bromide. Experience, seemingly unavoidable, is not manifest or discernible, evident or apparent to most people. The genius required in the observer is to squint into the world as we know it and look for the unmistakable, the factual, the indisputable, and the incontrovertible and by native wit and the accuracy of insight make it—convincingly—self-evident. Goethe said, "All writing is confession." I do suspect that for its strong opinions, without which no list of original truisms can exist, this book constitutes a kind of autobiography, as well. But you could also call it a joke book or a litany of laments or an examination of culture. I do not shrink from self-revelation. It may be charged against me that I have a haptic bias, an astigmatism regarding perception. A common cause of low visual acuity is refractive error (*ametropia*), or how the light is refracted in the eyeball. But no opinion does not reflect a bias, since it is both personal and subjective at the same time. Paradoxically, a strong opinion reflects a bold mind that is ideally also open, keen, inquisitive, unsparing, always attentive, a mind that notices habits, finds trends, detects customs and routines, perceives directions, discerns inclinations, distinguishes values, spots repetitions, marks traditions, and understands convention and change, the fleeting passage of thought and the vagaries of protean emotions, but in its iron assertions it also a mind that becomes closed, fixed, and final, one that posits permanent positions and identifies completely and wholeheartedly with universal thoughts of feelings. In 1853, Gustave Flaubert wrote to his paramour Louise Colet, stating, "Everything one invents is true, you may be sure." I would add that every truth one observes seems inevitable, coming to us with an assurance that rings with the sound of honesty, obliging us to recognize it.

While a delightful perspective to the curious mind like a special flavor to the palate and comforting to one's sense of recognition, a truism in a certain slant of light can come across as impolite, injudicious, impertinent, overstated, offensive, and to many a reader contestable. It is often politically incorrect, which is not a feature that can pass muster in this weak age of ours of self-consciousness and supreme scruple, when, for example, in ordering a chocolate ice-cream cone one can very well meet with the reproof, "What is wrong with vanilla?" Truisms are never *not* opinions, frankly an individual's insight into what is taken to be a universal truth, so that a subjective judgment is involved in the undertaking. Slant is therefore a standpoint, attitude a stance, perspective the persuasion advanced to produce the statement to prove the outlook true. The truisms presented here thus may fight another's sense of truth, the definition of which, for its mystery, its enigmatic depth, not only confounded Pontius Pilate, but kept Jesus wordless. I seek to assault the sensibility of no one; it may be the case that the only people who become angry at someone speaking the truth are those who are living a lie. Creeds are less healthy than tropes but may be subsumed in them, for, as I see it, they take on the symbolic truth of living emblems. As Ralph Waldo Emerson vigorously asserted, "The intellect is stimulated by the statement of truth in a trope." I only pray my efforts don't prove valid one of Thoreau's richest truisms: "Whatever succeeds with an audience is bad."

As St. Thomas More wrote in his amazingly invented Utopian language "*Voluala barchin heman la lauoluola dramme pagloni*," which translated literally into Latin is "*Libenter impar-*

tio mea, non grauatim accipio meliora" or translated into English, "Freely I impart my benefits; not unwillingly I accept whatever is better."

You cannot fail to note in your reading that I have discovered a petty side to human behavior often hidden behind otherwise politically correct conventions. I pray in this parade of my disclosures—sincere, if not seamless insights—that it be reckoned, nevertheless, I come to you with matter that has solidity of substance, even if in rigidity of form, smiling, in turn, like Horace or scowling like Juvenal.

Let us not lengthen the Prologue. I will conclude by echoing the startling assertion made by Machado de Assis in his posthumous memoirs that "the main defect of this book is you, reader," if for whatever reason, ingenious or otherwise, you feel the need to contest the veracity of assertions made patently clear. Speaking truth always requires exposure. A truth is a poultice over the wound of lies or denials.

Hearken then to the holy of what you hear in your own ear. Ramfit into memorable cartridges the inevitable of the available. It is an arrow against the false that targeting the need for verities acknowledges fact. I am sorry, but, taken altogether, this is the way I see the world. I bequeath my observations to you.

Truisms

A handshake's more than anything a code.
You rarely see a pretty woman walking.
Dryness never figures as a concept in a toad.
There's lassitude in every rumpled stocking.

Owls in Arab culture signify death.
Every egg carton must show a pack date.
Theater people shun the word "Macbeth."
A human skull, grinning, appears elate.

Chess pieces all have glum expressions.
One's true journey in life is the interior.
Autobiographies are never true confessions.
Safety resides in an airplane's anterior.

A diary that serves as a friend is an enemy.
English actors for sore throat gargle with port.
Auditorium seating is an aspect of entropy.
All snobbish people quite naturally assort.

Anticipation is inverted recollection.
Human skeletons all tend to look alike.
A pious Scientologist's a contradiction.
An empire, not a reign, denotes a Reich.

All apologies are basically forced.
No monarch may enter the House of Commons.
The Talmud is virtually unsourced.
The fairer the skin, the more valid the Brahmin.

No grape pulp yields a colored juice.
Exotic chickens are indifferent layers.
French films all tend to be abstruse.
Baseball managers were awful players.

Travel writers are dilettantes, not explorers.
The greatest creators manage it alone.
Injustice collectors are always secret scorers.
Our most cherished dreams have always flown.

Armenians look peculiar wearing hats.
Itches on the back are always out of reach.
Street filth created the need for wearing spats.
A raging storm leaves a smoother beach.

Eskimo teeth constitute another hand.
The Finnish language is rabid with N's.
Good paprika is far less hot than bland.
No boulder's stiller than sleeping hens.

TRUISMS

One should never clean mushrooms in water.
Menstruating women must be cautious of bees.
An indulgent father most perverts his daughter.
A gift is deemed worthless if given with ease.

The saffron of Kashmir is the world's finest.
All Western philosophy is a footnote to Plato.
Presumption is the singular failing of a dynast.
The world's most popular fruit is the tomato.

Walls have solid foundations, never fences.
Mezzo-sopranos in opera play evil figures.
Anything taken in abundance dulls the senses.
Every secret code has its specific triggers.

Pour white wine from a greater height than red.
Nouvelle cuisine eschews Auguste Escoffier.
Capitalism represents all of labor that is dead.
Chilling is mandatory to serve a perfect pâté.

Jesus Christ never spent a night in Jerusalem.
The archetypal stripper music is "Night Train."
Alzheimer's disease has been linked to aluminum.
A compulsion to queue comes natural to a Dane.

Never maintain tomatoes in your fridge.
No true teacher says something only once.
No lake exists in Barbados, nor a bridge.
The average pencil always weighs an ounce.

In polite circles, port's always passed to the left.
Peregrines attack other birds only from above.
The bereaved feel loss, the lovelorn feel bereft.
The only bird able to sip water is a mourning dove.

All L.L. Bean catalog models have to smile.
Jesus was a *tekton*, likely worked with stone.
There is no single source to the river Nile.
Facing east (to the sun) is a normal gravestone.

Warm water transmits sound faster than cold.
The Declaration of Independence is mum about Christianity.
So pliable is it, sewing thread can be made of gold.
The Japanese language has no words of profanity.

No wife is fully a man's who has a daughter.
Alcoholic drinks are generally stored in a tun.
Never get between an elephant and water.
No husband ever fully has a wife who has a son.

All newborns are fascinated with edges.
Mimosas look dead until they start to bloom.
Horticulture in England includes hedges.
Loudmouths crave the center of a room.

There were no maps in the Book of Mormon.
Horse fat is proven best for frying potatoes.
Goods are no longer touched by longshoremen.
A log cabin is the basic template for dadoes.

TRUISMS

A child actor is good for but two pictures.
One does not shoot quail on the ground.
True vision is throttled by any strictures.
No union management is strictly sound.

The CIA and the FBI are hostile rivals.
No animals are killed in the *Oz* books.
Nature everywhere is abundant in spirals.
Japan invaded China to steal their cooks.

Not one Allied boot entered Germany in WWI.
Only 30% of the ocean floor has been mapped.
Scatology informs the average Shakespeare pun.
The cheapest gifts are inevitably overwrapped.

Grace need not be said at breakfast.
Most nudists loathe the sight of tan lines.
Vintage types prefer wood distressed.
Fine embroidery uses quills of porcupines.

Not biology but worth defines a mother.
The ancient Greeks avoided glass in art.
Strengthening one thing weakens another.
Size always diminishes taste in a tart.

You can only explore when you are lost.
All candy tastes better when it is cold.
Rime, as such, is *not* a type of frost.
The most malleable of all metals is gold.

Jesus never set foot in Herodian Tiberius.
A dowser can only detect *running* water.
All yogurts are produced from bacterias.
A political hanger-on is but a human blotter.

You rarely see a marathoner smiling.
Freckles are rarely found on Asian skin.
A cat's tongue is suitable for filing.
Most Welsh in South Wales are kin.

A thing made clean has made another dirty.
Hats never appear in Roman sculpture.
Smooth skin in women disappears at thirty.
Talk shows are the opposite of culture.

Pendant earrings always clash with chokers.
The leaves of beets are healthier than beets.
Turks remain the most addicted smokers.
Every college girl loves memorizing Keats.

Move the left side counterclockwise once,
then the facing top clockwise once—keep
repeating these maneuvers from the front
to solve the Rubik's Cube, a simple sweep.

Thorns are but aborted branches.
Perfect circles don't exist in the universe.
A mediocre mind fixes on finances.
Most English poetry employs blank verse.

TRUISMS

All polar navigation uses nautical miles.
There are no nightingales in the United States.
Delay is great-grandfather of all denials.
The person prone to destroy never creates.

Bluntness is a major trait of the Viennese.
Toddlers hate foods touching on a plate.
Obfuscation is the design of all legalese.
Trespassing is the route of every roommate.

All whistleblowers are demonized as unstable.
Shakespeare's plots move from town to country.
Only the letter J is absent on the periodic table.
In all the world, Indonesians are the most runty.

All beauty contestants have a high smile.
Only 3% of men in the U.S. receive alimony.
Crows get along with so many to a mile.
No food requires sauce more than abalone.

Forgiveness always constitutes permission.
Inflation, farting goods, shits too much money.
True power never willingly joins a coalition.
Ushuaia in Argentina is virtually never sunny.

A salt dish should always have a glass lid.
The U.S. Constitution never mentions Christianity.
Not headfirst, but by tail, travels a squid.
Virtue is always half in love with vanity.

Frog-legs are almost always sold in pairs.
Weeds in general grow faster than flowers.
Filthiness is seldom found with bears.
Shakespeare's lovers always meet in bowers.

There are presently no Islamic democracies.
A catcher merits full credit in a no-hitter.
Not one written word survives by Socrates.
Although there's salt in sugar, it's not bitter.

Butternut hickory is best for smoking hams.
Tomato soup is almost never served in bistros.
If not open after cooking, avoid eating clams.
Yale secret-society buildings all lack windows.

Fungus forms the single food for ants.
The ancient Romans never trusted kings.
Carnations are grown in sand as plants.
A metal lobster-trap is useless, as it "sings."

Italians hate the concept of cold food.
Human graves are situated east to west.
In South Korea, smoking is thought lewd.
Mushrooms, when cooked, taste best.

Catalpas seldom live to an old age.
Russians play more chess than Americans bowl.
Elephants die sooner (by half) in a cage.
Aquinas called the intellect and will the "soul."

TRUISMS

Those who hate to go to bed fear death,
Whereas those who hate to rise fear life.
Kissing well's a way of regulating breath.
Deafness hears not silence, rather strife.

No Vidalia onion should really be cooked.
Smallpox conquered Mexico, not Cortés.
A bra with snaps opens faster than when hooked.
Lawyers mean the reverse of what they say.

No boat drills had ever been done on the *Titanic*.
Queen Elizabeth II does not sing "God Save the Queen."
Roundness is the unalterable shape of bannock.
Mona Lisa in her portrait wears a gown of green.

No serious cigar smoker ever inhales.
In South America only white corn's eaten.
Volume is a weapon in bull-market sales.
Gold becomes much shinier when beaten.

All autobiography is narrative of ascent.
No Protestant accepts the book of Daniel.
Half the hemisphere makes up the Orient.
A gun dog finds perfection as a spaniel.

No Englishman is ever waited on
at breakfast but must serve himself.
One surface surely never skated on
at the Pole is the Ross Ice Shelf.

Jesus never mentions the city of Rome.
You never get coffee hot in room service.
The most efficient building structure's a dome.
A cheetah of all beasts is the most nervous.

Vegemite should always be spread thin.
Second novels are somehow always jinxed.
Filipinos far and away drink the most gin.
No one ever notices the *tail* of the Sphinx.

A black bear does not bleed when shot.
Smallpox immunologically wiped out Aztecs.
Every senator, by any given gift, is bought.
Meek alone, dangerous in groups are rednecks.

Nothing's grimmer than pudding skin creep.
Clear glass on a bottle easily sours beer.
To grow asparagus, always plant it deep.
No dream should ever have a frontier.

Sitcom women always outsmart men.
The sound on 45s is crisper than LPs.
No serpent's killed more people than a pen.
No graceful handshake is a vulgar squeeze.

Those who say "I honestly believe,"
rather than "I believe," are lying,
like drunks while upright never leave
the premises unless they're dying.

TRUISMS

Never cover spinach when it's cooking.
Deep experience is never fully restful.
Expectation lies behind all looking.
The strictly natural alone is easeful.

Russians have a natural fondness for birch trees.
Cape Cod League baseball requires all bats be wooden.
Frenchmen are greatly attracted to female knees.
Rich in raisins and currants is every Christmas pudding.

Raisins rot teeth far worse than candy.
Dieting and mayonnaise exclude each other.
Smoking is the best adjunct to brandy.
Gays are manufactured by their mother.

In sports opinions, everyone's correct.
No blueprint for a lovely face exists.
Favoring a brand constitutes a sect.
Collecting is a form of making lists.

Lack of color defines a Dickens hero.
Korean dinners are all about plates.
As to doctrines, Unitarians have zero.
Terrorists prefer attacking on soft dates.

All Presbyterians as if by formal law
sing every single stanza of a hymn.
No artist is an artist who can't draw.
In Mauretania, ugliness is being thin.

A person half right is the worst kind of charlatan.
All great novelists are adepts at neology.
A certain lameness adhibits to every nonpartisan.
Profitability in business is wed to dishonesty.

A wave prefers to move uphill, not down.
Hex signs are *not* used by Amish folk.
Wistfulness defines the humor of a clown.
The finer pouring rain, the deeper the soak.

Diamond rings on men are in bad taste.
A trial has less to do with truth than winning.
Vulgarity is forever an attribute of haste.
Sin rarely admits to itself that it is sinning.

The circle is the beginning of aesthetics.
Haute cuisine in Italy ignores desserts.
Ill-temper is common in congenital diabetics.
A will proffers less than it perverts.

In poker never draw to an inside straight.
A Japanese soldier's uniform rarely fits.
Portugal is a refuge for evil heads of state.
A chicken may perch, but it never sits.

The name Idaho means exactly nothing.
Litigation is mainly undisguised thievery.
Indians mashed hardwood twigs for brushing.
Cold defines any wind blowing easterly.

TRUISMS

Light green is the color of male sexuality.
Dreams come true sleeping under a new quilt.
Bruckner's Symphony No. 7 in E Major is the great elegy.
Cheating pinball is prevented by machine's tilt.

The colder the air, the fluffier the snow.
To walk away is the best negotiation.
Birds take comfort standing row on row.
A runway model's fashion is emaciation.

The corollary of all speed is confusion.
Nothing natural's connected to monogamy.
Sex is but a variation of collusion.
Birch when stained resembles mahogany.

The color brown is really degenerate orange.
Use apple tree wood for the best saw handles.
Out-of-staters in Maine are deemed as "foreign."
Only one shape exists in the flame of candles.

Reading a cookbook is a way of eating.
Tea gives off cold energy, not hot.
A dreaming life's about a life repeating.
No truly wealthy person's not distraught.

Amish men abhor the use of mustaches.
Miss Judy Garland entered from the rear.
Nascar fans are hugely fond of crashes.
Hitler commanded people by his stare.

Being Christian in Asia's counter cultural.
Peeing outside always involves the feet.
Tabloid reporters to a man are vultural.
A Fijian woman is rarely found petite.

A paradise is always taken to be tropical.
Haters of Christmas are an ill-natured cult.
A teenager's moods are kaleidoscopical.
Blowhards love to be asked to consult.

Most shoplifters are store employees.
The denser the crowds, the faster they erupt.
Psychiatrists claim success improves with fees.
Every lobbyist in Congress is corrupt.

Barbershop quartets tend to sound alike.
The only metal found *en masse* is copper.
No one in Denmark's complete without a bike.
Everyone walks like Groucho leaving a chopper.

German beers are subject to *Reinheitsgebot*.
Calorie Guilt has ruined American beer.
No Raymond Chandler isn't muddled as to plot.
Caution is a positive element in fear.

No civic-minded person's not a bore.
The biochemical price of breathing is aging.
In every poison, what can kill can cure.
The key to joy in marriage is disengaging.

TRUISMS

Three right turns make one long left turn.
All Americans mispronounce *veterinarian*.
Whatever is fully oxidized will never burn.
Labor power is the muscle of a proletarian.

A wet face can never get any wetter.
Sacco and Vanzetti's name are never reversed.
Bankruptcies are valentines for debtor.
Roanoke Island, haunted, is said to be cursed.

Men are always drawn to girls of sorrow.
Lightning mainly seeks to strike what's tall.
No day can be experienced as tomorrow.
Every diamond's worthless that is small.

Librarians who love to read are lost.
Turkey stuffing is a bust when missing sage.
No design by any artist matches frost.
Adolescence chiefly defines the genital stage.

Country singers become patriots for money.
Any person who likes everyone likes none.
No constantly repeated joke is ever funny.
A lover's heart, for trust, is never fully won.

Cost 60 cents: the first Book of Mormon.
Patriotism is by its nature jealous and selfish.
Cancers can be killed with an antihormone.
No fish have anything to do with shellfish.

ALEXANDER THEROUX

None of Christ's Aramaic sayings have survived.
It is grain loads on cargo ships that quickly shift.
No truly fair tax system has ever been contrived.
Foraging on the wing characterizes the aerial swift.

Proportion in architecture grants repose.
Twelve minutes is the standard lobster boil.
No genius pays attention to his clothes.
Lust by definition is never true love's foil.

Marriage is the first step toward divorce.
Public laughter in Iran is held as rude.
Shapes of boomerangs are all retrorse.
The height of pilgrim fashion was the snood.

Angels in art are never shown as dark.
Jesus glorified menial work alone.
True wisdom never makes a slang remark.
No graceful invitation is made by phone.

An interviewer is nothing but an auctioneer.
Wasting—squandering—anything's a crime.
A barcarole is properly sung by a gondolier.
Entertainment is murdered by every mime.

To draw distinctions is never of the spirit.
An elegant house has no need for curtains.
Whoever looks for glory deserves no merit.
Stupidity is at its ugliest when acting certain.

TRUISMS

Colonial building only copied Georgian.
Alternating speeds in marathons is bad.
All comments on the future involve forging.
No violin concerto is not sad.

No North American bird has a purple feather.
The number 7 rules the book of Revelation.
Loving couples should never work together.
Without make-up, stands another female nation.

Jackie Robinson, oddly, is now a baseball god.
Van Dyck mastered capturing fabrics in paint.
All other fish are eaten by the carniverous cod.
No creatures are stranger than a Christian saint.

Rare is a black Tory MP in Britain.
Woman writers using three names suck.
Native Americans left us nothing written.
Good health is basically just luck.

Heavy curtains have an automatic drape.
Nothing gotten free is held sublime.
Cruel violence, not sex, defines a rape.
Dreams are constantly destroyed by time.

Game shows are inherently sadistic.
Everyone in Holland rides a bicycle.
No gambler's dream is ever realistic.
The perfect murder weapon is the icicle.

Museum silence is predominantly sexual.
Overfamiliarity is being rude twice.
All cowboys are basically anti-intellectual.
TV chefs overuse the word "nice."

Sacrifice explains what love is worth.
Woman basketball coaches all seem mannish.
Fate is mainly handed you at birth.
Happiness for ethnics lies in being clannish.

No famous poet was ever truly sane.
A choral singer cannot hear his voice.
Requests for cash render faith profane.
Anyone's a jailer who prevents a choice.

Earnestness is inherently quite funny.
An exile carries his country in his skull.
Only churls exclusively pursue money.
A Schoenberg fan has an ear that's dull.

Paella should be cooked over a *wood* stove.
No polite Arab looks at you when he talks.
Saltwater never adversely effects a mangrove.
There are thirty Biblical verses about rocks.

Inconsistency is the diarist's privilege.
Literal people are identifyingly stupid.
Hope without faith is a true sacrilege.
To blind is the essential job of Cupid.

TRUISMS

Fitness people rarely feed their minds.
Black women politicians love three names.
The principal signature of Nature is design.
Ingratitude pure ignorance acclaims.

Disc jockeys always expect free food.
Most baseball shortstops are Latinos.
Obedience is frequently mere lassitude.
No battleground is littered like casinos.

Planting time in Africa does not matter.
All vain authors hastily sign a book.
Greed is being overweight but fatter.
No loan company agent's not a crook.

Narcissists truly hate to be alone.
Gospel groups are the homeliest people alive.
Charity has nothing to do with a loan.
The most important goal in life is to survive.

Health food is always more expensive.
Cops at accidents make the traffic worse.
Tax fraud among farmers is extensive.
Pensions for state workers are a curse.

Impotence ads often run on sports shows.
Eiffel Tower color paint is never revealed.
Southern woman's fashion's fixed on bows.
A promise postponed is a lie concealed.

Port Orford cedar is the best for arrows.
All trees that are living bear flowers.
There are always thirteen steps to the gallows.
Affection for a single flavor always sours.

The promise of young girl's always porous.
A tiny diamond's barely worth a pebble.
Chauvinism always finds a chorus.
To be a serious Christian is to be a rebel.

Where celibacy leads, perversion follows.
Jingoism is the essential source of war.
Heights are always paralleled by hollows.
Cigarettes lack the flavor of a good cigar.

The best show-biz audiences are military.
Black people despise *Gone with the Wind*.
No thank-you note delayed is conciliatory.
All capitalists have, by definition, sinned.

The Met allows no solo curtain calls.
No good muralist *sits down* to work.
Success in a neighbor particularly galls.
A prelate paid is a priest who'll shirk.

Sherry, oxidized wine, loves exposure to air.
American weather always blows west to east.
Who is a couple is rarely what is a pair.
It is pretty girls whom pretty girls love least.

TRUISMS

Silenced for major funerals is the bell Big Ben.
A zoo sentences every poor animal to life.
Forgetting whom one's harmed only harms again.
Greek women keep their surnames as a wife.

Nachos served in Mexico are thicker.
Seed-packets are always one-tenth full.
Liquor always makes seduction quicker.
No toreador is worth the value of a bull.

Better walk than run boasts the sloth.
911 agents need everything repeated.
A vow to God is weaker than an oath.
No martyr executed was ever defeated.

Waiting—its perversity—cannot be hurried.
A Hebrew can't be purified in stagnant water.
No word in India exists for curry or curried.
A fascist note is distinct in every imprimatur.

A second child to parents is old news.
Snobs prefer words to numbers on addresses.
The Texas landscape is bereft of views.
All Wall Street marketeers rely on guesses.

Los Angeles skies are never fully clear.
Aggressive people's heads are spherical.
Flattery is incontrovertably insincere.
Ex-priests are invariably anti-clerical.

No ugliness exceeds an old sexpot's.
A muffin's a breakfast excuse for cake.
Infantilism is always attracted to dots.
It is far easier *to do* than *to make*.

There are no airplanes painted black.
Hollywood won't make pro-Arabic films.
No Biblical timespan is ever truly exact.
The letter of the law necessity kills.

A film cowboy's hat never blows off.
General law fails in concrete cases.
Many a fatality begins with a cough.
After American aid comes Army bases.

Beauty queens claim they're keen for school.
A good director presides over accidents.
Whosoever finds Congress honest is a fool.
No animal is not wounded by a fence.

A Tiffany lampshade, not its base, has value.
The kitchen is the dirtiest place in a house.
When you find fame, everyone wants to pal you.
Black is most alluring in a woman's blouse.

No Catholic saint has ever been quite normal.
No sexy woman is ever found in breadlines.
The purpose of etiquette is to be formal.
The cruder the paper, the bigger the headlines.

TRUISMS

Most poplar furniture came from New York.
Lipstick sales fall off during a recession.
The least necessary cutlery item is the fork.
All mortal sin is a variation of possession.

A terrible teacher is always overpaid.
Mediocrity is best met by being ignored.
Justice that is withheld is ever delayed.
A bullfighter should himself be gored.

Police in uniform feel eight feet taller.
Rain always brings a change in weather.
The Mediterranean nature is to holler.
No single color quite defines heather.

A football is designed to bring bad luck.
A human's natural scent is due to sweat.
The better the driver, the larger the truck.
A women pursued is always hard to get.

Needy people always feel betrayed.
Something of green resides in blue.
That man is more alert who is afraid.
A friend in deals banks on cheating you.

Hating an enemy makes us loathe ourselves.
Never watch a baseball game with a female.
Valuable books require durable shelves.
No significant meal truly depends on kale.

American breakfast cereals rot the teeth.
Brownies are burnt in a matter of seconds.
What is above, ridicules what is beneath.
With facts an adventurer rarely reckons.

Sex criminals were often earlier arsonists.
Garage mechanics are never talkative.
Literary obfuscators always claim genius.
Anything masked is always evocative.

To cure ham well takes more than a year.
All Civil War officers led from the front.
Purposeful narcissism focuses on the hair.
Good manners require often being blunt.

Every secret is dirty to a biographer.
Accumulation is the ambition of rubbish.
No real artist is ever a photographer.
Neo-cons and fascist folk are cubbish.

Travel writers all have bad marriages.
Every lake is yearly growing smaller.
Littering is the act of perfect savages.
Than *pro bono* doctors, no one's taller.

No statue has ever been erected to a critic.
The most popular films are always the worst.
Gardening correctly involves arithmetic.
Vanity is mainly the need to come in first.

TRUISMS

Minnesota is matchless for duck-hunting.
Shakespeare depicts no death of a mother.
Smart poles prevent death in train shunting.
For intimacy in a killing, look to smother.

No kiss without a taste of sin is sweet.
A corner location is best to locate a store.
Very few people have the same size feet.
The $2 bill died, being the fee of a whore.

Impatient souls loathe instruction manuals.
Climate we create, thrust on us is weather.
Perennials are never as colorful as annuals.
Sex addicts are invariably aroused by leather.

What looks solid in a cathedral never is.
Folks in old photographs rarely smile.
The cheaper the drink, the louder the fizz.
A car dealer's numbers never compile.

Jesus left us not a single written word.
Getting married is being out of luck.
Feminist fiction co-celebrates the herd.
Lawyers' zeal equals a client's buck.

Nothing's worse than an overindulged pet.
Real look less bright than imitation jewels.
A cat is never contented when it is wet.
Untalented painters blindly follow rules.

Insouciance in a buyer gets the bargain.
All bad singers record Christmas albums.
Bars suck where a mug is called a flagon.
Rapist contrition is nothing but pabulum.

Heroines of novels are always energetic.
Illness in youth often prophesies a scholar.
All conceptual art is a visual emetic.
The candidate who wins is always taller.

No problem's unrelated to one's parents.
Most *New Yorker* cartoons are nonsense.
No person is humorful named Clarence.
A contented pol is one sitting on a fence.

A sports fan's zeal exceeds the athlete's.
Cinnamon ruins everything it touches.
No bed-wetter is indifferent to sheets.
Packrats always tend to favor hutches.

Refinancing is a miser's nightmare.
Accordion music is an oxymoron.
Institutions mainly employ whiteware.
"Speed" always drives a whore on.

Marilyn Monroe always had a lover.
A single whale yielded 160 barrels of oil.
A hawk fully to see needs to hover.
A corpse takes two years to dissolve in soil.

TRUISMS

All squirrels in the world look alike.
Hispanics love Christmas lights on houses.
No painter liked brown more than Van Dyck.
Isolation is a danger sign in spouses.

Nationalism is a fascist's true religion.
Pigeons are all dirigibles of germs.
Anger's vocabulary is primarily derision.
A human's final bounty is for worms.

One's fiftieth birthday demands reflection.
No human head of hair is all one shade.
Self-pity finds a harvest in rejection.
The openly willing are always underpaid.

Eunuchoids prefer unsalted peanut butter.
Civil War soldiers hugely loved to sing.
At Oxford, it is considered chic to stutter.
The signature of any slavery is a ring.

An astute reader is any book's co-author.
Serbians all despise the "Radetzky March."
To proffer is far more polite than to offer.
Every fascist glories in a triumphal arch.

Charlie Parker, its innovator, hated the term "Be Bop."
Bobolinks migrate—entry and departure—only through Florida.
Affected was a WWI officer's swagger stick/riding crop.
Trajes de luces is properly yellow for the cowardly *corrida*.

Weeping is the way a woman sweats.
A talking blueberry picker never works.
He who has, ironically, always gets.
True need in greed rarely ever lurks.

A pun is a perpetration, not a gaffe.
Bullying goes against no U.S. law.
Authority figures always bear a staff.
Japanese much prefer to eat food raw.

Lovely women can't stand moderation;
they need an endless supply of excess.
A war results whenever haughty nations
ice-coldly regard another one as less.

The scariest people in life love no one.
Insurance salesmen overrate their skill.
A farmer knows a field who has to sow one.
A man who truly hates himself can kill.

Chestnut trees are always first to shed.
High heels are designed as sexual allure.
All whores highly esteem the color red.
Every non-reader is a crashing bore.

Every sanding tool should also have a vacuum.
D minor is the most melancholy of all keys.
Muslims choose water to absterge in a bathroom.
As unique as fingerprints are human knees.

TRUISMS

Baltic folk love mushroom-hunting.
Fat people hate the act of bending down.
Patriotism is identified with bunting.
A cross-dresser's joy is in his gown.

Scarves never go out of fashion.
Apple juice is the standard drink filler.
The Irish list last in physical passion.
Than winter midnight, nothing is stiller.

No U.S. tax brochures make sense.
The Grand Ol' Opry despises drums.
The truly avaricious tabulate to cents.
No moist bread is likely to leave crumbs.

All acts of haste are invariably comic.
The universe has neither a center nor an edge.
One's enemy is never not a heretic.
To condemn a person is easy: merely allege.

A barrel is no better than its shooks.
Short men all seek an occasion to sit.
The Amish, over buttons, prefer hooks.
A dangerous man is always definite.

No writer has had a happy childhood.
To torture is a cretin's high delight.
A romantic's heaven is the wildwood.
History is always made at night.

Psalm 22:16-17 predicts Christ's crucifixion.
No country's goulash beats that of the Csángós.
Conflict, not harmony, feeds the art of fiction.
Desperation and sadness are nuanced in tangos.

Writing hacks forever praise their like.
Women drivers always refuse to yield.
A cent costs more than a penny to strike.
No cop is ever as honest as his shield.

No Judeo-Christian tradition exists.
Farce, foremost, is always embarrassing.
A moron's eloquence is in his fists.
A neighbor, by definition, is harassing.

A pie should be cold before baking.
Old women insist on having permanents.
An erection is a constant upon waking.
Sacrifice proves passion's determinants.

Paintings in Hawaii never hold up well.
Uniqueness is the secret of all couture.
A huckster's eye is on something to sell.
A bad listener is, before all else, a bore.

A dream, by definition, is erased.
No human failing beats ingratitude.
A man dying rich dies disgraced.
An object's worth alters with attitude.

TRUISMS

No man hasn't somehow molested a woman.
A true New Englander eats pie in the morning.
A good winter stew can be warmed by cumin.
Aposematism in animals states a warning.

Every garden is a form of civilization.
Getting no mail is invariably a blessing.
Mystery is the soul of all creation.
When courting, keep a partner guessing.

Black walnut is the best for gunstocks.
When you're fat, your hair looks thinner.
To reek is part and parcel of a fox.
Noise of any sort is the bane of a dinner.

All campaign contributions are bribes.
Lobster should be eaten unadorned.
Irish satire has no humor, only jibes.
No Asian can abide being scorned.

Old folks seem of indeterminate sex.
Mobile homes invariably house a dog.
Never will a hurting bubo never vex.
A mist is part and parcel of a bog.

Socks never complement espadrilles.
It is not done to serve Chablis with meat.
No overhead power wires exist in Beverly Hills.
Ambiguity in essence is always bittersweet.

Never poke a hole in a bratwurst.
What animates a solon makes him bad.
Neglect ever creates a form of thirst.
Staring is a compulsive habit in a cad.

State workers tend to be lazy sods.
Initiative is destroyed by public funds.
Chewing gum alone is expressed in wads.
Psychoses come natural to nuns.

Cuban exiles are all right-wing.
Sportswriters are all envious of jocks.
To pray to heaven, one may also sing.
Laughter of any kind invariably mocks.

Subtlety is always lost in floodlight.
Harried men make the worse husbands.
Offering flowers for one's faults is trite.
Tight pants are the choice of scuzzy bands.

Jingoists thrive on patriotic songs.
Summits rarely lead to true solutions.
A cowboy for the sunset always longs.
Blood is the living fuel of revolutions.

Modern athletes are grossly overpaid.
Garlic should be planted in the fall.
For the poor, everything is delayed.
Show-business people thrive on gall.

TRUISMS

A nagging wife is first a nosy one.
The beautiful is always kin to sorrow.
Semitic is a language classification, not a racial one.
Comfort adhibits to the word *tomorrow*.

Nigeria is famous for the births of twins.
All small canines bite your ankles.
To comprehend mercy, understand sins.
Rivalry is known by what it rankles.

Imagination feasts on the hidden.
Americans have a genius for waste.
What lures is what's initially forbidden.
An indifferent girl is always chased.

No true father's daughter marries right.
A pantry's where a butler keeps his port.
Love and crime alone adhere to night.
Creation is a displaced person's best resort.

Infants are invariably homely to a one.
Fancy is always constricted by fact.
Poverty of language makes a pun.
A cord of wood is never quite exact.

Stating one's humility is vain.
No one has ever laid his eyes on God.
Recollection thrives in rain.
Everyone who hails from Maine is odd.

If it is not French, it is not Champagne.
Romans feared to open an unpierced egg.
Any plant with acrid milky juice is dogbane.
Mace is the true spiritual father of nutmeg.

The Old Testament is all about revenge.
Art history majors have learned nothing.
Offering mercy is, very often, to avenge.
Strike a light whenever going mothing.

All illumination comes from pain.
It is illegal to have as a pet a shrike.
The hope to win a war is never sane.
No tricycle should be called a bike.

Teens hate joining the family dinner.
Ninety percent of taste is due to smell.
A sorrow felt best describes a sinner.
Pressure is the very soul of any sell.

Doormen all tend to be awful snobs.
Everyone is a betrayer by nature.
Small goals all spawn large mobs.
Self-advancement makes legislature.

Every fish with scales has also fins.
The only goal of television is to sell.
Almost all Irishmen have whitish shins.
Any clock worth having sports a bell.

TRUISMS

Few paintings with surety can be ascribed to Verrocchio.
No country's capitol does not sit on a river.
A highly unlikable character was the original Pinocchio.
Every drug that's taken damages the liver.

The larger a belt buckle, the lower the IQ.
Book dealers are rarely readers of books.
Headlines alone comprise the nightly news.
Circumspection is the living soul of rooks.

Mayans drank chocolate but did not eat it.
There are no battle scenes in Trollope's work.
Eating flaxseed makes one quickly excrete it.
The mentally ill are agitated by fireworks.

All privacy is offensive to a wife.
The French refuse to use umbrellas.
To forego freedom is to forego life.
Buyers for virtue, vice for sellers.

Grief for Hosain is the sign of Islam.
Tchaikovsky's *Nutcracker* is unbearable.
To stare into a bear's face creates alarm.
The bane of polyester is it is wearable.

Pretty girls in ads always sell.
Never buy salt pork at a shop.
Every family is a little hell.
A merciless man defines a cop.

ALEXANDER THEROUX

Hangovers are rare with alcoholics.
Onions make every food taste better.
In the Book of Mormon are no frolics.
Cash to lawyers is the sole begetter.

Germany produces poor red wines.
Duncan Phyfe favored mahogany wood.
Forks for centuries had but two tines.
Anonymity historically favors a hood.

All methods of flight imitate birds.
Evangelists to a one sport hideous hair.
A woman is suspicious wooed by words.
Focus is essential to any serious prayer.

Always clean a trout on the spot.
The autodidact is always a prig.
Lovers of praise are easily bought.
Age at its saddest is wearing a wig.

To leave the ego is to forego talent.
Truth arrives at the end of conversation.
Hannukah, as an event, is irrelevant.
Reason ever seeks to avoid sensation.

Ivanhoe assassinates young readers.
Nobody has ever been a nobody.
Gluttons see rivals in fellow feeders.
All that's dire fades before a toddy.

TRUISMS

A flatterer is always a future enemy.
Umlauts are never used in Danish.
Money is behind all acts of venery.
Being short makes all girls plainish.

Only a half-wit can truly love a mall.
Christmas is a tightwad's nightmare.
No alternator is easy to install.
Anything marginal's denominated queer.

Mormon churches resemble Dairy Queens.
Nietzsche: the sole universal means of value is power.
No bad drivers match boys in their teens.
The character of sweet depends for its identity on sour.

Air is, ironically, the nemesis of freshness.
Sacrifice is the *sine qua non* of love.
Cholera may also be called Bangladeshness.
Below is always inferior to above.

Figwood is the best to conjure fire.
Gold is ductile and soft though heavy.
A bad memory always brings down a liar.
Woman's beauty is always lost in a bevy.

Air is nature's best insulator.
White oak is the best timber for ships.
Ego is the living essence of a creator.
Gulps badly malign a wine, not sips.

Orange may be called the wife of blue.
Belarus numbers the most alcoholics.
Interest invariably grows as debts accrue.
Trees fight insects by exuding phenolics.

A dark suit serves to flatter any man.
Snakes always swallow their prey whole.
Prejudice essentializes any living clan.
Symmetry is never lacking in a bowl.

Vexation is the beginning of all art.
Nothing fails for Christians who believe.
Who values a zoo is missing a heart.
Bank on political extremists to deceive.

The deeper one goes, the larger the squid.
No unmarried men recognize their faults.
All western cities bear a logical grid.
Questions asked are never not assaults.

Sole custody is frankly child abuse.
The Chinese were never a martial race.
Falling in love is always half ruse.
Every man at fifty deserves his face.

A scent of godliness pervades leaf mold.
No Shakespeare play is set at Christmas.
In poker, diffident players tend to fold.
Width is invariably narrow on an isthmus.

TRUISMS

Crabs are stale when their eyes look dull.
New grapes need new vines to grow.
Food eaten in darkness is rendered null.
To not love? Simple. No gratitude bestow.

Cruelty ever thrives in the face of fear.
LA's centerlessness embodies lack of soul.
Faith and good works always cohere.
The Soviets alone reverenced a prole.

The most impenetrable part of a castle is its keep.
Southern Poverty Law Center salaries are huge.
Acupuncture needle are inserted ¼ to ½-inch deep.
No evil was done by the pre-converted Scrooge.

Blue smoke indicates an oil problem.
Send wedding gifts only to the bride.
Any Puritan can understand a Moslem.
No human face has a matching side.

Garage doors erase a building's beauty.
Bare feet make old men of us all.
As a human motive, love surpasses duty.
A fully handsome man is always tall.

A non-cultic faith's a contradiction.
White, not green, in lemongrass is used.
Autobiography's the source of fiction.
Hatred is to self-destruction fused.

Rutabagas are properly food for animals.
Virgil felt only women were the cause of war.
The Korowai of Papua still remain cannibals.
The Panama hat is actually from Ecuador.

Craving ice is a symptom of anemia.
Every lie incurs a debt to the truth.
Fungi picking is the passion in Bohemia.
Wine spiked with brandy is vermouth.

Armida desires to kill, then kisses Rinaldo.
A Frans Hals grinning face indicates stupidity.
Countertenors match in voice a female contralto.
Baseball pitchers, in top form, convey fluidity.

Elephants are completely unable to jump.
Ireland and Côte d'Ivoire share the same flag.
Samoan men prefer their women plump.
The sap of fir trees constitutes a rosin bag.

Lake Ontario never freezes over.
An oblique confession is always a plea.
No creature relishes rain like a plover.
The most selfish of all words is *me*.

Women's underwear is meant to tease.
Christ never once described a heaven.
A hug is the gesture, not the squeeze.
The taste of bread has to do with leaven.

TRUISMS

All insects have six legs.
Whom you borrow from you're bound to.
Pride by definition never begs.
Forgive a debt? Banks are never found to.

Spiraling reduces the steepness of a grade.
Water is the foundation of all soup.
Shade is the comfort in every arcade.
A knot cannot be made without a loop.

Everything tastes better after midnight.
No British bobby carries a gun.
Everything is clarified in hindsight.
Cicadas revel in the blazing sun.

Don Quixote sustains any theory brought to it.
The poor are promised, or so Jesus said.
Choose a dry day in a field to pick a blewit.
Anyone walking on heels has a heavy tread.

One can never find a vista in New Jersey.
One cannot taste, merely smell fishiness.
Schoolboys beat up every boy named Percy.
Gold is to greed, as wheezing is to itchiness.

Mistletoe, parasitic, is also poisonous.
Hydrangeas only bloom on old growth.
The crime of commercials is in cozening us.
Each is never quite as holy as both.

Our best traits lie right next to our worst.
Army intelligence is an oxymoron.
To hurt innocence is to be forever cursed.
When you weep, you so forewarn.

Music never offers concrete meaning.
Cremation is illegal in Islam.
Insincerity is invariably overweening.
The fact of any firearm means harm.

Eating snow can lead to hypothermia.
No economic idea is ever truly dead.
The richer the lawyer, the wormier.
The poorer a nation, the less it is fed.

Than potatoes nothing feeds man better.
The Irish never produced an economist.
A president looks foolish in a sweater.
The faster the seduced, the slower kissed.

Women's figures approximate fruits.
Every living actors is grossly overpaid.
No female fails look sexy wearing boots.
Celebrity is all an engineered charade.

Victorian bedrooms had no closets.
Against knaves the best defense is knavery.
Withdrawals perpetually exceed deposits.
Dominance is the beating heart of slavery.

TRUISMS

Generosity describes no woman driver.
Child abuse fosters powder kegs.
Sincerity is wholly absent in a striver.
The glory of a model is in her legs.

French pastry is all about butter.
The Red Sox always swoon in September.
Diffidence accompanies a stutter.
To dream one must first remember.

Violence is ever the imperial tool.
Cows abhor the taste of flowers.
Turkish pornography is always cruel.
Weather change attends on showers.

A sibling never fails to be a rival.
Cook fish on each side only once.
Age makes anything archival.
Scratch a non-reader, find a dunce.

Swedes have a tendency to obey.
Guests after three full days are jailers.
Homophobes often prove to be gay.
Gentlemen never discuss their tailors.

A spider's web is all straight lines.
Every hosta plant despises sunlight.
Eggplants all have poison vines.
Diplomacy hides a private gunsight.

Few podiatrists have earned a degree.
The poverty of having everything is real.
Lunacy's having one name for the sea.
A popular Japanese entrée on rice is eel.

A thumbs-up gesture in Iran is offensive.
Orthodox Jews do not shake hands with women.
Stocks in October are historically ascensive.
Magicians like to feign affinity with the demon.

An organically dyed rug in green is rare.
A potato needs a sandy soil to thrive.
Sweets are the *summum bonum* for a bear.
An eagle's aim to kill is in its dive.

Littering is a criminal act in Singapore.
A lack of punctuality is always rude
Fatuity defines a yacht-club commodore.
A prig is far, far worse than any prude.

A poker player's "tell" defines his vice.
Gardeners on TV are always pleasant.
Praise is the Psalmist's main device.
Shyness is a teenager's suppressant.

All bag ladies look like Louise Nevelson.
One cannot be a collector and a dealer.
Who betrays a friend is the devil's son.
Nature is both a killer and a healer.

TRUISMS

Old Irishmen have hideous eyebrows.
An invalid exists in every unhappy wife.
Busty females prevail in boat prows.
State workers toil in moods of strife.

For Hell's Angels a Harley FXR is the bike of choice.
People who dance attendance have to learn new steps.
Virility often masquerades itself with a bass voice.
No government investigation isn't pointlessly complex.

All Red Sox/Yankees games are hateful.
Hibiscus flowers always appear unnatural.
A debtor in one's family is never grateful.
The human figure is basically contralateral.

It is impossible to overcook ribs.
Bald men invariably shower with hot water.
Wisdom adhibits most to female Caribs.
No living animal has thicker fur than an otter.

As oppression escalates, fear heightens.
Mafiosi love to operate funeral homes.
Aging, white wine darkens, red wine lightens.
Bacteria have circular chromosomes.

It is blasphemy to train a wild animal.
A dilatory girlfriend is a messy wife.
Abusing anyone is being a cannibal.
Lemons often figure in a typical still life.

To plant mums in summer is too early.
The Inuit never punish their kids.
RMV workers seem to exist to be surly.
Marriage proposals are merely bids.

One can see further in colder air.
In life, the rich are given huge head starts.
The Shaker mentality exalts the spare.
Greek sculpture shows no private parts.

Sapphonics can muster freakish fury.
An only child mainly goes unreproved.
Amateur writers concentrate on story.
A knave always shakes hands gloved.

A fat man looks for food to heal.
Bad nerves, not people, gnash gum.
No use of capers ever improved a meal.
Royal faces in playing cards are glum.

Crab grass can never be stopped.
Miss Shirley Temple was a genius at five.
Anything on sale is always shopped.
Even the evil dead, sentiment will shrive.

American breads are utterly tasteless.
The need to seem authentic only damns it.
Shifts in fashion are always baseless.
The worse the comedian, the more he hams it.

TRUISMS

A potato should never be refrigerated.
Military manuals are written in blood.
Every computer's immediately outdated.
Bangladesh is forever in flood.

Polytheism has no omnipotent gods.
A Shatoosh shawl should slip through a ring.
India and Pakistan are always at odds.
Humility is the *sine qua non* of worshipping.

All practical jokers tend to be cruel.
4,800 chemicals sit in cigarette tobacco.
Boy Scouts tend to be pedophile fuel.
The wind gives no comfort in a sirocco.

Red wine needs time to improve.
Ants in colonies are always equal.
An eagle to kill needs prey to move.
Sense is always sacrificed in a sequel.

Exaggeration is somehow always comic.
To interpret Scripture, use nothing else.
All oversimplifications end up gnomic.
America's first hunters sought only pelts.

The closer to power, the more morally blind.
Beware any household devoid of books.
The chronically immature always reply in kind.
Female power best resides in its looks.

A lover joins one who makes him suffer.
The worse the beer, the colder it must be.
Every boaster at bottom reveals a bluffer.
The greatest of water pumps are any tree.

No hate can match a poet's for another.
Life in its brevity allows no one to belong.
A zealous always has a lazy brother.
Nothing is filthier than an Asian klong.

Obstacles invariably swell the libido.
Plum seeds actually contain cyanide.
All straight ties clash with a tuxedo.
Los Cabos leads the world in homicide.

Dahlias flower throughout the summer.
Always fract a chicken when it it hot.
Than state policemen, no one's dumber.
DVDs in a library proves a sign of rot.

The Marx Brothers were never funny.
Any nude without a face is dishonest.
San Diego's weather is always sunny.
A man of faith is invariably a Monist.

An orchid needs a window west and east.
Estonian is quite impossible to learn.
All visits to a church presuppose a quest.
Nothing evokes sadness like an urn.

TRUISMS

Censorship is always born of fear.
Never in August trim a clematis.
An intelligent auto commercial is rare.
Celebrities expect everything gratis.

Never give a child an option or a choice.
Smiles are the hardest expressions to fathom.
Hypocrisy's best salesman is a voice.
Dauntlessness is the trademark of a madam.

An owl in a Bosch painting epitomizes malice.
Protestantism views the Virgin with a gimlet eye.
No cardiac glycoside can top the drug digitalis.
Shakespeare links orgasms with the verb "to die."

Dreidels began as a gambling game.
Leaves from the tops of trees fall first.
Love felt for anyone is always the same.
No human agony can supercede thirst.

A uniform makes any man a killer.
Every Japanese is born a Shinto.
The lyrics to most songs are filler.
Use no bean for chili but the pinto.

Autumn's always best for planting grass.
No post-WW II boy was named Adolf.
The vilest distinctions are those of class.
Ralph in the UK is called Rafe, not Rolf.

ALEXANDER THEROUX

For calcium intake nothing beats sardines
Approach a drowning victim from the rear.
Miners get to see only their own seams.
Government should not row, but steer.

Most law students crave only money.
Clapton always tried to imitate Muddy.
Most pregnant women prefer eggs runny.
The face of an Inuit is invariably ruddy.

Bells never signify in American cities.
Every set of keys is made to be lost.
Lewdness is the beating heart of ditties.
Owning a boat is a parable of cost.

Women other women always suspect.
Never use ground beef in chili *con carne*.
Innocence is a condition unable to detect.
Even a politician's dreams are blarney.

Never look at the bowl of water you carry.
The fourth Brandenburg is the most beautiful.
The credulous discover everywhere a fairy.
Custom alone gauges what is suitable.

A galantine is always served up cold.
Good editors are far rarer than good writers.
Reaching by definition is always bold.
Those who deal with nature must be fighters.

TRUISMS

The higher you go, the quicker the refund.
Wars always enrich the corporate sector.
A tree near any spreading vine is moribund.
To pay a visit unannounced is to hector.

The need to write a book a year's a curse.
Grapevines prefer their roots be dry.
No shine exceeds that on a coffin or hearse.
The sea is ever a mirror of the sky.

A police funeral is always maudlin.
Without Curly, Stooges movies suck.
Good lookers demand constant coddling.
All ball sports mainly turn on luck.

Use only naturally brewed soy sauce.
Anthony Trollope was fixated with suicides.
Cheap jewelry flashes major boss.
He who envies, compulsively first derides.

Blind loyalty is an aspect of unreason.
You never see the croc that kills you.
A charitable act is never out of season.
No actor's brainpower ever thrills you.

D=*daleth*=door=delta=the female pubic triangle.
Miro and Klee seemed to paint proto-Sinaitic symbols.
Armenians and Azerbaijanis perpetually wrangle.
Digitabulists are passionate collectors of thimbles.

Convenience not comfort applies to futons.
Never consume any oyster that is dead.
Uranium atoms fission when hit by neutrons.
Authoritarians all adore the color red.

Two billion people on Earth are unable to read.
The continents can be rearranged to form a chicken.
It was only slaves in Southern states Lincoln freed.
Liquids for safe swallowing can be made to thicken.

All shrouds in sailing need dead eyes.
All human conflict is theological.
Moisture in a lower crust redeems all pies.
Orchestra seating strictly geological.

One can never be sad and also whistle.
Italy exports far more wine than France.
Abrasiveness characterizes every thistle.
Sex in intention is a kind of ritual dance.

Wolverine fur will never mat or freeze the skin.
All map boundaries are subjective and artificial.
Under Israel, the most destitute are Bedouin.
Human law is less probative than prejudicial.

Eschew salt whenever cooking beans.
In a bar fight, always go for the legs.
Laws ever indulge anyone with means.
Any individual who flatters, also begs.

TRUISMS

Terrorism is the war of the poor.
Welsh language has no silent letters.
Everyone who is incurious is a bore.
Greed, not need, drives all bettors.

Over electricity, chefs choose gas.
Hope tends to be the mother of fools.
No occasion doesn't call for a Mass.
Reality destroys what romance fuels.

Rule: always split aces and eights.
Nothing with zero calories tastes delicious.
Falling in love involves swapping fates.
No nation-building dream is not fictitious.

No inmates shared a cell in Alcatraz.
All Ibos are abos, not the reverse.
Who denies he has sinned already has.
Length alone becomes a hearse.

No true Italian ever says pizza *pie*.
Cook Islanders are badly overweight.
To demand justice is to mercy deny.
Every honest wall eschews a gate.

Mysterious truth is never analytical.
All deep-down Marxists are compassionate.
A hypocrite's repentance is hypocritical.
No observer is worthy unless dispassionate.

"Best" lies close to "worst" in people.
Picasso reinvented the modern ceramic.
The prayer of a church is in its steeple.
Howling is an evangelist's sole dynamic.

Not a single thing exists without Tao.
A uniform disguises a person's uniqueness.
Intrigue in film loved locations in Macao.
Great spiritual power resides in meekness.

Folks in sunless nations rarely smile.
Hypocrisy is the gift that vice pays virtue.
Beauty in a human easily fosters guile.
Laws less often come to help than hurt you.

Politics is showbiz for ugly people.
Tigers always attack from the rear.
Molasses is much darker than treacle
To become elected, threaten fear.

Most cities emerged at river bends.
All quests involve seeking God.
No quality whisky involves blends.
Everything original is always odd.

The Incas valued the cacao tree more than gold.
Elvis Presley, hating them from youth, never wore jeans.
The Sadducees denied the immortality of the soul.
Packed in oil, as opposed to water, taste the best sardines.

TRUISMS

Chew oysters, never simply swallow.
Never vacuum an oriental rug.
Etiquette, unlike manners, is hollow.
Staring is the habit of a thug.

Age is the *sine qua non* of whiskey.
Mushroom pickers tend to be misfits.
Climbing in every sense is risky.
Real baseball requires fistmitts.

Berbers feel that washing is unhealthy.
Texas mesquite is the best grass for cattle.
The *status quo* is defended by the wealthy.
Alexander the Great never lost a battle.

World economy depends on microchips.
Asians are intolerant to alcohol.
Micronesians in the main are missing hips.
Thinness is a kind of horrible tall.

It is easy to be rich if you are cheap.
A yucca plant is impossible to kill.
At Gettysburg, one cannot fail to weep.
Prayer involves offering one's will.

Folks in Maine cannot bear idle talk.
The true smile is in a person's eyes.
Caution always tells the tale of caulk.
Guilt constantly sells what pity buys.

Dried rosemary is dead rosemary.
Eggs derive lutein from the yellow marigold
Biblical heavies are always hairy.
Darkness is inevitably a terrible kind of cold.

Smoking's never mentioned in the Bible.
Southerners all cherish the military.
The greater the truth the greater the libel.
Aimlessness is the joy of the fritillary.

Our bodies create cholesterol at night.
Hemlocks rarely grow on level land.
The truest charity is given out of sight.
A fiancée's request is always a demand.

The French tend to eschew spicy food.
No Christmas carol should be improvised.
Loudness is a major aspect of the lewd.
For every heat, a blister is devised.

Israel stole the land of Palestine.
Bosch believed sexual passion threatened the soul.
Grace does not eat but dines.
No pot should ever be called a bowl.

A balsam is the ideal Christmas tree.
Americans love happy-face theology.
Most Canadian Indians are Cree.
Loners gravitate to herpetology.

TRUISMS

All great poetry is essentially prayer.
Shape aids in the taste of falafel.
Than Vilnius, Lithuania no city is grayer.
A doughnut without glaze is but a waffle.

Seek a neap tide to swim a channel.
There's no place to hide on a rugby field.
Fix less on the portrait than the panel.
Achilles alone lived up to his shield.

A sushi bar is only as good as its tuna.
St. Paul mastered the epistolary form.
Masts are the soul of any schooner.
The antonym of study is a dorm.

Rising age leads to more suicides.
Louisianans pronounce pralines "prawlenes."
Suicidal risks are high in parricides.
Literary uncles are notoriously fiends.

Hawks are not hatched but *disclosed*.
Caviar is sampled from back of one's hand.
All things apposed are never opposed.
Every racist adores sporting an armband.

All crimes are variations of theft.
Petulance comes natural to a cook.
Right for total balance needs the left.
Suspicion is the fail-safe of a rook.

You cannot kill a rosy rugosa plant.
Every baseball pitcher's arm is doomed.
All of history's written at a slant.
No serious male is ever groomed.

The vileness of a rumor is it's spread.
A center airplane seat gets *both* armrests
What's remembered is written, not said.
Three days is the ultimate limit for guests.

E, a wind vowel from old proto-Sinaitic *heh*,
is the sound of breath, emanation of prayer.
No vowels exist in Tetragrammaton YHWH.
Napoleon struck in the Coup of 18 Brumaire.

The biggest bores are failure and success.
To "hold" a consonant no singer's able.
Of government we need more, not less.
Character in a house involves a gable.

No arbitrary tax is ever a low tax.
Solitude safeguards the self.
"Pitch outside, throw inside"—Koufax.
No soft shoulder is a shelf.

Bank on governments to waste money.
No real Italian refers to sauce as gravy.
Climate in the Faroes is never sunny.
No falcon flight is chronicled as wavy.

TRUISMS

Chinese restaurants all love awnings.
The secret of baklava is in the layer.
Know a politician by his fawnings.
Charity is the deepest form of prayer.

Lilacs thrive on fireplace ashes.
No matter who, the unhappy are dull.
Pimps cherish anything that flashes.
Elation characterizes every skull.

All Greeks pronounce cheese "*tzeese*."
No one in Paris works on Monday.
Bridges are always first to freeze.
Suicide-types fear a lonely Sunday.

No actual soil is found in potting soil.
Mormons are invariably Republican.
A fool is always valued as a foil.
Garrulity characterizes every publican.

Thumbs do 40% of a hand's work.
Women reviewers praise women writers.
A complimented worker tends to shirk.
Boxing is not always fit for fighters.

Chewers favor one side of the mouth.
Nothing breaks quicker than cookie jars.
Evangelism thrives mainly in the South.
A hockey player's badges are his scars.

Pruning always stimulates new growth.
Chinese loyalty's to family, not to state.
Be but loyal to fully pledge your troth.
Only the very first and last sons rate.

Every culture has its stuffed savories.
Statins have proven better than stents.
Water by itself establishes aviaries.
Sex for landlords is to dream of rents.

Children offer the best conversation.
Broccoli leaves are healthier than its florets.
State workers are always on vacation.
Any self-reliant man forgoes regrets.

Self-haters will not be told they're loved.
Americans hate the idea of a third party.
Born New Yorkers shove when being shoved.
To the Mennonite mind all color is arty.

Pedantry is fueled by self-applause.
Every living plant creates a flower.
To find deceit, simply search a clause.
Pity rarely corresponds with power.

Auto commercials are beyond vulgar.
Grapes never grow on last year's vines.
Force to a Prussian is finally fulgur.
Fingers taught forks the fact of tines.

TRUISMS

Iranians are ill-given to want to smile.
No politician is not a panderer.
The soul of selling is essentially guile.
The female form shapes a philanderer.

Indian kids win most spelling-bees.
Peat moss, dried out, never gets wet.
Dr. Fraud uses his honorary degrees.
Regret *sans* contrition is never regret.

Noon is midnight for garage sales.
Hummingbirds love trumpet-shaped flowers.
Intimacy is required for betrayals.
What is familiar always quickly sours.

All aspects of lobbying are crooked.
No one pronounces "February" right.
A Scientologist is someone snookered.
Sweet kisses dissolve the longest night.

Being tall is a national trait in Latvia.
Rapists all had terrible childhoods.
Style in Rome is found in its atria.
Quebec has miles of roadside roods.

Plants naturally grow in communities.
That meat nearest the bone tastes best.
All beautiful women expect impunities.
Severe solitude is sanity's surest test.

Poverty disallows any privacy.
The Sudanese rarely buy a book
Wars are the major source of piracy.
No living human can outfox a rook.

Basil under 50-degrees won't flourish.
Deer antlers sell pocket-knives.
Fail to praise, fail to nourish.
Sovereignty is the goal of wives.

Pharma in America is utterly corrupt.
Women pols try to sound like men.
Every savage ego seeks to interrupt.
Nonsense is the *sine qua non* of Zen.

True Communists are serious idealists.
Latinas tend to love hoop earrings
Cynics are synonymous with realists.
Weather is evoked in a tree's rings.

The prettier the woman, the more jealous.
Men when driving hate to ask for directions.
Than converts, no one is more zealous.
True love is never curbed by imperfections.

A pointing finger invariably blames
Baltic temperaments tend to the sour.
War is the subtext of all sport's games.
Hubris is the message of every tower.

TRUISMS

Stop signs in the USA mean go.
Never fertilize a thirsty plant.
Blueness as a color *whitens* snow.
Evangelists only speak through cant.

Bees favor the colors purple and blue.
Golf is a game, not at all a sport.
British everywhere compulsively queue.
Rank alone defines a royal court.

Dahlias longer flirt than any flower.
Postal workers feel constantly abused.
Sizes in tombstones reassert a need for power.
A bought diamond is immediately used.

Learning golf is basically pure mimicry.
Blond hair never really shines.
A bourgeois mind delights in symmetry.
No face is not enhanced by lines.

Bunnies all adore white clover.
Resting a steak's as crucial as cooking it.
When candor enters, romance is over.
One abets prejudice when brooking it.

Never water a garden after 6 p.m.
Hunters badly fear not being men.
A watch is most breakable at its stem.
Fear is the vice that wonders when.

No kipper tastes as good as it smells.
New Year's Eves always foster regret.
Any product aimed at vanity sells.
Natives abroad are all well met.

Kangaroos are unable to walk backwards.
Rh antibodies factor minus in fertility
The most prolific breeding avians are blackbirds.
Humility should never be taken for servility

African-Americans love to rhyme.
All hydrangeas start out white.
The greatest arch-satirist is time.
Independence gives every man some height.

Movie villains love smoking jackets.
Misogyny thrives in many a maxim.
Excess is what ruins crime rackets.
Congress's sole solution is "Tax 'em."

No Dane dines without a candle.
Donald Trump's rule: never apologize.
Money gives everything a handle.
All Thai women have lovely eyes.

Rain of all the waters is the purest.
High school bullies all became cops.
Distress proves friendship surest.
Computer speeds are gauged by MFLOPs.

TRUISMS

Sunshine's the ultimate disinfectant.
Wealthy heiresses are always homely.
A watch can make the perfect sextant.
No da Vinci woman is not comely.

Vowels are indistinct in an Arab's mouth.
Soccer in Europe is a religion.
Sloth is a condition in every country's south.
Sikhs famously revere the pigeon.

Masseurs in Japan are generally blind.
All cephalopods are carnivores.
Vitamin C is found richest in the rind.
Primitive cultures all eschew doors.

A creature's shell is a mobile home.
Bullfighting is symbolic transvestitism.
A jealous mate is always first to roam.
Americans are spooked by communism.

The skin of mushrooms holds the flavor.
Sports stars rarely kill themselves.
It is the *rarity* of certain foods we savor.
Spite is the special delight of elves.

A running child follows a rolling ball.
The *Titanic*'s sinking killed the Belle Époque.
A crow is doing algebra with its call.
Intelligence is strictly eyesight in a hawk.

Slice cucumbers from the thick end.
Animals compulsively live by routine.
No original mind ever follows a trend.
Miracles for faith need not be seen.

There is poetry in the fingers of cooks.
Two fingers always mean a curveball.
Sententiousness thrives in handbooks.
A short man in his dreams is always tall.

Any house is sterile without books.
No is the defining meaning of a wall.
Cruelty subverts anyone's good looks.
Aimlessness adores a shopping mall.

Foreigners always stand out in Japan.
Men's underwear is perfectly hideous.
Squareness never validly suits a can.
Having no opinions is perfidious.

India never wins Olympic medals.
A Serbian heart is always a bigot's.
The brawn of a bike is in its pedals.
Find no bunghole, see no spigots.

Colored candles are always tacky.
A clear conscience is a crystal ball.
No political booster's not a lackey.
An ugly man gains looks when tall.

TRUISMS

An overlarge robe is always best.
Sisters are proud of brothers' sex lives.
Over-planning a day insults a guest.
Any listener to gossip fully connives.

No joke is ultimately not serious.
A big game hunter never takes a risk.
Handshake shapes are multifarious.
Every true command is always brisk.

Reading is a form of thinking,
All New Guineans look like James Baldwin.
Submission is a way of sinking.
An empty mind is a zealot's cauldron.

No Indian buttons his collar tieless.
One is supposed to chew port wine.
Living without a dream is skyless.
The eight major planets never align.

Never put your plants to bed wet.
No one keeps to his lane in a roundabout.
Every actress yearns to play Juliet.
Truth inevitably arrives by way of doubt.

Republican Conventions all lack soul.
A cop-killer's legal defense always porous.
Roman Catholicism is crucial to a Pole.
Masks were always worn by a Greek chorus.

Lunch is the main meal for Chileans.
All barracudas zero in on shine.
Talk is a circus for sesquipedelians.
Savages eat, food lovers dine.

Footwear noise sends power to the wearer.
Always offer odd numbers of flowers.
Gifts to wives never make you dearer.
Males revel in the height of towers.

Graffiti indicates disaffected youth.
All great causes begin as a movement.
Wherever kindness flourishes is couth.
Contrition is the beginning of improvement.

Lingerie is code for emergency sluthood.
One hates one's roommate by definition.
All non-readers qualify for nuthood.
Amendment is the soul of all contrition.

If a woman's a cause, a woman's a cure.
Always cultivate a plumber's friendship.
Being clueless always makes a bore.
Hate and jealousy make a perfect blendship.

Nothing's happened until it's been described.
Everything tastes better wrapped in bacon.
Decency with money has never jibed.
Thrift, seeing waste, is badly shaken.

TRUISMS

Chowder's the most abused dish on earth.
It is not meaning that we need, but sight.
Of reason in matters of war there's a dearth.
No wind was ever mastered by a kite.

Travel nowhere without a book.
Everyone has a recipe for chili.
Every sheriff inside-out's a crook.
No French comedy is not silly.

Human conversation pets a cat.
A homosexual's mother is his wife.
Everyone looks a fool in a brimless hat.
A dash on a gravestone sums up a life.

Crows see very poorly in the dark.
No nutrients are found in sand.
The Apostles are fools in the Gospel of Mark.
An M is inscribed on every hand.

Love is a vowel. Marriage is a consonant.
Giving yellow flowers in Russia is a curse.
Menstrual pain's allayed by Shepherd's Purse.
Innocence in its only failing is improvident.

Writers using three names tend to suck.
Haters will always vote in the rain.
The need to gamble is to be out of luck.
Rarely is a stripper fully sane.

Asians in the kitchen are the kings.
No rejection's fiercer than a mother's.
Any wire in a window always sings.
Pain ignored is always another's.

Men have wishes, women have whims.
The more prolific, the bigger the hack.
Beauty, when cruel, immediately dims.
Where we hate, we reveal what we lack.

Neurotics all open mail right away.
Every racetrack payout is a bunce.
Showing mercy is a way to pray.
Patience is the politics of punts.

Art forgers in prison are never despised.
Electricity creates magnetism.
A plant with dead fish is truly fertilized.
War turns reason into cataclysm.

True jade lovers are usually Chinese.
Symphony conductors prefer birch batons.
No tight dress is not a tease.
Dutch words comprise 90% of Afrikaans.

Campaigning is poetry, governing is prose.
Unsprouted bud tissue makes wood burled
Rhythm is the key for anyone who rows.
Intentions in Maine are always furled.

TRUISMS

Buy mushrooms whole, never sliced.
Country votes are tallied later than city.
No high-quality stout should be iced.
True love is never expressed with pity.

All who hate the sacred, adore magic.
A servant glides away; a handler lingers.
No play where logic rules is tragic.
Cinema lust tends to focus on fingers.

Women who love horses usually love sex.
A Hell's Angels bike starts on the first kick.
The actor is directed, the real artist directs.
Nothing with a solution constitutes a trick.

No Republican ever wins Ohio.
Every golfing purse is an obscenity.
A waiter's manner is a form of bunco.
Solitude allows the only true serenity.

Gays tend to love Broadway Cast albums.
All little people sound like frogs.
Chocolate to horses is delicious pabulum.
Loyalty comes naturally to dogs.

Cook all turkeys at 325 degrees.
No one tenders tips in Israel.
The tastiest food is fresh, buttered peas.
Nothing healthy is found in a pill.

ALEXANDER THEROUX

The drive for power is born of weakness.
Chopin wrote only the briefest pieces.
Nothing like Lagos for utter bleakness.
Divorce addresses the nature of leases.

The biggest bores are failure and success.
To "hold" a consonant no singer is able.
Of government we need not more but less.
Character in a house involves a gable.

Snobs are perpetually insecure.
Gregariousness is the enemy of art.
A joy for the rich is to see the poor.
No target can ever avoid a dart.

All Bostonians look like William Demarest.
Plagiarism is a confession of weakness.
To descend is to have to re-climb Everest.
Transcendent joy is found in meekness.

In society, friendship amounts to zero.
The cripple wins all races in his dreams.
A woman's a fascist who admires a hero.
No true genius thinks in terms of teams.

Any serious vow is a godly oath.
A cretin does not believe in privacy.
State workers define the word sloth.
Tithing is, at best, religious piracy.

TRUISMS

Taste is wanting in the middle-class.
Telethons are an aspect of nagging.
Socialite's another name for bitch.
Military medals are only bragging.

Despair means having no alternatives.
Guys named "Bubba" look just like it.
Christianity shames all conservatives.
To enjoy water, always spike it.

Elephants loathe having to climb hills.
The rights of man were created by rebels.
All handshakes should avoid any frills.
Duplicity against a close friend trebles.

No tree ever dies of old age.
Mormon missionaries can never go swimming.
Motors always employ AC voltage.
Improvisation is the prime virtue in scat-singing

All definitions are re-statements
Suicide notes are always insignificant.
Every usurer reviles abatements.
Kneeling dignifies any communicant.

In clothing sales, it pays to be small.
Rodeo riders resemble stubby pliers.
No girl isn't propagandized by a doll.
The color red is never seen in fires.

ALEXANDER THEROUX

A friend in power is a friend soon lost.
One cannot be jealous without being in love.
Nothing in a tempest is not tossed.
Shape not warmth defines a perfect glove.

Saying "Bless his heart" precedes pity.
The secret to any good cookie is butter.
Country songs all revile the city.
Psychotic minds tend to cultivate clutter.

Street vendors insistently only accept cash.
Liars thrive on trust in the innocent.
No honest history describes the actual past.
A child rapist is never found repentant.

Every agnostic supposes he's the first.
A good cranberry always bounces.
Roses have endless hunger and thirst.
A conventional florist always flounces.

Clams should cook for seven minutes.
There are no Amish physicians.
Flax feeds both linen and linnets.
Sobriety is the smile of all morticians.

Good latkes are born of dry potatoes.
Chubby kids always play the tuba.
Shakespeare is the king of quotatoes.
Suicide rates are very low in Cuba.

TRUISMS

The history of Afghanistan is war.
The Irish tend to age very poorly.
Nobody ever washes a rented car.
The extremities in gout feel sorely.

It is very easy to make a bad pie.
Butchers in movies are always fat.
The task of a lawyer is first to lie.
Ash is the wood for a baseball bat.

In Arkansas, football constitutes a religion.
Queen Elizabeth II never said a memorable word.
Nothing transmits disease like a pigeon.
A good servant is never seen and never heard.

A sordid past explains many a carny.
Nobel Prize awards are always political.
Patriotic speech is always blarney.
No final confession isn't veridical.

Cocoa should properly be called cacao.
Tolerating delay offends a multi-tasker.
Pickpocketing is rife in Montevideo.
A rascal on ships is generally a Lascar.

Astringency points to dry, not sour.
Thin and warm are everywhere at loggerheads.
Johannesburg natives are perpetually dour.
The truest arrowheads are smallest arrowheads.

No truly great female humorist exists.
Cartoon figures all have three fingers.
Ambition alone yearns to be president.
Despair is the basic cause of anomie.

Dirty oil means it's doing its job.
Gold is always a ballast to inflation.
A worthy watch is partnered with a fob.
Chauvinism blasphemes a nation.

Gary, Indiana has most blacks America.
Vinegar gives soup immense mileage.
A feminine trick is pleading by hysteria.
An explosion lies awake in any silage.

Thrift stores reflect their neighborhoods.
Pissing outside flows to the shoes.
An original lie is still damaged goods.
Repetition expresses the blue of the "blues."

All translators are dreadfully poor.
Repetition is an indication of dementia.
Opposite orders are given by a door.
No mother-in-law isn't valued in absentia.

Trade deficits fall in a recession.
Envy is hatred's next-door resident.
Abasement is vulgar in a confession.
The Occident will fade before the Orient.

TRUISMS

Rarity alone generates demand.
Drunkenness is always another man.
Land is ruled by lip, sea by hand.
Anonymity rallies the Ku Klux Klan.

Familiarity is pernicious in a waiter.
Secrecy is indispensable for a tryst.
Lovelessness is the fate of every satyr.
Avarice holds sway in a game of whist.

Know yourself to know your enemy.
Indians are closer to sisters than to wives.
Silk is conducive to venery.
Whiteness for bees is required in hives.

Only lowbreds speak publicly on phones.
No red-headed person is truly normal.
Vanity and atheism are perfect clones.
A Mass is sacriligious if said informal.

Valentine's Day's for women, not for men.
Canadians, unlike Mexicans, stay put.
Wild chaos is the defining beauty of a fen.
Vinegar with water will erase black soot.

The Stock Exchange is run by fear and greed.
The meanest guest has the keenest eye.
Even beauty is not forgiven in a weed.
God a penitent soul will never deny.

ALEXANDER THEROUX

A pink turkey leg shows nothing is cooked.
Mathematics is a metaphor for reality.
A faultless restaurant is always booked.
Communism in perfection is pure ideality.

Rope is never coiled up, always down.
Immigrants tend to be fervently patriotic.
The world capital of gayness is Cape Town.
Leather is, inexplicably, weirdly homoerotic.

Psoriasis inclines to people with pallid skin.
Flowers buy wayward men easy forgiveness.
If it teaches feelings of shame, blessed be sin.
American baseball's not a sport, but business.

A newborn baby is three-fourths water.
All cops try to sound like John Wayne.
Every wife has a rival in a daughter.
No TV talk-show host is not inane.

All car mufflers are created to corrode.
Postal workers always feel interrupted.
Think of use, not charm, in a commode.
Any solon lobbied is a solon corrupted.

Many heads can't fit under one hat.
Confidence is the child of optimism.
Wine to age well needs a solid vat.
True sanctity exudes its own chrism.

TRUISMS

Moss has neither flowers nor seeds.
Childless couples always buy a pup.
An obese man never eats, he feeds.
To a mole, the direction down is up.

Every genius has a half-wit brother.
Conservatives dream at night of tanks.
The youngest is loved most by a mother.
Librarians are predominantly cranks.

A disappointing lover is always hasty.
Mexicans have no interest in getting tans.
Chucks of beef are never truly tasty.
Barbecue should be eaten with the hands.

Unblotted hands are rare with lepers.
Poverty should seek the warmest climate.
The sole vegetable Texas-grown is peppers.
A venomous squib sharpens if you rhyme it.

Airline pilots on intercoms always mumble.
Jews tend to avoid working in agriculture.
Every worthwhile cookie is low on crumble.
No horror on earth exceeds visisepulture.

George Bernard Shaw despised all traveling.
A fondness for trading is very Tunisian.
No mystery isn't diminished by its unraveling.
Spouses too long together form an adhesion.

An oversize zucchini tastes like clay.
No one drinks from the front of mugs.
The act of gossip is basically to betray.
Treachery is often linked with hugs.

Shape is the beating soul of seeds.
Poisonous are *all* parts of a buttercup.
Small talk is eschewed by Swedes.
Decolletage is standard for a pin-up.

Compulsive talkers hate loquacity in others.
No jellyfish, starfish, or crayfish is a fish.
Envy and greed are perennial brothers.
Acquisition is the beating heart of every wish.

Tomatoes in Hawaii cannot be grown.
Left from horses is the side to dismount.
Better than glued, a book must be sewn.
On movie locations, sex does not count.

Exactitude is the secret of all bonsai.
A porcupine's defense is walking backward.
Every emotion makes a woman cry.
A giraffe's every move appears as awkward.

Shaping is the work of symphony conductors.
Nobody's favorite month is March.
All locusts by nature are natural destructors.
Cones enhance the beauty of a larch.

TRUISMS

Durability is the perfect living proof.
Expert hypocrites have many styles.
Discernment demands one be aloof.
Women are very rarely pedophiles.

Nothing can ever kill a yucca.
Vietnamese people love to squat.
Kidneys suffer in a trucker.
By a solon's favor you are bought.

A cat's tongue is purest emery.
Alumnae waxing nostalgic are fools.
Hate is the harbinger of memory.
Sparkle elucidates all jewels.

Tigers always lie in wait downwind.
The cruelty of crowds cannot be matched.
Inquire about diets only of the thin.
No cold egg can ever be hatched.

A first request should always be honored.
No sex appendage rivals the tongue.
A dangerous beast is one that's cornered.
Psalms for beauty are always sung.

Polish names all sound like anagrams.
Redheads are notoriously irascible.
Discard when cooking any cracked clams.
Cleanliness makes poverty passable.

Butter is the living soul of cookery.
What's bred in the bone comes out in the flesh.
Noise is celebration in a rookery.
For sex in women's stockings, look to mesh.

There are no Chinese football players.
The color yellow denotes quarantine.
Hustle is the fuel of all purveyors.
Mozzarella dominates Caprese cuisine.

Siena and Florence never ceased to feud.
Everybody goes back home in September.
Hindsight is perpetually badly skewed.
No child abused will never not remember.

No floor should be darker than its walls.
Anything that's scarce will take on value.
Than legal torture, nothing more appalls.
Officialdom always seeks to corral you.

Every single wall has double faces.
A good boot touches the foot everywhere.
The working sea everything erases.
Does any still life ever exclude a pear?

Never cut what you are able to untie.
The worst plaque is on the lower anterior.
A secret wish slumbers in every lie.
The rapist is always the victim's inferior.

TRUISMS

Every angle creates another angle.
Old men are always poorly shaven.
No pygmy can't be bought with a bangle.
An attorney for cash is always craven.

No one equally likes both in a couple.
The sea can be brutal to a canoe unkeeled.
All true principles are never supple.
The wounds of childhood are never healed.

A wealthy man of God is an obscenity.
Women jazz singers tend to be lesbian.
Opposites are, perforce, complementary.
Charlie Chaplin was a true vulgarian.

A bull, even victorious, is never spared.
Only a deadline makes Washington work.
Originality strikes mediocrities as weird.
The bullied *in extremis* can go berserk.

Great novels are rarely greatly received.
To get a bank loan you must prove you don't need one.
Only a celebrity is publicly bereaved.
To become a serious Christian, go find and feed one.

Quakers avoid music at their service.
Cough drops are perfectly useless.
Any east wind makes a sailor nervous.
A Scottish Presbyterian is juiceless.

ALEXANDER THEROUX

New York City cops all live in Jersey.
Catholic baiting is the anti-Semitism of liberals.
Justice hates the lineaments of mercy.
Taboos are frankly prayers to aboriginals.

Tipping in Iceland is held an insult.
The fascist mind adores all marching music.
We are pawns of anyone we consult.
Foam is an impedance to anything acoustic.

Oxen naturally work in pairs.
Yellow should never be worn by blondes.
No one sentence should express two ideas.
High risk is godfather to all junk bonds.

Royals avoid wearing the color black.
Thursday is the maid's night off.
No one ever witnesses one's own back.
Aging actresses need lighting soft.

Leisure clothes should be anathema.
Banking policies are legal thieving.
Food preservatives can trigger asthma.
Country songs love the fact of grieving.

All vines need to climb to grow.
Dolls with closed mouths have higher value.
Blueness is the color cast by snow.
A base betrayer first will always pal you.

TRUISMS

Rustics on back roads always speed.
No lefty should throw a "changeup" to a lefty.
Pride is a major element of greed.
Television weathermen are always hefty.

What you'd have secret, never put in print.
Competition never fails to rankle.
A pocket is a show, its audience is lint.
No evening gown should show an ankle.

In their seventies, most people die.
A child's question is invariably deep.
Symmetry is always dull, style awry.
No unsalted fish will ever keep.

Large audiences laugh more than small.
A minister who is poor invites respect.
Perspiring can warn of high cholesterol.
Whom you coddle, you badly neglect.

Self-pity and self-hatred go together.
No diary is not a perfect soliloquy.
There is no actual scent to heather.
Standing water always kills a peony.

To test true feelings, contemplate a will.
Show business folk ignore humiliation.
Corn flourishes best grown upon a hill.
No spots are found on a baby Dalmatian.

Shy people always prove the nicest.
With stocks, buy on rumor, sell on news.
To fall in love is love's first crisis.
True poverty first forgoes its shoes.

Most human emotions are derivative.
God speaks clearly in the sound of bells.
All commandments are deprivative.
In short supply just about anything sells.

Sailors consider it bad luck to whistle.
Raymond Chandler's characters drink gimlets.
A priest must daily use his Daily Missal.
Panache on a bolo tie is in its *aiguillettes*.

No comic should step on a laugh line.
A man with an umbrella prays for rain.
All killers leave some one thing behind.
In every family, some member is insane.

Pity for the guilty is treason for the innocent.
Gauge friendship by the way you say goodbye.
You are always owned by what you rent.
True *al fresco* painters always master skies.

Posturers all insist on being gnomic.
It is envy that makes book critics critical.
Penis imagery is essentially domic.
Protest is ever shored up the anarchical.

TRUISMS

Thimbles are worn third finger, right hand.
Lavender flowers as a symbol are gay.
The best investment is to purchase land.
To best abide neighbors keep them at bay.

When you are heavy, the day is very.
The need to win kills most enjoyment.
No Christmas without Christ is Merry.
Medicines to savages are ointments.

A truly iconic individual must first look like one.
Huck Finn and *Moby-Dick* were first published in Britain.
A tonne's an imperial measure; metric for a ton.
"Elizabeth R" is the Queen's signature, handwritten.

Outcasts are without exception mourning.
No woman should wear velvet after March.
Salt's indispensable in the task of corning.
Adhesives all needfully depend on starch.

To teach too long always sterilizes.
Every flu is a kind of psychedelics.
All killer beasts sport big incisors.
Hustlers thrive in the sale of relics.

Any unjust law invites its own breaches.
There is no bad weather, only bad clothing.
A storm levels and smooths all beaches.
Fear is inwevitably followed by loathing.

Reality is the most effective mask of reality.
Parasitism is associated with the small.
No vileness cannot find its personal sodality.
Grotesquerie is an aspect of every doll.

A jabot should never lose its guimpe.
Plump women should avoid quilted fabric.
Spitefulness is characteristic of every imp.
Regret is as dense and dark as cambric.

Lebanese accept no money from a friend.
Denial's the most predictable human response.
A beginning is always at something's end.
Princely behavior requires nonchalance.

Growing tips tell the roots to grow.
Stubble persists with an electric shaver.
Above perpetually sneers at what's below.
Smell, not taste, is what basically we savor.

Any murderer can look like anybody.
A deep armhole serves a fattish women.
Drinking wine turns complexions ruddy.
Thoughts cannot be held while swimming.

Guilt is the church in which many repent.
No atmosphere means there is no sound in space.
By kisses given, kisses returned are meant.
John Newton, an ex-slaver, wrote "Amazing Grace."

TRUISMS

Surprise is the best element of attack.
The military mind is ever incomplete.
The most slimming of all colors is black.
Old age is registered first in the feet.

Stock markets at Christmas always boom.
A garbage-fed animal is repeatedly killed.
Circularity modernizes any room.
All design in an Irish cardigan is twilled.

Useless parents make a kid an orphan.
Raised heels on any shoe seems vulgar.
Strong emotions follow an endorphin.
Wrestling comes naturally to a Bulgar.

Purple never gives a youthful look.
One is a number you cannot divide.
Every room is sterile without a book.
To kill a person's spirit but deride.

All government awards are political.
Daughters badly need a lot of father.
A mother-in-law is naturally critical.
No white-collar work involves lather.

Koreans tend never to talk at table.
One should not wear lace with tweed.
To smile is automatically to enable.
Ambition is always a form of greed.

Rednecks are much crueler in a pack.
A beautiful woman talks only of herself.
Ramen soup is the popular inmate snack.
Every dentist's ambition is for pelf.

Pruning anything both kills and saves.
The "*hallali*" of a hunting horn sounds death.
No prelate's carnality is not a knave's.
To become homely and hideous, snort meth.

Humor is the enemy of infatuation.
Clothes were a Fifties woman's vocabulary.
Mexican skulls all express elation.
Bullying is standard with all constabulary.

January is the month for most divorces.
Chance is a busy servant to Destiny.
Deregulation is oxygen to all bourses.
Jesus's best friends lived in Bethany.

No American girl refuses a dare.
The larger the baton, the worse the conductor.
It is never said that Jesus had long hair.
Love is despondency's greatest instructor.

Seattle men favor lumberjack shirts.
The bigger the hat, the dumber the cowboy.
Caring, when it is real, always hurts.
An oboe in snobbish terms is called a hautboy.

TRUISMS

Avoid more than one fashion accent.
Genius alone finds success in music.
Penance, not joy, is the liturgy of Advent.
Perpetually rigid is a walrus's *oosik*.

Whispering is never not subversive.
A person dies when ceasing to be surprised.
Mediterranean men are forever coercive.
No liar can ever regulate his eyes.

A Jewish Christmas involves Chinese food.
Protestants very rarely kneel at church.
A Guinea hen will die defending its brood.
All Russian forests are nine-tenths birch.

Suspense from news is always torture.
A lie, with just some truth, is truly peril.
Absence always exacts some forfeiture.
All belated thanks are always sterile.

No alligator can catch an otter under water.
Julia Child preferred company at the stove.
3500 B.C. dates earliest pestle and mortar.
There is no better ant repellent than a clove.

One inch of rain equals one foot of snow.
Southern novelists thrive on nostalgia.
It is much easier by far to sail than to row.
Marriage regarding freedom is neuralgia.

Sentimentality creates artless poems.
The truly greedy always deal in oil.
A dauber's ocean always overfoams.
To have a spring, you need a coil.

No redheaded's hair is ever downy.
All women yearn for thicker hair.
Chew, not crunch, makes a good brownie.
Edgar Poe savored the word "weir."

It is sheer politics that establishes all wars.
Iron alone best sharpens iron.
Knives and forks are basically human claws.
Birth is the beginning of dying.

Midwestern Americans: the most polite.
No newborn infant has a facial profile.
The Israeli personality is wired for spite.
Every New Year's Eve crowd is vile.

Geniuses are always badly dressed.
Self-reliance defines the perfect guest.
An Irishman secretly adores an aristocrat.
A sexy quality adhibits to every brat.

Every museum is in fact a mausoleum.
Women, not men, write best of marriage.
A mosquito in Maine is called a "no-see-um."
To praise faintly is fully to disparage.

TRUISMS

Make-up is allowed in all passport photos.
Stage directors have a God complex.
Toyota's designs were stolen from DeSotos.
Worthwhile conversation's always duplex.

Orthodoxy is the grave of intelligence.
One lover always desires the other more.
Choosing anything a form of negligence.
Lobbying Congress is corruption at its core.

The main enemy of the lion is the lion.
All things that smack of wildness are good.
Every vision is always labeled Zion.
Hatred creates its very own neighborhood.

A shadow always follows a searchlight.
Balusters must go in before banisters.
A graceful curve is consistently a bight.
Nesting is the layout of true canisters.

Nothing dollar-worthy is ever safe.
Every Lincoln book depends on Herndon.
Sexual predators all prefer a waif.
When giving to the poor, you are turned on.

Thrills invariably seem never to repeat.
Colt guns made possible the West.
Passions are inflamed by eating meat.
Good is never not the enemy of best.

Buying in bulk is always cheaper.
American fictional detectives love the gin sling.
A bully in his other morph's a weeper.
True grace involves the state of owning nothing.

The cunning give gifts to obligate people.
A pillow is twenty percent of your bed.
More fertile the land, more fertile the people.
Without senses, nothing enters our head.

To notice unduly is always vulgar.
Fish are unable to consume any leather.
The world's oldest food is bulgur.
Nature's software is in fact its weather.

Movie stars ache to win awards.
There are no public toilets in Peru.
A big fascist collectible is swords.
If you despise torture, hate a zoo.

No insult to a Latino exceeds *tu madre*.
Aspen is best for making matches
Americans have never solved the bidet.
Dog and cats practice love by scratches.

An exit by definition is also an entrance.
Neglect is the best check for fanatics.
Whatever is unpredictable is chance.
Italians react solely by dramatics.

TRUISMS

The finer the grain, the better the salt.
Sex addicts rarely have sex with their wives.
Pork is the preferred meat of the Balt.
Insects cannot bear the smell of chives.

African Americans rarely ever ski.
That which is not just is never law.
The Spartans always met pain with glee.
Eating fish badly is eating fish raw.

Bad writing is full of much disclosure.
Soldiers in English novels always deceive.
Speaking truth always requires exposure.
A true victor, oddly, is the first to grieve.

Attending one wedding hastens another.
All professional boxers die penniless.
True effort is taking the time to bother.
Chauvinism roots for a rival's ugliness.

The highest clouds are numbered "nine."
The stink of cooking kidneys always lingers.
Anterior teats produce more milk in swine.
"*Brava*" is the proper call to female singers.

Libertarians struggle against authority.
Cruelty is the harbinger of coldness.
Mediocrity always defines the majority.
True consistency requires boldness.

ALEXANDER THEROUX

A lie is never so deadly as when it's nearly true.
Every empty or unused hotel bed robs the poor.
Napoleon Bonaparte never set foot in Waterloo.
Love for Muammar Gaddafi is rooted in Lahore.

Parsnips dug in winter are planted in spring.
Political partisanship is unpatriotic.
Continuity is symbolized by every ring.
Feathers in classical painting were erotic.

The top shelf of a refrigerator is the coldest.
All men hug each other awkwardly.
The dumbest in committees is the boldest.
Glaciers have all traveled rockwardly.

One woman never praises another.
A bottle of perfume loses scent when opened.
No radical idea cannot find a brother.
War has always open thievery betokened.

No one great has been a one-term president.
Gay men hold great love for Judy Garland.
Self-hatred in criminals is always resident.
Mercury toxins soar in sharks and marlin.

National anthems tend to make one weep.
Use egg-whites at room-temperature.
Smugglers all look for a tidal neap.
Nothing in nature has not an aperture.

TRUISMS

NHL skaters are very often bow-legged.
Lapsed Catholics fall for Scientology.
A perfect drink needs the measure pegged.
Female Studies are close to cryptology.

Vegetarians tend to miss the taste of bacon.
TV exists solely to sell advertising.
Lipstick curiously makes male lust awaken.
The act of dating is basically devising.

Everyone's own head describes a bum.
No one has never been molested.
A Swede contented is invariably glum.
A lover pitied is a human bested.

Exercise can shape a body, not a face.
Stand-up comics favor wearing plaid.
No flower does not improve a vase.
Manufactured sweet drinks are all bad.

Everyone who litters is mentally ill.
Dominant women hate opinionated men.
The cry of a peacock is always shrill.
Flocking comes quite naturally to a hen.

Silver is badly damaged by salt.
Tall women earn more money.
No authentic Swede dislikes a *palt*.
Texas wasps make toxic honey.

A literary agent is nothing but a pimp.
No truly religious war was ever fought.
A prawn is always larger than a shrimp.
Any fish bought is far better caught.

Human kisses began by exchanging food.
Pigeons have a hardwired need to return home.
Gentleman, except on purpose, are never rude.
Bees and ants all miss a sexual chromosome.

NYRB book reviews are painfully too long.
Surprises are hated by dogged rule followers.
Three chords constitute every country song.
Beggars have very close cousins in borrowers.

Jerusalem was always attacked from the north.
Suspect the worse, prevent the worse.
Pythagoreans are fascinated by anything fourth.
No single shape has found a purse.

Baseball movies are never any good.
Repetition invariably kills the soul.
Hack painters consistently rely on mood.
Every state worker's basically on the dole.

Man is half beast, exactly like a centaur.
All car commercials are moronic.
Storms were always "worse" in days of yore
Fear is by far the sharpest clonic

TRUISMS

Plant garlic on the shortest day of the year.
Vital hits quickly end all fights.
No blandishment is ever close to sincere.
Injustice is the mother of all spites.

The polio virus enters through the mouth.
Bribes bring alive every legislature.
Beauty contests flourish in the South.
The origin of a thing determines its nature.

Roses thrive when grown near garlic.
Daytime Emmy awards are offered anyone.
The mind alone creates what is phallic.
Anyone is, in point of fact, everyone.

A tent is only as safe as its fly sheet.
Gaffes occur when pols tell the truth.
The oldest human measurement is feet.
Jesus was part Gentile (cf. book of Ruth).

No horse may win the Kentucky Derby twice.
At Victorian dinners, everybody overate.
Copying in any shape or form is ever a vice.
No range-riding cowboy has a normal gait.

A revolution never goes backward.
No Jewish actors have ever played Oberammergau.
Only a public sign can be a placard.
An Angus cattle marbles better than a Hereford cow.

Perennials are drugstores for all birds.
Wedding cakes in England are fruitcakes.
Deepest vision renders useless words.
The Irish always drink with glee at wakes.

Greed kills what it manages to acquire.
A fish that sinks in fresh water is fresh.
The overuse of detail always reveals a liar.
Lust finds comfort only in the flesh.

Song and sorrow are standard playmates.
Thick-shelled nuts are commonly empty.
To hear a neighbor's radio always grates.
Adequate to any honest man is plenty.

Big car stereos usually represent
the bulk of the owner's net worth.
Love that is unspoken is hope pent.
Life's inequities begin at birth.

No coastal people are ever provincial.
Great waves always come in threes.
Death to anything living is essential.
Our largest body joints are knees.

Synagogue windows are above eye level.
Fertilizer grows a flower faster but weaker.
A man's fedora thrives on a bevel.
Squeak is the utterance of a sneaker.

TRUISMS

Squirrels bury acorns pointed down.
It is bad luck to give away your first quilt.
Every human face reveals a frown.
Any house unpaid for is poorly built.

Doing nothing is doing something wrong.
Giorgione and Titian vied with reclining nudes.
Any serviceable bookmark should be long.
Self-reproach is the subtext of all prudes.

Never cook asparagus over 5 min.
All Vermont churches are painted white.
Political TV ads are strictly spin.
Adages become the quintessence of trite.

Hobbies are a form of sublimation.
Every weed has a right to flower.
Sex generally abhors illumination.
Whiskey always sings when sour.

You will find no surfing in Jamaica.
Carrots flourish planted next to tomatoes.
Any formal oath offends a Quaker.
Yeses sing the sweetest *obbligatos*.

Every Russian craves good bread.
A square face is the most photogenic.
Thickness is unbecoming in thread.
Eating is man's favorite calisthenic.

Homelier people are likely to be poor.
Every single fascist has a following.
Snow is aggressive nature's way to snore.
A fat man wading is a fat man wallowing.

We all love a man who loves to listen.
No absurdity lacks a faith to back it.
Sweat makes a lovely women glisten.
Wisdom is hateful to those who lack it.

Graveyards are not found in San Francisco.
Italians rarely become alcoholics.
Tequila is the convivial essence of Jalisco.
Illiteracy is the happy patron of Ebonics.

Engines run happier rich than lean.
Midgets love Uncle Sam costumes.
Islam ever reveres the color green.
Perfume bottles cost more than perfumes.

One always laughs louder in company.
The lighthouse invites the raging storm.
All Native Americans grasp botany.
Matter badly yearns to find its form.

You never see a road-killed crow.
A cop will always another cop defend.
Gold rises in value at the year's end.
What you own is only what you know.

TRUISMS

Muses and Worthies come in nine.
Butterflies fly about only during day.
Nothing twining is never a vine.
Utterance is appreciated when you pray.

No hope can therefore have no fear.
Safe puffball mushrooms must be all-white inside.
No circle without dimension can be a sphere.
All swine obsessively sleep on their right side.

Continents are wider in the north than the south.
No museum paintings are for sale.
Sensuality's best conveyed by a person's mouth.
A wing is plagiarized by a boating sail.

Radio fascists always begin "Hello, America!"
Sex is the common connotation of bunny.
The worst form of human contagion is hysteria.
Earnestness in a person's always funny.

Armies are inevitably tied to roads.
The mystical is linked with albinism.
Anything repressed inevitably explodes.
Two willful parents constitute a schism.

Regimentation is by definition bad.
Silence is the voice of complicity.
Dating is illegal in the city of Riyadh.
Blood is by far the truest electricity.

Only where there's cover is there game.
No one understands quantum mechanics.
A pimp and an agent are exactly the same.
A dare and a dream are only semantics.

A translator's job is personally to disappear.
Little in art surpasses Giotto's *Ognissanti Madonna*.
More Jacobean than Elizabethan was Shakespeare.
No financial investor is ever recognized for honor.

Women often refuse to vote for women.
Astronomers are known for disliking each other.
No one has ever seen a giraffe swimming.
No hatred exceeds brother versus brother.

No clock-watcher ever enjoys his work
No animals traps and snares in the UK are for sale.
Driving culture is ignored by every Turk.
A Manchu shaved his top head and wore a pigtail.

Never try to mist a rosemary plant.
English swans are owned by the Queen.
A monk's prayer is his monastic chant.
Faith depends on nothing that is seen.

Few like the taste of black Necco Wafers.
No birds ever visit feeders after dark.
Surprise constitutes success for strafers.
All three religions accept Noah's Ark.

TRUISMS

Steak is nothing less than carrion.
Aussies aren't Catholic if named Bruce.
A woman rubbing her arms is a sexual clarion.
No mules can ever breed or reproduce.

Nothing's uglier than a room of naked men.
A horrible warning is always a good example.
The world's most secretive bird is the wren.
No prototype is not at the same time a sample.

Queen Elizabeth II never gives interviews.
Absence of evidence is not evidence of absence.
The nature of gossip is the essence of news.
Miss Gertrude Stein indited strictly nonsense.

Silver is the best electrical conductor.
Who owns more than three suits is a fop.
Error is far and away the best instructor.
For casual corruption, nothing beats a cop.

Every memoir is a tissue of omission.
All success begins with a fear of failure.
Avarice is the motor of all acquisition.
There is nothing attractive in genitalia.

Peas always ripen from the bottom up.
Cold water (not hot) erases blood stains.
The longer the snout, the better to sup.
Whatever permits equally restrains.

Sports fan nation is nitwit nation.
Fifties desserts thrived on Jell-O.
Only nincompoops love alliteration.
Wrath with guilt is always a fellow.

A child's is never a prudent soul.
Ill-repute is the connotation of a tinker.
Fear whatever you cannot control.
No non-reader can be ever a thinker.

Religious reformers are famously lusty.
Local celebrities are vainglorious buffoons.
No unused tool avoids becoming rusty.
Every question by definition impugns.

No American VP may ride with the President.
Black truffles need heat to release full flavor.
No tree will ever find a pigeon as a resident.
Success has never met an electric shaver.

The Pilgrims were promoters as well as evangelicals.
The best wood for toothpicks is paper birch.
No vowel sounds exist in Phoenician alphabeticals.
"God has a wife" declares the Mormon church.

Large birds never sing as well as small.
Composers are notoriously bad pianists.
Wearing skullcaps is based on no Jewish law.
The vainest person is always the tannest.

TRUISMS

Islam has avoided the West's spiritual decline.
C major is the musical key of exultant joy.
It is kinder to kill an Indian than to confine.
A baby girl talks earlier than a baby boy.

Politics can never be the subject of poetry.
The best way to make money is to lend it.
Southern women are mistresses of coquetry.
Employ water for wood to try to bend it.

No hero ever states that he's a hero.
Nothing is explained without interpretation.
Neither positive nor negative is zero.
Visions are enhanced during one's starvation.

No richer soil than at bends of the Tennessee River
To paint it, Constable breathed God into the Stour.
The only human organ to regenerate is the liver.
For pike, a light, fluttery spoon's the best lure.

Potassium thrives in juice of an apple.
Italians serve fish on New Year's Eve.
What nature camouflages it will dapple.
Gain is the inverse of what we thieve.

Never try to de-mold a hot cake.
Meditation is done best in early morning.
To do is the opposite of *to make*.
Red stands as a universal color warning.

There are no essential rules for fishing.
All salmon return to spawn in the fall.
Nothing comes from merely wishing.
Mercy running makes justice crawl.

All decomposition is re-composition.
Any essence is abstract by nature.
Customs officers have vile dispositions.
Sloth is the soul of every legislature.

Abstinence is easier than temperance.
A large vocabulary aids an invective style.
The truly unworldly are mendicants.
Capitalism flourishes by craft and guile.

A flaw's intentionally left in an Arab rug.
A good preacher is as rare as a unicorn.
The craving for fame is a fearsome drug.
No smoking pipe pulls well unless it's worn.

Dark fishing flies work best on bright days.
September is prime time for cotton-picking.
A labyrinths is unicursal, branching a maze.
Glue in a plastic bottle resists all sticking.

No one is ever patriotic about taxes.
A flicker of reason halts a person's instinct.
The hair of a Hottentot never quite relaxes.
Naïve perpetually marries Hoodwinked.

TRUISMS

The human thumb has a pulse of its own.
Every poet's juvenile poetry is bad.
What you ignore, you always condone.
Risibility resides in the fabric plaid.

Mount new tires always at the rear.
Wonderful guests are usually terrible hosts.
Always a metaphor is the word *frontier*.
Awards for aging are, sadly, feeble boasts.

Hitler's favorite author was Karl May.
Adriaen Brouwer delineated only brawling peasants.
Cardenio, once performed, is a lost Shakespeare play.
Totally different look male and female pheasants.

To a prudish mind, all sensation is vice.
Perfection admits exactly no one.
Over potatoes, Asians much prefer rice.
To best admire a tree, grow one.

Of all water, rainwater is the purest.
Never mistake motion for action.
One always travels lamest as a tourist.
Lateness characterizes all retraction.

No Champagne *sec* is sold in the USA.
Television is the arch villain of dialect levelers.
Lace is the *sine qua non* of women's lingerie.
Silence is to praying as noise is to revelers.

Everyone in airports feels important.
Schemes for making money are all low.
Gigolos thrive on sleek deportment.
Collectors thrill to see things in a row.

No businessman is ever truly honest.
Society fully despises its unmaskers.
All great poets have written sonnets.
Primates ever thrive in Madagascar.

Dress for court as you dress for church.
Not on the board, play chess in the head.
All birds face the same way on a perch.
Ancient Romans were poisoned by lead.

Baseball fans are foolishly sentimental.
Lower property values cause higher taxes.
Love matches are essentially accidental.
Seeing symmetry incontestably relaxes.

Killing a bull in a ring is justice gored.
Serial killers were invariably once arsonists.
Abuse a daughter, find a daughter whored.
Bluejays are nature's greatest larcenists.

It is the childless who plan for posterity.
Heat warps everything it touches.
For sainthood, join prayer with austerity.
The Norman arch invented crutches.

TRUISMS

Every anti-Semite has a Jew he likes.
Naked people will never resist.
Boys, never girls, are referred to as tykes.
Trickery is the beating soul of whist.

Commerce always follows the flag.
Daffodils have a proclivity to multiply.
The witch in all fables is always a hag.
Man's profoundest yearning is to fly.

Cowboys eat from the point of a spoon.
Replying to a cruel attack gives it more force.
Every dictator resembles a buffoon.
The backing echo of transgression is remorse.

Tongans prefer eating with their hands.
A pitcher at 0 and 2 should always nibble.
The drummer is the nitwit in all bands.
The need to cavil makes a need to quibble.

No butterfly can ever fly if it is cold.
Obsessions are by definition dangerous.
Something is hidden in every fold.
Routine makes a person languorous.

No pickle to eat should ever be heated.
Strong opinions are invariably strident ones.
The lower the job, the worse one's treated.
Prettier religious habits make for kinder nuns.

Nature instinctively abhors a garden.
All governments are selling propaganda.
The richer the crook, the faster the pardon.
Lame excuses comprise all memoranda.

Wind in Iceland blows from all angles.
Two million Americans live on less than $2 a day.
Most preferred road signs are triangles.
Arabic is spoken by half the people in Marseille.

Misogynists are basically terrified of women.
Ignorance is often a common trait of the fearless.
Models are perpetually obsessed with slimming.
Sunlessness by any measure is cheerless.

Red cedar is best for pencil wood.
Small seeds suffice for any pullets.
Better is ever the enemy of good.
Guilt easily kills more than bullets.

The absence of a denial is not an admission.
In the wild, never eat anything that's red.
Silence may be always taken as permission.
Race issues will only be solved in bed.

Italians never eat cheese with fish.
A cucumber is basically a beverage.
What you need is rarely what you wish.
Stealing is the quickest way to leverage.

TRUISMS

No wine goes well with chocolate.
Queen bees sting only other queens.
Clouds and moisture always flocculate.
The end never justifies the means.

The posture of myopes is always bad.
Only hard pears truly taste the best.
Style by definition is merely a fad.
Father and son should be host and guest.

Laughing juries will never convict.
Bermuda grows the best arrowroot.
Inflexible people's foreheads look strict.
Despair makes a person resolute.

Sushi with sake is disfavored in Japan.
Testosterone levels are highest in the morning.
Nothing ever exists the way it began.
Bright colors in nature indicate a warning.

There are, as such, no Jewish monasteries.
Soft toys are an industry in prison.
July's the highest month for picking berries.
Anything splitting involves fission.

Ownership universally adores a collar.
All government taxes constitute a heist.
Sin best flourishes in squalor.
The less of dogma, the more of Christ.

ALEXANDER THEROUX

The Chinese drink tea without milk.
Ant colonies are constantly at war.
Water is the nemesis of silk.
Salt in heavy rain will never pour.

Never wash or soak mushrooms.
Wounded always exceed the number killed.
Tasteful clothes are never costumes.
Potentiality by definition lies unfulfilled.

The earlier the service, the more devout the churchgoer.
Any waiter who tells you his name is crude.
Followed a devised grid whenever using a push-mower
Ex-athletes, discontented, show a tendency to brood.

Carping is the talent of the literary critic.
Sushi should be eaten in one bite.
Saying "sort of" is a snobbish PBS enclitic.
No one looks bad by candlelight.

Cheese tastes best at room temperature.
Cops love wearing aviator shades.
Translation itself cannot be literature.
Military minds just adore parades.

Every single Welshman loves to sing.
Bridesmaids' dresses are invariably ugly.
A toroidal shape describes an anchor ring
People tend to eat ice-cream smugly.

TRUISMS

Bees crave the flavors of a sedum.
No entertainment isn't also manipulative.
He who borrows sells his freedom.
The frailty of love is it is collaborative.

The palm is stronger than the fist.
Asians rarely smile in photographs.
A tasty light beer does not exist.
Senators talk in lengthy paragraphs.

Tuscans are highly spirited and witty.
The NE quadrant of hurricanes is worst.
Innovation is lost in every committee.
Charity is simply logic reversed.

Geese are more territorial than ducks.
Turner transformed energy into skies.
Pinyin Chinese never coos but clucks.
Government spending is never wise.

Caribbean natives all prefer pork well done.
Ex-pats make up 70% of Kuwait
Execrable legitimately describes every pun.
Sergeants feel obliged to be irate.

Hippies are despised in Singapore.
Andorra's the best place to buy pearls.
The portal to love is always rapport.
Spite is common among schoolgirls.

A sawyer pulls the saw *toward* himself.
Sapphonics love to join softball teams.
Doing onerous tasks is fabled job of elfs.
In morning hours occur the longest dreams.

One's always alone listening to Mahler.
Animals confined are animals provoked.
Privacy applies to no place in a parlor.
Oxen are never joined, merely yoked.

Every secret made is a betrayal.
Fruit is sweetest at the bottom of a pineapple.
Caricature defines all portrayal.
Compassion constitutes a personal chapel.

In the woods, eat nothing that is furry.
No great men exist without goodness.
Migraines makes the vision blurry.
Weak men find a strength in rudeness.

A man's thrown shadow spooks a fish.
Greta Garbo had no bad angles.
What is a whim is not the same as a wish.
The past the present always entangles.

Spices turn impotent with age.
The more lightning, the heavier the rain.
No living creatures belong in a cage.
That is also pathetic, whatever is vain.

TRUISMS

Roasted coffee has a lower caffeine.
All fashion is strictly plagiarism.
Clean water is the essence of hygiene.
Non-readers cotton to despotism.

A Scottish kilt should never be hemmed.
Americans denigrate subcompact cars.
Objects of rumor are already condemned.
Darkness permeates American bars.

That car is stolen with an idling motor.
Episcopalians love to feign they're British.
Logic demands one be a straight party voter.
Every egret is by nature forever skittish.

Go positive at the bottom of a market.
No left-hander should play third base.
Keep no car in Boston: no place to park it.
A true ignoramus thrills at baiting race.

No smell can strictly be defined.
No intermarriage for an Orthodox Jew.
A great thin cook's impossible to find.
Climbers prefer tea to any other brew.

Red roses mean romance world-wide.
Clocks are bad luck gifts in China.
Trout tastes much better when pan-fried.
Rarely used is the plural of vagina.

Biblical "marks" were always on the head.
Whom you trust alone can betray you.
Tradition, by definition, is held to be dead.
Never expect goodness to repay you.

Mankind is a zoological expression.
Formosa produces the best oolong tea.
Health-care jobs are proof against recession.
No male hairdresser is not twee.

American elections turn on trivia.
"I like both" is every solon's mantra.
No Latin country's poorer than Bolivia.
The spirit of joy defines the tantra.

It is rare for women to be pallbearers.
Old Italians called their firstborn "Sonny."
Mirrors must never be facing mirrors.
Losing begins by first winning money.

New York Times obits fix mostly on Jewish deaths.
Small boys eat strictly to fill up.
A cyanotic face attends one's last breaths.
Even steady hands spill a full cup.

Boston politicians always go to jail.
Mushroom cell walls are indigestible raw.
Canadian currency can be read in Braille.
Worthwhile cob depends on straw.

TRUISMS

Fawning comes natural to publicans.
Profit drives enterprise, not thrift.
Far polar regions boast no pelicans.
Never given is a long-awaited gift.

Sad music's always seen as beautiful.
Distraction is the enemy of learning.
Socks with sandals are never suitable.
A lover of flattery is never discerning.

Girls who hate pink hate other girls.
Aging athletes are perennially wistful.
Rare are completely round pearls.
Any bee in an aster is always blissful.

Florida leads all states in lightning strikes.
Tie-dyeing should only be done on cotton.
It is trepidation that fosters all dislikes.
Casu Marzu cheese is always savored rotten.

Whistling is booing in Argentina.
Helvetica is the best font for signs.
Soup is lunch for every ballerina.
Slobs eat, whereas elegance dines.

Logic and truth are direct opposites.
Gynanders love to play the game of golf.
Materials must differ to be composites.
No howls are made in rain by a wolf.

The mandible is the strongest part of the head.
Money donated is wasted on a politician.
The center of Mid-Eastern meals is the bread.
With no amendment there is no contrition.

Pillowy buttocks give the smoothest entry.
NHL wins are 50% puck-luck.
Ownership, not class, comprises the gentry.
Overdecoration profanes a Yupik mukluk.

There is a reason that there is a reason.
Morality is essentially self-evident.
Apostasy in Islam is deemed treason.
Every sacred vow is a sacrament.

Fruit orchards on a coast always fail.
Pro athletes should be paid at year's end.
Canary song is consistently always male.
Cows all sitting, dark storms portend.

Purple is by far the most imperial color.
Romeo and Juliet, not a romance, is a tragedy.
Coffee is perfect companion to a cruller.
Time, by definition, is Eternity's sole malady.

Mad characters in Shakespeare always sing.
Italian women always show a blouseful.
Be sure to kill him, when you strike a king.
Telling the truth is without exception hurtful.

TRUISMS

No couturier is not seriously creepy.
High barometer means low thermometer.
Sunshine on a windshield makes one sleepy.
No gauge is not also a speedometer.

Everyone in a Hammett novel imbibes.
Severe weather brings people closer.
The country of Syria runs on bribes.
Than a rotting corpse, nothing is grosser.

CEOs loved being sexually chastised.
Texans are loudmouths to a one.
Baltic amber is by far the most prized.
The weakest form of humor is the pun.

Every surplus wasted is immoral.
Half of country music deals with drinking.
Youth when cruel are always choral.
Acting is the opposite of thinking.

A recluse is the sanest of living men.
One's early fears never really go away.
To frighten the monkey, murder the hen.
Evenness describes no flower spray.

Ancient Trojan business was selling horses.
Laws perpetuate crimes they seek to abolish.
Iowa leads all states in the lowest divorces.
Stainless steel is made sanitary by a polish.

All crows strictly avoid eating onions.
Chlorofanatics are always bores.
Texas law is administered by trunions.
Money worship is the faith of whores.

Cold hands are every pianist's nightmare.
Improve yourself to better the world.
A woman's elemental beauty's in her hair.
Sails in an ocean storm are always furled.

Boiling kills the flavor in all stews.
Eraserless pencils keep all golfers honest.
Patton owned the Germans at the Meuse.
To appear dumbest, always be the blondest.

Mushrooms are all edible—once.
Bullying is a crime that is never policed.
Falling in love depends on bunce.
A heart victim's earlobe's often creased.

Reality TV is solely manipulation.
In extremis, all men search for God.
Superstition invigorates a Haitian.
Bankruptcy cases thrive on fraud.

To follow fashion is conformity.
Catering in any form is servitude.
Hatred is the worst of all deformity.
Noise of any stripe is turpitude.

TRUISMS

Chanterelles are found only in the wild.
Dreams are always our temptations.
It is stress that wets the bed, not the child.
Faith alone guarantees salvation.

Risk is the fulcrum of capitalism.
Shortbread gives the best cheesecake crust.
Human palms are prized in cannibalism.
The mother of certainty has to be mistrust.

Never call a Muslim a Mohammedan.
Ambition is a variant of greed.
Sex is never practiced during Ramadan.
Intolerance threatens every creed.

Food tastes better eaten in small rooms.
A valuable doll must have original clothes.
Wistfulness characterizes waiting grooms.
A dog senses all direction by its wet nose.

Any plants with white sap avoid eating.
E-flat major serves patriotic themes.
Sikhs always name the person they are greeting.
For flavor, cooking is best that steams.

Knit is the most unforgiving fabric.
Cowboys cherish large belt buckles.
Petulance is predictably geriatric.
No one ever thinks of a toe's knuckles.

Folded arms in Fiji show disrespect.
"Shrimping" entails the paraphilia of toes.
O blood and *A* blood badly disconnect.
English yew wood makes the best bows.

No human being is fully innocent.
Memory is a poet, not an historian.
Anonymous giving's the most beneficent.
Jehovah is forever the stentorian.

No thickness matches the yogurt of Bulgaria.
Holiness is the goal of personal prelates.
No working rasp is ever better than its farrier.
An owl's story is revealed in its pellets.

Never address Japanese by their first name.
No women are world chess champions.
Notoriety mainly generates world fame.
Animism is intriguing to every Gambian.

Seeking worldly glory is the route to hell.
Fat in food essentially means flavor.
Who loses to buy, can always win to sell.
Than a Christian martyr, no one is braver.

Southern folks adore baton twirlers.
You cannot make a soufflé rise twice.
No turn-off can beat a woman in curlers.
Northern Chinese prefer noodles to rice.

TRUISMS

Schizophrenics all love to smoke.
Evangelists all hale from the South.
Every subservience has its special yoke.
Drugs all cause dryness in the mouth.

Political protests are a sign of health.
Curly was the only funny Stooge.
Wars are waged for and by wealth.
No actor's brain has ever been huge.

Rage is the result of being helpless.
No house for style beats one of stone.
Every sow is less ferocious whelpless.
The more needed, the less likely a loan.

Rowers face the direction where they've been.
Climbing up is easier than climbing down.
A dray for every squirrel is a desiccated den.
Perseverance in the end will win the crown.

Wagner at Bayreuth is always sold out.
Never add cheese to a seafood dish.
Buddha sought to have all fires put out.
A flathead is the best-tasting catfish.

Short men are bred to be tyrants.
City areas are warmer than rural.
Exploitation is the fate of migrants.
The paucal loses funding to the plural.

Southerners prefer bourbon to Scotch.
Jacobean furniture is predominantly oak.
Before WWI, it was fey to wear a watch.
Honeybees are all becalmed by smoke.

Faith is good only for good people.
Business evokes the worst in human nature.
Every atheist despises a steeple.
Sloth is the teleology of legislature.

All lives reduce to partial recollections.
Nations with green in their flags are savage.
A committed lover's blind to imperfections.
Depend on marriage love to ravage.

Truth is the contradiction in a paradox.
Magazines are always ceasing publication.
Palestinian Christians are mainly Greek Orthodox.
Condescension is a kind of defamation.

A sculptor always fights the clay he works.
White oak is best for liquid containers.
Smiles are ever the antonyms of smirks.
Complaint is identity for chronic complainers.

Circulated news is always bad.
Cowboy boots are buckle-less and lace-less.
Fashion at its best is but a passing fad.
Cowardice is predominantly faceless.

TRUISMS

A football punter always faces adversity.
Nutmeg is America's oldest favorite spice.
A fool is one who gives up liberty for security.
No cigar box may legally be used twice.

Fishing guides traditionally are bullies.
Serve Welsh rarebit on *un*buttered toast.
Friction is the inevitable death of pulleys.
Accepting any prize is essentially a boast.

No defeat is ever fully a defeat,
Nor any victory complete success.
Westerners think Easterners effete.
Scorpions at night by light fluoresce.

A star will shine, planets never do.
A true German stein always boasts a lid.
Butter is the essence of any roux.
Ancient western cities never had a grid.

Body vermin always desert a corpse.
State workers invent holidays to loaf.
Heat in its every facet badly warps.
Every voter by bloc is a voting oaf.

Marginal people are invested in Hallowe'en.
For poetry there is no public passion.
Selling fear to the public is a cash machine.
A value's instantly created by a ration.

Solicitors earn more money than barristers.
American men feel queasy hugging another.
A plot in novels is created by its characters.
Narcissists rarely find a friend in a mother.

Cooking cabbage leaches off its vitamins.
Two thin garments are warmer than a thick one.
Responsibilities alone make citizens.
To flush out a fool merely trick one.

Doctors and nurses never shake hands.
Chubby men love wearing suspenders.
A perfect slave relishes commands.
Conformity by definition surrenders.

Jewish ladies are rabid book-buyers.
He lives happiest who lives unknown.
Sexually impotent men commonly start fires.
Failures in a marriage seek a clone.

Crooners love vowels in their songs.
Cypresses and cemeteries go together.
Servile husbands always serve as gongs.
The best stories thrive of heavy weather.

Every single rose is actually edible.
Women have worse reflexes than men.
No wealthy minister of God is ever credible.
True satire demands an angry pen.

TRUISMS

Black mambas always move in pairs.
Helium has never been frozen.
Freud claimed there's sexuality in stairs.
Duty over love is basely chosen.

No adult food involves marshmallows.
Never button the bottom of a waistcoat.
Fraternities create the harshest fellows.
Luck validates the owning of a mascot.

All realization is basically release.
Loneliness and illness correspond.
Cadging comes quite easy to police.
A toad will never inhabit a pond.

To examine the self, objectify the self.
A sorrow shared is a sorrow halved.
Flatness alone constitutes a shelf.
Vision comes with being starved.

Yeast adds brains to any dough.
Caking a brownie's a punishable crime.
Always use a mallet with a froe.
Shine is characteristic of a dime.

No passion exceeds adolescent love.
Humorless people love telling jokes.
A hawk finds no partner in a dove.
Every memory some shame evokes.

Sweet is war to those who never serve.
We all dig the ditch that we die in.
Fruit is not considered an *hors d'oeuvre*.
Jungles are *never* the habitat of a lion

Never look a howler-monkey in the eye.
Helium is much lighter than air.
Landscape painters love a busy sky.
Lust in a woman lowers her hair.

Everything lowers its energy if it can.
Magnets only other magnets attract.
Seduction's favorite prop's a wagging fan.
Potency by definition is not act.

Women adore military uniforms.
Every ism constitutes an isn't.
Cruelty kills less than it deforms.
A dwarf unlike a midget's wizened.

A pearl not worn will lose its luster.
Taupe for stockings is a flattering color.
To survive is, first of all, to cluster.
The female of a species is much duller.

Jury verdicts always come on Friday.
Entertainers in France are mostly Jews.
Thrice repeat the distress call "Mayday."
Cars come not in colors now, but hues.

TRUISMS

In Victorian homes, prayer began the day.
The first fact of peanuts, they're not nuts.
Poplars always murmur when they sway.
Every Hapsburg chin, by definition, juts.

Pioneers migrated west in straight lines.
A clematis cannot stand the sun.
Grace accepts less than it declines.
Custody of the eyes becomes a nun.

Road maps are difficult to fold.
Boston is America's windiest city.
Love of gain learns to first withhold.
It is strictly a vice, not a virtue, to pity.

Laugh and Cry live in the same house.
Momentum in political races brings cash.
Rankness in its meat flavors grouse.
The better the dive, the less the splash.

No one in whodunits cares about the corpse.
Show-tot mothers are without exception fat.
Cars make up the USA's largest imports.
Ash is the preferred wood for a baseball bat.

Fires move faster uphill than down.
Teeth are the most durable part of the body.
In Europe sadness is the mood of a clown.
Needy people love fashion gaudy.

Autobiographies never fully tell us all.
The brutalized become brutalizers.
Squeaking snow best makes a snowball.
UVa. dismisses anyone who plagiarizes.

No one visits Utah for the food.
Extreme is the forerunner of grief.
No Maori ever goes untattooed.
Rules to right-wingers are a relief.

There is no jazz without improvisation.
Lawyers are by definition pimps.
Plants need bees for pollinization.
Soft Rock music is for wimps.

Most ordinary men are actually significant.
For wooden handles select hickory.
Virtue is essential to the magnificent.
Indirection is the beating heart of trickery.

Political extremists are all unpatriotic.
No boss should not have a boss.
Comedians are borderline psychotic.
No flowers or seeds belong to moss.

The act of eating is highly unattractive.
An organ-grinder is the emblem of oneness.
Continuity can be retroactive.
Below the skin you never see a fungus.

TRUISMS

Micromanagers mainly thrive on spite.
Thin-skinned lemons are the juiciest.
All mourners in Vietnam wear white.
Without a priest, there is no Eucharist.

No saint has not a wilderness for a pillow.
A nighthawk, not a hawk, is not nocturnal in its habits.
No national cuisine hasn't a version of phyllo.
Carrots, high in sugar, should be limited to rabbits.

Every true answer involves a diagnosis.
Human ears generate their own noise.
Look to the past for a perfect prognosis.
Who does not create, always destroys.

All men feel uncomfortable hugging.
The Japanese turn out the greatest cars.
Strikeouts go hand in hand with slugging.
Darkness is the décor of American bars.

You never hear the missile that kills you.
St. Paul wrote the first Christian literature.
It is the fine print that ultimately bills you.
Simplicity is the soul of great architecture.

An *en l'air* in ballet must always be vertical.
Always blanch vegetables in an uncovered pot.
The Finnish tongue has no definite article.
Dampness is the essential grandmother of rot.

The quicker the loan, the worst the rate.
Hawaiian shirts are hideous to a one.
The hater is the first victim of hate.
First sounds the drum and then the gun.

Selling loose cigarettes is illegal.
Twisters require an unstable atmosphere.
Mercy alone makes any leader regal.
Parsimony's the reverse of debonair.

German theology is overly analytical.
Spoonerisms amuse only fools.
Skill requires that one be self-critical.
Dawn is officially the hour for duels.

Pulitzer Prizes are given to anybody.
All puts and calls in stocks are chancy.
The Road to Mandalay is the Irrawaddy.
Every eye fabricates its own fancy.

Store sweaters are folded, never hung.
Art is much older than is science.
Whole histories reside in fossil dung.
Freedom is the joy of self-reliance.

A flower has neither front nor back.
No one not needy becomes an actor.
Overeating commences with a snack.
Of snobbery insecurity's the factor.

TRUISMS

Nobody loves the head of a dandelion.
No medication has no side effects.
Irresponsibility typifies many a scion.
Social acceptance rides on dialects.

Power should be fought in any guise.
Substitute teachers are disrespected.
Tyrannical types never internationalize.
Nothing without friction is perfected.

Soda water very subtly leavens a biscuit.
The Parthenon initially was red, blue, green.
BBQ pitmasters despise sauce on their brisket.
A gastropod habitat is a whale's baleen.

Nuns, to a one, are standard Democrats.
All bishops tend to be Republicans.
Snobbery devised the act of wearing spats.
Most Mexicans are actually Indians.

Balkan women love dark lipstick.
Martinis are strictly an urban drink.
It is crude to gesture with chopstick.
You will find a snake will never blink.

France was Camus' father, Algeria his mother.
A yellow-bellied woodpecker is a glutton for sap.
Why is the question answers can never discover.
Rarest of all is the Martin Waldseemüller map.

Old men love the taste of licorice.
It is impossible to kill a yucca plant.
Episcopalians love a formal service.
Guile proceeds always at a slant.

License-plate framing is bafflingly vain.
A true cocktail contains no fruit juice.
Hyperglycemiacs habitually complain.
Any worthwhile powder is always loose.

Gold, where undervalued, never stays.
A pale moon rising portends coming rain.
Petulant divas are greatly revered by gays.
Love as sacrifice is all discounted pain.

When charmed, we feel charmless.
Chastity is sacred in a Muslim *hareem*.
A necessary lie is morally harmless.
Snipers invariably operate as a team.

Hungarians are addicted to dueling.
No war could not have been avoided.
Vascular diseases find blood pooling.
Swedish clothes are all embroidered.

Starlings always migrate during day.
Sherry before meal, port comes after.
No priggish fellow is not a gourmet.
Any passion is repudiated by laughter.

TRUISMS

Umami is the hidden taste in ceps.
History is unmoved by the poor.
Fakery is the fashion for all adepts.
12A often signifies the 13th floor.

Grapes only grow on newer wood.
Old age slowly softens all its profiles.
Should, first of all, requires could.
Passion pure reason often defiles.

Light unfailingly kills flavor in beer.
No round face should ever wear a bob.
Misconduct at all times fosters fear.
Any preposterous hat would fit a mob.

Pruning a tree stimulates its growth.
No marinade can penetrate without salt.
Allah alone can bind a Muslim oath.
Never equal are the legs of the halt.

American butterflies have tongues.
Almost every stutterer is a man.
Fish live without the use of lungs.
The color black was ignored by Cézanne.

Iceland's main vegetation is moss.
British wine gums are the best of all candies.
A sweet tooth is curbed by hot sauce.
Whatever ferments can be turned to brandies.

Soil good for wine is best for olive oil.
Mannishness unfairly stereotypes lesbians.
Steam all ears of corn instead of boil.
Hamlet is the desired role for all thespians.

Never open interviews with a large question.
The longer the barrel, the greater the accuracy.
Peppermint best can cure in human digestion.
Every dictatorship is a secular theocracy.

Large women should avoid large prints.
Good caviar is marred by any garnish.
Americans are indifferent to world events.
No human smile is not a form of varnish.

A warm ocean is always hurricane food.
Lobsters are scared to death of octopi.
Holly berries grow only on old wood.
The mouth of a diabetic is always dry.

Frost can make a mushroom toxic.
Vain authors give illegible autographs.
The merest curiosity is gnostic.
Sterile minds have faith in graphs.

Most jewelry store rings are size 7.
Bad teachers always take attendance.
No good literary take exists of heaven.
Solitude is primarily independence.

TRUISMS

Divas, to a one, are cartoon women.
Never run a hand up saw grass, only down.
Every redneck's hair needs trimming.
Evoking pity is the aspiration of a clown.

All drag kings are attracted to men.
The lunar day is longer than the solar.
The tongue of a fertile mind is the pen.
Spending is captivating for the bipolar.

Kids liked Shirley Temple less than adults.
Most quotations are meaningless generalizations.
A strategy only serves by way of its results.
Stubbornness is one of stupidity's manifestations.

UK elections are always held on Thursday.
Argentinean cattle are solely fed on grass.
Reaping is the *topos* of every doomsday.
Good acoustics greatly favor use of brass.

Every great metropolis is on a river.
French chefs use softer flour, thicker cream.
Easy bleeding indicates a failing liver.
Very few sales pitch do not hide a scheme.

Spinners and spoons should be kept bright.
A nick in a knife renders fowl unkosher.
A given day is usually longer than a night.
Coarse is crude, but gross is gaucher.

ALEXANDER THEROUX

Social programs irritate Republicans.
People expect free books from writers.
Aprons are the badge of all publicans.
No unambitious men sport mitres.

Italians have a racial obsession with fruit.
Envy is always the bookend of spite.
Bigness is ever the antonym of cute.
Women in a social mate crave height.

All dildos stand perfectly erect.
Never run from an approaching bear.
Pedophiles all constitute a sect.
No animal predator can abide a stare.

No blonde women can play an exotic.
Discard trays are always red in blackjack.
Over habit, always prefer the chaotic.
Even the worst of actors has his claque.

Too much water makes pie dough tough.
All actresses are masculinized with time.
A sailor to learn needs an ocean rough.
Poverty's the Mother Hubbard of all crime.

An old man constantly has to pee.
Angle is crucial in the placing of a trellis.
Own absolutely nothing—and feel free.
Hate needs love to make a person jealous.

TRUISMS

Misogyny flourishes in national proverbs.
The ardor of love increases through suspicion.
Public signs steer clear of using adverbs.
Abused women are comforted by coalition.

No Biblical angel is ever a woman.
Chefs are rarely invited to dinner.
No antiquity is a riddle to a Roman.
Models compulsively must feel thinner.

Chainsaws are a redneck's best friends.
Muscles cannot push but only pull.
Wind can never break a tree that bends.
No ancestral explanation is ever full.

In Japan, the hand is used as a knife.
No one eats as much as a teenage boy.
A mocker delights in creating strife.
The presage of grief is extreme joy.

History is basically a litany of injustice.
Birdsong is half questions, half answers.
No regime can match that of Augustus.
Courting depends entirely on advances.

Timidity is always fatal to experience.
Always turn your auto toward the skid.
Realists with romantics live at variance.
What you want to popularize, forbid.

Drought in one place means floods in another.
Half of any culture is a cult.
Everyone erases himself who attacks his mother.
Whom you ignore, you insult.

Everything exact is always brief.
Descriptions of Jesus Christ always fail.
Much knowledge means much grief.
Domesticity kills the hero in a male.

Carpeting absorbs the noisiest sounds.
Possessions are always lost in the possessing.
What marinades always slowly browns.
Ownership is a release made by confessing.

Girls always ask more questions than boys.
Iran alone makes the world's best rugs.
Pleasures are modest substitutes for joys.
More than love, desperation finally hugs.

No live cone-shell should ever be handled.
Too high's the lifetime cost of chasing money.
Every rapist as a baby went undandled.
Western pioneer clothes were mainly gunny.

A water current's fiercest at the outside of a bend.
Testosterone levels are highest in the morning.
Political solicitations crassly never end.
History's patterns prove our greatest warning.

TRUISMS

A qualified apology is never an apology.
To detect a government leak, seek who gains.
Fate is more than anything physiology.
Iron workers call off labor when it rains.

Anonymity is essential to the Ku Klux Klan.
Slow to pay was always quick to borrow.
Don't cook onions and garlic in the same pan.
The essential mood at graduations is sorrow.

No opinion isn't seasoned afterthought.
Admiration and familiarity are strangers.
Blue in a diamond is most often sought.
The abuse of liberty, liberty endangers.

No penis erects except in little jerks.
Mud flaps serve to abet fuel economy.
Bribing a policeman constantly works.
Elitism is close cousin to gastronomy.

The 21st century will center on Asia.
Raccoons all hate the smell of mint.
Millinery positively craves fantasia.
Prejudice is essentially a kind of squint.

A soaring bird always needs a thermal.
The olive abets the cooking of Provence.
Olive skin when pale is a green dermal.
Avarice is the singular motive of finance.

French cuisine tends to ignore desserts.
Weather is all—only—about wind.
Alleys are the thoroughfares of perverts.
Frosting and cake are always twinned.

Raymond Chandler was master of the simile.
Republicans despise every collective impulse.
Sex is found in every ad subliminally.
Two beauties meeting create instant repulse.

Vodka is best for making herbal tinctures.
Avoid going swimming in deepest Africa.
Gracility is acquired by mere cinctures.
Principle to all lawyers is fully anathema.

Suffering puts an end to suffering.
Ignorance more than anything is dangerous.
Scots love the business of publishing.
Gluttony at rest is impotently languorous.

Psychiatry rarely addresses the subject of hope.
Card dealers never put their hands in their pockets.
Disinterestedness alone gives a person scope.
Fuel ironically adds a crucial drag to rockets.

Only drones follow recipes exactly.
An automobile is useless in New York.
No "celebrity" isn't by definition ghastly.
Balto-Slavonic cuisine thrives on pork.

TRUISMS

There are no early warnings for earthquakes.
Mormons may swim without sacred underwear.
Unimprovement describes all movie remakes.
A subtle bias pervades every questionnaire.

Men tend to look at women in segmented parts.
A child should be taught to question authority.
Italians hear "*Va, pensiero*" with pulsing hearts.
Mediocrity is the condition of every majority.

Repression is always based on selfishness.
No one hasn't advice on growing vegetables.
Needful interdependence breeds joylessness.
Human innards are favored by cannibals.

To cross a fearful height, never look down.
Okinawan women live longest on earth.
Macho men are drawn to the color brown.
One's success in life originates at birth.

Garlic is the truffle of Provence.
All sixteenth-century folk wore gloves.
The only surety of law is expense.
Squabs equal pigeons equal doves.

Loving Corgis is a British royal tradition.
Professional chefs famously fly into rages.
Teaching is never a trade, rather a mission.
Capital holds workers as slaves for wages.

ALEXANDER THEROUX

Go to the top to get a problem solved.
Gout almost always begins in the big toe.
Revenge is a personal way of feeling absolved.
The Red River flows due north in Fargo..

Hatred can never drive out hate.
Movies never state the date they're made.
Nothing in nature is absolutely straight.
Red in sunlight is always quickest to fade.

The higher the water, the lower the waves.
Every Santander meets his Simon Bolivar.
The grip of obsession of any sort enslaves.
The third Brandenburg is the most popular.

Hand-signing officializes major receipts.
Changing one's name is a form of fraud.
Green is the color that nature excretes.
Human beauty is at some point flawed.

Jesus greatly preferred Galilee to Judea.
Remember to ski with your skis facing in.
Child-death's main cause is diarrhea.
Every lie is a small variation of treason.

Cover plants with straw—hay has weed-seeds.
A hitchhiker of color rarely gets a ride
White garments figure in all religious creeds.
Trust any word that is officially denied.

TRUISMS

Never prune a tree during summer.
A marten hates to go near water.
Stress is less when one is dumber.
What mother does, so will a daughter.

A plumber paid up front despises you.
Waste of any sort is blasphemy.
The least common color in food is blue.
Fate in mainly taken as catastrophe.

An unconvinced minority is healthy.
Depression is actually internalized rage.
No true Christian ever dies wealthy.
True neediness nothing can assuage.

Political partisanship is unpatriotic.
To serve God, one must be a servant.
Trusting a lawyer is patently idiotic.
A convert's faith is always fervent.

Guilty people always feel cold.
Never seed land that is lying fallow.
Fermented cheese is made to mold.
Suet can't be stored, unlike tallow.

Faith without action is woefully deficient.
A movie camera is a lie detector.
A novelist's ego says he can be omniscient.
One's image is one's favorite reflector.

Burgundy's clay soil perfects the wine.
Holy people tend to consume very little.
Both lust and asceticism scarily align.
Dryness in any kind of matter is brittle.

Force manufactures its own resistance.
Russian Mensheviks were mostly Jews.
Risk turns the flywheel of existence.
Loss is the theme of all the "blues."

Monochromatic flower arrangements pall.
Japanese need to keep up appearances.
Anything sublime must perforce be small.
Rich boys all achieve medical clearances.

Bake beans slowly with indirect heat.
Unofficial guides are illegal in Morocco.
A flower is the smile of every aesthete.
Every oppression has its own sirocco.

Drugs fuel the major crimes in cities.
American crooners are mainly Italian.
The fearful always form committees.
Megalomaniacs live for a medallion.

Wall Street always acts on instability.
There are no husbands in Hemingway novels.
Hollywood tycoons are averse to humility.
Public adulation in every instance grovels.

TRUISMS

Destruction forever breeds creation.
Cherry trees all have pest problems.
Boxwood despises any ocean location.
South Africa pullulates with slums.

Altruism always expects a fanfare.
No fish can be said to have a face.
A rabbit lives below ground; above, a hare.
The word "oriental" conjures up no place.

When hope is hungry, everything feeds it.
A river always narrows to a brook.
Fear, facing cruelty, only speeds it.
At home, chefs rarely want to cook.

Anyone's full history would shock everyone.
Any air angrily quarreled-in turns yellow.
No Victorian novel is wanting for a heroine.
Breathing from the chest is always shallow.

Academy Awards are strictly politics.
Revenge is the theme of all great novels.
Lewdness is the beating heart of limericks.
Love alone legitimately grovels.

What is too eagerly awaited always palls.
Hollywood royalty is a comic oxymoron.
A physician's script is always scrawled.
No insulation can't benefit from boron.

Those you cannot criticize, rule you.
Congress goes to sleep after an election.
Nothing asserted in terror is ever true.
Anticipation is invented recollection.

Unbridled nostalgia is a crippling vice.
All of literature is mediated gossip.
Any fighter with faith is armed twice.
Every actress over 30 fears a close-up.

Rich people get away with everything.
Nobody ever looks good in golf clothes.
Detachment to divide is never severing.
Hosta in sunlight ever grudgingly grows.

Men despise joining book clubs.
Shoulders matter greatly in men's suits.
Meek sex addicts thrive on sexual rubs.
Champagne aroma depends on flutes.

Smells always sharpen in the fog.
All new babies have grayish eyes.
A toad needs no water, unlike a frog.
John Constable painted perfect skies.

The English feel uneasy being warm.
Lazy teachers give multiple-choice exams.
American Indians generally hate to farm.
Psychic readings is another phrase for scams.

TRUISMS

Facts never fully tell the truth.
Every sane man is revulsed by aspic.
Any public riot is definitively uncouth.
Sikhs are said to be famously priapic.

Chinese surnames have one syllable;
but their first names have one or two.
No empty human heart is not refillable.
Every old proverb authorizes a new.

No metaphor is not, actually, a lie.
Strong opinions are considered rude.
To have true faith is never to die.
Naked is vulgar, virtue is nude.

Any good kitchen stock is never fat free.
Democracy is always portrayed as a woman.
The appeal of every prayer voices a plea.
A mustache always becomes a villain.

Mary Lincoln hated her surname Todd.
Books are dynamite where injustice prevails.
No diamond, in some way, isn't flawed.
Few dogs have prey instincts like Airedales.

A canary has the briefest of lives.
Self-control depends on rogation.
One knife can whet other knives.
Willow oaks love an ocean location.

Eskimos rarely die of diabetes.
All plants contain antioxidants.
America expanded by broken treaties
Romance turns solely on accidents.

Repetition always savages the soul.
All plants with white sap are inedible.
A deadline merely parodies a goal.
No life-after-death tale is credible.

Olives are always best bought loose.
A rough sea leaves a smooth beach.
Always mildly undercook a goose.
Southern boys have a yen to preach.

Arbitrariness rules all stand-up comics.
Any true chowder contains potatoes.
Greed ignites the study of economics.
Florida leads the country in tornadoes.

Your best teacher is your last mistake.
If you can't tie a good knot, tie many.
Never use sauce in a classic cheese steak.
Lincoln faces right on every penny.

Noël Coward hated a long play run.
All poinsettia plants despise the cold.
Every Texas native owns a gun.
Each new invention kills an old.

TRUISMS

Binoculars are always telescopes.
American rivers mainly flow south.
Satirists are classic misanthropes.
A bare mind matches a big mouth.

Easter is the primal feast for Christians.
Names in Henry James novels are plots.
Reciprocation is the key to pistons.
Germans no longer dare to be patriots.

Firefighters all avoid the word "Goodbye."
The blue field is the honor point of the U.S. flag.
Refinement is the secret of growing bonsai
Blue beads held highest value in Wampumpeag.

Crowd noise effects poorly coached teams.
Feminine boys are valued in Tahiti.
Never companion-plant onions and beans.
Damaged societies always spawn graffiti.

Stephanotis loves heaviest humidity.
More people are shocked by honesty than deceit.
No Latino is wanting in cupidity.
Saffron thrives when trodden by the feet.

Magazine advertisers control their content.
Cucumbers dislike growing by potatoes.
Funds to Nigeria are consistently misspent.
There are 7500 varieties of tomatoes.

A cannoli should always be served cold.
The poems of Conrad Aiken are too long.
South Africa grew with the discovery of gold.
It is worse to be vague than to be wrong.

Keep food hung out of a north window.
Lewis Carroll had no interest in little boys.
A bleached blonde promulgates a bimbo.
"Work from Home" schemes are all ploys.

Illiterate folk have excellent memories.
U-boats attacked from the windward side.
No modern country has legitimate boundaries.
The color yellow never becomes a bride.

There is no irony in the art of music.
Never dry your snowshoes near a fire.
None has more roving eyes than a guzik.
Pigs, having no sweat glands, don't perspire.

Every bibliography is always dated.
The thicker the ice, the slower a ship should go.
Praise is always worthless when belated.
Glycoalkaloids impart poison to a potato

College hoop coaches are mental cases.
Sears Roebuck catalogs are Bibles in Vermont.
Falsehood has no end of smiling faces.
Deceit and flattery make a perfect détente.

TRUISMS

True railroading begins west of Chicago.
The name Algonquin is spelled 100 ways.
Military prose is always a farrago.
Silence is the friend that never betrays.

Roads for Native Americans were rivers.
Bears always swim in a straight line.
No dietary claim ever fully delivers.
Israeli occupation throttles Palestine.

Thomas Jefferson's favorite home/dwelling
was not Monticello but rather Poplar Forest.
Health in cooking sees a vegetable swelling.
No ancient Greek drama was not chorused.

U.S. Commissions are always a dodge.
Nothing owned by force is ever owned.
No presumptuous guest is easy to dislodge.
A book stolen was ever a book loaned.

Looking at baby photos is the ultimate bore.
The best cask for wine is new white oak.
A wigwam's best bed is farthest from the door.
Every holy priest should always be broke.

January is the best month for trapping.
There is very little humor in Italian opera.
The genius of feathers is their overlapping.
Small businesses are slain by the corpora.

ALEXANDER THEROUX

War is always a crime—against peace.
Einstein refused the presidency of Israel.
Traffic jams are caused mainly by police.
Sugar infects all U.S. breakfast cereal.

Obsession is a notch below dementia.
Never smile in a formal photograph.
Toxic are the flowers of hyacinthia.
Only shits refuse to give an autograph.

Vastness of view is always sublime.
Great talk never reproduces in cold print.
Daring to excel is always found a crime.
Nationalism is nothing but a squint.

Chinese demons despise loud noises.
Good haikus cannot be written in English.
Death is widely recognized by white roses.
Napalm is impossible to extinguish.

Parsley turns yellow if it isn't used.
Goat, world-wide, is the meat of the poor.
Waste and need are eventually fused.
Too much is always the enemy of more.

Eat no oysters in months missing an R.
False modesty is a sign of ill-breeding.
It is the *wrapper* that flavors the cigar.
Praise is only a disguise for pleading.

TRUISMS

The more general a rule, the harder to find exceptions.
French women never get fat.
Strips of plywood, glued, run in alternating directions.
The more a woman's style, the less of hat.

Stop signs in parking lots are ignored.
Never use oily fish in a bouillabaisse.
To a novelist, journalism is abhorred.
Authority's a joy for all who acquiesce.

Buying on margin is always dumb.
The smaller the congregation, the shorter the sermon.
Africa labors to the beat of a drum.
A weasel in summer, in wintertime's an ermine.

Hints of the imperious reside in the serious.
Renoir never missed a chance to paint a breast.
Than ocean depth, little is more mysterious.
Cooked chicken always zings with orange zest.

Starfish are savage killers of oysters.
Anybody can conduct an orchestra.
Contemplation is the aim of cloisters,
just as light is the point of finestra.

Baldwin apples are the best for pies.
A bore, by definition, never knows he is one.
The Arrowhead Alpine plant never dies.
To have loved many women is to have loved none.

Highly nutritional foods cause farting.
A whale spouts air, but never water.
Of the human heart there is no charting.
A good wife has been a good daughter.

Russians eat a pound of bread a day.
Every undecided voter is a moron.
The memory of kindness does not stay.
Every actor is a playwright's pion.

No good mustard ever goes bad.
Daytime TV is the pornography of housewives.
Neckwear is fashion's constant fad.
White is the widely preferred color for beehives.

The simpler the explanation, the better.
Vultures never get to eat in peace.
A creditor is the jailer of a debtor.
No truly balanced person is obese.

Virility is undermined by pleading.
No words beginning with Q aren't odd.
Clichés murder the joy of reading.
You must disobey yourself to obey God.

Cold springs let maple sap flow best.
All veristic journeys are vertical.
Dutch elms are bedeviled with pest.
The highest revelations are musical.

TRUISMS

No Catholic cathedral exists for Dubliners.
Proper marmalade needs bitter oranges.
No beginner succeeds without true nourishers.
Six screws fasten all door hinges.

The shelf life of beauty is but minutes.
A stock portfolio without cash in inflexible.
Flax seed is the favorite food of linnets.
A neighbor is a horror because annexable.

Old Testament brothers often hated each other.
Sperm whales rarely go where water is cold.
For risk, sheer necessity is always the mother.
The marketing of diamonds is strictly controlled.

Inquiry is the beginning of all freedom.
Never cut polenta with a metal implement.
In Rabbinical literature, Rome is Edom.
Anger is, before anything else, impotent.

Height is never reached in a hurry.
Brittany is France's seafood Mecca.
Guilt is the driving force of worry.
Pettiness is virtue in a fact-checker.

No true lowland Scot will wear a kilt.
Yukon Gold is best for mashed potatoes.
It is bad luck on a Friday to begin a quilt.
A safe space sits within all tornadoes.

ALEXANDER THEROUX

Women accept flowers even from a shit.
All Russians love diminutive nicknames.
Every presidential debate is a comic skit.
In Iceland, there is no use of surnames.

Only an imbecile overfills an omelet.
There is no known reality without possibility.
A politician's worship is the voting ballot.
Vanity and faith define incompatibility.

A doe always tastes better than a buck.
Air is the ultimate enemy of wine.
Recipes written out in prose all suck.
Darkness is necessary to witness shine.

The physics of water is central to cooking.
Stabbing is the *personal* way of killing.
To find God, what's involved is *looking*.
No apprenticeship is ever quite fulfilling.

Richard Wagner hated everything French.
No joke you tell is funny to your wife.
Craven appeasement gives off a stench.
Oceans hold 95% of our planet's life.

Every golf course needs 150 acres.
Every affair is a series of betrayals.
Quietism creates good Quakers.
No portrait aims at true portrayal.

TRUISMS

Picture is always subject to text.
Saltiness in a food cannot be smelled.
Ideals in Congress are always vexed.
Cashew nuts are always sold shelled.

After any stock rally, seek to raise cash.
No Abstract Expressionists could draw.
For grey, mix poppy oil with cigar ash.
Lawyers subvert rather than obey the law.

White-flowered plants have the worst odors.
Female crabs taste better than male crabs.
Brazilian police fight with front-end loaders.
Always pan-fry—bone in—fresh sand dabs.

Wars invariably commence in the Fall.
One must speculate in order to accumulate.
Submission of any sort, to atheists, is gall.
The folly of a lover is to overestimate.

Golfers improve when they're playing faster.
The riper the pepper, the less the heat.
The most precious calcite is black alabaster.
Sleep proves the sagacity behind retreat.

Boys play in pairs, girls in groups.
All lotteries are taxes for dumbbells.
Memory works by leaps and loops.
It is against the law to pick bluebells.

Native Americans feel pity is a weakness.
Dahlias are ingredients in Oaxacan cuisine.
Patient suffering is the virtue of meekness
The best-tasting bacon is never lean.

Most flags queen it with the color red.
Woman authors never give their age.
Marx's *Das Kapital* is very rarely read.
Jealousy nothing can ever assuage.

Fame stultifies the creative urge.
Quince is only edible when cooked.
Every Andy Williams song is a dirge.
No-deposit trains are always overbooked.

Decadent types scorn the ordinary.
You never see pests on stinging nettles.
The truly virtuous are voluntary.
Paranoids tend always to trade in metals.

A tomato despises any tobacco near it.
Competition always engenders anger.
No noise is made an owl can't hear it.
Cruelty is at the source of all clangor.

An honest traveler is always a pilgrim.
Weather creates a person's character.
Blackness is the color of the Hasidim.
Pulling, not pushing, denotes a tractor.

TRUISMS

It is vulgar of guests to "notice" things.
The bane of vitamins are heat, air, fungi.
Parsley is oddly effective for bee stings.
Mating is the goal of glow in a firefly.

Scallops were once thought to be poison.
Artichokes and anchovies pair with no wine.
Integration finds a metaphor in cloissone.
The temple of love houses a fallible shrine.

The French refuse to drink tap water.
Little girls cannot play without screaming.
Every animal's final end is slaughter.
The past not the future informs dreaming.

Every parable is about light and dark.
San Francisco was always a city of misfits.
The spice called cinnamon is bark.
One yawn another always transmits.

A bareheaded Jew at prayer is a pagan.
Wine should only be served with food.
Two wheels a cart, four wheels a wagon.
French citizens are by nature rude.

Plagiarists all fear being stolen from.
The selfish are most likely to succeed.
Cut flowers need water, never sun.
All prosperity is married to greed.

No English country house is warm enough.
In Chinese, surnames precede first names.
Brinksmanship totally thrives on bluff.
Delight is felt by everyone who blames.

Every page of history is bloodied.
All serious action is a form of belief.
What's taken for granted is never studied.
Avoiding fame in life provides relief.

No yard sale sign should ever be prosy.
Alcoholics find aid in being anonymous.
Asian girls are often violin virtuosi.
Capitalism and theft are synonymous.

White truffles should be eaten raw.
There is no great history of Ireland.
Every Persian carpet shows a flaw.
Bees are needed to fertilize the almond.

Louisiana leads the nation in prisoners.
Every vaccine must be refrigerated.
Big talkers are never good listeners.
Objectivity in obsessives is obliterated.

Bikers have a love affair with chrome.
Heroine addicts are commonly impotent.
Godly faith in buildings favors a dome.
Every depressant calls for a stimulant.

TRUISMS

Pruning well stimulates later growth.
True tomato sauce is orange, not red.
Want of imagination is a form of sloth.
Depression indicates fury never said.

Nothing is not basically a chemical.
The Israeli is now as cruel as the Nazi.
Visual beauty is always asymmetrical.
Arabic script is employed in Farsi.

Non-existent is an *average* person.
Time forever speeds up as we age.
No worse exists that cannot worsen.
Arrogant actors crave a raked stage.

The now, the immediate, is never holy.
"Minor" can never define back surgery.
Intimacy can only develop slowly.
Need as proxy for love a sheer forgery.

All dictators demand super regalia.
Intuition is born of the mind's moral eye.
Fancy rarely jibes with proven behavior.
100% literacy exists in the nation of Brunei.

Right reason is never free of passion.
Obedience above all means sacrifices.
True style is rarely joined with fashion.
New England food eschews all spices.

Truth is treason in the empire of lies.
All nationalities as subjects are comical.
Blessings are always in disguise.
Insurance is at bottom uneconomical.

All victims, in the end, are dangerous.
The tail of every rat is always cold.
One's own spy is never treacherous.
A medal given is an act condoled.

Never play leapfrog with a unicorn.
A complete lie comprises a half truth.
Expect nothing good from a Capricorn.
A prophet to a degree is always uncouth.

Most miles of river exist in Nebraska.
Ohio buckeye's best for artificial limbs.
No state income tax is levied in Alaska.
Mystery writers treasure pseudonyms.

The Congo leads in U.S. foreign aid.
There is no copyright on book titles.
An English breakfast entails marmalade.
Exhibitionism typifies all recitals.

California has always been a mecca for lunatics.
Gentile's *The Adoration of the Magi* is Christmas personified.
The Inquisition held all Protestants to be heretics.
After three *consecutive* failures a high jumper is disqualified.

TRUISMS

Nothing at all is known about Habakkuk.
London is the busiest airspace in the world.
Gertrude Stein's opera is gobbledygook.
An Irish shillelagh is significantly knurled.

Devil's Island guards were always Corsican.
Bank balance sheets are mainly bonds.
Japanese women all have skin of porcelain.
Frippery is famously connoted to blondes.

Bullied teen suicides are always pretty.
No playoff begins until a game is lost at home.
The sea has neither meaning nor pity.
Tough girls paint their nails with chrome.

Obituary superlatives are only reflexive.
It is women who create all movie stars.
The effective is more forceful the affective.
Tilt allows for seasons on the planet Mars.

Kissing babies, above all, woos a voter.
Conflict is the beating heart of fiction.
Insecurity animates the gloater.
Every truth fosters its contradiction.

Circus people are itinerant folks.
Of jealous girls, pretty girls are prey.
No airplane wheels admit of spokes.
No formal wear isn't enhanced by grey.

ALEXANDER THEROUX

A friend of the world is the enemy of God.
The worst heretics are the purely selfish.
A lover when awed is invariably flawed.
Animals is the proper term for shellfish.

A German, seeking sunshine, goes to Italy.
The urge for fame is a desire for echo.
A politician always agrees, noncommittally.
Red wines are all predominantly *seco*.

Gambling is exciting only if you're poor.
Young school killers have all been bullied.
Though bent in the water, straight is the oar.
Any object best lifted is always pullied.

Shopping, done by the very rich, is dull.
Anglicanism was built on hate of Catholics.
There is no deader eye than that of a gull.
Courting a mate strictly deals in tactics.

A successful pie crust is kept cold.
The second harvest is rice's claim to fame.
You cannot live long without living old.
Envy going public gives slander its name.

Whiskers grow on cheeks, not the chin.
Smell is the sense in poetry least praised.
Vertical stripes mock any woman thin.
The tale of mothers is the tale of gays.

TRUISMS

A catcher needs the ball to block the plate.
The N.Y. Yankees always buy their teams.
Rudeness always registers by being late.
Bower birds are drawn to whatever gleams.

It is crude to cut lettuce on your plate.
Younger drinkers tend to avoid bourbon.
No bad weather deters voters who hate.
A man always looks virile in a turban.

Never leave well enough alone.
Low turn-out elections help Republicans.
Rhyme scone with "gone," not "tone."
The multiplying variable is the multiplicand.

The defect of symposia is lack of unity.
Oregano constantly takes over a garden.
Power breezily pre-assumes impunity.
No acrylic paints ever quite fully harden.

Women never have enough shoes.
Only a teenager should play Romeo.
Misery must be felt to sing the blues.
Every ration also always implies a ratio.

The French open oysters from the side.
Schoolboys always vilify eccentrics.
Gloom forever awaits a blushing bride.
No governing structure rules pandemics.

A poetaster's work is always crude.
Any discrepancy always fosters doubt.
A lover's vision is always skewed.
The best oily fish is the steel head trout.

It is harder to forgive those who've wronged us
than to forgive those whom we have wronged.
German philosophy has always been ponderous,
to which a simple sentence has never belonged.

True hula dancers never wiggle their hips.
Grapefruit grow best in alkaline sandy loam.
No planet without moons can have an eclipse.
The more elegant the car, the less the chrome.

Wasting food should be a criminal act.
A cavalry saber is always straight.
Inert gases with other elements never react.
Rabid fear eventually turns to hate.

Buy saffron in threads, never by bulk.
Irony is basically a form of retaliation.
Waiting is the force behind every sulk.
Twice blest is an anonymous donation.

Choose *lapereau* to cook for its soft ears.
Gardening gave to us the very first catalog.
Only empty promises are souvenirs.
Vladimir Nabokov hated use of dialogue.

TRUISMS

The need to be on TV is a mental illness.
To want to be an actor is to need therapy.
Bees have to move fast to know stillness.
Greed has always preceded philanthropy.

It is always colder in the Texas Panhandle.
Every Indian in Mexico cooks perfect beans.
Whom you love you inevitably manhandle.
Every fashion the previous contravenes.

One must never tower over a Thai royal.
Bad teeth in women can cause a miscarriage.
Love never ponders the need of being loyal.
It is lack of *friendship* that kills a marriage.

No one must ever touch the Queen.
Astronaut personalities are always flat.
Many headache drugs include caffeine.
All Hassids are required to wear a hat.

A true cassoulet must contain some goose.
 Spines constitute the leaves of a cactus.
A deer's no less a deer when called a moose.
Congenital diabetics are always fractious.

Greed is caused by the fear of want.
Inaccuracy defines all reflections.
Every boast is also a taunt.
White accurately describes no complexions.

Poets beginning adopt another's voice.
The Hershey Company never advertises.
Take away freedom, take away choice.
One's direct opposite best magnetizes.

No one ever feels at home in a motel.
Hawthorne's dialogue is always stiff.
Black's the chosen color of every rebel.
A true prose style bears its own glyph.

Cover-ups are part and parcel to the crime.
Christianity comes uneasily to Japanese.
No single life lived can be called sublime.
Humidity fosters many a human disease.

A good sauté pan always has a lid.
Television creates its own events.
Anally-retentive minds adore a grid.
Misfits are all by nature malcontents.

Non-existent is a purely English royal house.
Reaction always follows a revolt.
Nothing tight in a shirt can be called a blouse.
Noise is half of every thunderbolt.

Always slice a brisket against the grain.
The northern side of a house gets dirtiest.
A change of weather always follows rain.
The stoutest is universally the sturdiest.

TRUISMS

The worst drivers on earth are Belgians.
Frenchmen always stop for lunch at noon.
Greeks devised the horse, not the Trojans.
Sunlight is actually the light of the moon.

Every single force evolves a form.
Every true form evolves a subject.
No written history does not disinform.
Bad parents love, but duty neglect.

No rational man seeks to have a power.
The French avoid mint in cooking.
Without an abrasive, nothing can scour.
Airlines make money overbooking.

Ash, a coolant, should be kept on a cigar.
Magic, culturally, always precedes religion.
Veggies frozen trump any from can and jar.
Nothing enjoys a hole more than pigeon.

All forms of life modify their contexts.
Australians cannot stand authority.
Younger sibling's get the older one's rejects.
Avoid being on the side of the majority.

Canada geese migrate to keep a 35-degree temp.
Anything large is incompatible with beauty.
Make no effort, and from failure you're exempt.
Work done from love is greater than from duty.

Short-sighted people have large handwriting.
The best cheese is made with unpasteurized milk.
Chats with businessmen are always unexciting.
Carnality and lubricity are ever aligned with silk.

Time of death is an inexact science.
Refrigeration kills the taste of fruit.
Silence is a synonym of compliance.
Truth and logic are always in dispute.

The only true cinnamon is from Ceylon.
Midweek is always the cheapest time to fly.
Nothing exists a cheetah cannot outrun.
Tastelessness delights in wearing a string tie.

Every truthful proverb has its opposite.
Norwegians are generally taller than Danes.
Fear and hatred are always proximate.
Grapefruit juice every medicine disdains.

Girl babies smile much more than boys.
Coldstream guardsmen never will retreat.
Hell—pandemonium—consists of noise.
Rudeness in Asia is expressed by feet.

Scratch a conspiracist, see a bigot bleed.
When cooking them, never cover peas.
To achieve good pie crust never overknead.
Poppy seeds won't grow unless they freeze.

TRUISMS

Loopholes are *lingua franca* at gun shows.
There is a church every mile in the South.
The correct plural of the letter O is Oes.
A baby signals solely by its little mouth.

Sexually inconfident men use thlipses.
The bird world tends to dislike blue jays.
Cunning as a tactic thrives on paralipses.
No vegetable's not improved by a braise.

Corned beef is best when served cold.
A fish that sinks in fresh water is fresh.
No Camembert is not improved by mold.
Nothing sells better than human flesh.

Tinware may be cleaned with wood ashes.
Never buy a goose with few pinfeathers.
Stripes and dots are fashioned for clashes.
A biker's mind is rapturous for leathers.

Tibet was never a part of China.
Juries never convict celebrities.
NeoCons thrive in South Carolina.
Best-sellers are defined by banalities.

Never shoot dice on blankets.
Old age in point of fact has no gender.
Sex and slavery share anklets.
Plaid as a fabric is wanting in splendor.

Bishops have less power than rooks.
April is the best month for the Dow.
To be running is the nature of brooks.
With God omitted, there is no vow.

People who wake for breakfast are energetic.
What's unidentifiable in a fridge, throw away.
Anything over-large lacks a visible aesthetic.
Love, compared to duty, will always outweigh.

Women always order first in France.
Monday night audiences are the worst.
No meat exists that onion can't enhance.
The son of any famous man is cursed.

Experience is useless without memory.
A poem to be effective must be short.
All fashion is merely an accessory.
Any act with competition is a sport.

Littering is a sign of a sick society.
No Englishman tries to speak French well.
Any reverent act in public lacks piety.
Together no Jew and Arab will ever dwell.

A creased baseball card is worthless.
The sky gets lighter near the horizon.
Victor Mature preened on going shirtless.
That any law's obeyed is most surprising.

TRUISMS

Closers in baseball are easy to steal on.
Danes love to sport the tallest hats.
Vanity in a garrulous host demands a salon.
Social programs thrill Democrats.

Money is more than anything a fetish.
Americans see stop signs as mere guidelines.
All affectation is basically coquettish.
Idolatry is the nature of all religious shrines.

All the planets travel counterclockwise.
Cinnamon should be used solely in desserts.
You destroy what you dissect to analyze.
What the mind never questions it perverts.

Experience is useless without memory.
To translate non-literally is only to distort.
All fashion is merely an accessory.
Any act involving competition is a sport.

Resolve is 90% of any plan.
The taller the bamboo, the lower it bends.
The world's most popular book is the Koran.
Canadian whiskeys are always blends.

Salvation is linked to the eremitical.
Audiences laugh at a clown, *with* a comedian.
The French have never been musical.
Every geometric solid is Archimedean.

A holy fool—*yurodivyi*—is a saint in Russia.
Reindeer hooves change with the season.
After WWII, Allies banned the name Prussia.
Five years in jail is the U.S. penalty for treason.

Men's clubs love farcical rules of secrecy.
No one's childhood account is ever objective.
Quality in sex trumps sexual frequency.
Marriage to first love is a stern corrective.

Celebrity culture is worthless coin.
No one sounds intelligent in *People* magazine.
Holly trees and bird nests gaily adjoin.
A measure of vulgarity is length of a limousine.

Every Ariadne meets her faithless Theseus.
Dutch painters loved to do group portraits.
No great choir hasn't a patient Coryphaeus.
The ramparts are always circular on a fortress.

Why do UFOs appear only to fools?
Humans inhale mostly nitrogen, not oxygen.
Exceptions alone force the need of rules.
A body's most abundant protein is collagen.

No visionary ever attends law school.
Violins hold sway in any orchestration.
Democracy by definition fosters misrule.
Non-reading leads to mental retardation.

TRUISMS

Death in showbiz is hosting a game show.
Endurance is the Asian secret weapon.
Crows who fear black hate their shadow.
Perfume exists solely to tempt and beckon.

Never trust an opponent's flattery.
Lips are more sensitive than fingertips.
True greed renders gain unsatisfactory.
Animals are confused in a total eclipse.

A beard helps bury the human face.
Women tend to eat muffins by pinches.
Masai all move with a natural grace.
Who dies by famine, dies by inches.

Never plant azaleas in direct sun.
News and gossip are all the same.
History is merely fables agreed on.
Yellow and blue are seen in a flame.

The ovary is actually a female gonad.
Lawyers will do anything for money.
God, the one eternal, is primarily a monad.
Poisonous is all rhododendron honey.

Policy always strangles individualism.
Cape Codders rarely use their front doors.
Xenophobia is foremost a provincialism.
Each sex is inflamed by the other's sudors.

Bostonians rarely pronounce letter R's.
Patents seem to be forever pending.
Men keep weirdly remote in American bars.
Envy and greed are always contending.

Always wipe baby girls front to back.
The country of Brazil prevails in soccer.
A rainbow strictly abhors the color black.
No Irishman is not a verbose talker.

A physician's writing is tortuous scrawl.
Never plant vines directly on your house.
Coral reefs often abound around an atoll.
A monarch's consort is equally a spouse.

A fart by a baby's as good as a burp.
Mufflers go on the ride side of vehicles.
No twin the other's space doesn't usurp.
Ambiguity is the soul of all oracles.

Baby swings all play "*Frère Jacques.*"
No discriminating person joins a book club.
Delivered in flight is the song of the lark.
Laughter's the best way to reverse a snub.

In most fruit drinks, apple juice is used.
Black Muslims made NAACP acceptable to whites.
The broken learn much faster than the bruised.
The higher up it soars, the faster goes the kite.

TRUISMS

Trappist monks avoid soft clothes.
Cardinals prefer to forage on the ground.
Products sell better when shown in rows.
Every single vibration gives off a sound.

Hens that lay brown eggs have red earlobes.
"Talkers" hate the rude title carnival barker.
All garments need sleeves to qualify as robes.
Urine remains in nature a universal marker.

Horsehair plaster walls badly blocks Wi-Fi.
The energy of matter never diminishes.
Its pot determines size in Japanese bonsai.
With smart shoes, all fashion finishes.

Modern dance is extravagantly ridiculous.
Summit meetings are masked as convivial.
Repetition in children's games is ubiquitous.
No box isn't too garish of breakfast cereal.

Ferry accidents are the rule in Bangladesh.
MLB players keep a finger outside their gloves.
Nothing in car ads sells like female flesh.
Nothing negative is ever assigned to doves.

All winter motor oil is thin.
English upper classes keep separate bedrooms.
Hell in literature is characterized by din.
Haplessness defines all waiting bridegrooms.

Vernon Castle was a better dancer than Irene.
No Animal Crackers box can now depict a cage.
Psycho was first to show a toilet on the screen.
An actor's identity is borrowed while on stage.

Satin trousers persistently badly wrinkle.
The best tasting bear meat is from a dry sow.
A twinkle in youth in old age is a crinkle.
The better the harvest, the deeper the plough.

Tire dealers are without fail sleazeballs.
Yearning is ever riven with contempt.
Fractiousness is the point of bugle calls.
Holy people are rarely seen as kempt.

Always ease a boat's speed when she pitches.
Women universally gush over babies.
Warnings characterize the speeches of witches.
Bats are the main cause of human rabies.

Craziness has a significant shelf life.
Nineteen's the most marketable age for women.
Religion manufactures every kind of strife.
What is forgotten is automatically forgiven.

Insects are the husbands of all flowers.
Tightly taping envelopes is a sign of paranoia.
Church *ordos* follow designated hours.
A *grove* is necessary to have a living sequoia.

TRUISMS

Homelessness is man's essential fear.
You need dopamine to make testosterone.
Stupidity is posted by the shape of one's ear.
Knowledge is required in any cicerone.

The magnetic poles have no longitude.
Nothing can travel slower than "stopped."
A Caribbean manner is happy desuetude.
The move to adopt is a need to co-opt.

Never trust the deepest places of a river.
90% of humans live in the Northern Hemisphere.
Insecurity constitutes every reluctant giver.
Rhythmic chanting supports every auctioneer.

Never trust a piss-proud servant.
Israeli power owns the U.S. Congress.
No *official* prayers are ever fervent.
No change—therefore, never progress.

Kings must be loved, dictators dreaded.
White vinegar is potently anti-bacterial.
No human being is naturally redheaded.
The biggest supermarket mark-up is cereal.

One's answers signify less than one's queries.
A change of suit should include a change of shoes.
Envy finds action in the need to accuse.
The fat wallets of New York Yankees win World Series.

Wall Street speculators are all vultures.
A senator's only goal is re-election.
Rich and poor create opposite cultures.
Every narcissist abhors correction.

Very few individuals cannot sing.
Fifty miles can stretch one ounce of gold.
The oldest combat weapon is the sling.
Diamonds are not rare, only controlled.

NATO in crisis has never had teeth.
A good interviewer always plays stupid.
No one conceives a non-oval wreath.
Logic was never a major trait of Cupid.

Trust a lawyer, embrace and kiss a serpent.
The filthy rich never pick up checks.
Becoming master is abhorrent to a servant.
Breathing is best utilized on necks.

Birthdays and binge-drinking go hand-in-hand.
A piano should be tuned to standard pitch.
Cranberry growth is hugely stimulated by sand.
The American economy favors the rich.

Where you stand is where you sit.
A Leyland spruce is the fastest growing tree.
A passive policeman is a cop unfit.
No ball player entered the HOF unanimously.

TRUISMS

Rednecks are only dangerous in groups.
Corn is the primary American food staple.
The DNA molecule is a graphic of loops.
The standard American tree is the maple.

What he loves is the key to his torture.
Only the closely similar are truly rivals.
Every day in Libya is always a scorcher.
Old Testament justice is mainly reprisals.

The sartorial taste of golfers is hideous.
Soccer fans are notoriously hysterical.
Sapphonic clothes are rarely fastidious.
College humor is immaturely chimerical.

Only sons to a Chinaman are worthwhile.
Food is more ritualized and enjoyed at sea.
The nation of Singapore is the least fertile.
The majority of Britons prefer black tea.

A jack, a knave, a valet are the same playing card.
Microwaves always alter the direction of rotation.
A penis in 19th-c. pornography was called a "yard."
Quote is a verb, whereas the noun is a quotation.

Burgundy lovers hate their wine decanted.
"Cherry Blossom," an Asian delicacy, is horse meat.
A prevaricator's explanation is always slanted.
No tree served Indians better than the mesquite.

The smaller the country, the bigger the generals' caps.
Loving eyes never see the truth.
Stupidity is associated with wide dental gaps.
Wisdom is the antonym of youth.

Every green apple is a potential pie apple.
Hawaii weather sweats all works on paper.
Lyricists to church prefer the word chapel.
No Mediterranean cuisine ignores the caper.

Tunnels are all dangerous areas for hazmat.
No New Englander recognizes spoon bread.
To catch a mackerel, always use a sprat.
Hindu populations are notoriously inbred.

Sound is the manifestation of movement.
Cold air holds less moisture than warm air,
Reapplication is required for improvement.
A Muslim prides himself on public prayer.

Billionaires are their own political parties.
Grass seed is effective in any season.
Loud voices are taboo on African safaris.
The first casualty in any war is reason.

The Koran in Israel is officially suppressed.
Not a single thing can burn without air.
No noun exists for the perpetrators of incest.
All rubes head directly for Times Square.

TRUISMS

Contours are entirely lost in a true whiteout.
Oyster stew is not a chowder—no potatoes.
Rare vitamin K2 is abundant in sauerkraut.
Only *fake* beards were worn by the pharaohs.

Football fascinates the Southern mind.
Feelings of mortification decrease with age.
Every criminal act is personally signed.
A sneeze can badly fracture the rib cage.

Hedgehogs are badly prone to cancer.
Governments are poor at handling money.
Whatever greed asks never has an answer.
Practical jokes are in fact never funny.

African Americans rarely watch hockey.
Only male crickets will stridulate.
No person in Nauru is not also stocky.
It is intrepid people alone who migrate.

If triangles had a God, he'd have three sides.
Koreans have cornered the manicure trade.
The emotion of jealousy never subsides.
Hosta, the perennial, only thrives in shade.

Cruise lines are notorious for crime
Danes are the world's happiest people.
No human is boring as much as a mime.
Green is the unvarying color of a sepal.

Money's only worth the good it does.
A servant should always be inconspicuous.
Any burden gives every rebel a cause.
Square-toed shoes appear fairly ridiculous.

The poor are more enjoyable than the rich.
High end art-collecting is idolatry.
No singing birds have not a perfect pitch.
Depressives are inordinately crotchety.

Coughing during a play is criticism.
Realism does not exist in the theater.
Asians are fairly immune to witticism.
Bowl-shapes characterize every crater.

Staring is never not a hostile act.
The better the skier, the more dangerous the sport.
Science fiction cold shoulders fact.
No successful presidential candidate is short.

Nothing is as expensive as cheap labor.
Sarcasm comes naturally to feminists.
The useless quince embodies nature's disfavor.
Indirection is the ploy of illusionists.

Politics in Zimbabwe are utterly corrupt.
Posturing is a measure of self-protection.
Every convention it is healthy to disrupt.
Black is not a race but a complexion.

TRUISMS

Any falcon must never be eyed.
A cause can never be less than its effect.
Expectation is a source of pride.
Zippers, buttons are barred by the Amish sect.

No crocodile cannot stick its tongue out.
Endless are the hits of Vincent Youmans.
An elephant knows the ankus of its mahout.
Koala fingerprints resemble that of humans.

Shakespeare has a stage direction *"Enter fleeing."*
Black flags are signifiers of the Taliban.
Napoleon lost Moscow by the Russians retreating.
Race often stereotypes the character Caliban.

March is the favorite suicide month.
Car races are won strictly on tires.
A scoundrel act is playing a dunce.
A .38 Special frequently misfires.

It is hateful now to say Merry Christmas.
Wet with dark always breed a fungus.
All true contrition requires forgiveness.
Horns are never found on any Angus.

A goose will only lay eggs in spring.
Cynics are proven every time correct.
Many brides in India prefer a toe ring.
An orphan identifies only neglect.

Love your job, and you'll never work.
Geese can only be raised on grass.
Lechery legendarily connotes a Turk.
Marching bands depend on brass.

British castles are never solvent.
Amish limit schooling to the grade of eight.
Promise marks the season of Advent.
No high Peruvian walks with a normal gait.

Reading books forces a personality on us.
Cremation is forbidden to Orthodox Jews.
In law, an enforceable contract is a promise.
Monks alone make the liqueur Chartreuse.

Monday is the favorite suicide day.
Cold weather diminishes all car sales.
Neurotics tend to want to crochet.
Where there is money, power prevails.

A uniform by definition makes demands.
No automobile lover outdoes an Italian.
Buyers all cravenly follow brands.
Use high-quality fence to confine a stallion.

Glory is always aligned with soaring.
All Greeks yearn to run a restaurant.
Nascar events are the epitome of boring.
Highways do not exist in Vermont.

TRUISMS

A theme in every novel involves cognition.
Apatheism makes an atheist look godly.
Consistency is the bane of every logician.
Rare is a man who looks at politics broadly.

A baby's first two teeth come in below.
Never stare hard at a schizophrenic.
Misanthropy explains much of Thoreau.
Grilling foods can be carcinogenic.

Colder temps bring larger snowflakes.
Methodist steeples never have crosses.
Fraternal minds love secret handshakes.
Flowerlessness is the condition of mosses.

Every Hungarian craves good paprika.
Wahhabism fosters much intolerance.
The best tamales are made in Costa Rica.
Only change of mind is true repentance.

Sound travels faster in water than in air.
Every umpire has his own strike zone.
Big women paradoxically need big hair.
Avoid using yeast in making a scone.

Chairman Mao's favorite food was *hong shao rou*—
pork belly cubes all glazed with caramelized sugar
and Shaoxing rice wine, his unique choice of brew,
with certain pigs to be braised in a special cooker.

There is no actual God in Buddhism.
Pull of Gravity is actually Push of Space.
Collectivism is the worse part of nudism.
Earth's future entirely depends on space.

Black's the easiest color to remove in tattoos.
Fresh snow makes every white house drab.
Brisket is by far the nonpareil of barbecues.
If it is not a decapod, then it is not a crab.

No Frenchman ever kisses a gloved hand.
All train engineers have to "call the aspect."
Best-selling books are almost always bland.
Female birds, to hide, are never bedecked.

Never read a great novel when writing one.
Any human being can grow a radish.
Beware a firework whenever lighting one.
Eccentric is conjoined with faddish.

All NHL goalies are deeply superstitious.
Rice should be boiled for eleven minutes.
The Haitian mind is largely superstitious.
Apprehension creates the nature of limits.

Chinchillas are commonly constipated.
All old men look baggy wearing jeans.
Apathy greets anything consummated.
Recklessness defines the mind of teens.

TRUISMS

The Oscars over-reward Holocaust films.
A good Brie should ooze but never run.
Diseases and insects both cherish elms.
Weaving's required before you've spun.

No banana on earth is ever straight.
A hangover follows any taken drug.
Hating doesn't cease with the act of hate.
Iran is the land of the handmade rug.

A beet leaf is more nutritious than its roots.
Bureaucracies are by nature inefficient.
Hollywood money walks in empty suits.
Wordless love is always love deficient.

Cooking popovers, never check the oven.
The older the buck, the stiffer the horn.
Three women together constitute a coven.
To cherish a rose, one must accept the thorn.

White oak is much harder than red oak.
Most mutton eaters are in the Muslim world.
A flower un-bloomed is an artichoke
Not a single ocean seashell goes unwhorled.

Dahlias should be planted horizontally.
The devil inhabits all gold mines.
Fraternities thrive in acting irresponsibly.
Prohibition popularized jug wines.

For totem poles, always use red cedar.
Any dose of salt will always kill yeast.
Much of the hereditary is in a bleeder.
Loneliness plagues every Catholic priest.

Sunday morning radio is the pits.
Babies all prefer the wrapping to the gift.
No one size in any product ever fits.
To gain prosperity is to cultivate thrift.

Native Americans were Asian nomads.
True winners fashion their own trophies.
Humility generates a million comrades.
Living fish positively thrive on anchovies.

Every petunia seems to bloom forever.
A woman is only as young as her knees.
Any enterprise requires bold endeavor.
Danish language has no word for *please.*

Totem pole colors are red, black, and green.
No baseball hitter can bunt a high heater.
A carburetor manages never to stay clean.
No serious cook is not also a secret eater.

Liberal satire is an oxymoron.
Choucroute is always cooked in wine.
The Iroquois despised the Huron.
Rubbing alcohol and bleach never combine.

TRUISMS

Pumpkins tend to grow mainly at night.
Black is the world's most common hair color.
Purity was the prime virtue of the knight.
What is higher is not at all the same as taller.

Dango in Japan is always served in fours.
Grass seed comes mainly from Oregon.
Foods long in the stomach cause bezoars.
Corners equal sides in every polygon.

Models are obsessed with their clavicles.
Any explorer anticipated is a bitter man.
Militancy is the *sine qua non* of radicals.
Kinship is required in any Scottish clan.

The posture of myopes tends to be bad.
To Brits, heated air is found unhealthy.
Black-and-white is checkerboard plaid.
Every person in Qatar is wealthy.

The wish is father of the deed.
Winter nights call for smoked brisling.
Conviction is the soul of every creed.
An owl spends every minute listening.

Never add dairy or meat to a compost pile.
Few Arabs have not a passion for jewelry.
Baltic natives notoriously never smile.
The Somali mind delights in silly foolery.

No Edwardian meal left out ptarmigan.
Bread is cut even numbered for sandwiches.
Cashmere wool makes the best cardigan.
It's either alternate or opposite for branches.

Sunbathing makes many people horny.
With plastic trash, the Pacific is rife.
The rose *depends* on its being thorny.
Three is the legendary number for strife.

After five telephone rings, hang up.
All boats demand to have a name.
Trophies are invariably a given cup.
Whatever thing is pointed has an aim.

The very best of slate comes from Wales.
Loving eyes very rarely see clearly.
God's most enigmatic creatures are whales.
All flattery is proffered insincerely.

Never print a yard sale sign small.
Let no threat get within arm's length.
A tall girl always feels far too tall.
Silence is a source of great strength.

In port is a vessel's busiest time.
Climbing is a way of saying yes.
No herb dries better than thyme.
The killer mind excels at chess.

TRUISMS

Asian men are ignored as romantic leads.
Nothing in God corresponds to us.
Punctuality is characteristic of Swedes.
Lawyers crave the chance to sue us.

When you have truth, you pound the truth;
when you do not, you pound the table.
Every jealous lover becomes a sleuth.
An ogre is a giant in every nation's fable.

Wolves are always in a starving state.
Travel is by far the greatest educator.
Kuwaitis fancy women overweight.
No motive ever quite explains a traitor.

The best milking-stools are rump-fitted.
A nurse's first lesson is not fully to care.
Whites in Mississippi are ever acquitted.
Muslims discern hell in a woman's hair.

Psychopaths will never flush or blush.
Rap songs are universally inarticulate.
Paul McCartney's songs are always lush.
Every atmosphere is mainly particulate.

It is not done to dislike P.G. Wodehouse,
nor to criticize Mark Twain, James Thurber,
Robert E. Lee, Gandhi, or Mickey Mouse,
all of whom snobs find nothing superber.

No one can ever fully succeed alone.
Confrontation freaks crave the last word.
Dictators all adore a vivid cologne.
The noblest brother in fables is the third.

Autos always fade when painted blue.
Nothing is swisher than shoe designing.
Equal parts fat and flour make a roux.
A promise is by definition confining.

America wastes trillions on false wars.
A sunflower to grow must be well staked.
Crystallized white honey never pours.
Jewish corpses are not embalmed nor waked.

At night, vegetables do most growing.
A pitcher who has lost his fastball is useless.
Repetition is the *Tao* of mowing.
A child molester's resolve to stop is fruitless.

Watering the leaves of plants is bad.
The best anchovies come from Sicily.
Sexiness is always only *partially* clad.
Regrets are always given wistfully.

Weight loss programs all exaggerate.
A fictional character's name suggests a plot.
A liar is always forced to elaborate.
Not a single war has Nepal ever fought.

TRUISMS

Not a soul on earth is truly important.
No clam chowder should include tomatoes.
Religion and revolution are ever discordant.
The Asian palate cannot enjoy potatoes.

Calves' liver is best to stop anemia.
Cowboy songs, to soothe a herd, are slow.
Regulations are all taboo in Bohemia.
The promise of rain raises a tail on a cow.

Literature has no true child prodigies.
Giving cash is best for disaster relief.
Faith is the staple of world theologies.
No woman was ever an Indian chief.

Doubleday's the publisher of Republicans.
Harper's commonly shills for Democrats.
Jews are forbidden by law to eat pelicans.
Lack of imagination is the bane of technocrats.

All orchids are actually edible.
Polls shape rather than reflect opinions.
An agent's word is never credible.
Wars are fought by the poorest minions.

There is no single Mediterranean cuisine.
The French prefer Bordeaux over Burgundy.
The Islamic color is predominantly green.
Triumph is the constant dream of Germany.

Always beat egg whites in a copper bowl.
Bird nests for strength are always woven.
Hunting by pack is the way of the dhole.
All ladies when dining constitute a coven.

1960s color photography always skewed wrong.
Julia Child utterly loathed the use of margarine.
Nothing positive is ever suggested by a "throng."
No patriot is ever first or deep down a partisan.

Protagonists are ambiguous in all great novels.
Beauty contestants all want to work with paraplegics.
For political votes, every campaigner grovels.
Chess is the *ne plus ultra* of multifarious strategics.

Toddlers impulsively seek out the hazard.
Nothing fully square appears in nature.
The best dance floor is made of mazzard.
Compromise is what perfects legislature.

Any hot object gives off microwaves.
Women have an affinity for chocolates.
No correct Afghanistani ever shaves.
Nothing's lamer than honorary doctorates.

The best lentils come from Puy, France.
Than Ebola, nothing's more contracting.
Success in marriage depends on chance.
The craft of acting is basically re-acting.

TRUISMS

Desperation in anything is unedifying.
Hummingbirds are unable to smell.
The Cold War was fought by spying.
Every rock star needs a bold marcel.

China in every facet is dyed red.
Only cook a lobster when it is alive.
Every nation shapes its own bread.
TV gadgets always sell for "$19.95."

Great droughts always end in a flood.
Platinum hair is always from a bottle.
Spoor in crime is inevitably by blood.
No position will be 0% idle at throttle.

No American cars are ever firmly priced.
Reading is a primal obligation for writing.
No toy directions are ever quite concise.
Slender fish are invariably called whiting.

Every street in Manhattan ends at a river.
An avalanche is the married spouse of thaw.
India as a nation's the most grudging giver.
The poor, no matter its color, trust no law.

Lyric poets tend to flower early.
Satire is very rare in American lit.
No healthy Tahitian is not burly.
Rapists compulsively recommit.

No one impugns art more than a censor.
Motives of a burglar are never complex.
Of a Mogadishan head, nothing is denser.
Any lens thicker at the center is convex.

Religion is the leading domain of kitsch.
The Chinese are fanatical gamblers.
Only 1 person in 10,000 has perfect pitch.
Deer are the only animals with antlers.

A bowlegged woman loves a knock-kneed man.
Native Americans cannot endure confinement.
Laundry alone establishes bias of a sports fan.
Alaskans thrive in eschewing all refinement.

Women tend to make poor butchers.
Never let a soup stock come to a boil.
Only prophets can read stock futures.
Green tea immediately begins to spoil.

Never prolong a closing musical note.
Never simmer bouillabaisse: it's always boiled.
Asian students tend to learn by rote.
A machine over-oiled is a bad as never oiled.

Ought, ethically, always implies can.
It is not done to hive an old queen bee.
Pomegranates flavor much cooking in Iran.
Freedom is the opposite of wanton liberty.

TRUISMS

A used key consistently burns bright.
They are free of fruit who want an orchard.
Papal clothes are specifically white.
18th-century gardens were always bordered.

Courtesy always masks the wiliness of craft.
No one is more liberal than a beggar.
Every Comanche arrow had a blue/red shaft.
Stabbing is the ambition of a dagger.

San Franciscans loathe the term "Frisco."
Lamb has the greatest affinity to garlic.
Latex allergies include banana, kiwi, avocado.
No penguins can be found in the Arctic.

Only the hopeful benefit from tears.
Lepidopterists prefer mountain terrain.
Only vertebrate animals have ears.
Cherrapunji endures perpetual rain.

In the beginning always waits the end.
Voodooists work only with black fowl.
A solitary hiker is his own best friend.
The arch enemy of the crow is the owl.

Insight is gained through physical risks.
Nymphets manage never to have acne.
Eight legs are found on common ticks.
Crime rates are always high in Hackney.

Shallots are the key to every good sauce.
Turmeric is the secret to good curry.
Paradise is home to a thief on the cross.
Jewish mothers love to have to worry.

Socialism is alien to the bourgeois heart.
Babies catch colds at day-care centers.
Torture with Mossad is a perfected art.
Autodidacts make the best inventors.

Birds never change their perch at night.
Practical jokers are typically immature.
Native Americans have no fear of height.
Grass is the perfect green manure.

Tomato sauce is only good home grown.
A valuable item in the future will be sand.
Climate change is everywhere man sown.
Music in Saudi Arabia is widely banned.

Bermuda grows the best arrowroot.
No one ever refused invitations to Cliveden.
Hatred of men is standard with a prostitute.
Boys are mainly stricken with duchenne.

All autobiographies are success stories.
No one can enter the Big Ben Tower.
Failure compulsively magnifies glories.
A victim's fear will a rapist empower.

TRUISMS

Kiwi birds by day are never seen --
they are blind and nest underground.
Fossils are never found of baleen.
Not a single known planet is round.

Spite inevitably stems from failure.
Imagination is required to be afraid.
Conscience is ever the perfect jailer.
Begonias best flourish in the shade.

Inexperience creates misadventures.
Always fish around a fallen tree.
At night, one must not wear dentures.
Arctic explorers rely on the fuzee.

Russians love to offer apologies.
Diaries are surrogates for living.
India produces many prodigies.
Corsicans are notably unforgiving.

Salt-water oxidation destroys aluminum.
Bengalis are uncompromising fish-eaters.
No one faith or country owns Jerusalem.
Five minutes is the limit for strip-teasers.

Landing by sea to "Free Cuba" is mythic.
The best wood for bending is white ash.
True vision is by its nature beatific.
No bribe's more potent than straight cash.

Wind speed increases with altitude.
Southerners consider lawn decoration art.
True generosity overlooks ingratitude.
Philanthropy and love are poles apart.

Aluminum canoes are all very loud.
Asthmatics are sensitive to sulfites.
Tees over 4" in golf are disallowed.
All political lobbyists are parasites.

Rodents hate the smell of peppermints.
The last verse of a hymn is sung loudest.
Speed a canoe through heavy currents.
The blindest man is always the proudest.

Predominance of the stupid is inevitable.
Wisdom and power rarely go together.
Much cookery in New Guinea is inedible.
The prime sexual fetish is for leather.

No human feat remains a lasting record.
It takes 55 seconds to cook the perfect omelet.
Wine is given during tutorials at Oxford.
Jesus Christ did not avoid the word *vomit*.

Faith continues to faith increased.
The sole absolute monarch alive is the Pope.
All true wisdom comes from the East.
If it wavers, it (by definition) can't be hope.

TRUISMS

Vending machines proliferate in Japan.
Apples grow poorly in the South.
No knowledge's enough in one earthly span.
A person ultimately becomes his mouth.

All biographies are group biographies.
The French Left is all splintered factions.
Forced celibacy leads to improprieties.
Artists who can't draw rely on abstractions.

Eyeglasses in films are thought to hide beauty.
Crackpot folklore defined the 1960s.
The opposite of true devotion is required duty.
Scandinavians are fascinated with pixies.

Sports teams run America's schools.
There are no tides in the Gulf of Mexico.
Genius is defined by transcending rules.
Timber is practically depleted in Borneo.

Jews infrequently contract tuberculosis.
Parsley always grows near stones.
Americans mainly die from atherosclerosis.
Plants, fungi, and bacteria are all clones.

The NFL brass never apologizes.
U.S. support of Israel created radical Islam.
Poverty significantly radicalizes.
The Sargasso Sea is ever perpetually calm.

ALEXANDER THEROUX

Surfeit is usually the father of fast.
Always make a pie with cold ingredients.
Female beauty is persistently harassed.
A Congressman's sole rule is expedience.

Anything good is always better buttered.
No Jewish son is named after his father.
Prayer can't be thought, it must be uttered.
Charity's negated when it's seen as bother.

Nothing can stay swollen for long.
In the biker world, green is a bad luck.
Right alone teaches what is wrong.
Postal workers very often run amok.

Cowboy heroes are never overwordy.
A well-dressed priest is a blasphemy.
Every sex kitten is depleted at thirty.
The highest goals demand audacity.

St. Mark's Feast Day is considered to be unlucky.
Shakespeare named only two characters William.
An unheroic age prefers to call its heroes "plucky."
Every pedophile's gaze is inevitably reptilian.

Refs unvaryingly favor the home team.
No fanatical golfer is ever a good father.
Hedonism is tempted by the extreme.
Sweating on horse is denominated lather.

TRUISMS

War defeats no terrorism, ideology does.
High school life is rabid with cliques.
The lamest excuse is always "because."
Ants and termites comprise a lethal mix.

All lead compounds are poisonous.
Infants can die from eating honey.
Milk served with melons can be ominous.
Privilege inevitably depends on money.

Toddlers repudiate all vegetables.
Indian chutneys are traditionally hot.
Sugars all transform to indigestibles.
Good taste can never be taught.

Hard water leads to bathtub rings.
Sizes never quite match in human feet.
It exhausts him when a bird sings.
No tiny diamond isn't sold with deceit.

Kosher salt is by definition coarse.
All of Rimbaud's poems are juvenilia.
A sole source is not a single source.
European royalty breed hemophilia.

No more envious breeds exists than poets.
Baked beans marry very well with fatback.
Faith and patriotism make a man heroic.
Impressionists abhorred the use of black.

Subliterate writing is difficult to read.
Toddlers automatically seek to destroy.
People with low IQs delight in speed.
Neighbors, by definition, always annoy.

No noise ever exceeded Stentor's bellow.
Every autobiography is an abridgment.
Julia Child loathed the concept of Jell-O.
True freedom balks at any infringement.

An alcoholic's paradise is alcoholic hell.
War and Peace is the greatest historical novel.
Misspell is a word most people misspell.
No lodging in Tierra del Fuego is not a hovel.

A secret shared is a friend (or enemy) made.
Sinatra never appeared in Broadway musical.
The further off the shadow, the less the shade.
No vacuum allows for anything acoustical.

Vermont drivers never pass a car.
No female comedians are attractive.
No Northerner is ever named Lamar.
A mind with a dream is often inactive.

January is the month for "white sales."
Loving her enhances a loved one's beauty.
Insanity is fairly common in North Wales.
The voice of librarians seem always fluty.

TRUISMS

There are no such green mammals.
Hungary is least open to immigrants.
Nothing is wasted in the carcass of camels.
The *mind* is the locus of impotence.

Scared rabbits run about in circles.
Ocean cruise romances never survive.
Flowers are most lavish with purples.
Insurance companies always connive.

Table condiments are rarely clean.
Union bosses are guaranteed larcenists.
Peru has a fairly non-existent cuisine.
Vison is the vice of many an ideologist.

Blues lyrics are very easy to write.
Vermonters rarely sport sunglasses.
The sentiment of every war is spite.
Botticelli's *Primavera* is a paean to grasses.

Magritte's penchant was hiding the face.
If it is real mink, it will never shrink.
Madness is epitomized in the arms race.
Shakespeare never knew the color pink.

Chicago gave the U.S. it greatest architects.
The primary joy of dancing is conversation.
English contains the most diverse dialects.
Negro blood built every Southern plantation.

Cocktails should always be served cold.
Social reform depends on moral reform.
The true facts of history are never told.
A silent Christian is a Christian lukewarm.

Almost all popular songs are love songs.
Refugees comprise mainly women.
In money trading, honesty never belongs.
Human rights do not exist in Yemen.

The title is always the center of a song.
Gabble is the language of a hackney.
Opposites, uniting, to each other belong.
Any helpmeet may be called Ariadne.

Not one of Jesus's apostles ever fasted.
When Queen Elizabeth steps back, she disapproves.
Greek houses are universally plastered.
Whomever a woman smiles at, she openly approves.

Tax-free are banks of the Federal Reserve.
Celts rarely get along with each other.
Texas highways very rarely show a curve.
Of frustration, hope is indeed the mother.

Cowards are always worriedly inquisitive.
Herbs are mainly Mediterranean in origin.
Every nation's proverbs are derivative.
Smoke from whatever source is a carcinogen.

TRUISMS

Children memorize anything easily.
A writer's style cannot disguise itself.
Movie Italians always speak sleazily.
No campaign cash is a pol's own pelf.

Zionists seem loud and basically uncouth.
All politicians, from ego, deceive themselves.
Only a savage appreciates sweet vermouth.
Nimbleness is a feature common to all elves.

Every living dog abominates a door.
No one ever trusts a bow-tie wearer.
A rare silk deep gold sari is tussore.
A master of wind is every true seafarer.

Cynical describes literary detectives.
Mussels from a lee shore taste best.
China mastered productive collectives.
A North Korean ill resorts to jest.

A lisping lass is always best to kiss.
Brown is never found in a rainbow.
Never comment on a person's likeness.
No Senate speech isn't a dumb show.

Every child is fundamentally an artist.
Nothing is quite reliable regarding erections.
Readers of books are every time the smartest.
Thank Ptolemy for having invented directions.

Southern girls never try to look too bright.
Cornish folk are famously unclubbable.
The Parthenon was multi-colored, never white.
Chinese films are only just barely dubbable.

A carpet's worst enemy is the moth.
Vacations foster the worst emotions.
There is never lack of residue in froth.
70% of the planet Earth are oceans.

All witches notoriously hate salt.
Belgians, Swiss, and Germans hate corn.
Silence passes judgment by default.
A bell's main duty is primarily to warn.

Lettuce that is cut too early turns brown.
White Leghorns are the most prolific layers.
The apex headwear is St. Edward's Crown.
Formality becomes a refrigerant in prayers.

The art of writing always involves rewriting.
Publicly now shunned is the Christmas carol.
A craven need for justice causes backbiting.
Mules and hinnies are notoriously sterile.

The higher you tap, the sweeter the sap.
1960s hippies *boasted* of being inarticulate.
Not one thing artistic is connected to rap.
Terror strikes are always indiscriminate.

TRUISMS

Gazpacho should be served cool, never cold.
Maple syrup needs cold nights, warm days.
No nightmare is ever quite safely patrolled.
Satire to the stupid always looks like praise.

Misery is compounded by protracted goodbyes.
All ski caps resemble Nazi headgear.
Fishermen mimic dead insects with wet flies.
Variants abound in the spelling of *Shakespeare*.

In a father/son business, choose the father.
No bird migrations follow natural barriers.
Snow leopards are never found to gather.
China leads all the world in non-marriers.

The arctic tern migrates the farthest.
American students no longer use lockers.
Brazilian bathing suits are immodest.
Recklessness is what impels most stalkers.

No sane diet can exclude vegetables.
People taking books to the woods are sad.
Rapacity fathers the need for collectables.
Binoculars are not allowed in Riyadh.

Hating, fixing focus, can provide enormous joy.
Shakespeare's merchant is not Shylock but Antonio.
The Hebrew Bible refers to the *Israelites* as goy.
Haunted is the unearthly Kiyotaki Tunnel in Tokyo.

The color purple honey bees see best.
Overweight kids are always undernourished.
Ideally never save, try to reinvest.
Apples in Florida have never ever flourished.

British royalty never carry money.
Buckingham palace employs no married women.
Never order fish to eat on Sunday.
For invisible ink MI-5 frequently used semen.

A women's hair to the Arab is incitement.
Narcissistic actors all perform downstage.
No examination of conscience isn't an indictment.
Greek dramatists kept all violence off-stage.

People only show despair they can afford.
Academy Award shows are always tasteless.
The ocean depths remain fully unexplored.
Jealousy thrives when most often baseless.

Cyclotrons can manufacture plutonium.
All top brass are overpaid in the NFL.
Any music by airflow is a harmonium.
Doleful is the sound of every cowbell.

Nothing can travel faster than light.
The Great Lakes are fairly shallow.
Purity was the prime virtue of a knight
Thirteen steps lead to every gallow.

TRUISMS

A beaver's favorite wood is aspen.
Gold is by far much denser than lead.
To best clot the blood, take aspirin.
Hematite is the original source of red.

A toddler can show true baboon rage.
Manhattanites tend to be loud and pushy.
Mercilessnes is putting anything in a cage.
Every college president's job is cushy.

Behind religion lies the spoor of nature.
The sun never sets—it's horizons that rise.
Silicon Valley is rife with nomenclature.
Most jazz musicians merely improvise.

When in a hurry, never make a detour.
Surprising freedom is found in *downward* mobility.
No travel spot lives up to its brochure.
Miami, Florida, in all of its phases, teems with incivility.

Highest department store mark-ups are perfume.
Duccio's masterpiece, *Maestà* shows a bit of heaven.
The who is always the superintendent of the whom.
Of chakras (disks in our body), there are seven.

For Nobel Prizes the U.S. leads the field.
All publicly presented awards are political.
No childhood abuse is ever fully healed.
In matters of the heart, nothing's analytical.

Ambition is rarely found in a healthy form.
Forgiveness is an attribute of the strong.
The tax system is geared to misinform.
Dawn and dusk elicit the most birdsong.

Child play is the process of learning.
Instinct is the linchpin of romance.
The U.S. Congress is always adjourning.
Dating is at best a game of chance.

All truly serious thought takes time.
Girls who model girdles never need them.
Walrus, *month*, and *purple* never rhyme.
No repair corrects a wounded brain stem.

What's made, not bought, perfects a gift.
Always fry your chicken to 165 degrees.
Niggardliness is often claimed as thrift.
Alcoholism is not a vice but a disease.

Politics is show business for the ugly.
No one says the word *February* correctly.
Exam proctors state directions smugly.
Sales pitches are always made indirectly.

For strikeouts, always credit the catcher.
The shorter the wavelength, the higher the frequency.
Every "best man" lacks a certain stature.
The newborns of wildebeest have no nascency.

TRUISMS

Division is the inverse of multiplication.
A Las Vegas headliner must work one hour.
The Sudan is the cradle of starvation.
Foods that boost endurance are often sour.

Koreans all prefer short grain rice.
Divorces don't occur in Joseph Lincoln novels.
New autos never sell at an established price.
Irish Americans are energized by squabbles.

Broadcast news is elevated gossip.
The Conquistadors, to a one, were bad men.
New England weather is a toss-up.
Idaho and Montana spawn military madmen.

Seville oranges alone are fit for marmalade.
A chainsaw long left gasless will not start.
Zeal is the ruling villainy of every crusade.
Incomprehensibility explains abstract art.

Unchecked emotions ruin moral character.
All fish sing when cooked in white wine.
Firstborn children betray a yen to hector.
Boat necklines and youthfulness never align.

People are kindest to those they deceive.
Power, given license, becomes inhuman.
Processed meats help no woman to conceive.
British cookery ignores the use of cumin.

Comanches were the fiercest of Plains Indians.
The higher the dew point, the more humid it is.
The U.S. government ignores the Palestinians.
Prisoners in jail give respect to counterfeiters.

Diabetics always have to watch the clock.
More are slain by knives than assault rifles.
Network television consists of pure schlock.
Sports reporters spend their lives on trifles.

Every woman looks attractive in a sun dress.
Rich people fussily eat only small vegetables.
Brazilian women glory in a state of undress.
Coconut products are serious indigestibles.

Dentists are given to endless monologues.
Parallel fibers make a single ply.
Mexican leaders have all been demagogues.
Long fingernails decorate a Thai.

All revolutionaries are anti-clerical.
Olive oil is almost a religion in Puglia.
The sun is almost perfectly spherical.
The most popular name in Austria is Julia.

Every distinguished man has disciples.
Scientists can't create metallic hydrogen.
Stitched pillows express only trifles.
The best refrigerant is liquid nitrogen.

TRUISMS

Jews rarely open the New Testament.
Beans are always ruined by black fly.
No Hottentot has ever been eloquent.
Fat aims straight for a woman's thigh.

Illness often precedes spiritual illumination.
Lard makes for a most phenomenal pie crust.
South America is predominantly anti-Haitian.
American history teems with breach of trust.

Marmalade oversweet is liked by parvenus.
Three U.S. states can claim the Rio Grande.
Hair-fad fashions are a game of curlicues.
Grade B in graduate school is a reprimand.

Hearing is a way of seeing further—360°.
The Decalogue was engraved in proto-Sinaitic.
Stress in the human body is worse on knees.
Cold air, low humidity cripple an asthmatic.

Posterity blithely forgets its entertainers.
No call of a loon is not forlorn.
Repetition is the gambit of complainers.
An only child is every firstborn.

Regulations are tripe to a true artist.
Lending money always fosters hatred.
Of dogs, border collies are the smartest.
Disdain epitomizes anything belated.

Snow falsifies every color value.
The past is unfairly cast as old.
No vowels can be found in Hebrew.
Never serve any wine ice cold.

Hamlet is a study of the repeatedly rehearsed.
The Virgin on canvas wears lapis lazuli robes.
Roanoke island, N.C. is claimed to be cursed.
Both convenient and modest are Arabic thobes.

Typhoons are *always* described as roaring trains.
Anchovies are one canned food that taste great.
Rapists are all creepily drawn to lover's lanes.
The British upper classes all say "et" for *ate*.

Vogue models are all exotically ugly.
The 6-5-3 double play in baseball is the hardest.
Every knob is fashioned to fit smugly.
The kitchen door is always the farthest.

Misers delay in paying at checkout lines.
Maple sap runs better by day than by night.
Shouting in public places warrants fines.
Females tend to find masculinity in height.

Fathers are rarely the subject of songs.
Timing is a comic's best basic talent.
In Sri Lanka, only men wear sarongs.
Knaves are always described as arrant.

TRUISMS

Brazilians are suspicious of black chickens.
Children are mainly molested by relatives.
There is no particular liturgy for Wiccans.
Owning weapons pleases all conservatives.

No peoples are absolutely indigenous.
All postures of submission mean surrender.
Fundamentalist Mormons are all polygamous.
Short hair in women renders her less slender.

The best marmalade shows darker preserve.
Self-aggrandizement typifies every nation.
The British mode is mainly about reserve.
Money values all increase with deflation.

The oldest world rocks are found in Canada.
Youth ever wins among competing swimmers.
Europe's warmest winters are found in Malaga.
A Scottish boggle or ghost always glimmers.

Monasticism needs one's full detachment.
Chess is actually the show business of math.
Criminal liability decreases with entrapment.
Violence is the perpetual offspring of wrath.

A people is created by its places.
Poets rarely write well when they're old.
Whatever runs, invariably chases.
Revenge is a dish best served up cold.

Barnyard dust badly causes asthma.
Ugly mathematics are fully abhorrent.
A fetid odor defines any miasma.
No person can ever outrun a torrent.

It is the wronged ghost who will return.
Inappropriate laughter is always shrill.
No pain exceeds a first-degree burn.
Civil War strategy was to attain a hill.

NBA pros hate playing in new sneakers.
No costly food isn't considered a delicacy.
Data dumping is the bane of public speakers.
The prophet Mohammed denounced celibacy.

Children are never drawn to the morose.
Comic book heroes have strong jawlines.
Programming languages are always verbose.
Trash newspapers are only headlines.

Naught intrigues a spy more than an airfield.
Any egg that floats is contaminated.
A sap tree by the water gives the biggest yield.
No government agency isn't constipated.

Anything that is moving has energy.
Asia accounts for 60% of suicides.
Every immune system has its allergy.
Royal history is a document of fratricides.

TRUISMS

Scarlet red can never be seen in flames.
All taxes are theft, claims the GOP.
Jews show a penchant for changing names.
A Scot's favorite adjective is "wee."

A rooster's crow is unalterably dactylic.
Battle scenes don't exist in George Eliot's work.
No computer has fonts for early Cyrillic.
Smugness is perpetually the smile of a smirk.

Avarice is the mood at every auction.
Soft climates produce the softest people.
Rhubarb leaves all carry lethal toxin.
Aspiration has its symbol in a steeple.

Governments only reward the second-rate,
because they have nothing to fear from them.
Japan never allows anyone to immigrate.
Old Bethlehem is now called Beit Lechem.

You can never have only *one* tong.
Covert people often hide to be discovered.
There is never a single way to tie a sarong.
No dream dreamt is ever fully recovered.

No American shoppers bag their groceries.
New England is in its glory in every season.
Obsolescence is the story of all batteries.
Circumcisionist advocates are immune to reason.

Grapes must be picked by hand for Beaujolais.
Sun and frost collude to render maple sugar.
No holyday should ever become a holiday.
Every Middle Eastern ruler comprises a führer.

All high levels of thinking depend on language.
No writing about Zen is not complete nonsense.
There exists not a single rhyming word for *orange*.
To run for office, first set aside your conscience.

Every nation has a recipe for trahanas.
Ghanaians are the most hospitable folk on earth.
No Turkoman does not need a harness.
Stammering inevitably causes a reaction of mirth.

No man ever walks alone from choice.
Maple sap at daytime is the sweetest.
Every Welshman has a suitable voice.
J. P. Kennedy was the ultimate defeatist.

Tired children are noisier, not the reverse.
The phrase "beloved attorney" is never heard.
Robert Frost utterly abhorred blank verse.
Every archaeologist argues from a sherd.

War is the ugly spouse of chauvinism.
Only pompous asses travel with a retinue.
Socialism seeks mercy from capitalism.
Every assignation requires a rendezvous.

TRUISMS

Artists who need "residencies" are hacks.
Nothing original doesn't transcends rules.
Love needs but to wane for hate to wax.
The lars and penates of Jews are jewels.

Mistresses are easier to acquire than dump.
Oboes as instruments are piercing by nature.
Movie star lovableness is invariably plump.
Nothing wasn't liquid before becoming vapor.

Cruise ship life is an utter waste of time.
In deserts, travelers never see a twilight.
Teen age is a woman's beauty prime.
Native Americans must have a skylight.

Never employ sesame oil for cooking.
Russians fear sitting at a corner table.
Life is perilous for the good-looking.
The economy of Greece is never stable.

Slate roofs can not be made too steep.
Maine coastal waters are never warm.
Pakistani rugs are invariably cheap.
The urge to create is never to conform.

Black cattle command higher prices.
Math advances are rarely made by men past fifty.
Untapered strands make terrible splices.
A thief is everyone nicknamed "Swifty."

Whom many fear, must fear many.
Painting is but the shadow of sculpture.
No candy should cost more than a penny.
Stomach acid is a treasure to a vulture.

Most girls lose their virginity on Saturday.
Fashion magazines are sales catalogues.
Tomorrow is the enemy of Yesterday.
Every one of Plato's texts were dialogues.

"Home" is a real-estate industry term.
In Latin, infinitives are single words.
Nothing's as indiscriminate as sperm.
Any size design follows the rule of thirds.

Extremists hate apostates more than rivals.
Southern Italy was civilized by Greeks.
Hysteria animates all religious revivals.
All creatures bite that are sporting beaks.

No French woman hasn't a recipe for cassoulet.
Water, as it heats up, will consistently expand.
Sloth is denominated the "demon of noonday."
The most difficult surgery is on the hand.

Jewish jokes love mocking the city of Chelm.
To rabid citizens, every foreigner is an alien.
Salt-spray cannot blight or damage an elm.
No shill on a midway is not sesquipedalian.

TRUISMS

People love to see stereotypes confirmed.
Bullies feel peace only when they are cruel.
No true misogynist has not first been spurned.
Whales with giant squid fight a perpetual dual.

Veneration is a stop on the road to contempt.
Hummingbirds are found only in America.
Alaskan front yards are notoriously unkempt.
The past is unquestionably the future's replica.

All disappointment emanates from desire.
Sap early and late in a season is the sweetest.
To correct is the essential goal of satire.
Every amiable quietist is a true defeatist.

Most photogenic models have a heart face.
Corporations cultivate money for friends.
Proof of a bad movie is an extended car chase.
Fast math proceeds in counting by tens.

Contraltos in opera play grannies and witches.
Everything in excess is opposed to nature.
Feminism began with women wearing britches.
Procrastination is pronounced *legislature*.

A bed without a reading lamp is a jail cell.
Vermont is colonized by rich New Yorkers.
Anti-clockwise movement drives a carousel.
Arabs are the known world's expert hawkers.

Women visit powder rooms together.
Sectionalism is invariably heredity.
The greatest of all sculptors is weather.
Placating others is a theft of identity.

Stock markets love a divided government.
Drugs are essentially vegetable television.
Restriction invariably forges a covenant.
The ancient Greeks abhorred circumcision.

Chinese clothes are all drab blue or green.
A Briton to praise will often shout, "Chapeau!"
Hand the untalented one the tambourine.
Opposite the sun is where to look for a rainbow.

Americans have a huge appetite for guns.
Cruise ships never go anywhere important.
Groaning is consistently a reaction to puns.
Rudeness in NYC is standard comportment.

The fiercest ocean is the North Atlantic.
All Englishmen are naturally reticent.
All taken oaths are crucially semantic.
Good manners are tentative, hesitant.

Humor is rarely the trait of an architect.
Everybody in sports abhors a tie game.
Jewish men are notoriously henpecked.
Every stripper assumes a stage name.

TRUISMS

Always suspect a west-running brook.
Wars are never fought by politicians.
Southern Italy is rife with superstitions.
Nesting collectively strengthens the rook.

It is not done to capitalize the word braille.
Chinese food eaters need backscratchers.
Homemade bread soon goes quickly stale.
Fundamentalists are literal gnatcatchers.

Being poor at Christmas seems truly fitting.
Everyone in Iceland knows everyone.
Meetings should be limited to a single sitting.
Doubt is central theology for a Unitarian.

Bosnian women dye their hair Kool-Aid red.
The most salient fact of life is that it ends.
Diplomacy depends on what is left unsaid.
Pretty girls always choose homely girlfriends.

Wood is not and never a single substance.
Fidel Castro obsessively reviled prostitution.
In courting, an enticing quality is reluctance.
The U.S. has the oldest written constitution.

Memory compulsively warps original facts.
Secrets are defined by their disclosure.
No support clinics exist for racing addicts.
Detachment is the key to all composure.

To be best obeyed is simply to be loved.
A truly civilized man shows empathy.
A sexy woman to a male is often gloved.
Familiarity inevitably breeds apathy.

Any apology, exasperated, is meaningless.
No sailing vessel sails directly into wind.
Born diabetics are prone to peevishness.
Rosemary and thyme are always twinned.

Conventional rules never rule a genius.
Heroic poetry is essentially narrative.
Gambling tables seduce with greenness.
Nothing absolute is ever comparative.

Shakespeare's tragedies owe all to Seneca.
A copper beech tree raises arms in victory.
Every small town looks similar in America.
Freedom to commit sin is contradictory.

Greenland is the source of Atlantic icebergs.
Natural and Good amount to the same thing.
Jutting chins characterized every Hapsburg.
Smoking cigarettes quickly hastens aging.

Automobile horns always sound angry.
Homesickness is defeated by being shared.
Never a working rocket without a gantry.
No soldier leaves war action unimpaired.

TRUISMS

Christmas trees should come down on January 7th.
It's warm air that feeds instability in storms.
Any third on a scale is dissonant with an eleventh.
With insects, mating is aligned with swarms.

Cuts on the tongue all heal very quickly.
Habitual lateness is a passive-aggressive trait.
Royalty of the Incas were habitually sickly.
Every single cube will show vertices of eight.

No plants in the Arctic are poison.
No wind isn't unfavorable to some business.
To hand out awards is always to cozen.
Metaphysicians repetitiously depend on *isness*.

Nothing obliterates snow like rain.
Every pacifist finds a substitute for war.
Victorian preceptors favored a rattan cane.
Pollution very rarely fells a sycamore.

Extreme passions always end in hatred.
A hat on a bed for Italians is unlucky.
Jazz speaks subversively to the jaded.
Sour mash bourbon is the soul of Kentucky.

The shortest women alive are Guatemalan.
It is not power that corrupts, but rather fear.
Everyone tends to sleep in late in Harlem.
Makoko in Lagos is the epitome of drear.

ALEXANDER THEROUX

Every person has six or seven selves.
Only at the start of words do people stutter.
Councils are invariably groups of twelves.
Serious bakers strictly use unsalted butter.

Bedwetters hate the reality of waking.
Chess in Russia is a national religion.
A working sandhog's back is ever aching.
Always pejorative is the adjective *pigeon*.

Anxiety is an aspect of foresight.
There are 5,949 possible moves in chess.
All moonlight is actually sunlight.
No aboriginal doesn't admire headdress.

Bribery in Nigeria is a way of life.
Drakes are not highly regarded as food.
Rebels always flourish in a land of strife.
Food best digested is food well chewed.

Every gourmand is always a pedant.
Hawaiian songs are about saying goodbye.
Every nave in a church is transcendent.
There is no bread for good pastrami but rye.

One risks becoming what one opposes.
No Parliament should delegate a king's authority.
Semitic people have the biggest noses.
Democracy's weakness is tyranny of the majority.

TRUISMS

The wounds of love always go deepest.
Dido was a Shakespearean obsession.
Merlot steak is better than flank—and cheapest.
No answer's as deep as its asked-of question.

Pie is to the Midwest as rice is to China.
Hatred is weirdly akin to attachment.
The best lasagna is from Emilia-Romagna.
Objectivity comes only with detachment.

Israel gobbles up stolen land by the minute.
There is self-cherishing archness in all envy.
Frugality was the creator of the spinet.
Nothing's more superfluous than a penny.

No two cigars are ever alike.
Boston Brahmins found the Irish proto-human.
A downward stock turn is also called a spike.
Wistfulness typefies the music of Schumann.

A valid baseball team needs 19 signatures.
Faith can thrive only on a personal basis.
No perfect sculpture needs its armature.
The date palm plant is crucial to an oasis.

Jezebel loathed Elijah the prophet.
No grades render education meaningless.
No swallow does not love a soffit.
Conviction without conduct is worthless.

All good poetry springs from sadness.
There is infirmity in all of human laughter.
No alphabet is not in debt to Cadmus.
The sky is commonly taken as a rafter.

Capitalism, by any definition, enslaves.
Fidel Castro was an ice-cream addict.
All Bajan food was the food of slaves.
As a poem Milton's "Lycidas" is perfect.

Ants are nature's cemetery squads.
Ballpoint pens don't work in freezing weather.
Siena and Florence were forever at odds.
Red and purple should not be worn together.

Solitude is the best spur to insight.
Jingles have replaced hymns at Christmas.
No pure savagery exceeds a bullfight.
No metal is more diamagnetic than bismuth.

We all fear to abhor what we adore.
Women are never allowed at cockfights.
Reason is the first casualty of war.
Reversal characterizes all hindsights.

Bengal tigers have no natural predator.
Seclusion is a must for Papal conclaves.
No debtor has a memory like a creditor.
Unemployment spawns most crime waves.

TRUISMS

Curiosity always bespeaks complicity.
A Sikh's fondest relationship is with his sister.
An honest man baffles one of duplicity.
If business is the burn, avarice is the blister.

Affection in Hollywood's an affectation.
No sane man trusts power in any form.
Depression often causes severe constipation.
Child molesters are incapable of reform.

Reading is easily the best form of travel.
Sanity avoids the death of an over busy life.
Noise to the silent is a perpetual cavil.
Gauge a husband by the health of his wife.

Television is geared to the utterly IQ-less.
Habañeros twin perfectly with tomatoes.
Buying lottery tickets is sport for the clueless.
Wetness is to water as the Irish to potatoes.

Alfredo sauce is perfect for fettucine.
Wall Street's best days are unexpected.
No woman with a pot should sport a bikini.
Police crimes remain fully undetected.

Everything in Ireland is imported.
Puerto Ricans pay no Federal income tax.
Worse than lies are truths distorted.
Half a woman is a woman in slacks.

Gormless boys always play right field.
Sleep under your first quilt when it's finished.
It is always harder to fight than to yield.
Fat kids in grade school feel sadly diminished.

A diminutive to a pejorative detoxifies the word.
Eels are coveted by the Japanese.
A computer is the sports playground of the nerd.
No surety is had in verbal guarantees.

Only 250 South Korean surnames exist
among the vastness of 44 million people.
Speak not a word on cards, playing whist.
Nothing is not food for a common seagull.

Oak is the best-burning wood for winter stoves.
Chess masters regress after age thirty-five.
Only animals comfortably driven can be droves.
An entrance faces downward in a hive.

Outdoor faces are always the kindest.
No knife cuts sharper than a barracuda's teeth.
Racial bigots are ironically the blindest.
Purplish pink are the living tints of a heath.

Short hair can make a woman look malicious.
Learn Castilian Spanish to best be understood.
History books are straightforwardly fictitious.
Stars *pay* for their "fame" stars in Hollywood.

TRUISMS

Fidel Castro was angrily anti-Israel.
Incas wove palms to umbrella all rain.
Patriotism is subjective and, so, trivial.
No Galician has any loyalty to Spain.

Angels canonically are never female.
Latins celebrate *saints'* days, not birthdays.
Earth's largest creature is the blue whale.
Tree huggers positively live for Earth Days.

The eye of the owner fattens the horse.
Austerity is a virtue in all revolutionaries.
No Scandinavian is not also a Norse.
Religious leaders are all reactionaries.

Young to marry, young to be marred.
Guyana as a nation has most suicides.
Israel in Palestine practices apartheid.
Toxic at 90% sulfur are any fungicides.

Rembrandt never left the Netherlands.
Drakes lose their plumage after mating.
The very best oysters are Maryland's.
Greece's money is always deflating.

Chinese characters are never phonetic.
Climate change is reducing woodlands.
Schizophrenics are notoriously splenetic.
Muslims with women never shake hands.

ALEXANDER THEROUX

No rhino can bear having his path crossed.
A lawyer would fuck his mother for cash.
Armenians had their very own Holocaust.
Ford and General Motors repeatedly clash.

Mahogany is the main wood in Heppelwhite.
No one is more ignorant than actors.
Males almost never contract dimpled cellulite.
A sense of inferiority is felt by chiropractors.

Than royals, muzhiks have the stouter heart.
Confit is the pillar of cooking in Gascony.
Pacherenc is Madiran's white wine counterpart.
Nobles historically preponderated in falconry.

A popular book plate is bare-limbed trees.
Solitude is the raw material of greatness.
Drinking hot water is unique to Chinese.
A feeling of contempt subtexts all lateness.

If Bob Hope is in the movie, it is bad.
No suicide knows if he accomplished it.
Russian revolutionaries came from Leningrad.
Christ founded a faith; Paul refurnished it.

A violin is feminine, with soprano pitch.
Heat invariably hastens decomposition.
Paradox is the prerequisite of kitsch.
The Bill of Rights is electric with sedition.

TRUISMS

People eating ice cream blankly stare.
Bake apple pies in fall and early winter.
Melanoma plagues those with red hair.
Every secret cadre depends on a printer.

Anger is the first response at betrayal.
The rooves of houses are never white.
No film succeeds at Christ's portrayal.
Easter festivals favor use of the kite.

High anxiety approximates being devoured.
People go open-mouthed when listening intensely.
Kefir milk is best enjoyed when soured.
Nothing very small impresses one immensely.

Canada has by far the blandest profile.
Reunion accounts are inevitably a pose.
Showing a foot in Bali is held as hostile.
The Jacobeans loved convoluted prose.

Any assiduous Marxist pities a waiter.
Grasshoppers are a trout's special delight.
Gladhanding one is the mask of a traitor.
A squire is step two in becoming a knight.

Tomatoes love companioning with basil.
American culture has lost the fear of God.
Of all languages, Hindi is by far most nasal.
After *Parsifal*'s last act, one does not applaud.

One ankle sock seems forever missing.
Never plant onions with peas or beans.
With strangers, it is vulgar reminiscing.
Never kiss, touch, or speak before queens.

Imperialism is capitalism in the extreme.
Potatoes always burgeon in alkaline soil.
A moonbeam is in point of fact a sunbeam.
No microbe is not destroyed by a hot boil.

Scoundrels love to feign patriotism.
Aphids will flock to anything yellow.
Opposition incites all chauvinism.
Masculine (its tenor voice) is a cello.

No Islomaniac is not an anal-retentive.
Always sow winter rye by October 15th.
Japanese audiences are the most attentive.
American hotels delete the floor 13th.

Daylight in Greece is phosphorescent.
No blasphemy exceeds torturing a human being.
Only heated light can be incandescent.
Mensheviks and Bolsheviks lived for disagreeing.

When olive trees shiver, they turn to silver.
A spunky tomboy is her father's daughter.
Every chemical compound has a builder.
Nothing's more flexible yet resistant than water.

TRUISMS

No solids or liquids can exist in space.
Hand gestures in Italy are copious.
Whatever is running is always chased.
Rap music is aggressively unmelodious.

Shade rules the north side of a garden.
Connecticut (more N.Y.) is not New England.
A Christian judge tends to grant a pardon.
The Danish krone is the currency of Greenland.

The sacrifice of islands are frontiers.
Acid soil produces blue hydrangeas.
Elections are auctions, pols auctioneers.
Risk is inconceivable without dangers.

In no joint enterprise are both equals.
Rear tires wear out faster than front.
Movies are mostly failures in sequels.
No parade is not also a publicity stunt.

Screenplay *literature* does not exist.
All bosses look like Herbert Marshall.
Success in badminton pivots on the wrist.
Hung juries are never fair or impartial.

School shooters were often abused by bullies.
Veterinarians always badly overcharge.
Ancient pyramids were constructed by pulleys.
Democracy is pandemonium writ large.

Private eyes in fiction all dislike cops.
California is culturally a wasteland.
Quantum motion literally never stops.
Scissors forever disfavor the left hand.

What people show in starts, they are by nature.
Avoidance of anything posits its merit.
No intelligent design co-exists with legislature.
Thievery is the *sine qua non* of the ferret.

African potentates, to a one, are hoodlums.
Nothing in the Congo reflects breeding.
Jelutong latex is the best for chewing gums.
Israelis, like Nazis, forbid interbreeding.

Jehovah's Witnesses consider the UN evil.
Mormons cache their food like squirrels.
Overvaluing college football is medieval.
Our solar system moves in twisting spirals.

Going Hollywood is death to any writer.
Pictureless books bore all toddlers.
Power loves the snap of a pocket lighter.
Waiting for windfalls delights all dawdlers.

Los Angeles is the motherland of mammon.
Learning in the 17th century was play.
The healthiest eating fish is salmon.
Raccoons stay hidden during the day.

TRUISMS

Film noir is the history of lonely cynics.
The Orkneys are completely lacking in trees.
Money, not mercy, is the aim of clinics.
Epilepsy, while non-infectious, is a disease.

Repetition destroys every pleasure.
Only one in twenty-five succeed as suicides.
Covetousness circumscribes every treasure.
The Bible is the canon for genocides.

"Don't die on me" is a painful movie cliché.
Darwin, who couldn't draw, feared distortions.
Ragged—"*rege-rege*"—is the etymology of reggae.
China leads the world in medical abortions.

Far too much is anticipated of men.
Far too little is expected of women.
Nothing tenderizes meat like papain.
A martinet's favorite switch is vimen.

Any object may belong to a collection.
Banks grant most loans in January.
Smoking cigarettes indicates self-rejection.
Justice is consistently abolitionary.

A billionaire's reach has to do with gluts.
The royal Stuarts had the Catholic vote.
Assembly lines are now best served by bots.
The truth will always be found in a footnote.

Nature rarely allows a happy ending.
No Hollywood actor is married once.
A child molester isn't worth defending.
No town selectman is not a dunce.

Greek cooks make things salty by design.
Satisfaction means the end of liberty.
Never fold a quilt (which leaves a line).
No woman's ever happy with her body.

Rebel Yell bourbon was only sold down south.
Crotch wood yields the loveliest patterns.
The axis of a portrait attends on the mouth.
Icy Titan is the largest moon of Saturn's.

All television is children's television.
A *wai* is the signature greeting of every Thai.
Umpire calls are the height of imprecision.
No one fully grows until both parents die.

Most every prayer is offered up to win.
Greenland is extraordinarily treeless.
In Qatar, virtually not a single soul is thin.
Manners, in the end, always reveal us.

Music with dinner irks a serious cook.
Chinese cuisine takes no notice of bread.
Humidity is always murder on a book.
Normalcy is forced on all who wed.

TRUISMS

Traveling carnival folk are all marginals.
Pink ivory wood is rarer than diamonds.
There is no migration with cardinals.
For good health eat only *raw* almonds.

A paper cannot be folded more than nine times.
Pigs should never be fed meat or scraps.
Six to eight rods best satisfy for wind chimes.
"Snake eyes" in thrown dice equal "craps."

Whom we hate is often our own double.
New Zealand lancewood is best for fly rods.
Cavitation is the joy of a blown bubble.
Anise is the flavor of French Pernods.

Change of mind defines repentance.
Chicken thighs are tenderer than breasts.
Oil is universally the blood of engines.
Three days is the outer limit for guests.

Monday night is industry night in Vegas
Brazilwood is the best for a violin bow.
Every practicing Zoroastrian is a magus.
No sea depth can match Deep Mindanao.

Momentum's next day's starting pitcher.
Olive oil should not be used in baking.
To the rich, any richness must be richer.
The lowest form of life is money-making.

Rest home help are largely bullies.
Dogs can thrive exclusively on vegetables.
Mud and dirt can be listed as edibles.
Hustle is all about levers and pulleys.

The Japanese never give combs as presents.
Justice and mercy are competing imperatives.
French cooking was conceived by peasants.
The Hebrew language has but two infinitives.

Italians knock on iron for good luck.
Recollected love is always sweeter.
World War I was fought in muck.
Insincerity is a plus for any greeter.

Yellow underwear in Columbia means success.
The *foco* is the best way to spread revolution.
Playing hopeless positions is seen rude in chess.
Self-interest serves all political contribution.

Nativist thinking is fully based on hatred.
Jazz drummers are often high on dope.
Illinois voting polls are often manipulated.
Any Roman Catholic can be elected Pope.

Treachery at one time passed for love.
Never pass food chopstick-to-chopstick.
Heart patients are dependent on foxglove.
Lord Horatio Nelson was often seasick.

TRUISMS

Abused children are orphans with living parents.
Mince pies embody the manger of infant Christ.
No mother-in-law is not suited for interference.
To the British, beer is not enhanced when iced.

Mistletoe, the kissing plant, is toxic.
American sycamore is best for butcher blocks.
Satire is by its nature always caustic.
Greenland is a nation riddled with barren rocks.

Internationally, Jews are "temporary locals."
Switzerland is sanctuary for Russian exiles.
Melody precedes adding lyrics and vocals.
Amusement parks use exit-only turnstiles.

Cuba internationalized guerrilla warfare.
Russians suspect gifts of oddly numbered flowers.
Fog characterizes every French *Brumaire*.
Bathing consumes far less water than showers.

Manufactured pride is pure hypocrisy.
Swedes are leery of bringing heather home.
Every theocracy is basically slavocracy.
The best water on the planet's found in Rome.

History as written is merely headlines.
An upside-down shoe spooks an Arab.
No work is not sharpened by deadlines.
Heavenly cycles made holy the scarab.

Black vultures always mate for life.
Strippers look inward in the act of stripping.
Stealing in the land of Nigeria is rife.
Pigs are all terribly fearful of slipping.

A letter is a substitute for private conversation.
An epistle takes the place of a public speech.
Lies, nevertheless, indicate some aspiration.
Every office is improved by who's impeached.

Too much analysis leads to paralysis.
Male sexuality daily peaks at dawn.
The body functions by way of dialysis.
The Last Frontier is the American lawn.

War renders savagery acceptable.
A quarter of American adults haven't read a book.
A person's faith is never perceptible.
Diamond dealing is the trade of crooks.

Overplotting is a sign of amateur novels.
A mustachioed Bogart performed poorly.
African townships are a *kraal* of hovels.
Unsafe is that man who feels securely.

The Jew is ethnically unamalgamable.
Asians in the U.S. are seen as indelibly alien.
Argentinian taxi drivers are all unamiable.
A party with nudity is suitably bacchanalian.

TRUISMS

Lying comes naturally to children.
Hawaiians never bring bananas on a boat.
All actors yearn to play the villain.
Jehovah's Witnesses choose to never vote.

Housing prices are never fully fixed.
Drill instructors are madly egotistical.
A Southern nightmare is racially mixed.
All etiquette is basically hypocritical.

Arkansas is low on the civilization scale.
Police never attract the highest type of men.
The index finger's best for reading Braille.
Every lottery store is also a gambling den.

No anomaly exceeds "Hollywood Royalty."
Danish smørrebrød is served solely on rye.
A frisson is felt in every act of disloyalty.
Becoming ever states what Being must deny.

Zunis and Hopis are prone to albinism.
Fentanyl ever imparts a glorious slumber.
Pride is the dragon breathing chauvinism.
Krill all other creatures easily outnumber.

Deception occurs in matters of volition.
Miami is the hive of age-inappropriate clothes.
Excessive drug-taking leads to inanition.
A major sexual fetish is apparently human toes.

ALEXANDER THEROUX

The supper/dance club is now extinct.
California is the commonwealth of transplants.
Adenine and thymine are always linked.
Case names will always first list the claimants.

John Ashbery never wrote a lucid poem.
Only vulgarians stare at a shopper's purchases.
To Romani people, anywhere is home.
White is the unvarying color of all surplices.

Coffee fixations are the American fetish.
Wednesday is amateur night at the Apollo.
Hebrew's a semitic language, German Yiddish.
Hollow is always understood as shallow.

The Japanese embrace every new fad.
Israel is a true diasporic agglomeration.
All vaudeville comedians favored plaid.
No vegetable doesn't require pollination.

San Diego is nothing but a climate.
No one's more sexist than a womanizer.
A pump cannot work until you prime it.
Blue is the favored color of an advertiser.

Mystery writers are slaves to similes.
Round-end shingles have long disappeared.
There is a barbless sting in bumblebees.
An Indian fakir never shaves his beard.

TRUISMS

No oldster should drive a convertible.
No one is more sentimental than a bully.
Master and slave are perniciously invertible.
The wheel is fundamental to a pulley.

Ants cannot abide wet soil.
A lupine never lasts a lustrum.
Gullibility is ever beauty's foil.
Repetition alone creates a custom.

Odor tends to excite deep nostalgia.
Mosquito repellent is a sting in itself.
Taxes create a form of neuralgia.
The true index of wealth is good health.

From wolves, come all domestic dogs.
Initial waves aren't strongest in a tsunami.
Rolling is apposite to heavy fogs.
Dominican Republic has no standing army.

The ambiguous exists for no fanatic.
Deuteronomy is a book of savage punition.
Calla lilies are strangely never aromatic.
The Sudan is ground-zero for inanition.

Cranes look nothing at all like herons.
Every Scotsman is a Jacobite at heart.
A coronet is the privilege of all barons.
Control is the rationale of the flowchart.

Arab-Americans are rarely hired at NPR.
No woman has money ready at a checkout.
The true spice islands are in Zanizabar.
Bonded forever are elephant and mahout.

Rumor is the beating heart of every panic.
The Bard's goriest play is *Titus Andronicus*.
Proprietary of his tools is an auto mechanic.
Every buzzer-show host is Mr. Sardonicus.

Hebrew prophets were savagely intolerant.
Reds have a predilection for provocation.
Charity heads appropriate huge emoluments.
Prelates rarely offer a brief invocation.

A Scoutmaster is often an ephebophile.
North windows get strong light without glare.
The colors red and pink never reconcile.
A distinguished kind of rectangle is a square.

Silence at nature's heart is non-existent.
Fashion labels avoid using Jewish names.
To be unrefined, merely be persistent.
Insurance agents are suspicious of all claims.

The worst Old Testament curse is drought.
A rich vocabulary abets invective style.
African American males are victims of gout.
Estonians, culturally, very rarely smile.

TRUISMS

Thrust must have lift for any flight.
Mary Queen of Scots deserved the English throne.
One-word answers are always impolite.
Woodiness is at the core of men's cologne.

Obsession is, perversely, an end in itself.
One of 131 Americans was once a prisoner.
Learn to dress only to please yourself.
A talker, by definition, is never a listener.

China never mentions the word Manchuria.
A serious exile misses the taste of threat.
An actual court comprised the Roman curia.
Asian girls fear wearing a white barrette.

There is self-comfort in anyone's bias.
Nova Scotia breeds ratty hockey players.
Nobody, who claims to be, is pious.
Man, not God, is the fulcrum of prayers.

There was never any balm in Gilead.
Money, fame, and status are human gods.
No death is not made glorious in the *Iliad*.
Experience is what suffering rewards.

Cucurbits love being planted together.
Best leaves for sandpapering are teak leaves.
Old people look revolting wearing leather.
True faith without seeing still believes.

The Battle of the Somme: pointless slaughter.
Toddlers best perform with none in sight.
The Citarum River is pullulating with toxic water.
In Laos, its men are of the shortest height.

St. Sebastian in art has become a gay icon.
Yellow had negative connotations in the Middle Ages.
The first autofocus camera was a Nikon.
A virus, parasitic in bacteria, are all bacteriophages.

Russians carry a genius for confession.
Shrewdness is a hideous characteristic.
One always devalues an easy possession.
Nationalism in any form is jingoistic.

A demolished castle is half rebuilt.
Dependence always fosters resentment.
No cancer acts as thoroughly as guilt.
Lassitude is a colleague of contentment.

James and Althea Thurber embody marital discord.
Farmers disvalue education in the work ethic.
International rules demand a *wooden* chessboard.
Whatever is artificial is always also synthetic.

"Acme" is the standard cartoon company.
To be without ambition is a blessing.
Bombast is every Congressman's tympany.
Taking college boards, avoid guessing.

TRUISMS

International Morse Code is out-of-date.
Gone is the sacramental view of kingship.
Fashion, once accepted, has sealed its fate.
Love, *despite* knowledge, is friendship.

Showbiz people are suckers for flattery.
"That's a great question" means "I hate it."
A beauty parlor's nothing but a cattery.
Dishonesty lives where one can't state it.

Gaza is now the equivalent of Auschwitz.
Fear of loss diminishes what we possess.
Fishnet stockings men invariably bewitch.
Hebrews' ancient enemy was Damascus.

All acid heads yearn to philosophize.
Faith attaches to no dogma or doctrine.
Gold, not reacting to oxygen, won't oxidize.
It is strictly illegal to hunt musk oxen.

Looking back is always done regretfully
No nation officially owns Antarctica.
A movie never films a book respectfully.
The torero's "salute" is the veronica.

Asian politeness: never cold, never effusive.
Manure piles sit, commonly, behind barns.
The urge to wield power is itself abusive.
Edgar Allan Poe imagined horror in tarns.

Picasso loved to wear a sailor shirt.
Kneeling is the proper shape for prayer.
The American cowboy is an introvert.
Scripture sees all women as a snare.

Nijinsky danced from his pelvis, not his feet.
Asian Americans have problems with alcohol.
A fatty liver makes the human body overheat.
Arabs say "*el mabka*" for the "Wailing Wall."

Sunshine in England always comes in shafts.
The more universal a work, the more divine.
Vanity gives—never collects—autographs.
Clay soil, without exception, tests alkaline.

A paranoiac is one who knows the facts.
Knitting backstage in ballet brings bad luck.
Clichés are the enemy of creative syntax.
Loveliest of birds is the male wood duck.

Great flyrods are made of bamboo culms from China.
Mormons claim for joy in heaven we need the human body.
No trees should ever be cut in the holy city of Medina.
Béchamel sauce is the true crowning glory of manicotti.

The Academy Awards are an *eventus nullus*.
Time is to eternity as a locale is to space.
Local mayors are the emperors of dullness.
The anchor is the linchpin of a relay race.

TRUISMS

St. Luke's Jesus was a paragon of revolution.
Influence turns college admissions into a con.
Social movements thrive by persecution.
The best mustards come from Saskatchewan.

The art of ballet is logically absurd by nature.
"*I need you to . . .*": the nurse's hateful tocsin.
The gaze is the declaration of all portraiture.
In either bow *or* a stern may sit a coxswain.

A flaw in all Utopias is purposelessness.
Rudyard Kipling refused to be interviewed.
The world's oceans define measurelessness.
Beauty in Pacific women means amplitude.

A face changes during the course of a day.
Stand-up comedians do so for easy money.
The natural camouflage for animals is gray.
No honey can match raw Manuka honey.

Immaturity aids in enjoying science fiction.
Wearing yellow in a theatre spooks actors.
There is nothing healthy in any addiction.
Arcane jargon is the bane of chiropractors.

Charles Dickens couldn't write (and disliked) poetry.
Protestant dogma pooh-poohs reality of ghosts.
Chefs notoriously withhold secrets to a recipe.
Unaccomplished snobs thrive on pedigree boasts.

The thumb is the master finger of the hand.
All pelicans make short migrations.
Guns in the United States will never be banned.
Butterfly flight is merely divagations.

None means "not one" *and* "not any."
Scribblers all rely on cliché and bromide.
Canada no longer mints the penny.
All funfair games are skewed cockeyed.

All true gardeners vacation in August.
Tabloid photographers are scoundrels.
Hairy bodies prove men to be baldest.
Simonists are the very worst of vandals.

Contempt for God is also way of wooing him.
GOP/Democrats pursue the same untruth.
Dark maroon is traditional color of theater scrim.
Everything that is new appeals to youth.

One-parent families are death to society.
Close acquaintance always lessens fame.
Sadness, regarding sex, follows its satiety.
The sterile are also often found to be lame.

The tendency to over-tip is vainglorious.
For porches and doorways, choose wisteria.
Named philanthropy is never meritorious.
Kitchen sinks are swarming with bacteria.

TRUISMS

Woodland soil is extremely nutritious.
Crosse & Blackwell mastered sauce for shrimp.
Blandishments are always meretricious.
Monkey meat is a gourmet meal for a chimp.

The weak find refuge in consensus.
Furniture gets lower as civilization declines.
Trust is the asset of an amanuensis.
Litterers should be given massive fines.

An unbalanced wine will never improve.
The Knesset finds panache in an open collar.
Laundered stains are impossible to remove.
No fishing vessel working is not a trawler.

Italians greet you by grabbing your chin.
Any good historian must be a revisionist.
The 18th-century English preferred gin.
Look for the bigot in every partitionist.

No person is as dangerous as a group.
It is traditional in Sweden and Finland
on Thursday eve to eat yellow pea soup.
All deserts in Australia are found inland.

Suspense has more potency than mystery.
Americans crave remembering war dead.
The Ark of the Covenant is lost to history.
Erythrophilia filled the Soviet Union's head.

The English language has the most curse words.
Girls are slighted in all Horatio Alger novels.
Statelessness is the perpetual state of the Kurds.
Disciples after Jesus' ascension were apostles.

Left-handed glass hand-vases are rare.
TV prefers the telegenic to the talented.
A stigma of fury attaches to red hair.
With a cause, no one defeats a paladin.

It is never sunny in Constable country.
Gossip is the very worst of stolons.
Scandinavians say everything bluntly.
Avoid using hyphens after colons.

Arrogance provides great height to smallish men.
Shakespeare had 70 words for female genitalia.
The McDonald's chain is banned in Phnom Penh.
Gender reversal is customary in any saturnalia.

A nation always needs an enemy.
The best art solvent is spit, on a Q-tip.
Imperialism is father to hegemony.
No person has ever seen a black tulip.

Private enrichment kills a commune.
The majority is very rarely correct.
San Diego Junes are filled with gloom.
Parallel lines can never intersect.

TRUISMS

Ancient Rome did not invent the stirrup—
the barbarians did and prevailed in battle.
Obscure is the chemistry of maple syrup.
The Klondike Gold Rush settled Seattle.

Travel writers all purloin their subjects.
Garlic is not allowed at Buckingham Palace,
nor are potatoes, rice, pasta, or Tex-Mex.
Nothing's more authentic than plain malice.

Old baseball players look bad in uniforms.
Few are ever loved for any logical reasons.
Wind both fans and exacerbates firestorms.
New England's beauty resides in its seasons.

Cucumbers are always best cut paper-thin.
No shades of blue are ever quite colorfast.
Farming is alien to the mind of a Bedouin.
England's most polished sons are pederasts.

None are more psychotic than religious leaders.
Blurb writers are never entirely of good faith.
Musk is the aesthetic secret of all cedars.
Gay designers demand a model be a wraith.

Vulgarity's prime passion is to snoop.
Finnan haddie must be used for cullen skink.
Wooden staves espouse a metal hoop.
The British Empire on maps is always pink.

There are 5,000 varieties of the potato.
Lincoln was obsessed with the play *Macbeth*.
Washington's favorite character was Cato.
It is fear of life that leads to fear of death.

Famous men's children suffer tragic fate.
All victors make the vanquished the accused.
Every dissenter lives in a perilous state.
A child without books is a child abused.

William Blake despised all landscapes.
The louder the cry of rapids, the wilder.
No color ever distinguishes moonscapes.
Cases of autism rarely become milder.

Cedar is by far the very best kindling.
A beaver dam entrance is always underwater.
No U.S. bank is uninvolved in swindling.
The Congolese have no respect for a daughter.

All 1950s television humor was the pits.
Anger is an integral part of mourning.
The Finnish are found wanting as wits.
Bright color in snakes is a grave warning.

No crowd isn't impressed with its own sum.
Food critics virtually *live* to be fussy.
Yahweh enjoyed striking people dumb.
No radio housewife wasn't also a hussy.

TRUISMS

Hippopotamuses rarely attack in water.
Mountains are natural refuges for revolutionaries.
No joy can quite match having a daughter.
Kyrgyzstan goes unmentioned in printed itineraries.

Jesus Christ clearly favored socialism.
It is a cliché that most clichés are true.
Bellicosity animates most chauvinism.
A rain burst can be terrifying in Peru.

Barbecue obsessives are hugely fat.
The sea, dark, absorbs ice, being pale.
A mackerel is best caught by a sprat.
High jumpers in the end always fail.

A bride's face is always graced by tulle.
Adele Astaire called George Gershwin impotent.
To employ the exceptions, first know the rule.
Modesty by lavish praise is soon made insolent.

No Jew is allowed to marry his aunt.
Guys in Las Vegas love pinky rings.
No insult hurts like a graceful taunt.
Bullet ants have the fiercest stings.

Scientologists, in that cult, do not pray.
Asian women are crassly domineering.
Southwestern France wears the black beret.
Wax moths have the world's best hearing.

It is fully impossible to train a cat.
Thieves feel deserving of their booty.
The Law of Talion takes pride in tit for tat.
Love as a motive far exceeds duty.

Drawing came naturally to the Neanderthal.
Weight loss books have the largest sales.
Never recite Shakespeare with a Southern drawl.
Fraction-pricing began at Bloomingdales.

A lawsuit's goal is always strictly money.
L.A. is ground zero for religious cults.
Rhododendrons in fact intoxicate its honey.
The flaw of science is it needs results.

Beavers have iron in their (orange) teeth.
Unrelieved certainty approaches real vice.
Moor is Scottish highland, lowland heath.
Craven obsequiousness is a cad's device.

No baseball writer is not sentimental.
Staleness is hastened by refrigerating bread.
Commitment is ever avoided by a rental.
Texans like buckles as big as their head.

Stylishness in clothing execrates velour.
Fingertips are actually a source of sparks.
Scent in every single instance is a lure.
France limits three months to trailer parks.

TRUISMS

A group of resting otters is called a raft.
Vicks rub is vaporized by body heat alone.
A ship glides faster when the wind's abaft.
Christ's robe was seamless, although sewn.

Atheists love to refer to themselves as "brights."
John le Carré's institutions are all male-dominated.
Viaticum alone is the Eucharist for the Last Rites.
Mercury fulminate always explodes when agitated.

One in every family thinks he's God.
Sibling treachery is the most barbaric.
Always look for a coward in a tightwad.
Most travel writing is strictly generic.

White birch works as the best tinder.
D-flat major is the best key for the flute.
It is always flammable if it is a cinder.
Nothing truly small is ever cute.

The smaller the pepper, the hotter it tastes.
Full of courtesy indicates full of craft.
Any foot aimed at an Arab is a disgrace
Every single island is but a larger raft.

Cheapskates have a withholding nature.
A peacock-proud novelist is a bad one.
Easy grace is every gentleman's arcature.
To make paper wisely, find an aspen.

Sprezzatura is a staple of all courtesy.
"They," in common parlance, are always wrong.
Vulgarity is always manifest in urgency.
An assemblage, when unhealthy, is a throng.

Big men who abuse small men are dwarfs.
Anthracite emits more heat than soft coal.
High school girls gravitate to mesomorphs.
For the rich, there's always a tax loophole.

People yearn to be close to a truth-teller.
Canada could have flourished as our fourteenth state.
Temperature swings threaten a wine cellar.
The skull of every human being looks elate.

Dachshunds all come in fifteen colors.
The Great Pyramid of Giza faces due north.
Opposing pigments are always lovers.
Onward, farther, forward all define forth.

An artist looking out a window is working.
A size of a watermelon can become a womb.
The unforgivable crime in Islam is shirking.
Stasis is a metaphor for every waiting groom.

Daughter and laughter are a *klang* link.
Calvinistic minds hold grudges against jewelry.
Women prefer their baseball caps in pink.
No substitute teacher doesn't engender foolery.

TRUISMS

Fiction makes moral the pathology of lying.
Clubmanship is a decadent person's goal.
All drugs the U.S. wants, Mexico's supplying.
Precisely, 3.75 cups equal a single bowl.

Bad weather here is good weather there.
All prayer that's institutionalized is bogus.
Bistro cuisine is pleasantly *peasant* fare.
Every satisfiable negation is tautologous.

Sewage sludge contains heavy metals.
White birch structured the Indian canoe.
Officialdom by law defines decretals.
Generalizations, yes, are generally true.

The best-tasting potato is the Pontiac Red.
Frogs consume their skin when molting.
A third of a whale comprises its head.
Casu Marzu as a food is most revolting.

Alaska harbors the most butterflies.
Every square is always a rhombus.
Pity—a vice—is never to empathize.
Tabloid papers thrive on jaundice.

Tall women are more likely to have twins.
Transgendered males love twinsets and pearls.
Actresses face aging holding up their chins.
Courting a guy shows desperation in girls.

Christians should be buried east to west.
Excellence is perennially its own excuse.
Revolution is the right of the oppressed.
Assembly instructions are ever abstruse.

A true glacier must be at least 25 acres.
Squareness oddly describes a boxing *ring*.
No clergy are ever utilized by Quakers.
A fat person looks a fool in a golf swing.

Volume is what drives stocks higher.
All buildings at Yale are faux-Gothic.
Hypocrisy and smiles forever conspire.
Nationalism is by nature catastrophic.

Apple seeds are poisonous to birds.
Lots of acorns promise a hard winter.
All great art follows the "rule of thirds."
Calcareous limestone yearns to sinter.

The best educated of nations is Canada.
Jokesters rarely have a sense of humor.
Pigs refuse to eat the skins of a banana.
It is mainly haters who employ rumor.

Leather is unpalatable to microbes.
The fable *Bambi* is an indictment of men.
A string tie is anathema to wardrobes.
All advertised watches are set at 10:10.

TRUISMS

Mormons believe that God has a body.
Cowboy boots with formal attire are ludicrous.
Service on American airlines is shoddy.
Opaque rice is served predominantly glutinous.

Vermonters hate submission in any form.
Any and every attempt that falters, fails.
Mediocrity is, conventionally, the norm.
Only true savages dock Rottweilers' tails.

Literary critics are mainly failed novelists.
The Irish temperament never forgives.
True botanists are all phytopathologists.
Talk-show hosts prove that duncery lives.

A brother is before anything else a rival.
Wise professors shun contact with students.
The most basic human drive is for survival.
Tact is ever a spinster courted by prudence.

The rich become rich on top of the poor.
Women's clothes have buttons on the left.
Humorlessness is death in any raconteur.
Tax loopholes are merely sanctioned theft.

Television anchors all have asphalt hair.
The fact of inequality begins at birth.
To glimpse a hammerhead shark is rare.
Potassium's found in every plant on earth.

No caiman has not a fearful maw.
Bad taste consistently tastes bad.
A crow orders its life by every caw.
Any man sporting a cape is a cad.

Nostalgia is habitually a cul-de-sac.
The venation of the oak leaf is pinnate.
A brilliant mind brews an insomniac.
The richest of all salmon is the quinnat.

To choose canned tomatoes, buy them whole,
for it is the bruised ones that are crushed.
Every promise made or pledge is on parole.
No passionate heart can ever be hushed.

Latent in electricity is a corona discharge.
The older the maple, the sweeter the sap.
No flat-bottomed boat is not also a barge.
The lower on the tree, the more you tap.

Mormons may lie, if for a higher cause.
Pinecones can be found in both genders.
Wind is more stable than popular applause.
A skinny belt a woman's waist slenders.

The word "vocabulary" applied to art is a joke.
Liberals find a sunset harbor in conservatism.
Antioxidant capacity is strong in an artichoke.
Tolerance, not compromise, forms ecumenism.

TRUISMS

With no point of view, there is no story.
Predicting fate is way of determining it.
Insight, regarding non-readers, is nugatory.
Protesting a lie is a way of furthering it.

The greatest Roman poet by far was Horace.
Tattooing is forbidden in the book Leviticus.
Traveling as a female's safest, says Jan Morris.
Army language is mercilessly acronymous.

Give odd numbers of flowers to a Rumanian.
Coulrophobia is born of manufactured grins.
All yogurts are a miracle food to an Iranian.
Directionals and rudders work a fish's fins.

The sun will eventually consume the earth.
Marijuana is actually legal in North Korea.
Slightly squatting is best for giving birth.
A prostitute was wife to the prophet Hosea.

Hack writers all lack prosody in prose.
Hatred and jealousy are magnetic Scottie dogs.
Every Shakespeare has his Robert Greene.
Twelve windows are required in synagogues.

No Bengali ever sleeps alone.
Moss always grows north of a tree.
The penis of a walrus is solid bone.
Crows at any moment are ready to flee.

Predations deplete every pension fund.
Legal correspondence is always curt.
Operatic tenors are inevitably rotund.
No native Greek is not an extrovert.

Book-a-year authors are hacks to a one.
Marriage demands all others forsaking.
Only impoverished minds cherish a pun.
Time as such is memory in the making.

The seldom right are always very certain.
Everyone's libido is a *chambre de débarras*.
A Hindu is only as holy as his kirtan.
Size consistently shrinks in a candy bar.

The bane of conservatives is rude surprise.
Grab, grab, grab is the American direction.
Baseball is a game played counter-clockwise.
Extension is the very opposite of flexion.

Floods are the living scourge of Sri Lanka.
Soy in a diet defeats the pain of menopause.
The most quoted-from movie is *Casablanca*.
America, not France, invented Vichyssoise.

The Chinese do not have an alphabet.
Caldecott Awards favor books on diversity.
Egg hunters have rendered extinct the avocet.
Blind obedience is but a radical perversity.

TRUISMS

Never pound, but press, chicken breasts.
Every wannabe President writes a book.
After a merger, every stockbroker invests.
A component of any barrel is a shook.

If blood is thicker than water, water is purer.
Abraham Lincoln never traveled abroad.
A jutting chin provides profile for a führer.
Tentacles indicate every cephalopod.

Magnets have two poles, north and south.
The gang instincts of critics are notorious.
Deceit in a kiss can be felt in the mouth.
Few Oscar winners are ever meritorious

Humor and finance are lethal opposites.
Nothing solves Seven Bridges at Königsberg.
Tension failure is the bane of composites.
A distinct sorrow haunts fields at Gettysburg.

Every Indian village has a sacred grave.
Encrusted lobsters in a tank taste best.
Nutrients are all zapped by a microwave.
A born host is usually an uneasy born guest

The sexual life of eels remains a mystery.
There are endless popular songs about Paris.
A Germans is quite at ease with pedantry.
Every opera singer needs an open naris.

Families know the art of being dangerous.
The palate is the softest part of the head.
None matches Puccini for the canorous.
It is in city slums that all thug life is bred.

Mother-hatred creates true monsters.
Diaghilev commissioned no American composer.
Money is the *lingua franca* of all sponsors.
The Polaris star is every mariner's cynosure.

Dictators have a predilection for pet dogs.
No Hell's Angel ever wears a crash helmet.
Rednecks employ as bumph farm catalogs.
A precious individual is attracted to velvet.

The truth is told by babies and lunatics.
Travel direction and wind rarely coincide.
A verbal anomaly describes any testatrix.
Every political convention is undignified.

Falling in love obliterates self-esteem.
Harlem is an armamentarium of drugs.
No scald exceeds the pain of live steam.
Traveling on its mucus aids all slugs.

A French baguette must weigh 250 grams.
The Yo-Yo was first designed as a weapon.
Of equal size are the two shells of clams.
If not religious, the art is never Tibetan.

TRUISMS

Autobiographobia is a vain man's fear.
Most transvestites are not transsexuals.
Wildness defines a dreamer's frontier.
Balance is the debility of intellectuals.

The less intelligent, the better the actor.
Portable solitude is the artist's biggest gift.
Anonymity most acclaims a benefactor.
Females, far more than males, shoplift.

Admiration is an aspect of humility
Jealousy is the terror of juxtaposition.
No water flows out of the Dead Sea.
Practice in any form means repetition.

Emulsifiers make semisolids congeal.
All Somali troops are uncommandable.
Conformity is the mediocrity's ideal.
A true writer finds everything understandable.

The *deep* South led the way to secession.
Accident is the greatest inventor.
A storyteller's biggest gift is digression.
A tortuous hell waits every tormentor.

The purest voice on earth is a treble's.
No politician dares visit the front lines.
Neutral people are allies of the devils.
Cheese marries well with *vin jaune* wines.

Ash wood is best for woodturning.
Most prostitutes become lesbians.
A hint is eloquent to the discerning.
Progressivism is natural to Wesleyans.

Equatorial Africa leads the world in lightning strikes.
King Lear, of pagan Britain, was coeval with Isaiah.
Realms, not empires, are defined by German *reichs*.
Ten miles above the Earth's surface is the ozone layer.

Christian Scientists never salute a flag.
Murderers have a fetish for tattoos.
English actors are devoted to wearing drag.
Homoerotic is the color chartreuse.

Never poach an egg over four minutes.
Kneading—anything—is therapeutic.
Allergies marry happily to peanuts.
The best teaching methods are maieutic.

Dill is the herb of choice with salmon.
French chefs refer to their stoves as "pianos."
Avarice is always linked to mammon.
C6 is a way of preening for operatic sopranos.

Political odysseys always go left to right.
The safest Mexican drug to buy is mota.
Phantoms are always visualized in white.
Nothing is ever cloudier than a quota.

TRUISMS

Arguments rarely shift intuitions.
Most fashion models are cocomaniacs.
Overreaching taints all ambitions.
Sexual paraphilia drives pyromaniacs.

Crazies always recognize each other.
Diamonds are neither rare nor valuable.
No enmity exceeds a rivalrous brother.
Nothing ever lasts that is fashionable.

The tallest people all suffer feet trouble.
Purity campaigns always end in scandal.
An echo will always the noise redouble.
Vietnamese footwear is solely the sandal.

Literary agents as being worthy is a joke.
Satirists do their best work when dissatisfied.
Only being harnessed to another makes a yoke.
Salaries of actors and athletes are unjustified.

Ignoring a narcissist is his worst penalty.
Half of Italian immigrants returned home.
True hatred always accrues, incrementally.
Native brome best flourishes in gloam.

Military poseurs adore swagger sticks.
The "mob" was created by Prohibition.
Protestant churches never display a Crucifix.
No expert on women beats a beautician.

Cancers love energy-carrying blood.
No G. A. Henty hero was ever corrupt.
The process of rumination produces cud.
Applause is never taken to interrupt.

Every movie celebrity is an *arriviste*.
Males are weaker than females when young.
Democracy never succeeds in the Middle East.
The sexiest part of the body is the tongue.

No opinion is better than information.
A Caucasian Ovcharka is the fiercest dog.
The land of Bulgaria was once Thracian.
Prejudice is a companion to a demagogue.

Cowboys and outlaw bikers hate each other.
David Ben-Gurion, of Israel, was not religious.
Treason quadruples in horror in a brother.
Any grudge-holder is by definition litigious.

Dental floss grows flimsier each year.
Aspen trees, alone, encompass the USA.
Any innuendo is always a smear.
Refinement is the boast of a gourmet.

Always water tomato plants in the morning.
A circus clown's face is essentially sinister.
Stigmergy is the linchpin of all swarming.
The CIA finds torture a delight to administer.

TRUISMS

May is the rainiest month in Yellowstone.
Night-blooming cereus flowers are all white.
Bellicosity is a by-product of testosterone.
The demand for equality defines most spite.

Casinos are arranged to steal your money.
Consistently expanding is our universe.
No animal scientist uses the term "bunny."
Paradise Lost is the masterpiece of blank verse.

"Happy Birthday" in Japan is sung in English,
but "Auld Lang Syne" sung always in Japanese.
A coal mine fire can never be extinguished.
Ceilings always fascinated Signor Paolo Veronese.

Every individual acts out of short-term interest.
Chinese cyberspace is perpetually fire-walled.
Loudest graduation applause goes to the dumbest.
Italy yearly sees a new government installed.

A whale has no bones in either back fin or tail.
Crisis conversions lead to opposite positions.
Officially languages do not include Braille.
Torture skews all confessions in inquisitions.

All blister packs are impossible to open.
Secure people never feel a need to belong.
Dried beans need an overnight soaking.
Gregorian chant is the acme of plainsong.

ALEXANDER THEROUX

Publicity is kryptonite to anyone sane.
One duck in children's stories is ever a straggler.
China manufactures the most acid rain.
Making a vendor lose face is a crime in a haggler.

Gullibility is the primary trait of scryers.
A prince in fables is always most heroic.
Pointless detail is characteristic of liars.
Lawyers and jackals are both saprozoic.

Stepmothers in fables are legendarily cruel.
Ants love to walk on butternut leaves.
Ku Klux Klansmen loathe parochial school.
Silence can wound a person who grieves.

Plums never thrive in tropical climates.
"Preventive war" is an immoral doctrine.
Cartoonists, for jokes, fixate on islets.
Horses are more excitable than oxen.

Gambling to the Chinese is endemic.
The British Navy favored oak for hulls.
A toddler's linguistic awareness is phonemic.
Mexican art is fascinated with human skulls.

A distiller's worthiest asset is pure water.
Cornwall, England is famous for wrestlers.
What the mother did, so will the daughter.
Giving bad news to kings was saved for jesters.

TRUISMS

Skill, not strength, governs any ship.
New Englander nor'easters blow from the south.
Cigarettes are no less harmful with a filter tip.
The process of digestion initiates in the mouth.

Africans love to greet the dawn with song.
Polar bears savor the taste of anti-freeze.
Burning coal and asthma never get along.
Still living in caves are 35 million Chinese.

Publicity intentionally disfigures the truth.
Mafiosi wit is limited to silly nicknames.
Not to burp at an Arab meal is uncouth.
All television game shows are shell games.

Shakespeare used tact in Henry VIII's past,
knowing the Tudors' shaky claims to kingship.
A pedophile very rarely becomes a pederast.
Ancient Egyptian eyeliner favored a wing tip.

Southerners refer to midday lunch as "dinner."
Picasso's "Blue Period" was by far his weakest.
Every Catholic saint is a reconstructed sinner.
Dhaka of all the world's cities is the bleakest.

Whiskey can be aged in barrels only once.
Chint, the plural of chintz, is never used.
The ears most publish the face of a dunce.
Harshly shaking gin can leave it bruised.

Upstage occupies the rear of the stage.
Missouri was always hostile to Mormons.
Tropical humidity helps teens come of age.
Cancers can be cured by anti-hormones.

Wealth constitutes merit in U.S. politics.
No conspiracy exists without a crime.
A sexual paradox defines every testatrix.
Tomatoes are a happy co-partner to thyme.

Graphene paper is stronger than steel.
Hair band divos looked like Charles II.
Braking is improved by an orbital wheel.
Computers do not discern but reckon.

Seamen are conservative in everything.
Salary caps in sports are manipulated.
Hoodlums have a yen for the pinky ring.
Detroit remains notoriously segregated.

Cigarette butts lead the world in litter.
World sailors favor a compass rose tattoo.
Laser printers delight the counterfeiter.
Asians eat the young shoots of bamboo.

Israel is approved as an apartheid state.
Fair and equal are not and never the same.
Mass should not be confused with weight.
Self-regard is necessary to feel shame.

TRUISMS

No invention is not indebted to others.
Delight glimmers at the edge of recall.
Freud believed heroes hate their fathers.
Carnality underpins every masked ball.

A harp's plucked with fingers, not a plectrum.
Bikers hate the bind of a snug-fit helmet.
The large intestine, not the anus, is the rectum.
Only a dilettante would fret about a pelmet.

A crow never takes food, he *steals* it.
To cynics, law is best served by religion.
Trying to hide a habit always reveals it.
The insanest eye belongs to the pigeon.

The world's great beers are brewed all-malt.
Porter is a traditional drink with oysters.
Sweet foods (check!) have lots of added salt.
Rectangular is standard shape for cloister.

Platinum dye volumizes a woman's hair.
A whaler's wife is ever a whaler's widow.
Presumption is the antonym of despair.
A circle is the actual shape of a rainbow.

All cultures spring from religions.
No one can read Los Angeles graffiti.
Diseases are spread by feral pigeons.
The U.S. stole Indian land *by treaty*!

No definition of psychoanalysis exists.
The way to heaven is by wholehearted repentance.
Encyclopediac novelists all favor lists.
Yale's secret society buildings show no entrance.

Navy and Merchant Marine despise each other.
No symphony was ever written in D-flat minor.
Mr. Rogers's sweaters were handknit by his mother.
Half of the world's pigs live in mainland China.

Bruckner is the kindred spirit of Mahler.
Venus and Mercury have no moons.
The face and palms first register pallor.
Individualists abhor the nature of communes.

No diver should descend past 200 feet.
Diapason is the principal pipe of the organ.
Vileness is suggested by a person discreet.
Only female demons can be called a Gorgon.

Japanese men bow with hands at sides;
Japanese women with hands touching thighs.
Envy in its most bitter form derides.
Geometry is the science of cutting pies.

A bronco rider must ride for eight seconds.
Catholics say "blessed" himself, Protestants "crossed."
True flirtation never, *ever* directly beckons.
No human artistic patterns can ever compete with frost.

TRUISMS

Space is upset by the passage of time.
The diamond market is completely rigged.
Underpayment is an embezzlement crime.
Caucasian hair costs most for anyone wigged.

A drawstring is the *sine qua non* of a seabag.
The Danish word *kong* actually means king.
Nothing should ever be placed on the U.S. flag.
The U.S. flag is considered a living thing.

Papaya juice makes tough meat tender.
A man with many women has no woman at all.
Oregon recognizes a third (non-binary) gender.
One blue cord is required in a Jewish prayer shawl.

Friday is a Jonah for the sailing of ships.
Never accept any human doctrine in full.
Symbols define but obscures apocalypse.
Gravity, in fact, is neither a push nor a pull.

All Korean Christians reprehend smoking.
Without love, nothing feels well placed.
Parrots—"sky-threat"—loathe human poking.
Red dots connote blood in Queen Anne's lace.

Barding a game bird induces moisture.
Geography is destiny to an astrologer.
Nothing filters water better than an oyster.
Nosiness animates every biographer.

Human motives are invariably mixed.
Polar bear liver is highest in vitamin A.
Wrestling matches are officially fixed.
Grace insists on the privilege of delay.

Die Zauberflöte is rife with Masonic symbolism.
Britain is the gout capital of Europe.
Traveled in America, but *travelled* is a Britishism.
A maple tree needs 40 years to produce syrup.

"Laplander" to Sami people is racist.
One walks on a pier, never on a dock.
Illnesses, oddly, rarely plague a sadist.
Transvestites adore the word "frock."

The loris is the sole venomous primate.
Narcissists name kids after themselves.
Many black slaves owned real estate.
Dwarves are often conflated with elves.

A Jew may legitimately get drunk on Purim.
Learn to trust the authority of your *doubt.*
The best wheat for pasta is glutinous durum.
Rings of age, as with trees, are found in trout.

Autodidacts are predominantly cranks.
There would be no USA without France.
Pygg, a clay, etymologizes piggy banks.
A truly great dancer becomes the dance.

TRUISMS

Noticing is first required for charity.
Both law and order foster conformity.
Intelligence in siblings shows no parity.
Drug use guarantees any deformity.

St. Francis most loved the crested lark.
To deny accusations is to have to repeat them.
Vietnamese is nonpareil of the diacritical mark.
Every single fruit has a seed and a stem.

Singular fame brings extreme disquiet.
No one invents a persona like a Pisces.
Jains exclude all roots from their diet.
Gauging self-reliance centers all crises.

Mohawk Indians have no fear of heights.
The blood of every octopus is blue.
Ideally cut a cookable hare into eighths.
Repeating the act mocks a good shampoo.

Buffalo hugely dislike being corralled.
Every consommé should be crystal clear.
No used-car dealer's promise is ever fulfilled.
We inevitably come to hate what we fear.

Only 5% of plant species are dioecious.
Jews and Muslims can't eat birds of prey.
Efficiency ever wars with the expeditious.
Comedy abounds about making soufflé.

New Guinea grew the very first banana.
The fiercer the trespass, the better the poem.
No non-American may be called *chicana*.
A caterpillar craves the taste of brome.

Male elephants do not have a scrotum.
Hallucinatory voices are suppressed emotions.
The color black is ever a negative totem.
Hot-air ballooning is big with Cappadocians.

Soviet hair dyes play unpredictable tricks.
The beaches in Guam are coral, not sand.
Bleach and ammonia must never be mixed.
No dairy products should ever be canned.

In 1890, virtually all men wore a mustache.
Mr. H. Thoreau disapproved of Mr. A. Lincoln.
The best wood for handles is white ash.
Tribal land for Native Americans is *still* shrinking.

Wind blows from oceans by day, to oceans at night.
"Quizzes" at MIT are mellow-speak for tests.
No Fundamentalist isn't also a born-again Luddite.
St. Paul as a Christian proselytizer never rests.

Rafflesia has no stems, leaves, or roots.
Locust is the best wood for railroad ties.
Cucumbers as such are technically fruits.
Psychology is the art of feeble surmise.

TRUISMS

Ferns produce spores and never flower.
Every computer boot-up presents a surprise.
Arcane symbols in Revelations never scour.
The sun persistently appears larger at sunrise.

The crown of oak determines the number of acorns.
Intention has to be involved as regards sinning.
Dental fricatives—consonants—voice runic thorns.
Every ending constitutes another beginning.

Black walnut is the best wood for gun stocks.
Paranoids find even a casual look an intruder.
Language is a human being's working toolbox.
Wales gave England the notable House of Tudor.

All euphemisms are a kind of posturing.
The French are supreme at frozen desserts.
Child abuse is often prevalent in fostering.
Every wild boar always pisses in spurts.

All home ice-cream freezers pall.
Rosin is only one kind of resin.
Every country has a version of a shawl.
Blindness is a virtue in a *mu'adhin*.

A luckless bishop is hampered by his pawns.
The French refuse to eat oysters with milk.
The first alloy used by humans was bronze.
Every pitchman's essential motive is to bilk.

White wine misappropriates all pâtés.
Spin is intrinsic to elementary particles.
Saudi Arabia as a nation is hostile to gays.
Ancient Latin uses no definite articles.

Matter is but another form of energy.
Ostrich is a hungry lion's favorite food.
The malady of monks was always lethargy.
All Scottish clans lived by the feud.

The Maasai go hunting only with spears.
Without humor, satire is pure invective.
Few Jews are left in Algeria or Algiers.
Irony is used by every fictional detective.

Male rhinos, so dangerous, very seldom fight.
The greatest soccer players wear number 10.
A disguised conscience finds itself never contrite.
Tempeh is best when eaten close to rotten.

Colors all have different frequencies.
Southerners eat red beans and rice on Monday.
Sex informs all laws regarding indecencies
"Babylon" refers to slavery regimes in reggae.

Formality is scarily the severest form of grief.
North and south in most countries are rivals.
There's no better bug repellent than a bay leaf,
The American South loves religious revivals.

TRUISMS

Gambling casinos are banned in Hawaii.
The perils of investing is a working-class topos.
The best pioneer scouts were the Pawnee.
British almost exclusively prefer brown sauce.

Red was Georgia O'Keeffe's favorite color.
Confrontation freaks hate to lose an argument.
Circulation lasts only eighteen months for a dollar.
Duplicity is ever associated with "*no comment.*"

Pedophilia necessitates alert vagabonding.
Cycling as a sport is compromised by drugs.
Peak drives of genders fail in corresponding.
The Virgin Mary lends her name to ladybugs.

One's very first book is worth the library.
Boston baseball fans never wave towels.
There is no such thing as a vintage sherry.
Gangster rhetoric consists of disavowals.

Japanese are contemptuous of Koreans.
New faces frighten Alzheimer patients.
A true patrician understands plebeians.
Agony for misanthropes is adjacence.

The extreme is the forerunner of grief.
It is derogatory to use the slang word *goy*.
True eloquence always aims to be brief.
All excesses are guaranteed to cloy.

No lottery winner feels he deserves it.
All lottery losers feel cruelly passed by.
Testing one's freedom alone preserves it.
Legal prose is guaranteed to stultify.

San Luca, Italy, is the kingdom of crime.
Never eat a parasol-shaped mushroom.
No loss of flavor is found in dry thyme.
The intrigue of acting is to wear a costume.

Alders always grow close to water.
A roulette wheel's numbers add to 666.
No native is not also a squatter.
All girl schools pullulate with cliques.

Fungi feed on anything detrital.
The best products are never sold but bought
God should allow one's life to be a recital.
No refrigerant can match a woman's culotte.

No two atoms share the same velocity.
A broken bat heartens a baseball pitcher.
Manic episodes thrive on grandiosity.
Biblical proverbs oddly applaud the richer.

Love for others always makes one vulnerable.
Avoid eating mushrooms with white gills.
All Khoisan speech is maddeningly unutterable.
Disease is spread by the use of dollar bills.

TRUISMS

Losing at gambling oddly assuages guilt.
All Liberty Caps are psilocyban ceps.
It is the female alone who is able to jilt.
Heights have a waking dream of depths.

Food somehow all tastes better at sea.
Sententiousness defines all epitaphs.
The magic fairy tale number is three.
An idiot does not indent paragraphs.

Poison is ingested, venom injected.
Hummingbirds co-evolve with each chosen flower.
Show business folk are all affected.
High heels on women's shoes greatly empower.

No symptoms are linked to tapeworms.
Parasitism describes all political groupies.
Dish rags—yes—pullulate with germs.
An open mind is bliss for any newbies.

Each plane disaster calls for new discovery.
Kissing sounds hale a Burmese waiter.
For any garden transition employ shrubbery.
To a scoundrel, truth is always a traitor.

All should feel shy writing about happiness.
Weakness is guaranteed in anything plied.
Simplicity is the lesson of the wilderness.
There are twelve hours between every tide.

The *Nakba* fills every Palestinian with dread.
Jehovah's Witnesses can be notorious anti-intellectuals.
In the Middle Ages, currency was often bread.
Transgender is the term preferred by most transsexuals.

Sufi anecdotes are all paradoxical.
Adhering strictly to law is to disobey it.
A Gascon is by nature thrasonical.
For any valid prayer, you have to say it.

Christ's crucifixion was to torture, not dispatch.
All Zen koans are intentionally baffling.
A Serb and Croat put together make a mismatch.
A state tax on simpletons is legal raffling.

Every congressional lobbyist is a *maquereau*.
The female dominates in the hyena world.
All hurricanes create an ocean undertow.
There's no need to salute a flag when furled.

Koreans love setting furniture at angles.
No crocodile ever stops growing.
It is Hindu married women who wear bangles.
Every last coming involves a going.

Left-handers are notorious for cacography.
The Joint Chiefs of Staff allows no women.
Any life is too complex for any biography.
Sperm don't define—are *included* in—semen.

TRUISMS

Go to Friuli to get the best prosciutto.
"Talk about..." tocsin of the lame interviewer.
An eleven-year-old girl named the planet Pluto.
Proselytizing is done precisely *for* the evildoer.

It is harder to be a guest than to be a host.
Wallis Simpson never once telephoned a man.
The Bible actually declares it evil to boast.
The ritual book of the KKK is the Kloran.

All graffiti is low-level dissent.
Urine (from a healthy bladder) is actually sterile.
Chinese roses have no scent.
A rapist's heartless grin is disconcertingly feral.

A cluster of rooks is called a "storytelling."
The nature of evil is that it is mysterious.
Arguments for torture are never compelling.
Nothing in asbestos is not deleterious.

No spotted cat skins may be imported.
Colombians clasp forearms to shake hands.
Every autobiography remains distorted.
The faith of every folly is accurate plans.

Both sexes of the rhinoceros have horns.
Italians prod and probe all new produce.
Depression in an eerie way actively mourns.
Birch bark canoes must be sewn with spruce.

Always add cornstarch with a liquid.
Eskimos rarely have more than three kids.
Servitude is often comfort to the timid.
Old Testament ethics basically *forbids*.

Eating too often causes hunger quickly.
Whales actually follow specific roads.
Every moral issue is angled very thickly.
Moisture for frogs, dryness for toads.

Female land does not crag, it arcs.
Psychoanalysis is a strictly pseudoscience.
None loved children more than Karl Marx.
Poverty slaughters all self-reliance.

Englishmen write letters on a Sunday.
The New York Yankees stole their logo from Tiffany's.
Dabbawalas are all male in Mumbai.
Homophonies are in fact also polyphonies.

Vermont has no major east-west roads.
The act of circumcision is perfectly useless.
Lack of water does not bother toads.
Trying to convert a Czech to God is bootless.

No one wins an argument with a child.
Control freaks despise surprise parties.
Subjects in old portraits never smiled.
Aesthetes were ever the bane of hearties.

TRUISMS

Advocacy exceeds proposal by having solutions.
Alleles are most commonly found in pairs.
Humbug is the grandfather of circumlocutions
M.C. Escher's rabid with never-ending stairs.

Long Tibetan coats obviate a need for gloves.
Harold Bloom sees Shylock as "inglorious."
The male alone sings with mourning doves.
The body's longest muscle is the sartorius.

Kashmiri dishes always ride on yogurt.
Masculine men hate military women.
Congressional lobbying is always covert.
Bowdlerizing is the worst form of skimming.

Frank Sinatra never once apologized.
Reformers are to a one wanting in humor.
Russians and Ottomans never fraternized.
Any abnormal mass of tissue is a tumor.

Laughter in *Hamlet* is completely bitter.
Dull people maintain formal categories.
An excitable person is often a mad knitter.
No idea was worse than coed dormitories.

A musk ox hide is best for warmth in bed.
Strenuous lying always begets credulity.
Toxic fabrics that kill never, ever shred.
All beauticians are fiends for garrulity.

ALEXANDER THEROUX

Japanese view Negroes with revulsion.
Guile has 100 faces, not so innocence.
Only liquids can comprise an emulsion.
Falling in love is always a coincidence.

The Windsors are actually Hanoverians.
Secrecy is incompatible with democracy.
Using a left hand is anathema to Nigerians.
Discretion is the persona of hypocrisy.

Philip Larkin's poems are all valedictions.
Ballet is about women, and women alone.
Democracy and efficiency are contradictions.
A school bully is the most widely known.

All U.S. family courts show gender bias.
City newcomers settle at the point of arrival.
Spiritual boasters with gall are most impious.
A Christian cross is found in any arch ogival.

Child prodigies never enjoy true childhood.
In Greece, a valid will must be handwritten.
A fairy tale setting is perpetually wildwood.
An uncomely person is always easily smitten.

Euphemism for a horse penis is a sheath.
Purchasing a rug is a courtship in Iran.
A halo clearly recapitulates a wreath.
Stairways strangely never figure in a barn.

TRUISMS

To seek the *whole truth* in courts is a joke.
In Sri Lanka, a waggling head means "yes."
It takes forty years to get acorns from an oak.
A fatwa in Saudi Arabia has banned chess.

The Chinese refuse to learn Japanese.
Courting popularity is uncommonly vulgar.
Wealth is the fuel of party nominees.
Rose oil is a cuisine delight for any Bulgar.

Ducks are suffocated at the Tour d'Argent.
Never look back—a circus taboo—on parade.
No fable is complete without a dungeon.
All materials, wherever water flows, corrade.

Anyone associated with Elvis was a celebrity.
First names aren't used in English public schools.
All political appointments lack integrity.
Only a jack and a mare mating can make mules.

Power is a hideous, inhuman phenomenon.
Aragon natives are legendarily hot-headed.
Albertans irk the folks in Saskatchewan.
A perfect quilt is always invisibly threaded.

A nook is a corner, a cranny is a crack.
Neurotics have a need to scratch off labels.
Henry Ford demanded every car be black.
Roosters are cheekily boastful in fables.

Eight-year-olds seek complete orthodoxy.
No guest can visit the Porcellian Club twice.
Etiquette is hypocrisy's constant proxy.
Throwing as a unit is law when rolling dice.

Maxims in Paris is always closed on Sundays.
To sit *facing out of* a circus ring is taboo.
Homophobic pejoratives are rife among gays.
Berets are fashionably meant to be worn askew.

Cocktails love the company of citrus.
Demagogic factions prey on scapegoats.
Easter is anathema to a Jehovah's Witness.
Although lithium is a metal, it still floats.

A skipping child in films is always murdered.
No bride should walk the aisle in rehearsal.
No petition to a losing pol is ever furthered.
Abhorrence for child molesters is universal.

Cold cynicism makes conspiracies flourish.
Troubled people gravitate to bus stations.
All pranic pathways always seek to nourish.
Trees are weakest at areas of any furcations.

Roses are never found in black.
Truly to see wilderness one must be alone.
Habitually canoe to water that is slack.
A smile is forever hypocrisy's clone.

TRUISMS

Lead newspaper weights have long gone.
For compressed air canisters, avoid agitation.
Scorpios and Virgos have never got along.
Seashell's construction is found in its striation.

No one has ever climbed Everest's south face.
True royalty takes time to notice servants.
The cripple in his dreams wins every race.
Chinese eschew western religious observance.

Activity is prayer to a Trappist monk.
All birds have evolved from reptiles.
An atheist's faith is the need to debunk.
Jews to Mormons are called "Gentiles."

Dead bodies—corpses—never bruise.
Kites fly higher against a headwind.
Scandinavians are notably avid for tattoos.
Always approach a bear downwind.

No Indian tribe possessed an alphabet.
Claret should be served slightly warm.
'50s lesbians signaled by way of violet.
Safety is always secured in a swarm.

Money is the plot in all of Balzac's novels.
Headway is lost when driving through sand.
Most South African townships are hovels.
Beans often taste better when they're canned.

Oysters always thrive in brackish water.
There is no real number having a negative square.
Light is the Creator's eldest daughter.
A rabbit has much shorter ears than a hare.

Wipe but never wash cast-iron omelet pans.
A talent for receiving gifts is rarer than for giving them.
A woman's brain is 10% smaller than a man's.
A Muslim population predominates in Bethlehem.

Protocol is inherently inflexible.
Seawater is never merely water.
Waste in any military is unindexible.
A milksop focuses on his alma mater.

An Atlantic Ocean liner crossing take five days.
Leos and Capricorns never get along.
Loops are in repugnant in any standard maze.
Melody is the beating heart of song.

All mail from a lawyer is bad news.
Serving at landed estates is done with gloves.
Every tuxedo abhors brown shoes.
Wars have been fought with passenger doves.

Oregon is celebrated for its lilies.
No American heiress can't buy an English title.
Wildlife is the expertise of ghillies.
Free trade for any healthy economy is vital.

TRUISMS

To be a girl in Sierra Leone is misery.
The parrot thinks of *you* as the parrot.
Cancers can be traced to the rotisserie.
For sweetness in cooking, add a carrot.

Prosperity conjoins to wartime spending.
Hell's Angels only ride U.S. machines.
A new Israeli land-grab's always pending.
No estimate is ever truly what one means.

A human frown is another kind of fist.
He has a hemorrhoid who has to grow one.
Obedience is often a tactic to resist.
Nobody ever leaves someone for no one.

A cool exterior implies sexual heat.
No Native American in films has a mustache.
A woman's dress is made sexy by a pleat.
Any fertilizer is improved with bone ash.

Every animal on earth eats plants.
Servitude is work an evil prig calls duty.
Sex is the *sine qua non* of every dance.
Symmetry is an essential trait of beauty.

Meat always tastes better on the bone.
Hierarchy is always based on power.
Defaults increase the smaller the loan.
Bees can make any elephant cower.

ALEXANDER THEROUX

No divorcee was presented at Queen Victoria's court.
A fish fork should ideally be made of silver.
Fortified wines reach their highest perfection in port.
A thief always begins his life with a moderate pilfer.

A crown prince always opposes the crown.
Fate, to conceal, names someone Smith.
Fright, more often than not, defines a clown.
No inner layer of any object is not pith.

Walt Whitman was deficient in humor.
Tears shed on it can badly stain a fur.
Truth is far less exciting than rumor.
Obsequiousness well befits a chauffeur.

Seeking publicity is a pathetic fetish.
Old wooden bundle handles have disappeared.
To speak Latvian is to speak Lettish.
A hated person is also always secretly feared.

Inexperience creates misadventure.
Longevity involves a degree of spite.
Worry is forever a loan's debenture.
The firmest traitors are never contrite.

All good writers have written less well.
Vodka is a part of all Russian cuisine.
No whorl is ugly on an ocean shell.
A woman's bum loves a shoe chopine.

TRUISMS

A fool pronounces lasagna "lazagna."
Fishing guides, traditionally, are bullies.
Oranges were originally called *naranja*.
Multiple ropes can never work pullies.

Awkwardness is the mother of error.
A car horn is created to be dissonant.
Facelessness is the nucleus of terror.
Pondering often needs to be indolent.

Superiority is the ugly sister of pity.
Inhumanity, sadly, is typically human.
Efficiency is victim to any committee.
Coriander is the ex-husband of cumin.

Forest fires move fastest going uphill
It is tasteless to prolong life artificially.
Any emptied space demands a refill.
Method acting operates superficially.

Nature glories in utter simplicity.
Toasting anyone with water causes death.
It is oddly the public that craves publicity.
The mouth is the very first victim of meth.

Never kick paper cups thrown down at a rodeo.
Angry honey badgers go straight for the scrotum.
The first vegetable grown in space was the potato.
The antithesis of a taboo is specifically a totem.

Troubled women need to sit down.
Christmas cookies quickly turn stale.
No pederast bypasses a playground.
Earrings alone glamorize a female.

Israeli crimes receive no press attention.
All U.S. presidents have married above them.
Love both pro and con's defined by tension.
All human prayer constitutes a stratagem.

Political appointees are often made a judge.
Chimney sweeps bring good luck to a wedding.
Automobiles in Cuba perfectly define a kludge.
Rain pattering on a roof softens all bedding.

American Indians lost their Black Hills
to the greed of U.S. political treachery.
Most poisonous mushrooms sport gills.
Asceticism's countervailing vice is lechery.

No passage in the work of Camus is comic.
Farting is an integral rite in Ugandan dining.
Sudden fame engenders suspicions anomic.
No meat is not greatly enhanced by brining.

Russians prefer hanging ikons in a corner.
Athletes go unshaven at playoff times.
Joy is characteristic for an Irish mourner.
Wind is the secret seducer of chimes.

TRUISMS

Taciturnity is a blessing in a barber.
A sun's rays kill viruses and bacteria.
A horseshoe shape well befits a harbor.
Wistfulness is connoted by wisteria.

Most game fish are, queerly, inedible.
Finland leads the world in coffee-drinking.
Tabloid stories are rarely ever credible.
Eyes shut simultaneously when blinking.

Glumness in a mouth is hippocrepiform.
Bad dress rehearsals bode good openings.
Graffitology is now considered an artform.
A head (not chest) voice allows yodeling.

Gamblers are given to nervous punding.
Cilantro stems are sweet, parsley's bitter.
Waste delights in government funding.
Aggression explains a compulsive knitter.

Noise is the camouflage of inattention.
A low outside pitch stymied Ted Williams.
Mongoose and cobra live in constant tension.
Over Italians, natives identify as Sicilians.

Cowboys never set their hat down on a bed.
Seven is the most often rolled number in dice.
Sew a garment with a lesser strength thread.
Ritual actions are superstitiously done thrice.

Shakespeare favored Roman (or Italian) names.
Nerds prefer doing other students' homework.
Professionalism has killed the Olympic Games.
Glass predominates in Native American beadwork.

Learning is a greater thing than being taught.
There is always a trace of remorse in satiety.
Indians, curiously, often call India Bharat.
Well-hidden are the traits of the truest piety.

All explorers are psychological oddities.
Lovers of Darjeeling tea never use milk.
Workers to line bosses are commodities.
Metal wire is weaker than a rope of silk.

No-eye-contact people fear wasting time.
The deeper the water, the higher the pressure.
Public housing environments foster crime.
Chardonnay wines taste best younger, fresher.

Cowardice adores the middle ground.
Germans dislike spicy or pungent food.
Guesstimates love numbers in the round.
Concealment in its every form is crude.

Carbonated drinks foster eructations.
Vaishyas control all of India's main business.
Women's shoes are shaped for seductions.
Any and all flirtation is an act of accismus.

TRUISMS

No Chasid feels kindly to a Misnagdic.
The fulcrum of nostalgia is dislocation.
Coca-Cola is a miraculous anacathartic.
War was mother's milk to every Thracian.

Duck confit is cabbage's best friend.
The Israeli lobby owns the U.S. Congress.
Any mistress has the right to misspend.
Fables ascribe dumbness to a laundress.

No extreme paranoiac is not credulous.
Translation inevitably distorts all meaning.
Fawning as an act is always sedulous.
Wearing a paper hat at work is demeaning.

Second visits are never as successful.
Toasting with water to Germans means death.
A sick baby renders every heart stressful.
Aping marriage is adultery's last breath.

There is a distinct biology in someone watching.
The John le Carré plot: individual vs. institution.
Always turn all clothing inside out when washing.
To waist chop was China's old way of execution.

Reform rabbis virtually believe in nothing.
The English exonym *squaw* is a sexual slur.
A kiss is given in Europe for blushing.
The first anointing oil for Christ is myrrh.

Dark beans have more vitamins than light beans.
Andrew Lloyd Webber's only flop was *Jeeves*.
Toy guns are never allowed in the Philippines.
Fall actually reveals the *normal* color in leaves.

The proper Galician pronunciation is "beigel."
Only a moron can enjoy a surprise party.
Repentance is the quintessence of all revival
Sweet marries acidic in Danish havarti.

Monkeys always peel a banana from the bottom.
Every cubic mile of seawater has 25 tons of gold.
Nature in its decay shows its brightest in autumn.
Bible enumeration favors the term sevenfold.

To New Englanders, a Yankee is a Vermonter.
No human being can outrun a polar bear.
Codes of four digits are transmitted by transponder.
Soulful pleas are better than fixed prayer.

We best remember what we want to forget.
Women, not men, are partial to yard sales.
No true-born traitor feels an ounce of regret.
U.S. main roads were initially Indian trails.

Cities—not country—more connote vice.
Mother hatred is always self-repudiation.
Whoever denies a compliment, seeks it twice.
Unions are the embodiment of defalcation.

TRUISMS

Never descend to eating green potatoes.
To disbelieve truth is to invite deceit.
In Antarctica, there are never tornadoes.
Boxes serve for bread, not mail, in Papeete.

Twins comprise a gang in miniature.
Lizzie Borden killed with a flat iron.
Seminarians are notoriously immature.
Biscuits taste best cooked on cast-iron.

Tonto was always sent to town to get supplies.
American gymnasts are over-muscled gnomes.
Left-handed people draw their circles clockwise
Bacterias proliferate in musty Roman catacombs.

Courtship rushed is a courtship lost.
Marble is common in a baptismal stoup.
No horse's nose is not nursery soft.
A jeweler always magnifies his loupe.

Nobody is prouder than a Corsican.
Prejudice is but second-hand hatred.
Toilets are almost always porcelain.
Dates on LP albums are never stated.

Frictionless love is literally non-existent.
"*Interesting*" is the lamest of all adjectives.
A judge shows thought when inconsistent.
Teenage girls abuse the use of laxatives.

Family gatherings are acrimony pageants.
For "blue trout," it must be freshly killed.
Smallpox led to the use of beauty patches.
Every medieval profession had its guild.

Worldly wisdom is very rarely wise.
The heavier always floats the lighter.
It should be a criminal act to plagiarize.
You will never see solid crystals of niter.

Wild bananas are pollinated by bats.
Orchestra conductors seem ever exasperated.
True fury is defined in a clowder of cats.
A father undermined is a male emasculated.

Boredom is an aspect of anxiety.
Never wear diamonds in the daytime.
Charity is the truest form of piety.
Hope forever soars in Maytime.

Red flowers, odorless, are fertilized by birds.
Mongolian "death worms" inhabit the Gobi.
A banana splits down the middle into thirds.
No matatu is not brightly painted in Nairobi.

Civility is paper-thin in rural Lithuania.
One sits twenty feet from an eyechart.
Doubt is the arch enemy of every mania.
Anything separated is also taken apart.

TRUISMS

All games aspire to the condition of war.
Every legal mediation is a game of bluff.
The Royal Ontario Museum is an eyesore.
Only amateurs sneeze when taking snuff.

Rooks are far smarter than chimpanzees.
Shadows in *noir* films do all the work.
No single chief ever ruled Comanches.
Satin stitches work to flatten crewelwork.

Every delusion contains a grain of truth.
No one will ever learn who Datchery was.
All Welshmen weep upon hearing a *crwth*.
Lessons done well were taught with a tawse.

Politicians are a professional criminal class.
Sweet Vermouth is Italian, dry is French.
Anything colored red will attract a bass.
Torque is the backbone of a serious wrench.

Class is always reflected in a costume.
No one actually won the First World War.
Coyness describes every *nom de plume*.
The smallest of bluefins is the albacore.

Psychotics excessively seal their letters.
The book of Esther never mentions God.
A creditor's memory exceeds a debtor's.
Salaries with charities make them a fraud.

Wide spaces breed narrow minds.
Psychiatry is one way that Jews pray.
Light fights to maintain straight lines.
To woo with success, always delay.

No nation loves poetry like the Russian.
In life, Harpo Marx was the most talkative.
Pedantry rules in all fastidious discussion.
Black in frillies are sexually evocative.

Altruism to any lawyer is strictly off-piste.
KFC is the last-meal choice of death-row inmates.
Ancient Greek and Persians could never co-exist.
To a feeling of failure, everybody donates.

Chinese chestnuts, not American, are edible.
You never leave a cult, you merely escape.
Faith always asks us to believe the incredible.
Being crinkled is the native language of crepe.

"Tiresome:" favorite British word of censure.
No soldier ever hears the shot that kills him.
Collateral is missing in any form of debenture.
Gluttony demands every portion overfills him.

Yeast produces alcohol which kills the fungus.
Those who come in need never come in judgment.
Cancer is attributed to everything plumbous.
The point of all kinds of peppers is being pungent.

TRUISMS

Strip-mining always scratches at the eyes.
Joy turns to tears in proper resolution
All with full knowledge comprehend lies.
A reactionary prays for counter-revolution.

The piano is, all by itself, an orchestra.
Self-help books nobody admits to reading.
A sin against the Holy Spirit is anathema.
One hazard among Mormons is inbreeding.

Histamines badly make the back itch.
Dinner plate geometry greatly favors meat.
Greeting card verse is the sheerest kitsch.
Antarctic's the highest continent by ice sheet.

The eye of an owl is fixed in its socket.
No buckler doesn't call for a shield.
Never wear earrings accompanying a locket.
A woman's smile is as good as a yield.

Every baby-kissing solon is basically craven.
Few in show business use their real name.
An "unkindness" is group term for the raven.
Rehabilitation is mainly built on shame.

Swifts feed exclusively on the wing.
Yemeni coffee is the world's most prized.
Ancient Romans abhorred the idea of a king.
Child abuse begins with the circumcised.

ALEXANDER THEROUX

Chefs are notoriously the hardest drinkers.
Ferns were banned as a Cliveden centerpiece.
Inaction is often linked to overt thinkers.
Abstruseness is the lingo of the legalese.

Japanese students are competitive zombies.
Most women disdain underground comics.
Costa Rica has no—and never had—armies.
Geometry is the key to all chordal diatonics.

Mentioning #7 at a craps table is bad luck.
The sun is actually an admixture of colors.
Aqua =water, but *e* is used in "aqueduct."
Full disclosure ends the dreams of lovers.

Henry James never once refers to movies.
Organized money is an organized mob.
Two rubies, adjacent, stain both rubies.
It costs money to keep one one's job.

Whippoorwills perch *parallel* to a limb.
Dry cleaning cannot restore a doited tie.
Neither giraffes nor rhinoceroses can swim.
Tall buildings are proscribed in Kauai.

Mozart composed no solo work for viola.
Holden Caulfield is never physically described.
No Sunni could ever become an ayatollah.
A person in your debt is, by definition, bribed.

TRUISMS

Third parties in America always lose.
Rumors spread more quickly than the truth.
Bumps with hemophiliacs turn into a bruise.
Car accidents are caused mainly by youth.

Butcher blocks are made from sycamore.
The nature of pity is it always comes too late.
Actually, quite bad for the heart is a snore.
A person's face becomes largely his fate.

Ocean travel kills quotidian realities.
Whites know nothing of the lives of Blacks.
All graduation speeches float on banalities.
Bipolar victims suffer a mental parallax.

Palm trees in Los Angeles all lean south.
Religious fanatics despise education.
A wise man's heart teaches his mouth.
Poisonous creatures feature coloration.

It's offense in sports that sells tickets,
but championships are won by defense.
Chirping's not done by female crickets.
Cowardice for the Nazis was capital offense.

The tallest of candidates, whosoever,
consistently wins a presidential race.
When planted, bamboo lives forever.
Moles live their lives without a face.

Nothing's so fleeting as a permanent wave.
In every decade, Israel bombs Beirut.
One pulls but never pushes a drawshave.
All awards are given to codify repute.

Most books have been sold by Mao Zedong.
Grandma Moses confused every perspective.
The hermit thrush is perfection in birdsong.
Vice in an astronaut is being introspective.

Soil west of the Missouri is sedimentary.
Presidents, in a scandal, do a "prayer breakfast."
Nothing reorganizes reality like memory.
Not a single Old Testament story is not sexist.

Soil east of the Missouri is glacial.
There are no battle scenes in Dickens' novels.
Racism in the last analysis is facial.
Outdated fashions are little more than fossils.

Laws never address our truest emotions.
No single rule of beauty is ever universal.
No holy person's seen at his devotions.
Television wall-to-wall is all infomercial.

Everything that matters must be proved.
No male Jew has not a yen for a beard.
No accurate rifle has not been grooved.
The Papal tiara has always been tiered.

TRUISMS

All vodka by law must be tasteless.
Peppermint is the very trash of candy.
Jealousy thrives best when baseless.
Land, to perk, needs soil that's sandy.

No martini should be mixed in advance.
The act of memory reorganizes all reality.
Circling most characterizes a square dance.
The average bloke is suspicious of originality.

Truth by any fanatic is actively disliked.
Ovenbirds sing, "*Teacher, teacher, teacher.*"
A cheerful buyer's offer is invariably hiked.
A caricaturist fixes on one's ugliest feature.

We never become what we pretend to be.
The butter plate is placed above the forks.
Gunflint (for acidity) is the taste of Chablis.
Airlines serve it cheapest meals with *sporks*.

Irony is in every instance a disguise.
No wine snob isn't critically insecure.
Only the best honey will crystallize.
Vietnamese women excel at pedicure.

No duet is not also a competition.
Good taste is never on parade.
A seeker of gossip makes a coalition.
Any vow ignoring God will abrade.

ALEXANDER THEROUX

Adolescence is a Piranesian chamber of horrors.
The costlier the tequila, the lesser the hangover.
Tests of self characterize all true explorers.
Matzah must be made in eighteen minutes for Passover.

To the blind person, all things are noise.
Telephone and telegraph created the stock market.
Geniuses are found less in girls than boys.
A rug—smaller, impermanent—is not a carpet.

All love for what is distant is delusion.
Craps dice must always be transparent.
Istanbul traffic defines utter confusion.
A single mom's spouse becomes a grandparent.

It is bad luck to give knives as a wedding gift.
French women always eat prunes to detox.
Business and godly ethics can never coexist.
The deepest of private visions are heterodox.

Male sperm dies sooner than female.
Beaujolais is meant to be served young.
Pressure of any devising is blackmail.
No cattle feed around their own dung.

No one is mocked who first laughs at himself.
Women have destroyed the cigar business.
200 nautical miles defines a continental shelf.
A strait is the exact opposite of an isthmus.

TRUISMS

Black cars are the most accident prone.
Every gamekeeper in sleep kills a poacher.
Heroism can only be accomplished alone.
A screaming hot oven cooks a superb turkey.

Complainants are always quickest to write.
Egotism in American generals is matchless.
After Labor Day, fashion wears no white.
Nothing hides construction flaws like a mattress.

The soul is composed of intellect and will.
"Miss USA" is different than "Miss America."
Feminist arguments are predominantly shrill.
Obscurantists wear the mask of esoterica.

If it's not true for you, it's not true is false.
The least popular car color is Kelly green.
Triple time is standard tempo for the waltz.
High NPR salaries are patently obscene.

The Olympic Games are strictly political.
No earthly horizon is factually real.
Moral confusion is a synonym for Levitical.
All glaciers are the exact color of teal.

The success of a throw depends upon release.
Scots pronounce scone to rhyme with *gone*.
Female flesh sings covered with nylon.
Films with black actors sell poorly overseas.

All beauty contestants have high smiles.
Great decisions are always improvised.
Anal retentives take comfort in turnstiles.
An unloved child is forever tyrannized.

Potatoes fried in fish oil never brown.
Blacks are rarely seen at a Nascar race.
Rooms don't exist for tourists in Bhutan.
Asians loathe being touched on the face.

Gridlock in Congress makes Wall Street pleased.
Truman Capote loved writing about kites.
Women in a see-thru blouse are always teased.
Salat al-Janazah comprises Islamic last rites.

Hangmen tie the noose behind the left ear.
The manicure sticks come from sour orange.
What a glow illuminates is obscured by glare.
A rhombus is standard shape for a lozenge.

Crows suspect anything symmetrical.
Restaurants in France let dogs come in.
Arnold Schönberg's music is numerical.
To Baptists, boozing is the vilest sin.

Asians go to movies in the afternoon.
Texture is, in fact, a kind of color.
The grayest month in San Diego's June.
Than hockey coaches, no one's duller.

TRUISMS

Mallomars are never shipped in summer.
A shepherd has a spouse in a sheepdog.
Than auto dealer ads, nothing is dumber.
A low-flow toilet is guaranteed to clog.

Abraham was not, and never was, a Jew.
Low self-esteem mainly causes frigidity.
Lard is preferred to butter in a Cajun roux.
Prejudice demands a mind of rank rigidity.

A prophet with piety aches to be stoned.
Flatbreads exist in every world cuisine.
Gregorian chant is not sung but intoned.
All short women need a shoe chopine.

To press a tweed suit always sponge it first,
More than 60% of the tango is just walking.
A victim of poverty is everywhere coerced.
Government taxation is form of stalking.

A gift of yellow flowers brings bad luck.
The British smoke Cavendish, not Burley.
Nesting in trees is safety for a wood duck.
An actress should break her mirror early.

Pemmican is the ultimate survival food.
The more ignorant the man, the firmer the belief.
A perizoma graces Christ on every rood.
Of wanton cruelty there is never full relief.

Doctrine is comfort softer than a pillow.
No child molester isn't a human cold front.
Aspirin is extracted from bark of a willow.
No hard-hitting slugger should ever bunt.

Trial is properly coupled with error.
The Holy Koran is banned in Israel.
All anticipation carries an aspect of terror.
Metal caskets transgress a "green" burial.

The true outlaw hog is a Harley-Davidson 74.
In novels Dickens ignored Canada and Australia.
As long as two people live, there will be war.
Incomprehension characterizes all glossolalia.

All great houses in England have hidden a Cavalier.
American Indians never fought except on horseback.
"Gay"'s about men to men; ambiguous is "queer."
Shouting is considered vile in games of blackjack.

The Chinese economy is based on irrigation.
Yellow surfboards are a taboo, inviting sharks.
The brilliance of any spy is infiltration.
Disgruntled describes the Hebrew patriarchs.

Feta is not a traditional cheese on Crete.
Intense pain on a chin can indicate heart attack.
Smell predominates in the fetish of feet.
All four-funnel ocean liners had one fake stack.

TRUISMS

Jewish folks rarely become alcoholics.
Chinese wines are never taken seriously.
Always a euphemism is the word *frolics*.
Marches convey might imperiously.

The English butter bread before slicing it.
No President wants to leave the White House.
A gift is cheapened by someone pricing it.
A perfect warble is the *lek* of a black grouse.

John Wayne thought *High Noon* un-American.
All servile gratitude harbors keen resentment.
All women hugely dislike eating terrapin.
Autocrats delight in the Second Amendment.

Antagonism often constitutes courtship behavior.
No detriment in dating surpasses a runny nose.
Snails—escargots—have no natural flavor.
Great writers excel at both poetry and prose.

Envy is the only deadly sin that gives no pleasure.
Gertrude Jekyll called gardening "making pictures."
What we are is divulged by how we use our leisure.
The structures of all religions are mainly strictures.

Picking up a check is a macho reveal.
Trig formulas hail from image of a circle.
Preciosity is the vice of the genteel.
Fish speed is aided by a tail heterocercal.

Every nation produces its own flatbread.
H. L. Mencken hated reading fiction.
Society dies downward from the head.
Love and duty stand in contradiction.

Popping off a rubber lid sounds B-flat.
Money has value because we agree it does.
Sweetness is lost on the taste of a cat.
One ancestor of Jesus Christ was Boaz.

Filial piety is central to Confucian ethics.
Foxglove is poisonous to human beings.
Dried fruit is unhealthy for asthmatics.
Fleeing contextualizes the act of skiing.

All cancer drugs are carcinogenic.
Slow-witted people cannot be hypnotized.
New Guineans are rarely photogenic.
Money being passed is never sanitized.

A scar on any human is a trophy.
Undefeated despair is very dangerous.
Darkness is to rain a natural strophe.
Every hunt in a handbag's clangorous.

Lek behavior is a courting display.
A man who loves uniforms has a troop for a soul.
UK elections are held on Thursday.
Revolution is ever spoiling in the heart of a prole.

TRUISMS

The sound of a crowd is a single voice.
California surfers wear shades in the water.
Between two bad options is never a choice.
Than the Carolina Reaper, nothing is hotter.

Tsunamis travel faster in deep water.
Suffering is often linked to beatitude.
Every father is hostage to his daughter.
Vice always begins with ingratitude.

Errors are invariably caused by speed.
There are no literary programs on TV.
No Southern state managed to secede.
Black tea in China is called "red tea."

It's perfection in marriage vows that suborns.
Looking at it never fattened a pig.
Every dilemma faced has officially two horns.
No Ivy League sophomore isn't a prig.

An Irishman argues even with himself.
The Pacific Ocean usurps most of Earth's space.
A lawyer's nose can smell only pelf.
A woman's plucked eyebrows empty her face.

All national flags (but Nepal) are rectangles.
Art galleries trade not in paintings but assets.
It is envy in the jealous lover that strangles.
Never fail to serve toast points with *rillettes*.

Colonialism is a greedy reach of capitalism.
Perfumed is the scent of pencil shavings.
The United Nations judged Zionism racism.
A frontier virtue was ever thrift in savings.

Every single snowflake has six points.
Facing death reduces everything to nothing.
An act of charity itself blessedly anoints.
True innocence is incapable of blushing.

Long emails virtually never get read.
Americans love ignoring speed limit signs.
The Middle East is woefully inbred.
Hucksters, to avoid taxes, become "divines."

To catch a mackerel always use a sprat.
Confidence is the child of optimism.
Wine to age well needs an oaken vat.
True sanctity exudes its own chrism.

The Koranic verse the 9/11 hijackers followed
is Surah al-Anfal 67, a chapter on the spoils of war,
where vows against one's enemies are hallowed
and in the sacred name of the Holy Prophet swore.

Nothing familiar can ever seem sublime.
It is always easy to demagogue the poor.
No war ever waged is not a violent crime.
Jealousy as a mood is a perpetual sore.

TRUISMS

Using potato water perfects a bread dough.
Saudis disdain gold less than 24 carats.
Human remains are prohibited air cargo.
Rare insight is a gift of Russian *starets*.

Asians have no interest in playing hockey.
Dams and reservoirs cause earthquakes.
Treading on new uniforms calms a jockey.
Wiccans and Odinists revere mandrakes.

Exhibitionism is a self-hater's disease.
Toxic rapeseed gave birth to granola.
Arabic and Sicilian comprise Maltese.
No vaccine now exists to fight Ebola.

One finger over, one under properly plucks a rose.
Coffee for iced coffee should be heated first.
No gentleman, dining, accepts the slightest noise.
A law that has passed must be duly coerced.

35% of blacks have a white male ancestor.
Bees only wake up when weather is warm.
Trust provides access to a child molester.
The craven mind yearns badly to conform.

Early Christians were authentic socialists.
Any interest over 25% is strictly illegal.
The state of tree roots is never motionless.
The female is larger than the male bald eagle.

ALEXANDER THEROUX

Water weighs 800 times more than air.
Doctors, outside their field, are poorly educated.
Pater Noster is the paradigmatic prayer.
Mandarin Chinese is never conjugated.

Houdini relocked the handcuffs he escaped.
Viruses resist all antibiotics.
To fit nests, not to roll, eggs are so shaped.
Graffiti is proletarian semiotics.

Pulp fiction is the *id* of modern literature.
Money—plain cash—is the universal belay.
The Japanese adore anything in miniature.
There's always a watered appearance to moiré.

Any charity congratulating the giver is false.
All science fiction shows low literary strain.
Oceans are mainly polluted by earth's salts.
A priest is *forever* one by act of holy ordain.

Scandinavian women favor a formal tress.
Bulgarians nod their heads when saying "No,"
but they shake their heads when saying "Yes."
Driest climates produce a premier guano.

Vodka, a distilled beverage, has no taste.
Elvis Presley had zero interview skills.
Computers, TVs, telephones are toxic waste.
Everyone is divorced in Beverly Hills.

TRUISMS

Salzburg was never warm to Mozart.
No one ever acts on single motives.
Every marriage has a weird flow chart.
No vow holds without godly votives.

It is illegal to hunt doves in Vermont.
Never vote for a political incumbent.
Steve Jobs created the first digital font.
Neither prone nor supine is recumbent.

You never see Native Americans with a beard.
Headway is lost when driving through sand.
A black stone by Muslims is highly revered.
Canaanites inhabited the original Promised Land.

Letters are the actual sounds we see.
Apostates yearn to justify themselves.
Mount Rushmore is 50% scree.
It is not fear we conquer but ourselves.

Never allow a fruit orchard to get warm.
Domestic cats go unmentioned in Scripture.
To stifle your best talents, only conform.
For boxers, a corrupt retinue is a fixture.

In college, women aren't allowed to wrestle men.
Republican conventions are never disorderly.
The designation for U.S. Interstate (freeway) is 10.
The adjective for decimal, never used, is denary.

Judge a baseball manager by his handling a bullpen.
No religion stands for the empowerment of women.
Tarantula kebabs are delicacies in Phnom Penh.
A working battery can be constructed from a lemon.

A motivated seller immediately loses leverage.
Maria Callas believed singers part of an orchestra.
Over 190% proof is allowed no alcohol beverage.
In France, no schoolboys can wear a yarmulke.

Smiling in any Congo wedding is forbidden.
American Hasidim disvalue spoken Hebrew.
Beauty secrets advertise what is to be hidden.
Every vision, by definition, creates a preview.

Credit card companies are usurers to a one.
In Schubert's *Winterreise* the piano is a singer.
Suicide, by the mere thought of it, has begun.
Egalitarianism animates a true left-winger.

Books written on economics are never lucid.
Rainer Rilke was always hostile to America.
Mystic vision is often a gift to the reclusive.
The credulous find great refuge in esoterica.

Italian products have always set the style.
A manservant is worth a hundred gadgets.
Every realtor's rhetoric thrives on guile.
Grandiosity is a major trait of psychopathics.

TRUISMS

No Frenchman goes without his Laguiole.
Forests in Shakespeare are free from constraint.
Always disconnect first the negative pole.
Monomania is the main trait in a Catholic saint.

Queen Elizabeth never wears colored nail polish.
Policy is the godfather of all strategy.
To deconstruct is the living antonym of demolish.
Logic, compared to truth, is a tragedy.

Wisdom was once ascribed to court fools.
Seal meat never tastes of fish.
Fishbones, millennia ago, were held as jewels.
Truly to communicate, a gay must dish.

Swag is customarily stolen property.
Mafiosi always seek golf courses to talk.
Mona Lisa: painted on wood of a poplar tree.
Any mimic of a baseball pitch is a balk.

Standard eye charts always start with an E,
but best to determine one's visual accuracy
the letters C, D, E, F, L, N, O, P, T and Z
turn out to be the only letters you will see.

Filipinos are crazy about beauty pageants.
The Masters starts on the back nine, Sunday.
Memory at best is shattered fragments.
Denial is often a major protraction of delay.

Gasoline prices in summer always increase.
Yiddish butchers the poetic German tongue.
Thieving is a commonplace among police.
The merits of volunteers always go unsung.

All art is basically stylish propaganda.
The Ulster accent is the ugliest on earth.
Bamboo alone satisfies the giant panda.
Of Earth's diamonds there is no dearth.

A mocking Irish honorific is "Himself."
A forgiving man never gains great power.
No Ghibelline ever cared about a Guelph.
No Scot even in happiness is not dour.

Opposition is the prerogative of all writers.
Robert Benchley never wrote a funny line.
All garlics are natural infection fighters.
Every criminal sanction is a monetary fine.

The unpredictable plays to the unexpected.
A major hallmark of a bore: retailing dreams.
Aid to the Third World is always misdirected
because it is siphoned off by corrupt regimes.

No one correctly pronounces "clothes."
Pick Brussels sprouts after a freeze.
Many a spinster had too long a nose.
Someone sneezing makes you sneeze.

TRUISMS

Women's facial creams are basically lard.
Climate in the Sudan turns every native a wraith.
British upper classes snub those trying hard.
Cradle believers tend to be casual of their faith.

Condors are notoriously heavy sleepers.
Assume every downed power line is live.
Brutal dictators are famously all weepers.
Most apple trees down South rarely thrive.

Genetically, there is no such thing as a Mexican.
Marathoners run faster in 40-degree temperatures.
The smallest bones are in the ear of any skeleton.
No Congressman doesn't pad his expenditures.

Improbability is never a barrier to gossip.
Princess Margaret hated being seated next to women.
Any milk needs alcohol to make a posset.
There are generally eight seeds in any given lemon.

Freshwater has a lower density than saltwater.
Maple sap best flows during winter thaws.
Nothing lacks definition more than manslaughter.
A person's vulnerability depends on flaws.

Shakespeare's kids neither saw nor read his plays.
Only a half-wit hasn't strong opinions.
To mimic a lawn, gaming tables bluff with baise.
Brits called all early natives "Virginians."

ALEXANDER THEROUX

Sexual attraction clouds the purity of love.
The Lone Ranger shot to wound, never to kill.
Rue is evoked in the coo of a mourning dove.
The world's most glorious beaches are in Brazil.

Brown is inarguably the color of flavor.
Deceit is often purveyed by way of charm.
Waiting to be served food is often to savor.
Women say male beauty is found in the arm.

Actors—*flaneurs*—love to sport ascots.
Sex is essentially an enemy of the head.
Goofiness describes all product mascots.
Renaissance painters used poisonous white lead.

Photographic subjects, sitting, are tentative.
Locations of Biblical sites are all uncertain.
Scripture encourages the philoprogenitive.
Fabric, not the lining, is face of the curtain.

Many battle re-enactors scarily transform.
All earnest people are immune to irony.
A blowing west wind is legendarily warm.
The one and only British gourd is bryony.

Mack Sennett did not believe in re-takes.
Good-looking women cultivate plain-looking women.
Quark is always used in Polish cheesecakes.
Nothing soothes a strained voice better than lemon.

TRUISMS

Cruciferous vegetables offend your smell.
China boasts more than half a billion bicycles.
Accord with Corsicans and Italians never jell.
Inversions in scouting are no longer obstacles.

No Mt. Rushmore figures face same direction.
Every filled *jardinière* constitutes a flag.
Between Greek and Turk there is little affection.
A mattress cover was the World War I body bag.

In China you often see a plate that's square.
Most folks surnamed Washington are black.
The fewer the words, the better the prayer.
There are no detectable odors on a yak.

Jealousy is not a Polynesian characteristic.
Heavily garnished cheeseburgers taste worse.
Camels in the Old Testament are anachronistic.
Poetry looks down its scornful nose at verse.

A small uncircumcised penis pisses fifty ways.
When royals travel, black outfits must be packed.
To cook you boil, but to tenderize you braise.
If not written down, it is never formally a pact.

Russians fanatically love the play *Hamlet*.
Emptiness is a natural condition in South Dakota.
A determined handshake is invariably a gambit.
Water constitutes half the county of Sarasota.

Marriage is a sideshow to an ambitious man.
South American cities ride on syncopation.
The lower the IQ, the more important the tan.
A Chinese cook is flattered by an eructation.

Television—the first fifty years—was junk.
British royalty do not eat shellfish or wear fur.
Self-denial and prayer identify the true monk.
Jesus' body was wrapped in aloes and myrrh.

Great wealth at birth cultivates the eccentric.
Campaign promises when not lies, are juvenile.
Ripples in water are customarily concentric.
Unknowable to human sensation is the noumenal.

Always leave a little on your plate in France.
Chivalry always effects a check on passion.
Disapproval's eyes necessarily look askance.
A lackey mind inescapably relies on fashion.

Old money flaunts wealth by countersignaling.
Propinquity is the *summum bonum* of the lonely.
Hiding, not joining, marks compulsive mingling.
Diplomatic graciousness is of necessity phony.

In an egalitarian age, royals receive no respect.
The Kaaba was originally, green, red, and white.
Flight 13s or Row 13s are not found on airline jets.
Changing his mind makes a person truly contrite.

TRUISMS

Cheyenne used horses for hunting, Paiutes ate them.
Grieving people are prone to mad behavior.
The Elizabethans kept wild bears solely to bait them.
We are all sinners in need of Christ, the Savior.

Mississippians pronounce the river "*Missippi.*"
Sodomy was an American felony until 1962.
A faux Indian became the profile of a hippy.
The true full Indian name was *Nadoues*sioux.

Mama is the Tamil word for uncle.
North and South American Indians are one race.
Garlic is by its nature anti-fungal.
Due to the Vietnam War America lost its face.

Romance is invariably luxurious self-deceit.
No graceful lover hugs but rather caresses.
Arches do not exist on an infant baby's feet.
Charity given, eternally that giver blesses.

Close female friendships are dangerous.
Thirst is actually a primordial emotion.
Uncertainty, by definition, endangers us.
Explored is only 5% of the world's ocean.

Justice to be truly balanced must avenge.
Presbyterian hymns are always multi-versy.
Forgiveness is the most complete revenge.
Nothing is more admirable than mercy.

Gustave Mahler never wrote an opera.
Oxen were cheaper than mules for pioneers.
Flavorlessness is the key to a premier vodka.
Claude Monet's *Sunrise* was initially met with jeers.

Canvas was denominated *twill* in the old west.
No Tiffany box may leave the store empty.
To stare at inordinately is unfailingly to molest.
Greed is never satisfied with merely plenty.

Buddhist teaching focuses most on diligence.
Any animal bellow is strictly called a *"wrawl."*
American pioneers were called emigrants, never immigrants.
Monkeys consume whole bananas, peel and all.

Tiffany cuts diamonds for brilliance, not size.
Marlborough fought no battle he did not win.
Lustmongers manifest strangely dead eyes.
Idioglossia is quite commonplace among twins.

Pornographers are sworn enemies of women.
Graffiti is always assured of an audience.
Both adding and subtracting apply to "trimming."
Othering in any form betrays intolerance.

The Greeks have always fought the Persians.
1852 led western migration in the 19th century.
All written history recounts merely versions.
Major crimes are forged in every penitentiary.

TRUISMS

Christopher Marlowe signed his name "Marley."
Conestoga wagons (too heavy) rarely went west.
The first grain in the Fertile Crescent was barley.
Legacies of rickets are bowlegs and pigeon breast.

Each new Shakespeare book apologizes for its existence.
What's sought in love are the missing parts of ourselves.
Sabotage was the essential tool of the French Resistance.
The Library of Congress has 838 miles of bookshelves.

A collapsed crater is more circular than a caldera.
The Turn of the Screw, a puzzle, should not be solved.
Honey with crocodile poo formed Egyptian mascara.
Quietism is the wan, decrepit faith of the uninvolved.

Rapists begin as ransackers of houses.
All blue jeans are white cotton, dyed.
Hazel twigs are the favorite of dowsers.
The toxic in nature is commonly pied.

No wedding reception excludes "Blue Moon."
No poaching liquid should reach full boil.
At Christmas, slaves traditionally ate raccoon.
Most of the world fertilizes with night soil.

Birth matters more than effort or talent.
European chocolate is the best for desserts.
Vaingloriousness open poses as gallant.
In blind dating, neediness always subverts.

Spring buds bloom faster at the treetop.
White chocolate is not legally chocolate.
The lawn is America's most useless crop.
Greed finds its spouse in anything corporate.

Israel's largest export is *African* diamonds.
In con man lingo, "Roscoe" is a boob or idiot.
Without bees, there would be no almonds.
No one's more immune to reason than a bigot.

Cholos passionately love chrome on a car.
All round-cut diamonds boast 58 facets.
The South Celestial Pole lacks a polar star
A Trappist seeks meditation in the tacit.

Codemakers are unrivaled codebreakers.
Islam maintains a bias against shaving.
Grizzle (black & gray) sells best with wigmakers
Self-control's offended by obstinate craving.

While geese in air are called a "skein,"
on land or water they're called a "gaggle."
Water on silk will invariably stain.
Causing loss of face is cruel in a haggle.

Most Korean men are filled with anger.
Ford takes credit for the grill of Jeeps.
Tranquility turns to sloth via languor.
Conscience without action only sleeps.

TRUISMS

All eyeglass frames are hugely overpriced.
Puns are intellectually clever, never funny.
A spliced rope's stronger than one un-spliced
Not a speck of paper is used in U.S. money.

Given names are shortened in Australia.
Tapestries don't wear out but merely shrink.
Nectar and leaves are poison on an azalea.
A green blood is actually found in a skink.

Thick tweed never moves with the body.
Chicken raising is now hideous manufacture.
Daily executions are nothing to a Saudi.
A falling dollar bill is impossible to capture.

Utah's the land of the open-pit mine,
A weed is a plant in the wrong place.
Justice and mercy almost never align.
Jellyfish seem never to have a face.

A standard postage stamp contains 5.9 calories.
Stage left or right is from POV of the performer.
A certain sensuality pervades museum galleries.
Excess zeal is the bane of every reformer.

The smaller a chili pepper, the hotter it is.
Alexander Pope claimed he never laughed in his life.
Speed characterizes each and very quiz.
Every wetland is threatened by invasive loosestrife.

ALEXANDER THEROUX

Only an ignoramus scribbles in a book.
Baking soda and baking powder are the same.
Employ a crook to find another crook.
Human nature exults in the downfall of fame.

Sri Lankans are fanatics of horoscopes.
Bald men with long beards are terrifying.
Monasticism is sanctuary for misanthropes.
Handling rubber cement is super-satisfying.

In China not a single thing is wasted.
An average wing beat takes a bird three feet.
A tonsillectomy kills anything tasted.
Oak trees mysteriously all tend to accrete.

The Amish only use tractors with iron wheels.
Queen Victoria was never fond of bishops.
Every traduced Irishman is closed to appeals
The compulsions of any habit are vicious.

Joy is a gourmet dinner on a racing train.
A held pigeon will never struggle or bite.
Swastikas are a symbol of a gate to a Jain.
Self-loathing is the sole cause of stage fright.

Acronyms fascinate the military mind.
Spitting in Iceland is a national habit.
Tamil and Sinhalese are never aligned.
Every women's group resembles a *sabbit*.

TRUISMS

Everything that exists is created by God.
Aromatic herbs all prefer a sandy soil.
Confederate soldiers all were poorly shod.
Apple trees suck nitrogen from soil.

Capitalism is an adversary of democracy.
Only female mosquitoes deliver a sting.
Tolerance is absent in every last theocracy.
No quartet is not enhanced by the string.

Altoona as a place name elicits chuckles.
Embassies abound with small gilt chairs.
Bullies and gorillas depend on knuckles.
Nothing's briefer than shelf life in pears.

Nowhere in nature can be found pure cobalt.
On his art Michelangelo rarely left a signature.
Slapping a person is battery but never assault.
Only tiny *versions* can be called miniature.

The Porcellian drink of choice is beer with gin.
Every nationalist dines out on being a patriot.
An insouciant loser is far more prone to win.
No Irish immigrant isn't a saccharine expatriate.

Everyone who accepts payment is a menial.
Hitting high C is a requisite for an operatic tenor.
Repetition is at the heart of anything remedial.
A man's handshake evinces a persuasive thenar.

Television's principal god is commerce.
A head of a screw should always face out.
Pierced noses were rare with tribal Nez Perce.
Inquisition victims were first splayed out.

Strict Jains eat neither onions nor potatoes.
Nothing is beautiful from every point of view.
Nicotine traces can be found in all tomatoes.
Every bunion can thank a pointed shoe.

All permafrost is thousands of years old.
Wild male pigeons never migrate.
Silver is the secret alloy of green gold
Gaza is an enslavement prison, not a state.

Advertising is the crowing of abundance.
English servants keep their palms turned backwards.
"Corrupt politician" is classic redundance.
Sexually dimorphism characterizes blackbirds.

Reserve is often mistaken for intellect
Shylock disappears in Act V of the play.
Every form of spoken English is dialect.
To shape it correctly, always wet a beret.

Lament by repetition defines the blues.
Kitsch prefers to say *homes*, not *houses*.
The best soft cow's-milk cheeses ooze.
An animal stays thin because it browses.

TRUISMS

Lingerie predominates in lesbian pulp fiction.
Adolf Hitler started a war he wanted to lose.
Pectin as a gelling agent increases excretion.
Eros, not height, governs all stiletto shoes.

Swedish women are reputed to be termagants.
Albany, London grand flats, one never calls *The* Albany.
Possession is insulted by impermanence.
Medieval Catholicism originated almonry.

Scots never hyphenate double surnames.
A birdhouse with any side open is useless.
Midway shills luxuriate in word games.
Rednecks predominate among the toothless.

Tassels are inherently provocative.
Airplane intercoms have yet to be perfected.
The Swiss, who rarely entertain, are untalkative.
Every obese child's personality is badly affected.

Homosexuals make successful spies.
No wool, without a mordant, dyes well.
Tartness is the secret to key lime pies.
Death is the message of any bell's knell.

Wearing hats prevents mastoiditis.
The queen in chess was originally male.
Slavs in general venerate St. Vitus.
Hard candy is almost universally stale.

Anything referencing turtles is a slur in China.
Jane Austen's Darcy is never physically described.
The South has a birthright on the name Dinah.
Wearing a Muslim veil in Quebec is proscribed.

Chinese love stone, wooden, and ceramic pillows.
Solitaries exaggerate the importance of their thoughts.
Only single corridors are ever dug by armadillos.
Sexlessness is perfectly embodied by severe culottes.

Killer Jeffrey Dahmer was movie star handsome.
The Alice Blue garment wasn't a gown but a wrapper.
The practice of towing vehicles is vile ransom.
Ash is the perfect wood to construct a tailor's clapper.

Phlegm in the lungs, in fact, constitutes pus.
Vegetables are the *sine qua non* of any diet.
Apostasy to a believing Moslem is treasonous.
Only a thousand people can speak Paiute.

Faces on "missing" posters always look naïve.
No woman has ever been Senate Majority Leader.
Stress makes it difficult for a woman to conceive.
The best wood for making pencils is incense cedar.

No two ever know the same in their knowing.
1940s lesbians all wore T-shirts backwards.
Unhappily married men are forever seagoing.
The carol's "four calling birds" are blackbirds.

TRUISMS

Collecting in the final analysis is hoarding.
Black is never allowed on any prison garb.
Tinfoil was employed in the first recording.
The sweeter the taste, the redder the rhubarb.

Shakespeare gave wit to sinners, never to saints.
Unlike other planets, Uranus rotates on its side.
A gentleman's grace is evidenced in his restraints.
Mr. Hyde knew not Jekyll, but Jekyll knew Hyde.

Only nine official public schools exist in Britain.
In Japan no formal guest may pour his own drink.
A brief shelf life exists for anyone who's smitten.
Parrots can quite unnaturally be poisoned by zinc.

An ancho pepper is simply a dried poblano.
Everything is changed but nothing ever perishes.
The violin has the female pitch of a soprano.
There is extremism in any mood that cherishes.

Birds prefer grapevine bark for their nests.
Chinese men are rabid cigarette smokers.
Amazon warriors amputated their *right* breasts.
Submission is signified by fashion chokers.

Rich old ladies have faces of expensive cats.
It is the *blandness* in eating liver that appalls.
Americans show a frenzy for baseball hats.
Fish use their internal organs as mating calls.

The human hand is a natural funnel.
A hot knife spreads anything that's gooey.
Every biome has its very own tunnel.
Any agglomeration can comprise chop suey.

Artichokes, when cut, quickly oxidate.
Ambition is almost always unstable.
Processed foods invariably constipate.
A wimperg makes the noblest gable.

Always discard any clams that float.
True evil *gently* courts an opponent.
Any inherent minor tonality is a blue note.
A debate is ruined by an interponent.

The best soil for vegetables is sandy loam.
Refreezing thawed foods is perfectly fine.
Drought has negligible effect on brome.
The archaic plural word for cow is kine.

Charlotte's Web is a Jain nightmare.
The thigh bone in the human body is the hardest.
One is literally cooked in the electric chair.
Making money is never the goal of the smartest.

Complaisant virtues soon become vices.
Birds flock to divide a raptor's attention.
Anti-oxidants abound in herbs and spices.
No drink is not improved by gentian.

TRUISMS

The Crow Indians despised the Dakota.
Regardless of the source, sugar works the same.
Toyota Motors founder was Kiichiri *Toyoda*.
No A.com is available as a domain name.

A stream never rises higher than its source.
Europeans find American bread too sweet.
Texting/driving laws are impossible to enforce.
1 Timothy 4:3 prohibits the eating of meat.

Manhole covers need to be round.
Mangoes, hard to peel at one end, are easy from the other.
Tomorrow's dreams are never found.
No rapist ever had a loving mother.

Birgit Nilsson *was* Wagner's Brünnhilde.
Jesus never once refers to a mother's love.
Beheaded means one's *given* a head—*de*headed, killed.
Mating for life is a trait of a mourning dove.

The best human possibilities lie close to the worst.
Sixteen tablespoons equal a single cup.
Fatty buildup in the liver can never be reversed.
It is lethal for humans to eat a fresh buttercup.

Hip-hop lyrics must attest by being "street."
No rabid sleuth on the web has a real job.
Healthiest by far is a crab's *brown* meat.
A mustache was a must for a 1930s heartthrob.

Sea breezes occur by day, not at night.
The most common anti-oxidant is lemon juice.
Joan Miró preferred to paint on Masonite.
Blandishments in any business deal is a ruse.

An east wind always blows west.
No recipes ever call for roasted chestnuts.
No one's more amiable than an uninvited guest
Every shape can be found in doughnuts.

The English fancy using initials for first names.
Any knot weakens any rope's strength.
Professionalism has tainted the Olympic Games.
Depth of acquaintance depends not on length.

The blazing sun is a star and not a planet.
Smoking *and* cigarettes are banned in Bhutan.
There are no external nostrils on a gannet.
Tree nuts come every two years on a pecan.

Optimum temperature in a fridge is 38 degrees.
The best coffee comes from Arabica beans.
A major paraphilia fixes on a woman's knees.
Democracy in fashion is the story of jeans.

Most outlaw bikers have swastika fetish.
Many aspiring musicians attend art school.
Deception is a compulsion of the coquettish.
Any northernmost land is considered Thule.

TRUISMS

Being a royal bastard is considered to be chic.
The scents jasmine and patchouli go well on furs.
Any statesman of conscience is driven to leak.
Ingratitude is a preconditional vice in curs.

Never decant a red wine 20-years-old or older.
Illiterates believe good grammar an affectation.
Term limits are abhorred by every officeholder.
Beautiful women cannot endure moderation.

The Hell's Angels major event is the Labor Day run.
Wives conventionally claim men wash dishes poorly.
Shakespeare over 3000 times depended on the pun.
The scientific is hobbled by thinking prematurely.

No American in Charles Dickens' work is admirable.
There is no Christian equivalent to Yom Kippur.
Every last planet in our solar system is inhabitable.
A person has to be terrified in order to abhor.

Each branch of the U.S. military wears different shoes.
Nothing is worse than outlasting your applause.
Literally, to sin by keeping silent is to be self-accused.
Parvenus refuse a final S to the word *vichysoisse*.

Most left-handers in baseball are low-ball hitters.
Speaking with an arm outside one's toga was bad manners.
Most right-handers in baseball are high-ball hitters.
Handling chemicals shortened the lives of tanners.

Shakespeare's teacher, Simon Hart, was a Jesuit.
Purgatory, according to Protestants, does not exist.
Great chefs handling an ingredient never measure it.
Every last used car salesman is a proctologist.

Toothpicks are made mainly of birch.
NYC imported Chicagoans to build its skyscrapers.
Catholicism's cheek to jowl with Anglican High Church.
Serious art is ascribed to significant wallpapers.

A plan, like a tree, must have branches.
Everything is taxed in Massachusetts.
Virtue is claimed by refuge in ranches.
Kindness is the essential message of Confucius.

Every single marine is a rifleman.
No great western trail went through Arizona.
There is no F, G, H, I, or J vitamin.
A couturier sells not product but persona.

Peanut butter is not available in France.
Presidential candidates' books all suck.
Conceiving a baby is an act of chance.
A serious loner yearns to drive a truck.

Mining takes an appalling toll on the landscape.
No black man could become a Confederate soldier.
Mourning officially utilizes the fabric called crape.
Mobility and stability war in the human shoulder.

TRUISMS

Baptists pray no prayers for the dead.
One never says "Amen" to his own blessing.
No Frenchman can enjoy a meal without bread.
The Puritan locates his worship in repressing.

Silver greatly alters the taste of caviar.
Caste is only another name for control.
The best dugout canoes come from Zanzibar.
No one country owns the North Pole.

Art school is a holding pen for rejects.
St. Patrick—cf. *Hamlet*—is patron saint of Purgatory.
No one can explain the allergy to latex.
A bent, creased old baseball card is basically nugatory.

No cooking substitute exists for saffron.
Chinese have deathly fear of the number four.
Domestic deaths predominate in bathrooms.
Enough in avarice is the opposite of more.

Herbaceous borders were created for economy.
No American wife can share her husband's title.
Explorers' discovery dreams include eponymy.
The rhetoric of all barflies is endless self-recital.

White divisions on a volleyball are hexagonal.
A tattoo of #13 indicates a marijuana smoker.
Broken pediments in British estates are fashionable.
Tribal African women love the adornment of ocher.

When a hero succeeds in Shakespeare, disaster ensues.
Conversing on a telephone in public is ignorant.
Angels and hearts mainly predominate in human tattoos.
The Romani, or Roma, are traditionally itinerant.

All the members of the Hell's Angels hate the AMA.
No whitebait meal exceeds that in a London tavern.
Depend on selfishness in the mien of every gourmet.
A *kludd* is designated chaplain of any Klan klavern.

Elephants cannot stand exceeding cold.
No fireman ever wears another's helmet.
Numerosity in Biblical terms is sevenfold.
Egyptians consider immodest any anklet.

Salt pork is an essential chowder ingredient.
Social chaos is fertile ground for extremists.
An ultimatum is catnip to the disobedient.
Fashion models are templates for bulimics.

The feudal system actually comforted all classes.
A "prairie schooner" was twelve feet long and four feet wide.
Seen in a positive light are Scriptural wild asses.
A gay not interested in anal sex is called a "side."

Imitation in its every form is praise.
Goliath never precedes the name David when cited.
Béarnaise is child to its mother hollandaise.
No slums compared to Dhaka's are more benighted.

TRUISMS

Colossal egotism in a person is never sane.
Son Willie's death made Lincoln hate Thursdays.
The Hindu religion refuses to include a Jain.
A summary is less detailed than any paraphrase.

Satisfaction with the world is of no poetic use.
Waterways gave formula names to Civil War battles.
Always serve medium rare the breast of goose.
No singular exists for the noun cattle or cattles.

Milliners have exploited the scarlet tanager.
Proust's work of art in fact *rediscovers* lost time.
Button Gwinnet's is the rarest U.S. signature.
The nadir of all entertainment has to be a mime.

Sun and heat after rain bring out butterflies.
Network nightly news is one-third commercials,
Fastidious people are difficult to hypnotize.
Plots of crime novels deal solely with reversals.

Both of Shakespeare's parents were illiterate.
Jews are manufacturers of most children's toys.
Bone-crushing handshakes are always deliberate.
Girls tend to be slower visual learners than boys.

Jesus avoided the terms "father" or "mother."
A pacifist wants to be right, not to *do* right.
Wisdom is presumed by every older brother.
A critic relishes an opportunity for spite.

A wine must be sweeter when paired with a food.
Paint failures are caused by moisture and damp.
Scandinavians by their nature are born to brood.
Work, pathopsychologically, is agony to a tramp.

Jews never call their Bible the Old Testament.
R. W. Emerson refused to lecture in the South.
Seawater will induce low slump in making fresh cement.
Snake migration greatly increases in a drought.

Shakespeare wrote mainly for commoners.
Physical traits usually jump a generation.
Singapore is a city-state quite hostile to foreigners.
There is in bananas a measure of radiation.

Vladimir Nabokov never once visited Moscow.
Baedeker guides all dealt in racial stereotypes.
It is strictly counterproductive to pull a Dutch hoe.
It is illegal to throw away the Stars and Stripes.

Few are your chances surviving slab avalanche.
Searching for similarities discovers differences.
For virtuous boasting visit an American ranch.
The cross is anathema to Jehovah's Witnesses.

"White trash" as a phrase is a racist slur.
A stutterer need not be a stammerer.
No one in show business is not a poseur.
Every street in London sports a camera.

TRUISMS

A pity Thoreau wasn't with Lewis and Clark.
The Kikuyu won't eat hens, dismissing it as women food.
The spice of cinnamon is from evergreen inner-tree bark.
Unprotected indicates naked, whereas unclothed is nude.

The tallest men in Europe are from Montenegro.
Referring to oneself in the third person is paranoid.
Six different states have all claimed Sarajevo.
All neurosis was sexual to priapic Dr. Sigmund Freud.

Ballplayers should only be paid at season's end.
Boasts of genius bespeak underlying uncertainty.
Frankness is the speaking language of the friend.
The most *terroir*-conscious of wine regions is Burgundy.

Wearing mufti detracts from being a nun.
The Huron were the most easily converted by Jesuits.
An almost perfect sphere is described by the sun.
Rare and unvoiced is the obstruent consonant tenuis.

Homosexuals, strangely, never get the gout.
Silk is invariably reeled, and never spun.
The best of campfire meals is rainbow trout.
A certain laboriousness attends to every pun.

Free will is but another name for fate.
The most unhittable strikes are always low.
To be rude, a guest need only be late.
One always flirts with tragedy to know.

ALEXANDER THEROUX

A dead clam—trash—will always float in water.
Herman Melville attended all Emerson's NYC lectures.
Chicanery is not uncommon on a police blotter.
Wildness is ever at war with landscape architectures.

Belief can never be compelled by violence.
Hamlet is precursor in literature to all Romanticism.
Overkill both defines and mocks opulence.
Imperialism, to Lenin, was the height of capitalism.

Any intern who goes unpaid is exploited.
True eloquence makes fun of eloquence.
Memories recalled are invariably disjointed.
Inferiority always encourages arrogance.

Dawn is predominantly yellow, dusk red.
The best guidebook is the red Michelin.
A 100 billion neurons function in the head.
Order is provably maintained by discipline.

Misers rarely bathe and often smell badly.
Racing horses, safer in herds, fear to be first.
Burial of Trappist monks is never done sadly.
Maori warrior masks are said to be cursed.

Curiosity ends the plod of doing homework.
We know nothing at all of Shakespeare's youth.
Every novelist should pay to be a motel clerk.
Candor in most of its morphs is truly uncouth.

TRUISMS

All tea comes from only *one* plant, *camellia sinensis*.
Emerson opposed allowing Texas into the Union.
One can rarely find in the South dry rock fences.
Between a Turk and Balkan is slim intercommunion.

No magazine finds its voice in the first edition.
The most favored animal of the two is the nigh ox.
True teachers see work not a trade but a mission.
Flight recorders, orange, are never a black box.

The violence of love is as terrible as that of hate.
American Indians love the beat of four-syllable names.
The racist numerical code for "Heil Hitler" is 88.
A pedophile charge, though false, one never reclaims.

Getting low school grades in Japan loses you face.
Anger, basically, is used to counterbalance fear.
Fish served with chips in England is mainly plaice.
George III banned all performances of *King Lear*.

Rural England is the domain of detective stories.
O negative blood can transfuse to everybody.
Sexual peculiarities exceed the nature of categories.
Not a thing can be serious and also be bawdy.

Russians have always been obsessed with French.
The thinner the chopsticks, the higher the social status.
To lie down is impossible on any public park bench.
Moisture is the cloudy promise of every cirrostratus.

Butterflies all abhor manzanita.
Over 90% of fish are caught in the Northern hemisphere.
Salt is the brain of a margarita.
There are only eight oar maneuvers for a gondolier.

More red blood cells mean more oxygen.
Henry James never wrote about Herman Melville.
Stronger than steel is fibritis in type 1 collagen.
Predestination is the opposite of free will.

Edward Gorey never used the alias Edward O. Grey.
Monasticism is a social form of autism.
All cartoonists rely for depth and contrast on Benday.
Nationalism is the unattractive brother of fascism.

A goat being sacrificed must first nod its assent.
Self-righteousness turns idealism into smugness.
Hand sign-language can actually reveal an accent.
Every single mushroom is technically a fungus.

Rats are actually allergic to blue cheese.
There are always "three nights" in fairy tales.
Lipstick ads lend themselves to sleaze.
Crashes are caused, not prevented, by guardrails.

Shakespeare's five collaborations are his weakest plays.
Touching a child's head is frowned upon Taiwan.
The fabric of casino gaming tables is unfailingly baize.
One breast is always missing in a true Amazon.

TRUISMS

Always introduce a younger to an older person.
Menstruation is a major taboo in Nepal.
Multiple sclerosis as time passes tends to worsen.
To inhale insecticide, smell a mothball.

Bears sense fear as a sign of aggression.
Pioneers habitually collected arrows.
Surveillance is unconscionable oppression.
Commotion is a way of life for sparrows.

Chewing gum is outlawed in Singapore.
A jiffy is an actual period of time (1/100th of a second).
Jaws can only move up and down in a carnivore.
Horse-donkey hybrids as a species prove never fecund.

No female of any sort can be a Hell's Angel member.
It is bad luck for ex-cons to visit former prisons.
Shakespeare never mentions the month of November.
The Fathers of the Desert all thrived on visions.

Myanmar's northern forests are unexplored.
The Chinese will never offer clocks as gifts.
Cold always precede hot dishes in a smorgasbord.
It is the wealthy not the poor who shoplifts.

Anemia is the *sine qua non* of poverty.
The mountain decides who will first reach the summit.
Stability can only be found in property.
No line or rope is ever secure without a grummet.

You never hear "It's too bad to be true."
No one knows why we have different blood types.
Greeks and Romans rarely used the color blue.
Slimness is enhanced by wearing vertical stripes.

No gentleman raises a lady's hand to kiss—he bends.
40% of Caucasians have type A blood.
A recovering alcoholic often irrationally misspends.
Cowboy shirts invigorated the press stud.

Orcas are the apex predator of the ocean.
The most spiritual people live in the highest places.
In every U.S. county can be found a Goshen.
Loss of identity plagues people of mixed races.

"Top o' the morning" is not a greeting in Ireland.
Most HIV victims worldwide are female.
In the Orkneys can be found not a single highland.
Weave, and not the material, defines percale.

In South Africa, giving with a left hand is rude.
Guinness stout should be served at room temperature.
Arab and African cultures own the name Masud.
Church and State are forever at odds over investiture.

No climber in storms unropes from a partner.
Religious revelations all become doctrinal.
Philosophy comes quite natural to a gardener.
Deterioration is faster in records colored vinyl.

TRUISMS

The Hawaiian alphabet has only twelve letters.
Poaching is the illegal cousin of hunting.
Garishness is the bane of Christmas sweaters.
Open air when flying encourages stunting.

World War I popularized blood transfusions.
No gentleman wears cowboy boots with a suit.
Any seeker of truth avoids easy conclusions.
A Pilgrim of the Absolute is forever *en route.*

Clenching one's buttocks helps the flow of blood.
Intuition apprehends all reality from within.
Nothing is more cooling for animals than mud.
No confession takes without proper chagrin.

The French love music on an accordion.
Russians never gives scarves as a gift.
Excesses were typical of an Edwardian.
Waste is pure agony to the mind of thrift.

Snobs loathe the democratization of luxury.
Mpingo wood is the costliest in the world.
Congressional lobbying is criminal jugglery.
Clamping grips of all pistols are knurled.

A mirror is a window with the harshest views.
Modishness jumps from disfavor to camp.
Men were the first to wear high heels on shoes.
Secret language signs aid a traveling tramp.

Crocuses and snowdrops are best seen *en masse.*
Edward Murrow and Walter Cronkite hated each other.
Not a single Russian novelist fails to mention kvass.
Heterodoxy marks the work of every Church Father.

Whoever asserts something, denies something.
Embalming is forbidden to Orthodox Jews.
Pork barrel funds forever back a dumb thing.
Confinement is a misery for animals in zoos.

Sport teams in domes grow soft in January.
Macho men call the game "*foopball.*"
Islamic sects are hopelessly contradictory.
Asian penis length is reported small.

Children playing alone take refuge in dreams.
Jews must be circumcised during day, not night.
In every religion, contrition alone redeems.
White contains all wavelengths of visible light.

TV evangelists consistently sing off key.
It is harder to write a poem of hatred than of love.
Butter has less calories and fat than ghee.
Toxicity abounds in the plant called foxglove.

All woodpeckers tend to love suet.
Ligurian people have a fetish for blondes.
Small fluids alone need a cruet.
No leaves undivided can ever be fronds.

TRUISMS

No door slams louder than an old screen door.
Faith is not mentioned in the Old Testament.
All insects (but flies) with wings have four.
Not one legal decision is without precedent.

Prayer in the ideal should be spontaneous.
Every uniform worn induces a rigid posture.
Inventive thought turns on ideas extraneous.
Envy, which never praises, can never foster.

Omitting a salient fact strengthens a short story.
No prohibition exists on gambling in the Bible.
"*Jaune doré*" (golden yellow) is a fish: John Dory.
Slander involves *speech*, what is *seen* is libel.

It is sacrilege to light a cigarette from a menorah.
The New Yorker rejected *The Catcher in the Rye*.
As names, magicians pick "Mandrake" and "Mandragora."
Shiny things do not tempt, rather *scare* a magpie.

To flaunt is the opposite of to flout.
"Where are you from?" is an allegation.
Arckaringa daisies very rarely sprout.
Skin color—variable—mocks segregation.

Only *seven pairs* of animals were taken into the Ark.
Every J.D. Salinger short story features a crucial letter.
Tornadoes always, weirdly, destroy a trailer park.
1940s actresses and glamor girls posed in a sweater.

ALEXANDER THEROUX

Nothing matches for beauty a young girl perspiring.
The Torah allows no knitting on the Sabbath.
Women are held as anathema for baseball umpiring.
The richest soil on the planet is Russian black earth.

Manhattan parties are all about connections.
Never lie on the ground floor in a hurricane.
Liturgical reverence is shown by genuflections.
Eastern Europe is the fountainhead of acid rain.

Only a barbarian enjoys a fruit pie hot.
Kipling's tales are riddled with insomnia.
Horseshoe crab eggs alone feed a red knot.
Everybody is poverty-stricken in Somalia.

Jewish lore offers no wisdom on an afterlife.
Point a boat bow in the direction of a storm.
To save wetlands, kill all purple loosestrife.
Any fully closed mind is well beyond reform.

Ginger hair is considered a Jonah on ships.
There's no mention in the Bible of an immortal soul.
Every horse racetrack configures an ellipse.
Eggs are never used in the wrappers of a spring roll.

Setting sail on a Friday is a sailor's taboo.
Komodo dragons all saunter laboriously.
Steel has less tensile strength than bamboo.
$20 bills are most counterfeited spuriously.

TRUISMS

Christopher Columbus never set foot in America.
Nothing is more uniform in width than bamboo.
U.S. income tax laws are inexplicable chimerica.
A lobbyist's sense of ethics nothing can imbrue.

The pitohui bird of New Guinea is poison.
A bride walks down a *nave*, not an aisle.
The sole crime defined in the Constitution is treason.
Men's starched, stiff collars were a killer style.

Jockeys never glory in victories, only the champion horse.
Christ performed no miracle in his Jerusalem ministry.
Sperm can be found to improve with frequent intercourse.
The Republic of Angola is virtually bereft of industry.

No significant songs are sung of Washington, D.C.
No person has ever been born a Shaker.
Poles and Basques are utterly fond of the letter Z.
Still a mystery is the formation of nacre.

A perfect meringue should never weep.
Never wax, shellac, or polish a good wooden bowl.
Gold buttons always bedeck a chimney sweep.
The world's busiest air route is found in Seoul.

Avery Fisher Hall has terrible acoustics.
The Polish, oddly, spell Rome (*Ryzm*) with a Z.
Nothing sharpens crueler than bamboo sticks.
Ecuadorians and Peruvians will never agree.

Two blades are a paddle, one blade is an oar.
The word *the*, not a definite article, is an adjective.
77% of the Earth's surface is the ocean floor.
Bowel tumors can result by overusing a laxative.

Korean hospitals never have a 4th floor.
Vanity in politics always leads to disloyalty.
Slumping is standard for a sophomore.
Signing autographs is never done by royalty.

An opera house is a hotbed of superstitions.
FDR loathed an unyielding conservative.
Theorists is the connotation of academicians.
Any psychoanalytic catharsis is a purgative.

Statistics are the lifeblood of baseball.
The human hand is the instrument of instruments.
Stone fruits are subject to crown gall.
All blood thinners invariably lead to impotence.

Fondant should never be described as food.
Westminster Abbey is a stolen Catholic Church.
Tardiness is in almost every instance rude.
Pathogens have an appetite for every birch.

The witless live under the protection of God.
Japanese hide their thumbs from funeral cars.
Televangelists' voices are riddled with fraud.
Beauty's announced in a Yoruba's tribal scars.

TRUISMS

Wind is not blown, but rather sucked.
American men hug each other like lepers.
A chef is praised in China if you eruct.
Unblock your sinuses by eating peppers.

An egalitarian is inevitably a leveler.
Suicides are common at firing ranges.
A sadness adhibits to the loudest reveler.
Our truest self-images to us are strangers.

Being over-polite is being impolite.
Bullfighters greatly fear the color yellow.
An open fire will never burn anthracite.
A human voice is best mimed by the cello.

Hitters look away from their fans after a K.
Modesty is invariably a matter of geography.
A chicken without water can die in a day.
Sexual assault is increased by pornography.

Showing up early in Venezuela is rude.
Diet means limiting food, not *not* eating.
A legitimate noun for a deceiver is a pseud.
Only what disappears fast can be fleeting.

Pond ice—cracks, it bears; bends, it breaks.
Venezuela's gas prices are the world's lowest.
More power goes a car's engine than its brakes.
Black-on-black crime goes forever unnoticed.

Pineapples always taste sweeter with salt.
"Barbie's" full name is Barbara Millicent Roberts.
The Congo has the largest reserves of cobalt.
Less sugar is found in ice cream than in sherbets.

There are 177,147 possible ways to tie a tie
A baby rabbit is technically called a "kitten."
Nothing thrives in poor soil better than rye.
The Celts first called a Britisher a "Briton."

Most Western lodges plagiarize Hopi pueblos.
Young adult fiction is almost totally prurient.
Funerals are actually held by murders of crows.
Far, Middle, and Near East constitutes the Orient.

All elm trees are shaped just like a vase.
San Luca, Calabria is Casa Nostra central.
European brides insist on wearing lace.
John Steinbeck would only write in pencil.

Eating coffee-grounds will kill a dog.
Impotence is common among sports fans.
Hickory wood proves the best of fire logs.
A ballerina's beauty is seen in her hands.

Maasai, regarding them ancestors, never kill flies.
A male tango dancer never steps backwards.
Laurence Olivier could not act without a disguise.
Liking to sing after rain is typical of blackbirds.

TRUISMS

By showing enthusiasm you lose a bargain.
Time is not about passing but something to be spent.
True meaning is purposely hidden by jargon.
Only one ingredient of actual concrete is cement.

Number 191 is bad juju to airplane pilots.
Foliage is frequently incorrectly pronounced.
Scent lasts but a second inhaling violets.
Anything subject to stricture is denounced.

One can never overcook mushrooms.
Italian tenors are notoriously crazy.
Silence is a law in British club rooms.
For tattoos, women prefer a blue daisy.

Celebrities all pretend to know each other.
Agencies rarely hire redheaded models.
Grave doubt is a firm faith's twin brother.
Hugging a child, for a lifetime swaddles.

Strippers love the stage-name Cheyenne.
Simenon protagonists are always male.
Classic French building? Visit Phnom Penh.
No Gucci merchandise ever goes on sale.

Skiing *haute couture* is utterly repellent.
Begin no interview with your core questions.
No rocket fuel sans an oxidizer is a propellant.
Orders are the wicked uncle of suggestions.

You can never learn from someone you resent.
All innovation is forbidden by the Torah.
Truth regarding "we'll call you" is never meant.
Gone is the fashion accessory called the fedora.

No one can cut a hot or cold soufflé neatly.
Jerusalem is Israel's capital only to the U.S.
Expensive jewelry cannot be worn discreetly.
Always Mr. or Mrs. on an envelope address.

Claymation constitutes the nadir of art.
Flavor *in se* can spoil taste in meat itself.
An honest yogurt should always be tart.
Endorsements in ads are done solely for pelf.

Bureaucracies by nature all disincentivize.
Never meet a writer if you like his books.
Schizophrenics are impossible to hypnotize.
Tetchiness typifies most professional cooks.

The partisan spirit makes people blind.
Athletes celebrate victory by wasting champagne.
Our Declaration, eight delegates never signed.
For the best natural pearls shop in Bahrain.

A Corsican brother is devoted to his sister.
The bison's hump provides the best eating.
SW to NE is standard direction for a twister.
Touching fingers is the Malayan greeting.

TRUISMS

Onions are fiercely toxic to a horse.
Fashion is what goes *out* of fashion.
Many fear marriage who fear divorce.
Want of hydration turns all skin ashen.

Africa leads the world in pedophilia.
Racehorses in Europe run clockwise.
Always plural is the word memorabilia.
Pot roast should be sliced crosswise.

Regional speech is slowly disappearing.
Every MI6 chief since 007 is identified as C.
Teaching more than anything is steering.
Water is anoxic (oxygenless) in the Black Sea.

The albino gene in a horse is lethal.
John Gotti let no one walk in front of him.
Supervision informs every bequeathal.
Inflexibility is the iniquity of being prim.

Giraffes always browse into the wind.
It takes two hands to don a hat correctly.
Small fish taste better when tinned.
Avoid drinking from a can directly.

For luck, nail a horseshoe both ends up.
No one maintains lanes in traffic circles.
The point of pastiche is mainly a send up.
The artifactual thrives on using purples.

Divas always have milquetoast husbands.
Bone marrow is what makes our blood.
Mohammed is *not* worshipped by Muslims.
Judas hanged himself on a crooked redbud.

Fashion models are all extraterrestrials.
Shakespeare's sonnets deal with sex, not love.
Proximity creates spark in all adversarials.
Pigeons are all descendants of the rock dove.

Divorcees tend to migrate to Alaska.
All American replies start with "Well..."
In football, Kansas always loses to Nebraska,
and Navy to Notre Dame, as well.

Every classic popular love song is sad.
The further north in Scotland, the fiercer the sermons.
Flannel as a fabric is the trampoline of plaid.
Discipline constitutes a kind of faith with Germans.

Paprika has more vitamin C than any citrus.
Civil War soldiers aimed for the mounted man.
The Puritans banned the feast of Christmas.
Nazi *left* arms are raised in the Ku Klux Klan.

Non-voters are the largest political party.
Minor key music is always heard as sad.
Overly robust defines a British "hearty"
All diet regimes constitute the latest fad.

TRUISMS

It's working folk who now wear spats.
In human life, there are no accidents.
Depth of sleep is foreign to all cats.
An obese official centers all events.

No singers should improvise a Christmas song.
Traditionally kilts are worn without underwear.
70 million deaths are attributed to Mao Zedong.
Arriving late in Tanzania's considered debonair.

Africans are the world's heaviest smokers.
Ballpoint pens fail to work in cold.
Prison guards are famously dishonest brokers.
Every good wallet has a natural fold.

Adding a rupee to a gift in India is auspicious.
Over long term, markets always trend upward.
All Israeli customs agents are rudely officious.
Every American male-to-male hug is awkward.

Any official spy may kill with impunity.
Air fresheners smell worse than bad odors.
Mediocrity is ever exalted by community.
Psychotherapists are notorious encoders.

Rapallo is a preferred option for exile.
Atheists feel candor merits God's approval.
Wasting food is a sybaritic lifestyle.
Nothing Gert Stein wrote doesn't bamboozle.

Nothing is ever at stake in architecture.
Marcel Proust's characters have no jobs.
All divorce is the story of misconjecture.
Passion, nor brains, animates all mobs.

Crabs should be cooked right after capture.
Satins for most women are unforgiving fabrics.
Evangelicals fixate solely on the Rapture.
Bending over is truly agony for most geriatrics.

Steers are tender eating, bulls are tough.
The words *liberty* and *system* are antonyms.
Too much for the rich is never enough.
Choose buckeye wood for artificial limbs.

No actual entity exists as the "present."
Pain lurks forever in good fortune.
Oxygen kills whatever tries to ferment.
No cable can exist without torsion.

Always spoon vertically into a caviar tin.
Rosemary grows where mistress is master.
Only blackthorn makes an honest sloe gin.
A head to a hat is as a column to a pilaster.

Acne sufferers are all phototropes.
Dogwood trees are famously frangible.
Hollywood types swear by horoscopes.
Faith is, by definition, intangible.

TRUISMS

Yugoslavia was the embodiment of fracture.
Good writing is an assault against cliché.
Aggression animates men of smaller stature.
The bass guitar is dominant in reggae.

Losing hurts more than winning pleases.
Never invest money in anything that eats.
Quite ruined is a garden hose that freezes.
For good health, never overcook beets.

Left-hander pitchers rarely throw straight.
Mohammed never left anything in writing.
Women look on perspiring men as bait.
Extreme loudness in a voice is disinviting.

The world of couture pivots on neomania.
Nazareth is not mentioned in the Old Testament.
No European country has more gold than Romania.
The flow of currency is a significant pestilent.

Jefferson yearned to checkerboard all land.
Hebrew and Yiddish use no capital letters.
Violence prevails in all kingdoms of sand.
Forgetfulness is as a pillow to all debtors.

Nothing takes place that does not matter.
Mixed concrete must be poured in two hours.
Chemicals, curing felt, often crazed a hatter.
Healing is validly linked to yarrow flowers.

Cranberries will not grow in water.
Businessmen see framed plaques as trophies.
Brutality fails to stun a beast before slaughter.
Intuition proves valuable in major diagnoses.

Ironing cashmere is a grave mistake.
Truman Capote had a predilection for straight men.
Inherently comic is any double-take.
The word Vatican is not Latin nor Greek, but Etruscan.

Marcel Proust took no interest in commas.
No British spy can hold diplomatic rank.
Desertion leads the list of childhood traumas.
Foreigners own the Swiss National Bank!

A turkey is cooked thirteen minutes per pound.
Yellow worn by dancers is considered taboo.
Chance is implied in anything that's found.
Tutsi are exactly the same people as Hutu.

Than political memoirs, nothing is duller.
Alcohol prices are the highest in Norway.
Every fog has its own distinctive color.
Native Americans have no official holiday.

More English words begin S than any other letter.
It is illegal to jump a queue in the British subway.
Every creditor owns a slave who boasts a debtor.
Horny boys love joining pretty girls in a bobsleigh.

TRUISMS

Never bet on a horse with four white legs.
Evelyn Waugh's fiction eschews prole characters.
It is physically bigger hens that lay brown eggs.
Shaking hands is avoided by opposing barristers.

Right wing satire is incontestably weak.
Other people's hobbies are always ridiculous.
All superstition is abhorrent to a Sikh.
The pebbled shape of taste buds is calculus.

To know only partially is to misread entirely.
Saffron is literally worth its weight in gold.
No compass near an MRI will work reliably.
The paranoid mind cannot bear being polled.

Stationary fish in currents always face it.
Every tatami mat consists of three parts.
Each stamp price costs more to replace it.
Any open top uncovered by pastry is a tart.

Beaujolais marries best with charcuterie.
Kosovo and Serbia have never gotten along.
Modern banking is little more than usury.
Anger is expressed in most birdsong.

Shape always trumps color in a fishing lure,
but its action's more important than its shape.
The evil goal of all advertising is to procure.
The tastiest part of grown garlic is its scape.

Never enter a tatami room wearing shoes.
Any good fisherman brings a spare knife.
Until 2006 Oklahoma forbade all tattoos.
Capitalism is the basic cause of racial strife.

Bets should be legal in games of skill, not chance.
The reveries of every stage mother are tasteless.
No legal refinement isn't a song and dance.
Ku Klux Klan adepts thrive on being nameless.

A politically biased reporter is merely a pimp.
Resin is the bandage over a pine tree wound.
Fishermen ruin ocean beds who fish for shrimp.
Any sentimental song that is sung is crooned.

No sport displays better manners than curling.
Japanese were held to be white under apartheid.
A fluent walker constitutes a special yearling.
Daily Mass was originally required of a knight.

Prestige in fact means illusion and imposture.
Screaming at an infant or child is morally harmful.
Dried, rather than hot, air is better in a defroster
Both arms being full technically defines an armful.

Ocean tides are actually a form of current.
Y-crotch in trees snap faster than a U-crotch.
Inconsistency is truly a vice in any parent.
Scots dislike being referred to as Scotch.

TRUISMS

Mattress ticking is invariably blue striped.
No cross-eyed man gets work on a railroad.
Everyone in *Gone with the Wind* is stereotyped.
Symbols operate the cipher, semantics a code.

A trainman never adjusts his own watch.
Forethought is the significant key to chess.
No Barbie Doll has been given a crotch.
Every last straw poll constitutes a guess.

No railroad engine in the U.S. is numbered 13.
Yiddish means Jewish in the language itself.
The color yellow predominates in Paris Green.
Animal life finds heaven in a continental shelf.

There are no railroads in Iceland.
Every marriage unites balloons and ballast.
No butte is not also a tableland.
All routes to political victories are calloused.

Psychiatry is extremely punitive to mothers.
Almost no first-century Jews spoke Hebrew.
One's recollection is never, ever another's.
All of East Asian land is ploughed by a zebu.

In the rigidity of law lies its strength;
In the rigidity of law lies its weakness.
No century was darker than the tenth.
Every bully is infuriated by uniqueness.

Jesus never visited the town of Tiberias.
No true genius is not a troublemaker.
All rocks are mineralized by bacterias.
Sewing is the main skill of an undertaker.

Macerating fruit educes its keenest flavors.
No prophet bows to accredited authority.
Show business parties turn on insipid clavers.
Intimidation constitutes its own majority.

Almost all of *Macbeth* takes place at night.
Silver is the best metal for conductivity.
Greeting card poetry is the epitome of trite.
Innovation is the soul of all creativity.

Vermont makes the best roofing slate.
Nothing cannot be made into a pie.
No stop sign has not sides of eight.
Shellfish weaken as oceans acidify.

Lists are notable for what they exclude.
Brewer's yeast has no leavening power.
Good writing is murdered by platitude.
Cooking kills enzymes in cauliflower.

A tree has only two inches of sapwood.
It is rude to leave a diplomatic function early.
Adolescence is the uncle of childhood.
Than a New Yorker, no one's more surly.

TRUISMS

People honor Jesus but ignore his message.
Confederate gray was dyed butternut bark.
Rain is of a change in weather true presage.
Scarcely a hill can be found in all Denmark.

To a bully, tolerance means weakness.
Always use wet hands to release a fish.
Patience, not timidity, defines meekness.
Every single culture has its form of *knish*.

Netherlands and Luxembourg share the same flag.
A generic noun for the Rat Pack was "clyde."
All infectious cadavers require a yellow body bag.
An intact hymen gave reason for riding astride.

Improvisation has its own formal rules.
No Texan ever eats brisket with a fork.
Sterility is a natural condition in mules.
Conscience is a source of moral torque.

Pericles is Shakespeare's least performed play.
Organic compounds derive from *in*organic elements.
Fishermen never head out to sea on a Friday.
Tusks are actually the large incisor teeth of elephants.

In Mexico it is gauche to eat tacos with a fork.
Cape Codders never disclose best places to clam.
Force and hinge are required for torque.
Every midway carnival game is entirely a scam.

Indonesia is the greatest exporter of coal.
Batman, a hero, has no supernatural powers.
Roundness is required to constitute a bowl.
Virtually never seen are bamboo flowers.

Wine is named for the area, not the grape.
Renaming any boat is thought to be bad luck.
World maps always show a distorted shape.
Bambi was made a mule deer of a roebuck.

The pharmacist's skill is to titrate doses.
Crime in Agatha Christie is always murder.
Many are self-ordained to save tax grosses.
No fanatic exceeds a "twitcher" in a birder.

No knit dress on a woman isn't provocative.
There is a biological basis to racial differences.
Every American cowboy hero is untalkative.
Christmas is abhorrent to Jehovah's Witnesses.

People who tape shut envelopes need therapy.
Cooking with salted butter is always precarious.
Great chefs create rather than follow a recipe.
Uncontacted tribes are by nature ungregarious.

Three kisses constitute every Breton *bise*.
California East Bay is ground zero for food loonies.
Chinese don't use police dogs but geese.
Shia follow guides and leaders, the scripture Sunnis.

TRUISMS

No Old West town became one 'til it sold whiskey.
Shopping late at Christmas, boasting men find virile,
A single drink for alcoholics is already risky.
American television will any healthy child imperil.

The worst crime in a small town is to be lazy.
The brain alone fails to tell you it's malfunctioning.
The air in air-polluted India is perpetually hazy.
The center of anything is all-encompassing.

North American maps have a west-east orientation.
A gallery of similar suspects fits every crime novel.
Symmetry is the living soul of botanical estivation.
Any political candidate for funds will always grovel.

Every Caesar has his treacherous Pompey.
Porpoises are portly, dolphins far leaner.
A bark can be heard in every poetic spondee.
The New York City mode is rude demeanor.

A choker worn by any woman exalts her looks.
Only the feeble-minded believe in astrology.
Rage notoriously describes most chefs and cooks.
Eastern Africa best rewards paleoanthropology.

We, all of us, have our origins from Africa.
No ocean whirlpool has a deeply vertical pull.
The strongest of world's natural fibers is abaca.
Nothing regulates body temperature better than wool.

Sufis are hated by all dogmatic Muslims.
Alpha Centauri, say mavens, is UFO central.
Routine is the parent of a culture's customs.
No creature survives a bullet in the ventral.

Every true fakir always sits cross-legged.
Belgians are the least patriotic of people.
Cinderella was more beautiful when ragged.
Integrity always lapses in a sequel.

Theory is far more fully liberating than dogma.
Longing is the agony of the nearness of the distant.
Tortellini heralds a meal in Emilia-Romagna.
The Kurds are a nation without a state existent.

Everything that we observe equals its meaning.
No Italian would ever eat out at Thanksgiving,
Feminists find most rules of etiquette demeaning.
Grudging Corsicans are notoriously unforgiving.

Whatever your job, you are selling a product.
No son grows to be a man until his father dies.
Passing times do not allow variance in conduct.
In a Constable painting are never sunny skies.

The more a loony demands release, the sicker he is.
A proper "canoe" birch tree always forks at the top.
Deformed or spotted leaves prove how sick a tree is.
Countries run by the military never have a bookshop.

TRUISMS

Every conclusion needs two premises.
Most African nations are ineptocracies.
Adjacent states are natural nemeses.
Class systems exist in all democracies.

Cooks abominate other cooks' kitchens.
Partiality is every instance is a discount.
Smiles are invariably tacit permissions.
Iraqi elections invite an instant recount.

No cult will ever call itself a cult.
Buses use separate traffic lanes in Quito.
True learning brings change as a result.
The most food-friendly wine is merlot.

No tourist ever constitutes a traveler.
Vicissitudes make manners variable.
An outspoken person is a born caviler.
A niggardly roommate is unbearable.

Every bird is related to the dinosaur.
Europeans have no concept of breakfast.
One's conscience is always a saboteur.
Generalizations are by definition reckless.

Sailmakers never refer to twine as thread.
Belgians are Flemish, Walloons, and Germans.
Every child not read to goes to bed unfed.
The center of a Presbyterian liturgy is sermons.

Neo-Nazism still flourishes in Croatia.
Every decision skews its alternative.
Marriage is not an option for a geisha.
Conservation defines a true conservative.

Nothing on earth can go faster than light.
Money-grubbing is the vice of parvenus.
Slower growing trees are less prone to blight.
No jingoist matches Southerners on barbecues.

A resemblance is the persona of a difference.
Mexican cooks beat every stirring clockwise.
Direct observation is the enemy of inference.
Divorce is not prohibited whatsoever to rabbis.

Never drink the water of the Trevi Fountain.
Essays are etymologically an *attempt* at truth.
We conquer ourselves by climbing a mountain.
Complete and utter candor is unfailingly uncouth.

Danger comes soonest when it is denigrated.
There is never a last word between friends.
Gold hoarders are economically constipated.
An inverted yield curve a recession portends.

The French people admire agile thieves.
Seeing both sides of a debate is a vice.
Pine needles on evergreen trees are *leaves*.
The Great Wall of China is bonded by rice.

TRUISMS

Aristotle privileged line over color.
Scythe-mowing bouts are big with Balkans.
Curved is ever synonymous with cruller.
Hawks kill with claws, beaks with falcons.

A "girl" in Chaucer could be of either sex.
U.S. dialects lessen the further west one goes.
A geometric triangle is a polygon N convex.
It is impossible to oppose anything apposed.

No anythingarian isn't an indifferentist.
Singers consistently sing behind the beat.
Power and happiness very rarely coexist.
Socks are included in a fetish of the feet.

No leaf venation fails to show a midrib.
Shakespeare disappeared from 1584 to 1592.
Gay pride is the cornerstone of gay lib.
Fat and flour are twin sisters of a roux.

To stop a cattle stampede, circle them.
A honest-to-god cowboy says "*Ro*deo."
Whenever we eat ginger, we eat a stem.
The Rio Grande is really the Rio Bravo.

Oral contraceptives owe a debt to yams.
Humans have only one more bone than horses.
Religious pitches for cash are all shams.
The sunny Maldives leads the world in divorces.

The best cowboy boots are made of French calf.
Cappuccino is drunk in Italy only before noon.
Whatever we hate, in us lies the other half.
Eclipses reverse when viewing from the moon.

All wood is naturally anisotropic.
A Bedouin shakes his cup to refuse more coffee.
Illusion shapes anything stereoscopic.
Matte photo finish, for texture, is better than glossy.

Conspiracists all suspect there is a "plan."
The Kaddish never mentions dying or death.
The oldest dessert on the planet is the flan.
Shakespeare pronounced the word heath "heth."

A tall woman dressed as a man looks shorter.
The English burnt Joan of Arc, not the French.
Envy is admiration's secret bastard daughter.
Greed is a thirst no liquid can ever quench.

All Methodists are properly Lutherans.
No picture or photo exists of Chief Crazy Horse.
Soil is notorious for harboring pathogens.
Carême discounted hollandaise a mother sauce.

Habitual lateness indicates secret resistance.
There are 40,000 varieties of beans.
Farming worldwide is mainly for subsistence.
Islands alone constitute the Philippines.

TRUISMS

Aprons on a woman have a fetishistic lure.
Nothing is truly mixed unless immiscibly.
In England, first floor is above ground floor.
Until next time is always said dismissively.

New Englanders don't go in for psychiatry.
Chutney on a shelf grows better with age.
Conformity is the ugly twin of propriety.
*Down*stage is at the *front* half of a stage.

Most women yearn to have a "past."
Usury was the only resort for the Jewish.
The British wanted pine for sailing masts.
Green meeting violet makes for bluish.

All steroids are derived from cholesterol.
Russia never once suffered from fascism.
The center for the slave trade was Senegal.
Boys are five times more open to autism.

Not a single wading bird can sing.
Few things are uglier than ballet slippers.
Every donut shape is a toroidal ring.
"Night Train" is the classic theme of strippers.

Dictators are the popes of nationalism.
A football punter needs at least 16 yards to kick.
Voice alone is the vehicle for mesmerism.
Ketchup is always best when pouring thick.

Heads-on shrimp deliver the best flavor.
Fans need sports to find *self*-distinction.
The voice of fear has a distinct quaver.
96% of species died in the Permian extinction.

Piano music hears terrible while jogging.
Seagulls never fly 200 miles from land.
Rainforests are half-gone due to logging.
34 muscles work the complex human hand.

Over-refinement in every instance distorts.
A lean human body is 70% water.
Much college tuition is wasted on sports.
No joy matches childhood in a daughter.

Little girls' clothing is devoid of pockets.
Every wedding's a triumph over democracy.
Teeth mark an infant's signature on lockets.
Pulling piety is the primary face of hypocrisy.

The book one writes is one he wants to read.
Bird plumage is about courtship features.
Nothing is quite as exhausting as greed.
Educing, not inducing, defines good teachers.

No Nobel Prize is given for mathematics.
The Canadians never had an Indian war.
The Lydian Lion coin is oldest in numismatics.
Nothing tastes better from a can than from a jar.

TRUISMS

Supreme Court justices shake hands every day.
Equivalence as to any translation is a fairy tale.
The passive to the active is perpetual prey.
No food exists that tastes blander than kale.

A foghorn at sea emits only bass notes.
Lettuce is never sold frozen, cooked, or canned.
A house with uncut lawns burglary promotes.
Black is very rarely seen on a comestible brand.

Mournful idealizing is the trope of courtly love.
Italian bakers use *lievito naturale*—natural yeast.
The *most of* is invariably never the *best of.*
Once a Catholic priest always a Catholic priest.

Shakespeare loved onomastic predestination.
The moon stabilizes the axial tilt of the Earth.
Every true reformation demands modification.
Being a parent is a matter of biology, not worth.

All Supreme Court justices are multi-millionaires.
U.S. submarines are named after marine creatures.
Statistics fall short of truth in any questionnaire.
Personal wealth is an obscenity with preachers.

Italian ricotta is made solely from ewe's milk.
Henry Cabot Lodge despised Thomas Jefferson.
The strongest of all natural fibers is silk.
Encumbrance is implied in the verb *to jettison.*

A bad background ruins any photographic portrait.
An affected stutter makes American snobs feel British.
Reality for an artist is merely a quiddity to interpret.
The *perceptions* of *shtetl* Jews inform all Yiddish.

Lichens need ruin to make them grow.
Durand is to French as Smith is to English.
Celsius and Fahrenheit match at 40 below.
No alligator has a bite that it will relinquish.

Rose oil is worth its weight in gold.
A standard *sari* is seven yards long.
There are half a million kinds of mold.
Servility flourishes in a great throng.

Patriotic expats are often anti-U.S. at home.
In every eulogy, the truth is sanded down.
Man's most efficient structure is a dome.
"Tea color" is the Japanese word for brown.

Yes in referendums has advantage over *no*.
Proper names are a subdivision of language.
Translucent, not white, is the color of snow.
No juice exists from (very healthy!) cabbage.

Serial killers tend to go by three names.
Final S's are not sounded in Gregorian chant.
Imagination palls in players of video games.
No condition asks that whiskey one decant.

TRUISMS

The real Western cattle rustlers were wolves.
Intolerance figures in every religious belief.
Vapor is loved by but liquids hated by wools.
Da Hong Pao is the most expensive tea leaf.

Every single fact needs an interpretation.
An animal is ontologically itself regardless of name.
A woman at age fifty experiences ablactation.
Contempt is the opposite of guilt in feeling shame.

Snow has never been reported in Key West.
A coin is placed on a ship mast for good luck.
Cold temps can hurt someone who's depressed.
Antlers increase a full inch a day on a buck.

Always dissolve yeast in 105-degree water.
The universe contains 70 billion trillion stars.
English law punishes corporate manslaughter.
Cherry-picking is a theme in written memoirs.

No parents ever name their child Hamlet. Why?
White quill pens still appear in the Supreme Court.
There is no universal term for the word *goodbye*.
Soldiers kept silent the night before Agincourt.

High jumping as sport always ends in failure.
Fashion always comes to an end with ridicule.
One nail bought sex for an 18th-century sailor.
Minorities ever suffer by way of majority rule.

Irish fathers and eldest daughters emigrated first.
Ignorance surrounds the death of Shakespeare.
Coconut water is better than regular to quench thirst.
A child molester is often a quondam puppeteer.

Fish of all kinds invariably love shade.
Ramen noodles contain more salt than pasta.
No girl looks homely wearing a French braid.
Than Quarter Horses, for sprints, nothing's faster.

Hawks are never overweight, but *high*.
Never use a metallic spoon for caviar.
The U.S. Congressional lobby is a living sty.
The world's best beaches are found in Zanzibar.

Every Cajun carries—totes—a jackknife.
Amerindians had a horror of facial hair.
An expiry date is specific, not so shelf life.
Cinderella's slipper was not *verre* but *vair*.

All men entered the Americas as invaders,
Wool actually becomes warm when wet.
To Luther, a Papal evil were the Crusaders.
In the Bible both mother and father can beget.

The trait of all literary heroines is energy.
Only 150 F. water temperature will kill lice.
The Quakers are bereft of any liturgy.
New car costs are intentionally imprecise.

TRUISMS

Bad poetry induces an actual auto-hypnosis.
Political cartoons are a form of hate speech.
No professional welder escapes siderosis.
For the most durable floor, use red beech.

Neanderthals never existed in the Americas.
The nature of fashion is to become obsolete.
The Tempest sets out only magical characters.
Submucosa (collagen) is wrap for sausage meat.

Las Vegas leads all suicides in America.
No Americans habitually eat cardoons.
The idea of perfect marriage is a chimera.
The stock practical joke is water balloons.

Bacteria cannot thrive in acid soil.
Infrared radiation is the heat of sunlight.
Only the blunt tip scores with a fencing foil.
Sadism is involved in every bullfight.

One always returns with more than he has packed.
March is the fastest month for daylight gain.
At a slant of 90 degrees light will never refract.
Only 5% of world's populace has flown in a plane.

Sardinians never die of cirrhosis of the liver.
In great fiction, most love stories will end badly.
A splinter is far more severe than a sliver.
Any land U-shape indicates a glacial valley.

Camembert cheese is best enjoyed when runny.
No photos of FDR and Eleanor's wedding exists.
Cotton and linen—not paper—make up money.
Perfume on the radial pulse sexualizes wrists.

Never attempt to hug Parisians—who hate it.
Offense always has the advantage in football.
Sharpening's required in any edge serrated.
Perspiring can raise a person's cholesterol.

All mammalian life lives on water and grass.
Italy traditionally produces the best hemp.
Predatory fish to be clean depend on wrasse.
All Shoshone held the Apaches in contempt.

A raw carrot is still alive when you eat it,
The French loathe the phrase "*Bon Appetit!*"
Capitalism thrives by what it sees defeated.
All paperwork is now close to obsolete.

There are 100 folds in a chef's formal toque.
Leonardo da Vinci never painted a crucifixion.
No tree courts a lightning flash like an oak.
The Bible literally teems with contradiction.

There has never been a fully vegan culture.
Lady Macbeth's full name was Gruoch ingen Boite.
There is no syrinx in a (mostly silent) vulture.
Hypocrisy and self-contempt as moods abut.

TRUISMS

Bactria was the ancient name of Afghanistan
Shipwreck capital of the world is Bermuda.
Flattery is currency for a confidence man.
Every object that is shiny attracts a barracuda.

Glazomaniacs crave to see things in a row.
A football shape—prolate spheroid—is unpredictable.
Histoplasmosis is spread solely by bat guano.
Njerep, a rare Bantoid language, is fully inexplicable.

There are no casinos in Paris—gambling is illegal.
A strict vegan's adrenals are often in deep fatigue.
A bullet has less force than the strike of an eagle.
Only polished shells constitute true *wampumpeag.*

It is illegal for U.S. citizens to eat penguin.
No French person doesn't drink red wine.
Bluster is a main trait in someone sanguine.
An acidic burn is not as bad as an alkaline.

Parisian women wear their jewelry to bed.
Human bone is four times stronger than concrete.
A woman looks fuller when wearing red.
The upbeat always anticipates the downbeat.

American Band-Aids are flimsy and useless.
Anywhere in France not Paris is a province.
All true mosses and liverworts are rootless.
Only the deluded have a clear conscience.

Artists fit badly into whatever organization.
Radio in Great Britain is an art form.
Sherlock Holmes took cases via provocation.
Christ abhorred anything lukewarm.

To Elizabethans, a comedy must end in marriage.
The biggest port in all of Europe is Rotterdam.
Taking folic acid can prevent early miscarriage.
Three major faiths claim the patriarch Abraham.

No one who can't make a *beurre blanc* is a chef.
An Inuit in a frost pays most attention to his feet.
G clef is always treble clef and F clef is bass clef.
A delicious port wine can be made from the beet.

Most Christians in Israel are in fact Arabs.
Salt is a completely inorganic compound.
Egyptians linked the daily sun to scarabs.
Solar panels should be facing southbound.

No portrait of Christopher Columbus exists.
Resistance to New Englanders is unwritten law.
The tail of a pig or a swine never untwists.
Neither of the two match in the lobster claw.

Buddy cops are a tedious television cliché.
Shakespeare disdained masques as ephemeral.
No bridesmaid's should match a bride's bouquet.
Perspiration can bring about good cholesterol.

TRUISMS

Concepts as facts have no real existence.
Hymns are known by first lines, rarely titles.
Antibiotics can grow bacterial resistance.
Orange not white should color film subtitles.

For sugaring, seek maples with the most limbs.
Sifted mouse brain was a dentrifice for Romans.
Deception is never the prank with orthonyms.
A side-facing wall is ideal for vertical gnomons.

Searing meat never fully seals in juices.
Rejection in love exceeds physical pain.
Human clitorises also have prepuces.
Petrichor imparts an earthy smell to rain.

Cabernet Sauvignon grape plants love gravely soil.
Bedwetters sleep deeply to escape the real world.
Gasoline makes up as much as 45% of crude oil.
No American flag should be raised when furled.

The act of sifting flour is utterly unnecessary.
People of low self-esteem tend to humiliate others.
The link between word and meaning is arbitrary.
Nature's the paradigm for empowering mothers.

Chinese medicine has never used dissection.
Use of pressure cookers Julia Child abhorred.
Every Arab rug has an intentional imperfection.
Vale do Javari, Brazil, remains till unexplored.

Whales have roads that they travel in.
An adze man sharpens his tool after 80 strokes.
Gloves may not be worn throwing a javelin.
The Cardiff Giant has been fully proven a hoax.

Organic compounds all contain carbon.
Jesus never once mentions circumcision.
No revolution ever took place in Japan.
No convert to a religion is not a precisian.

No wine grapes to grow need deep top soil.
Bowhead blubber is thicker than sperm whale by 3 inches.
Gasoline is composed of only 45% crude oil.
A "charm" is the formal collective name for goldfinches.

Business as a rule attracts business.
A perdix wants to be braised in cabbage.
Easter rates higher liturgically than Christmas.
Mediocrity always exalts the average.

Whisk*ey* is Irish, whis*ky* is Scottish.
Any sensitive worker in a slum becomes a socialist.
There is no true substitute for potash.
In Egypt and Iraq it is illegal to be an abortionist.

Gandhi on trains traveled only third class.
Incentive fades when an athlete's overpaid.
Metal always contracts faster than glass.
Nothing is ever quite equal regarding trade.

TRUISMS

Personality invariably constitutes policy.
Rolling disclosures are inevitably lies.
Prejudice informs all documented history.
Any serious question expressly defies.

Pub ciders always tend to be too sweet.
Everyone mispronounces the word *fuchsia*.
A woman flirting will always spread her feet.
The Sicilian flag bears the image of Medusa.

Never blender-chop basil—heat kills its oils.
Two leaps per chasm is automatically fatal.
Pressure will effect any liquid while it boils.
Lung problems are issues in babies pre-natal.

Every true Tuscan has a reverence for bread.
Most late-night radio listeners are half insane.
Even plants strategize against being in-bred.
A bicycle is a crucial accessory to a Dane.

Onions are marked up in groceries 800%.
Camel as food is prohibited by the Torah.
Concrete is not even 10% cement.
"Halo" (fluffiness) is best found in angora.

Every operatic tenor began as a baritone.
Great-horned owls love the meat of skunk.
Our most unstable bone is the ankle bone.
No woman can be touched by Thai monk.

To doubt nothing is to learn nothing.
Giraffes always browse into the wind.
The scalp, not hair, is improved by brushing.
Intention alone matters in what is sinned.

Baseball on-deck circles exist no more.
A hungry people is ever a barbaric people.
Money being counted rarely records a crore.
Theology is involved in any decretal.

Amish men grow beards but never mustaches.
No book of the Bible was written by a woman.
Recollection comes only in isolated flashes.
Failure's understood as a synonym for human.

Great architects are painfully narcissistic.
Thunderstorms in Texas predominate in May.
The redneck mentality is madly nativistic.
U.S. ships, for camouflage, are painted gray.

Characters provide the fuel to writing fiction.
A taboo is firemen saying, "It's quiet tonight."
Rural Americans find comfort in bad diction.
Purity was the principal virtue of a knight.

Chilled plastic wrap is easier to handle.
Ovolactovegetarians all value protein.
A thrown shadow beautifies a candle.
A skin derivative, not bone, is baleen.

TRUISMS

Adding salt to it makes ice colder.
Most philosophers have never married.
Illusions increase as we grow older.
A lazy man feels perpetually harried.

A tubby woman's always in the way.
Teenagers hate to read a book.
The Boston Irish outlook's always gray.
A martini's better stirred than shook.

Disguising food is a way of murdering it.
Wagnerian opera is an all-inclusive art.
Confessing a crime is unburdening it.
The cradle of auto manufacture is Stuttgart.

Ginger that is turning white is bad.
All obfuscatory poetry is trash.
The key to grandpa is the key to dad.
No life is wasted more than chasing cash.

All lawyers should be banned from politics.
A teaspoon of dry sugar will cure hiccups.
Any and all lists compiled are gimmicks.
Pick-up lines are as fatuous as pick ups.

Infants have no knees at parturition.
For pulled pork, select a Boston butt.
Hostility is encouraged by bipartition.
Every shell is toxic of a cashew nut.

America fetishizes its own nationhood.
Tactlessness is the vice of all upstarts.
For anything to float use balsa wood.
Sequence is the tongue of flowcharts.

No human commune is not a cult.
The ephemeral is generally putrescible.
Animals figure in every Chinese insult.
Guns in America are always accessible.

Every pointed arch re-directs gravity.
Cynics crave the pleasure of displeasure.
A subtext in jazz music is depravity.
Flirtation best succeeds by countermeasure.

To listen is held more virtuous than to watch.
Palestinian deaths always exceed Israeli's.
It's the barrel that gives its color to scotch.
A golden eagle's favorite food is capercaillies.

Lobster roll buns are side split the better to grill.
Japanese never write a person's name in red ink.
Krill eat plants, and all whales to subsist eat krill.
Prison walls stem violence when painted pink.

Debt makes every man a coward.
The U.S. has no possessions in Africa.
Every arch strives to move outward.
The strongest of natural fibers is abaca.

TRUISMS

Nothing can match in beauty a Veldt sunset.
Ted Williams never sat at the end of a dugout.
Sauce is the *sine qua non* of any croquette.
Every consequence involves negative fallout.

Pursuit of one thing also causes its opposite,
Were there no uniforms, there'd be no armies.
Sterility adhibits to anything corporate.
It is always recommended to eat *cold* salamis.

A given loan is a hate that you incur.
East in every country's saner than the west.
Of occupations that pedophiles prefer
to drive a musical ice-cream truck is best.

Children of suicides are prone to follow suit.
Sartre merely channeled German philosophy.
Cecil B. DeMille invented the fascist salute.
No good biography is a worshipful biography.

Jews don't like the use of the word Jew.
Orson Welles hated to be seen laughing on screen.
The British method is always to queue.
Cooking with aluminum turns egg yolks green.

Birds when scared will always fly in circles.
Lear's bias for Cordelia causes her sisters' hate.
Violet is a spectral color, not so any purples.
Urine is the tincture of New Jersey license plate.

A great wine is never drunk but chewed.
The totalitarian mind is always patriotic.
Birds most favor sunflower seeds in food.
Volleyball is understood to be homoerotic.

Every barbershop quartet looks alike.
Vending machines don't take half-dollars.
No toll-less road can be called a turnpike.
Administrators disesteem true scholars.

Pressure diminishes as altitude climbs.
The taste of lobster is ruined by any sauce.
Guns equally foster and prevent crimes.
Japanese gardeners highly value moss.

Guinness stout that's imported loses flavor.
Financial crises happen every seven years.
Women's beauty parlors thrive on claver.
Bite-crushing a bowling ball is possible for bears.

A natural frontier becomes a manmade border.
Anchorage, Alaska has never seen 90-degrees.
Space is experienced as a horror to a hoarder.
Helium in a liquid state will never freeze.

The only reality among politicians
is what's perceived but never meant.
Calumnies—slander—are dry crucifixions.
A peony is by far Nature's greatest scent.

TRUISMS

Wales has its own postage stamps, not its own money.
Nothing loves to re-seed itself more than day lilies.
The city of Loja in Ecuador is perennially sunny.
The entire Caribbean comprises the so-called "Antilles."

All Utopian dreams are built upon exclusion.
Dieting means eating, not *not* eating.
The only true desert in Europe is Andalusian.
Snapping fingers in Nigeria's a greeting.

Only 7% of the land in China is arable.
New England taste excludes blackfish.
Analogy is the intention of every parable.
The U.S. tongue is not officially English.

The art of decorating is all about space.
Yawning is an unacceptable act for a Muslim.
Expressions are symmetrical in a human face.
Showing up late in Venezuela is a custom.

Silent movies derive from the 19th century.
A promise broken to a child is a form of murder.
All satire of any kind is a type of flattery.
Pedantry is the vice of every serious birder.

Movies are valued by sales, not worth.
The banana cannot reproduce by itself.
Antarctica is the driest place on Earth.
Only ill-gotten money can be called pelf.

Drake Passage weather is tempestuous.
Aristocrats are very rarely nationalistic.
The phrase "prepared mustard" is ludicrous.
The Balkan mind is largely pessimistic.

Drying kills the scent of the herb cilantro.
God's *understanding* forgives all our sin.
No one ever looks good in a passport photo.
Diary-keeping is argument you always win.

True kin are only those that we have chosen.
The letter J is missing in the periodic table.
Bahai and Shia can mix only in an explosion.
One true pervert will another always enable.

Ancient Greek temples always faced east.
Anyone who is outnumbered fosters pity.
Drinking beer's essentially drinking yeast.
Country connotes boobs, suavity the city.

A comet's tail always points away from the sun.
Wordsworth in poems never mentions his father.
Upholsterers and drapers both prefer cretonne.
Norwegians for durability use salmon leather.

Bananas are a type of herb, not trees.
An angry camel's shit immediately liquefies.
Sunlight can cause people to sneeze.
The nature of rudeness is, primarily, it defies.

TRUISMS

The French hate that Napoleon was Italian.
In his books. Darwin never mentions "evolution."
Any parvenu can be bought with a medallion.
Ethics, not religion, interests a true Confucian.

Flax plants are pulled from the ground, never cut.
Show biz wives in Las Vegas are never welcome.
The oldest tree food on the planet is the walnut.
Both adverb and adjective is the word "seldom."

Nine out of every ten living things live in the ocean.
Huckleberry Finn never once refers to his mother.
Every Thai as to language can understand a Laotian.
A sister helps find boyfriends by way of a brother.

The happiest creatures on earth are birds.
The UPenn faculty has never been unionized.
All designers depend on the rule of thirds.
Everything that is paraphrased is plagiarized.

Circles are always constructed from triangles.
Nothing should be shorn that does not grow back.
No one from one's genes ever disentangles.
Yugoslavia formed the Slovene, Czechs the Slovak.

Larch though a conifer is a deciduous tree.
July is the wrong month to visit Hawaii.
Nothing subtly flirts like a woman's knee.
Earth's largest canyon is in the Bering Sea.

Cold weather both induces and increases joy.
Nothing explains Supreme Court judges being nine.
In China and India parents welcome only a boy.
Skin diseases can benefit by the use of brine.

All Australian elections are held on a Saturday.
Public decorations should only come from royalty.
Only the Gamay grape is used in a Beaujolais.
Staying with a brand is the modern idea of loyalty.

All of Hemingway's novels are love stories.
Government awards in a republic are ludicrous.
No better fishing boats than Nova Scotia dories.
The Book of Mormon narrative is stuporous.

Permanence is transfigured disposability.
A slump is a grunt is a buckle is a cobbler is a crisp.
Coconut meat is the nadir of digestibility.
Sibilants pose a true agony for anyone with a lisp.

Fresh tomatoes need not be peeled for sauce.
Mothers never signify in George Eliot's novels.
Christ appears only on the Roman Catholic Cross.
Greed in performance characteristically grovels.

Tact is the essential quality of a doorman.
Only marginalized people live on mountains.
Eating while walking is thought rude in Japan.
Two streams are employed in water fountains.

TRUISMS

A perfect circle is never seen in Nature.
Freedom is always taken, never given.
The Antarctic ice sheet is in fact a glacier.
Creases enhance the beauty of linen.

No meal ever failed for want of a chive.
Fabric bias is technically not a grain.
Southeast facing is the standard beehive.
Victorian lung tonics favored mullein.

The larger the room, the emptier the space.
Painting a ceiling makes the room look taller.
Whiteness opens up any rooms with grace.
Rugs make a small room look even smaller.

Americans have never understood cheese.
Virtually every girl in Somalia is circumcised.
Coin currency is not used by the Burmese.
Thailand by Europeans has never been colonized.

There have never been maharajas in Ceylon.
A diamond shape was Picasso's signature image.
A chicken is always less flavorful than a capon.
Only the *appearance* a face makes is a visage.

Terrorists favor the use of bombs to kill.
Men, unlike women, love to read maps.
Asparagus is the perfect match with dill.
Potatoes are the beating heart of schnapps.

In the ancient world, all wine was sweet.
Muslims who are pious sleep on their right side.
Cancer is often caused by processed meat.
One large, long wave constitutes the ocean tide

Strong leaders make a weak people.
No McDonald's burger isn't 3.875 inches in diameter.
Everything faecal is different from fecal.
A pyramid is the standard shape every single balsam fir.

Ugly violinists tend to marry beautiful wives.
Every piano makes seven octaves available.
Insects in general are all repulsed by chives.
Finches of all the birds are the most tamable.

Diplomacy is nothing but political strategy.
John Bardeen transformed the modern world.
Memory is the first sign of a child prodigy.
Fungal disease can cause a tree being burled.

Generalizations are always lacking in total truth.
The Adams family felt never at home in Boston.
Soda pop, more than anything, decays a tooth.
No state law requires human burial in a coffin.

Comedians are invariably despondent people.
Stainless steel knives cannot properly be sharpened.
A perfect match is the fungal and the beetle.
Old jewelry can be restored when work hardened.

TRUISMS

Actors idiotically feel ascots look dynamic.
Diary entries made in the morning are crueler.
No megalomaniac's dream isn't panoramic.
His booth, alone, makes paranoid a jeweler.

Anything *between* is the cause of limitation.
15th-century wealth meant nutmeg and mace.
Letters in Christmas cards constitute retaliation.
Seriousness in gambling is *not* a straight face.

Most chefs in France are also Freemasons.
No Apollo 11 astronaut ever returned to space.
No professional butler or servant ever hastens.
Virtually any flatfish is denominated plaice.

Avalanches plague Switzerland's valleys.
Golden Delicious are best for apple pan dowdy.
Most book collectors covet bound galleys.
The color green provides comfort for a Saudi.

George Washington never wore a powdered wig.
The English language was *imported* to England.
Sleeping nose to nose is favored by the pig.
There are no significant roads in Greenland.

Hens of all foods preferably prefer ripe fruit.
Shakespeare never had permanent lodging in London.
Women feel empowered wearing a high boot.
Wearing flip-flops fosters painful growth of a bunion.

ALEXANDER THEROUX

Raspberry bushes propagate with abandon.
No one more than a Welshman loves a hymn.
Old movie stars paid their favored stand-in.
A tyrant's most feared characteristic is whim.

The prophet Mohammed outlawed all usury.
A quarter of world languages are spoken in Africa.
The nature of anticipation is at bottom delusory.
For the best hemp rope always choose the abaca.

! is how linguists denote a click in print.
Wyoming's Madison River never freezes over.
Life in the Stone Age depended solely on flint.
A starving lawn grass will always breed clover.

No rivers can be found in Saudi Arabia.
All talk radio is largely inconsequential.
The world's richest digs are in Belgravia.
No swamp on Earth is not pestilential.

American flags must be folded as a triangle.
Modernism is the death of religious conviction.
A half of a circle is never not a straight angle.
Every commitment made announces a restriction.

Sexuality is inflamed the prevalence of mists.
Pigs, who have four toes on each foot, walk on two.
Flexion in all sports hinges mainly on the wrists.
Popular magazines sell best when the cover is blue.

TRUISMS

Moses Mendelssohn dismissed Yiddish as jargon.
Every ballet plot is banal because uncomplicated.
Nothing given away free is technically a bargain.
No inveterate pedophile can ever be rehabilitated.

The mineral cryolite has been fully depleted.
A bee's *wings* are never touched with pollen.
Scotland's National Monument was never completed.
Only a reconciled enemy has officially fallen.

The choke of every artichoke is inedible.
The Inuit use igloos only for hunting camps.
No circle touches or surrounds a pentacle,
unlike that which every pentagram stamps.

Only 1% of college students are American Indian.
A lobster's eyes are little more than an ornament.
Dinner at midnight is common for an Argentinian.
Shapes that are equal are not necessarily congruent.

Shepherds are always favored in the Bible.
Whoever asks, "Who me?" yes, it *is* you.
Slander comes under speech, writing libel.
Americans have no conception of a queue.

A hen lays eggs standing up, not sitting.
Shakespeare never once traveled abroad.
The human need to climb is unremitting.
There is no actual fish called "scrod."

Stock markets, even with rules, allow thefts.
There is no folklore in Wordsworth's poetry.
Over-planning their stay is ever rude to guests.
Hand fans constitute a language for coquetry.

Violinists begin their every piece on an up-bow.
No Utopia does not exclude someone.
What the English call claret is in fact Bordeaux.
Enzymes are destroyed in food overdone.

Nothing of love exists that is not an echo.
Any true victim relies heavily on intuition.
Speed lines superanimate all Art Deco.
No eunuch isn't an authority on abscission.

Critics have killed more writers than liquor.
Rabbis still debate whether Jell-O's kosher.
Victorians held as sanitary anything wicker.
Magicians see deceit in any trick disclosure.

Lipstick kills the effervescence of champagne.
Rivers in India are the world's most polluted.
Always *organized* is a whispering campaign.
Stock market terminology is always convoluted.

The Korean language is neither tonal nor inflected.
There is one ocean tide, with no beginning or end.
Protecting a U.S. president never been perfected.
Nausea results in almost each and every scend.

TRUISMS

War crimes, taken as a phrase, is redundant.
All Texans love drinking Dr. Pepper.
Not only common, diamonds are abundant.
Armadillos carry bacteria to make a leper.

A writer's faults become his style.
The most common surname in Quebec is Tremblay,
Chewing is impossible for a crocodile.
Straining is definitely required for making true purée.

A chef's toque blanche has 100 pleats.
People hate to be sold but love to buy.
No ancient Mayan cities had any streets.
Belief in God is not required of a rabbi.

It is considered highly rude to shout in Jordan.
The oil business is the oil *shortage* business.
Police have less power than a game warden.
Hollywood agents' handshakes are viscous.

People are thinner in mountains than down below
Never open a letter with no return address.
Southerners still refer to a boyfriend as a beau.
A knight can move 122 million ways in chess.

A green hat in China indicates a cuckold.
Dental floss is stronger than sewing thread.
Of earth's rare elements, ranked 58th is gold.
The most appetizing of all colors is red.

A "tramp' travels, but to work is not willing.
A "bum," who hates travel, of work will cavil.
A "vagrant" less prefers traveling than milling.
A "hobo," always itinerant, is driven to travel.

A "Royal stag" has antlers with 14 points.
Girl scouts shake hands with the left hand.
The human skull has no movable joints.
Preservatives are absent in vegetables canned.

Actors all crave "celebrity adjacence."
Ancient Greeks rarely committed suicide.
Inadequacy is snobbery's basic nascence.
Beauty can never another beauty abide.

Credulity is the twin sister of skepticism.
A raven has as many as thirty distinct calls.
Monastic life is lived in perfect communism.
In Portugal, fish are served with eyeballs.

The Arctic, a desert, has less rain than Arizona.
Blackstrap molasses has more iron than spinach.
Greta Garbo's face adorns the Swedish 100 kroner.
No passport embraces more countries than Finnish.

A walrus must be shot six inches behind the eye,
since the rest of the beast remains a solid blubber.
For breakfast, old New Englanders always ate pie.
Newspapers can't be made without natural rubber.

TRUISMS

No cider apple beats a Yarlington Mill.
A scratched seed needs a smooth tilth.
A dog will sicken eating any daffodil.
No recovery exactly replenishes spilth.

Flatware originated as fashion.
Every mountain man was raised by a hostile father.
No genocide exceeds that of the Circassian.
Proposal is for consideration, a proffer is an offer.

Dry oak leaves rustling sound exactly like rain.
For good luck, opera singers say "*Toi! Toi! Toi!*"
Every country on the map has a variant for Jane.
Blacks say "man," for despising the word "boy."

Tire rubber is basically polybutadiene.
A seal surfaces for air every twenty minutes.
Extracting money lies behind all chicane.
Flax is the favorite munch for all linnets.

Impotence ads flourish on sports talk shows.
Nothing attracts a grizzly more than the smell of fish.
Renaissance women loathed having eyebrows.
A large size is counter-productive in a Petri dish.

No orchestra is ever completely in tune.
Bark left on logs badly darkens a log cabin.
Code is the central tenet of the Nordic rune.
Sex in women's fabric is the sheen of satin.

Victorian pornography is riddled with incest.
All school bubblers have a low arch of water.
Ovate forms mainly predominate in bird nests.
No living animal has thicker fur than an otter.

Girlfriends of gay men are their mothers.
Genius is never found in a committee.
Best friends are chosen, never brothers.
In all lawless societies, you find graffiti.

Pink flamingos are always sold in pairs.
No one's more savage than women in a strike line.
Stupidity is best published by a person's ears.
Re-sign is the direct opposite of resign.

A lobster goes fastest moving backward.
The human femur is stronger than concrete.
No ballet movement isn't basically awkward.
His crime a pedophile will always repeat.

All trees are "dwarf trees" in the tundra.
Kids dislike *cornicione*—the edge—of pizza.
The darkest part of a shadow is the umbra.
No world alphabet is not indebted to Phoenicia.

Salt cod was the staple of the British Navy.
Any republic tolerating a privileged class fails.
No true Italian refers to sauce as "gravy."
No Duke of Cornwall isn't the Prince of Wales.

TRUISMS

Insect repellent is ineffective against gnats.
Strangers in Maine are said to be "from away."
Their teeth will never stop growing in rats.
The first gender-equality sport was croquet.

Capitalism does not have a human face.
Speaking when hunting is the worst sound to make.
Nutmeg from the seed, from its cover mace.
Liquor is most essential to any decent fruitcake.

Water extracted (distilled) from beer makes whiskey.
All right angles are equal to one another.
The American flag should always be hoisted briskly.
Cookbook authors favorably blurb each other.

Claret, or Bordeaux, comes in a bottle with shoulders.
Ethiopian food is eaten mainly with the hands.
Burgundy is sold in a bottle smoother than boulders.
Ecologic degradation occurs fastest in wetlands

Tulip buds are perfectly symmetrical.
Always shoot a moose near water, for transport.
French philosophers are all born skeptical.
The penchant to exhort is to frequently extort.

The Chinese Exclusion Act banned a nationality.
Living in tap or fresh water will kill a lobster.
Negative are all Bible references to sinistrality.
Kidnapping was never the crime of a mobster.

ALEXANDER THEROUX

Gladiola bulbs are not true bulbs but corms.
Never invest emergency savings in stocks.
A person's *gestalt* is enhanced by uniforms
Discerning colors is a special gift of hawks.

All bourbons (from oaken casks) are brown.
No Confederate leaders appear on U.S. currency.
Bring no entourage to choose a wedding gown.
Nothing spots cowardice like an emergency.

Cows can produce milk only after they calve.
John Constable never painted a scene of autumn.
There's no verb form of half, but only halve.
Negativism thrives on imagery of the bottom.

Chewing kisses in movies are revolting.
Leonardo da Vinci never signed a painting.
A lobster sheds its exoskeleton by molting.
Ladies once proved their charm by fainting.

Southerners always say Mama and Daddy
but literally never say Dada and Mommy.
Airtightness is a necessity in a tea caddy.
Seiza is the proper way to sit on a tatami.

Plot is an irrelevance in a great novel.
Above the Kaaba in heaven is its replica.
It is illegal in America to advertise a brothel.
Only plays as tragedies interested Seneca.

TRUISMS

A draft will consistently collapse popovers.
There are no inferior poems by John Milton.
Hasty selling is the plague of bondholders.
A cheese license is required to make Stilton.

Sartorial lace has signified status for centuries.
Fathers don't exist in *Where the Wild Things Are*.
80% of those released return to penitentiaries.
One crucial aspect of memory is the human scar.

Writing screenplays is the death of writers.
The Seven Years War was the first world war.
"Goodbye" is never uttered by firefighters.
Filleting tuna is impossible with an albacore.

Capitalism is thievery at best.
Pigs loathe drafts and easily sunburn.
Hate the oppressor, fear the oppressed.
To acknowledge a landlord is to *attorn*.

Animals all eat with a sense of stealing.
A billionaire reveals somewhere a policy failure.
Worshipping, Jews avoid the act of kneeling.
Mere tradition constitutes a serious jailor.

Sheep sensing danger always run uphill.
Leo Tolstoy despised William Shakespeare.
Duty is at bottom an antonym of free will.
Chanting is *lingua franca* for an auctioneer.

Every exit always involves an entrance.
Siblinghood is naturally contentious.
Nothing agreeable constitutes a penance.
An oversized restaurant menu is pretentious.

The lowest sea levels on earth are in India.
Bing Crosby hated singing "Polka Dots and Moonbeams."
No gentleman regards the worth of media.
TV commercials sell far less well than ads in magazines.

True sovereignty can never be shared.
Letters in ancient Rome were never signed.
Sweet and salty are always perfectly paired.
The eight major planets are never aligned.

All revolution is legitimate retribution.
Lincoln personally disliked the nickname "Abe."
Acceding to lobbyists is a kind of prostitution.
A clock functions in every was as an astrolabe.

"The Birth of the Blues" is not a blues song.
Under the law, the dead cannot be libeled.
Horse-racing alone uses the word *furlong*.
Satire conventionally borders on the ribald.

The name Marx derives from Mordecai.
Darkness in its gloaming muffles sound.
A knife can cut all and any metals alkali.
A stew meat should always first be browned.

TRUISMS

Granite is the chief material of the continents.
Piano keys are fashioned mainly from holly.
Mother love gives a child lifetime confidence.
Seeking pity from bankers is the height of folly.

Selfishness as a personal vice self-victimizes.
All of Lewis and Clark's expedition was uphill.
Knowledge of the ocean deep is all surmises.
Tamizh is the correct pronunciation of Tamil.

Baseball's Ty Cobb hated Rogers Hornsby.
Every torturer is the lowest trash on earth.
Strict laws protect every camel thorn tree.
The word *frith* can also be spelled *firth*.

Sentimentality is the opposite of sentiment.
Ancient Greek choruses numbered fifty.
Wealth makes even common slobs pre-eminent.
Long-term growth makes vision thrifty.

Franklin Roosevelt disliked Charles De Gaulle.
American Irish invented an imitation homeland.
Promiscuity is the subtext of every masked ball.
Fully out-of-date is the practical use of shorthand.

Any sugar in its sap is useless to a tree.
The strut of grandiosity always comes up halt.
Dandelion's the best plant for an ersatz coffee.
The U.S. product most often recycled is asphalt.

Hands most betray any person's age.
Plants need iron to make chlorophyll.
The fashion world is beyond outrage.
Whatever is fed pigs is technically swill.

Every tree is an upside-down river.
The English are clueless when it comes to jazz.
Our only regenerative organ is the liver.
Every rainbow color can be found in topaz.

No one can accurately judge the age of lichen.
Jewelers preponderate in France.
Every paint stroke is a prayer making an ikon.
Ears to hear do not exist in ants.

Poltergeists only manifest through children.
An elephant's trunk is as much lip as nose.
Anything learned by rote has been drilled in.
Humans control balance by their big toes.

Science fiction is utterly bereft of humor.
Mock anger is a mask for the real thing.
Reputations essentially pivot on rumor.
Fascists compulsively lean to the right wing.

Concrete is always alkali and never acidic.
Tree sap contains no bacteria or organic matter.
No fundamentalist sermon is not bromidic.
Untried land's a casino to a gambling wildcatter.

TRUISMS

A typical woodchuck tunnel is 25 feet long.
About half the weight of a fresh log is water.
Cowardice prospers best in midst of a throng.
Wet is to a hard rain what heat is to a potter.

Ceramic knives are harder than steel knives.
Tree leaves are both air- and waterproof.
Divorced women are still considered wives.
Proof is unalterably sufficient to be truth.

Teenage love is mainly a primitive illness.
No Amish people today remain in Europe.
Heavy perfume exudes a distinct shrillness.
There are six different spellings of Zurich.

Israeli *haute couture* is in fact anomaly.
Refrigerated tomatoes lose their taste.
A polka played well is played abominably.
Political donations are a form of waste.

No water outside Earth exists in our solar system.
After Pearl Harbor, no ship is named *Arizona*.
Only the correct *use* of knowledge is true wisdom.
The saltiest water is Don Juan Pond in Antarctica.

Wearing civilian attire diminishes a nun.
When ocean water freezes, it loses its saltiness.
No Boston butt that's cooking can be overdone.
In anything legal a shyster can find faultiness.

Only a natural scent becomes a potpourri.
Third base in baseball is the easiest base to seal.
The deepest canyons on Earth are undersea.
The sledge was always used before the wheel.

No one has ever seen an H_2O molecule.
The most brutal 19th-century slaveholders were devout.
Every world religion has its Golden Rule.
The healthiest food for humans is said to be sauerkraut.

Routine is fortification for a butler.
Striking an Asian is seen a monstrous insult.
Of floral scents nothing is subtler.
Faith is to religion as knowledge to occult.

Ho Chi Minh never bothered to marry.
Sassafras trees have three types of leaves,
Health greatly benefits by ditching dairy.
Hollywood producers are kings of sleaze.

Brown in nature is a degenerate orange.
To keep alive is hard without growing bigger.
No green sauce isn't enhanced by adding borage.
A true bartender never measures a jigger.

A green costume is taboo in a circus
Function not beauty serves mortar and pestle.
Most state workers serve no purpose.
Every married couple is sadly sessile.

TRUISMS

Bay leaves protect against all moths.
Behind every great fortune lurks a crime.
Germans insist that a good beer froths.
Robert Frost preferred that poetry rhyme

November 1 is the best time to buy candy.
"Methods" is Communist code for torture.
A cracked clam or oyster is always sandy.
In fraud technique alone describes a forger.

An English butler is invariably married.
An English valet is commonly a bachelor.
The monotonous is invariably unvaried.
The right-side tip is longest on a spatula.

Vietnamese never abandon their relatives.
Place books forward, not backward on a shelf.
All vintners are fanatical about appellatives.
Dishonesty is forever identified with pelf.

Bacteria highly figures in plant life.
Totalitarian governments require enemies.
Serration is the fulcrum of a bread knife.
Omission's an implied option in parentheses.

Only deludinoids find meaning in politics.
All archives are by nature incomplete.
A true Christian embraces all derelicts.
Pasta is made best from hardest wheat.

Bette Davis had no vanity as an actress.
Corn-brewed beer makes an inferior product.
Housebreakers first search under a mattress.
Disorder is defiance in childhood conduct.

In the human finger there are no muscles.
Tobacco thrives only reddish sandy soil.
Three languages are all official in Brussels.
Only wood pulp properly yields tall oil.

Coercion always manufactures consent.
An average hen lays 260 eggs a year.
Oxygen is the enemy in foods to ferment
Humans have 32 teeth, so do deer.

Greta Garbo never once appeared on stage.
Mules, with odd chromosomes, cannot reproduce.
On hills trains prove best on narrow gauge.
Pepsin's the chief digestive enzyme in gastric juice

Beer mats (coasters) always have a border.
Left side of a face looks best in photographs.
Cops are main culprits in traffic disorder.
Warnings comprise most colonial epitaphs.

A fresh egg in water will never float.
Visibility is key in a conductor's baton.
Harmonically nonessential is a grace note.
Tenderness of meat adhibits to a capon.

TRUISMS

Serial killers are commonly active in church.
No one values their king more than Thais.
The most popular tree in Russia is the birch.
Envy can only be registered by the eyes.

A standard ear-to-ear smile is always false.
Greta Garbo loathed wearing long dresses.
Sorrel is the preferred color in a Belgian horse.
Morals in human history never progresses.

There are 600 rooms in Buckingham Palace.
Hay is a mix of clover, alfalfa, and timothy grass.
Due to brevity in sex no bone exists in a phallus.
Bronze is more expensive than brass.

Repetition is usually found best in threes.
Cemetery headstones generally face east.
For 90% of history Earth had no trees.
Being wealthy is disgraceful in a priest.

Black locust is best wood for fencing.
Waste, unlisted, is the Eighth Deadly Sin.
Both giving and taking defines dispensing.
The greatest misery in prison is the din.

Hurricanes occur only over warm seas.
The Atlantic cod population has disappeared.
Authority is universally symbolized by keys.
Dishevelment describes an old man's beard.

No one knows how large lobsters can grow.
Wierpole wood in a fireplace flares best.
Yamaska, Quebec is ground zero for clan Theroux.
A good host never makes plans for a guest.

The tip of a knife is not the *point* of it.
Vessels cruise *in* water *on* a coast *off* a cape.
No cider apple beats a Black Dabinett.
Sunlight alone makes a raisin from a grape.

Thomas Jefferson hated all monarchies.
Hair infuses good nitrogen in compost.
No African nations function as autarkies.
Emptiness constitutes 99% of the cosmos.

Every needy mother dominates a child.
Fresh olives are all virtually inedible.
Bu the Japanese Koreans are reviled.
No political primary promise is credible.

Run if it is a moose, stand if it is a bear.
Forged chef knives are better than stamped ones.
Fluorescent light is deleterious to beer.
20% of gun owners entirely own 65% of guns.

Our eyes originally evolved to see water.
A fence that can't hold water can't hold a goat.
A pestle is male, and a female is mortar.
English school children mainly learn by rote.

TRUISMS

High air pressure badly hurts birds' ears.
Severe frostbite cannot heal on its own.
Cows give less quality meat than steers.
Mating is the sole purpose of a (bee) drone.

Shine in any clothing implies wear.
No one knows what makes cells divide.
Brown hair grows faster than blonde hair
Radical feminists began the ride astride.

Short vocal cords produce a higher voice.
Halibut is but a distinct kind of flounder.
Refusing to choose is also distinct choice.
Scolding *outspoken* is a scolding rounder.

Fever is the body's attempt to kill viruses,
No bouillabaisse isn't improved by a rosé.
Both its scientific and common name is *irises*.
To sing, said St, Augustine, is also to pray.

Moods are the cause, not the effect.
Shop-bought Melba toast is execrable.
Anything flecked is equally specked.
A chosen group is by definition select.

Distrust a condiment that bites too soon.
Millers were legendarily hated by peasants.
Fried food is king in every greasy spoon.
Its whirr, not the hunter, murders pheasants.

ALEXANDER THEROUX

Warm *sake* tastes the best at 121° F.
To dismember an eel is to *tranesse* it.
Sharp knives are icons to a serious chef.
A dog feels unloved lest you caress it.

Border Terrier dogs flourish on killing rats.
Statins are rendered useless by grapefruit.
Bananas and mangoes are pollinated by bats.
No better thickener exists than arrowroot.

Back braces pained faces in old photographs.
A good blurb is only—always—pithy.
No narcissistic celebrity ever gives autographs.
The biggest canard is there's a holy city.

In bad weather, teams *run* the football.
Every plate of figs deserves a sauterne.
Tuna is/are a specific species of mackerel.
Look to make investments on a downturn.

Good taste is invariably simple taste.
St. Luke the Evangelist was a Gentile.
The United States is indifferent to waste.
Any worn perfume is meant to beguile.

A Malbec pairs brilliantly with beef.
Warm steamy climates produce short noses.
Politics understands nothing of grief.
Polystyrene foam never decomposes.

TRUISMS

To cut up quail is formally to "wing" it.
Flounder is also often referred to as *sole*.
A Homeric epic was written to sing it.
Romans loved jet jewelry made of coal.

Plaid is essentially the fabric of a buffoon.
Feathers are most easily removed when a bird is warm.
Farce adhibits to singers who overly croon.
Female insects, gnats, and midges never swarm.

Two in the same trade will rarely agree.
Never apply the American flag to commerce.
Self-promotion is invariably rapacity.
Spontaneity can be a hazard writing verse.

Football practices are built on repetition.
Gin will badly spoil without a cover.
It was *women* who demanded Prohibition.
Overintensity is oppressive in a lover.

Mexican wine does not in fact exist.
The term brunette includes all dark hair.
A double fisherman knot will not untwist,
Medieval robes were trimmed with *vair*.

Fans care far much more than athletes.
To win Three Card Monte's simple: never play.
Vertigo is often suffered in tiered seats.
Massachusetts bans hunting on a Sunday.

Caviar as food has never been kosher.
Reporters within campaign bubbles are hacks.
Racism has been notorious in Nova Scotia.
Theories tend to float on the absence of facts.

No true gambler ever frankly "gambles."
A hawk does not clean but *freaks* its beak.
An impromptu speaker will forever ramble.
The *politique* is antonym of the *mystique*.

No gentleman ever competes for money.
The smaller a fishhook number, the bigger it is.
Italians called their oldest son "Sonny."
Rudeness in conversation is found in the quiz.

Liquor bottles never yield refunds.
Orthodox Jewish coffins comprise no metal.
Stature is, sadly, prohibited to dachshunds.
It is dangerous to cook in a pewter kettle.

The flabby League of Nations birthed fascism.
Freckled kids are thought commercially cute.
It is fear and insecurity that prompts narcissism.
Bald men are invariably extravagantly hirsute.

Most speak Hawaiian only in phrases.
Irascible people have a passion to jaw.
No woman's mind isn't a map of mazes.
Rabbis are masters at circumventing law.

TRUISMS

No wealthy minister is ever a true minister.
Southern women all adore chenille.
A lawyer's smile, a rictus, is darkly sinister.
No automobile dealer lacks a turgid spiel.

A quince is completely edible when raw.
No one has ever crossed Antarctica alone.
Conscience should prevail over any law.
Fashion models worship the collarbone.

No one's forgotten sooner than an athlete.
Obsession is never noticed by its victim.
Sycophants are by their nature all effete.
Communication by a bully is by dictum.

A *doux* Champagne is now no longer made.
No infantry should advance over a bare skyline.
Jealousy is an emotion that refuses to fade.
The number of fruits cited in the Bible is nine.

Women dislike Gilbert & Sullivan operettas.
Chalk is 100 feet deep in good French vineyards.
Creditors have better memories than debtors.
Prescience is a gift that appertains to bards.

Capitalism is the enemy of true democracy.
Burgundy red grapes alone make Pinot Noir.
Most temperance meetings are a gynocracy.
Vegetable gardens are helped by coconut coir.

ALEXANDER THEROUX

Waiting is never not a form of sloth.
Translating is literature's thankless task.
No godless person can swear an oath.
A public face is a variation of a mask.

An international air pilot must identify in English.
Swimming is the most economical means of locomotion.
A petrol fire by water is impossible to extinguish.
Ancient Greeks linked anything pejorative to a Boeotian.

The younger a Muscadet, the better.
A cannon in the Navy's always called a gun.
No down payment isn't suddenly a fetter.
Cooked lamb is ruined when it is overdone.

All gin stills are given female names.
Spartans owed their martial gifts to steel.
The best short stories are by Henry James.
Abstract art defines that of the Ndebele.

Japanese never pass food with chopsticks.
Juniper berry is compulsory in making gin.
Adolf Hitler loathed any and all lipsticks.
The largest organ of the body is our skin.

Spoons are mankind's oldest eating utensil.
Sexy Shakira loves performing barefoot.
Truman Capote always wrote in pencil.
Input needs throughput to become output.

TRUISMS

Every map is strictly a point of view.
The best wines grow on the 45th parallel.
Relentless is the growing of bamboo.
Only clockwise goes a British carousel.

No arrangement with a blackmailer is ever safe.
Horseshoe counters in diners force community talk.
Exhaustion in fiction characterizes every waif.
Gamblers in westerns are frequently called "Doc."

Mister Rogers avoided watching television.
The signifier underlying pretzels is to pray.
All natural growth depends on cell division.
Only the *climbing* mountaineer is on belay.

Tobacco barns are all built to face west.
Power concedes nothing without demand.
A horse's gallop sounds like an anapest.
Only one's birth country is a Fatherland.

Structurally, fingers are modified hairs.
No recording exists of Eugene V. Debs' voice.
Single scissors are referred to as pairs.
Emotions trump logic in the average choice.

Chlorophyll is forever seeking carotene.
No cigar wrapper beats Connecticut Shade.
Nature explicitly *rejects* the color green.
The *peel* is essential in good marmalade.

Sins of politicos always end with a prayer breakfast.
Sing Sing executions always took place on Thursdays.
No California religious cult is not also a sex fest.
Jewish Sabbaths start eighteen minutes before sunset Fridays.

Sympathy badly enables a desperate alcoholic.
Boiling water at high altitudes is nearly impossible.
Hollywood praise is overweeningly hyperbolic.
Silk, burlap, and rayon fabrics are unwashable.

Most firehouse calls are not fire related.
Thunderstorms rarely occur on the open sea.
A church with locked doors is desecrated.
Composed entirely of fat is bovine ghee.

Snakes hear by resting their jaws on the ground.
Nietzsche's *Ecce Homo* is a book about himself.
The royal dog of Scotland is the deerhound.
The lighter the volume, the higher the bookshelf.

Blacks are shunned as iconoclasts as jurors.
Wagner's *Rienzi* is never performed anymore.
Exploitation is the ambition of all insurers.
Never respond whenever you're whistled for.

Lamb finds loyal sisterhood in mint.
A biker's rider must be at least eight years old.
Any hue with white added is a tint.
Each cubic mile of sea water has 25 tons of gold.

TRUISMS

There is no such thing as a black orchid.
Where we cannot reconstruct, we cannot interpret.
A graduation speech is always florid.
Supplication is the message of every self-portrait.

Never trust any organization's treasurer.
All wild orchids are considered endangered.
Excessiveness is implied in the word plethora.
All alcohol is toxic that has been denatured.

Hatred, it is claimed, can invigorate coition.
The Hebrew bible does not acknowledge the Maccabees.
Einstein claimed our most valuable trait is intuition.
No afterlife was a tenet of the old Hebrew Sadducees.

Seafood is always ruined in a cocktail.
Synagogue seats all face toward Jerusalem.
The circular saw was invented by a female.
No known form plant life uses aluminum.

A truly valuable cigar humidor is furniture.
The book of Ezra is seldom read by Christians.
A dutiful spouse is before anything a servitor.
Circumspection is a gateway to premonitions.

A squeezed cigar that makes noise is too old.
Most world languages face imminent extinction.
The Irish potato blight was caused by water mold.
Pols named on city sites boost their own distinction.

Any movie with an overture badly oversells.
Muslims believe ten animals live in heaven.
Suppression always inflames rather than quells.
Secret societies all revere the number seven.

Goldfish will grow pale if left in a dark room.
No restaurants in China serve fortune cookies.
The stronger the power, the narrower the flume.
More bettors improve money odds for bookies.

Nothing in existence is chemical free.
Korean Hangul is the world's simplest script.
France drinks Chardonnay, exports Chablis.
Beneath a church apse belongs a true crypt.

The blood of eels is toxic to humans.
Judeans consider Galileans country bumpkins.
Bringing home seashells is taboo to Cubans.
There are 500 seeds in your average pumpkins.

Frederick Nietzsche despised Christianity.
Ecclesiastes is never quoted in the New Testament.
Cults invariably center on a single personality.
Two parties alone comprised a Biblical covenant.

Amish call everyone by his and her first name,
Sherlock Holmes had no love for suffragettes.
No prison suffocates more than extravagant fame.
A creditor remembers for him a debtor his debts.

TRUISMS

Black people love to say the word "situation."
In Scripture, St. Joseph's age is never given.
No lowbrow need exceeds that of retaliation.
Resentment is soon felt by the quickly forgiven.

Oxford is a city, but Cambridge is a town.
Power favors the creditor, never the debtor.
The burden of identity is born by the noun.
Always refuse the friendship of an abettor.

Moray eels when they bite never let go.
To Arabs, 14-carat is not considered gold.
The less it is handled, the better the dough.
A bright light on any compass is too bold.

Bunts fail using a metal baseball bat.
Eating macadamia nuts will kill a dog.
Glossy is forever the archenemy of matte.
No softshell clam is ever a quahaug.

All birds possess a poor sense of smell.
No great diarist isn't a true ventriloquist.
Monopoly is the goal of every cartel.
Overcharging is the goal of a psychiatrist.

No father is not very distant territory.
70% of French-produced wines are red.
Digression is death to a good short story.
The go-to Mexican staple is fry bread

Crossbreeding strengthens every race.
Sound is unable to travel through a vacuum.
Utter silence characterizes outer space.
Real flowers today are never used in perfume.

No ruler can be tried before a foreign court.
David is the only person in the Bible so named.
No Nobel scientist had skin that was swart.
The zebra in its wildness has never been tamed.

Melancholy songs *please* the melancholy.
Hebrew Bibles don't recognize the book of Judith.
Fully toxic are all the berries of a holly.
Everything not lovely becomes obscene in a nudist.

When thirst is dominant, hunger is absent.
Jesus Christ personally never baptized anyone.
Dante held Alexander the Great as a tyrant.
France does not recognize the Breton tongue.

No flags are displayed in an Amish classroom.
Snobs eat chicken manually, but only *one* hand.
No judge can be sued for conduct in a courtroom.
The drummer is always the cutest in a band.

Slavs have an aversion to anything Teutonic.
No flower has a need for its own nectar.
Clockwise is a southern hemisphere cyclonic.
Greed is the propulsive for every collector.

TRUISMS

No automobile clock is ever quite exact.
Offense improves in a domed stadium.
Every crank distributes a religious tract.
All non-metals combine with radium.

Ryegrass and clover are bad for horses,
Cross-dressing need not mean gender dysphoria.
After a day, rigor mortis dissipates in corpses.
Dionysianism in every form is phantasmagoria.

Every Depression pop song exalted money.
By Roman law, no Jews were crucified nude.
Until fortified with bee saliva, no nectar's honey.
A sitting greeting in China is considered rude.

One can never sneak up on a squirrel.
Amish men and women seldom cut their hair.
Savage, without fluoroscopy, is an epidural.
A fictitious name is every *nom de guerre*.

Old fashioned melodies are always diatonic.
Procedural law favors landlords, never tenants.
Grand opera is by every standard histrionic.
Contrition is at the beating heart of penance.

All mid-ocean islands are volcanoes.
There was never an *Ursprache*, a primeval language.
A tranquil spot sits within all tornadoes.
Denial of any kind in any form is always a bandage.

Hot dry climates produce longer noses.
A glass of Sauterne begs for Roquefort.
Of all colors, there are no black roses.
Pacificism is the faith of a Doukhobor.

All biography falls under historical fiction.
Without resting, a horse can travel for only an hour.
Earth and its air battle in a constant friction.
Sexual ambition explains the need for human power.

No explanation exists for the dog in Tobit 6:1–2.
Man has lived in Africa longer than anywhere else.
The less thickening power, the darker the roux.
Tungsten in its brute ferocity virtually never melts.

Only a bee twenty days old is able to hunt nectar.
No archaeological finds confirm the existence of Jesus.
The epitome of perfect fatherhood is Trojan Hector.
Every masterful oration made is finalized by auxesis.

Always keep a boat's bow facing a storm.
A pollen grain is the male germ of a plant.
Reproduction is the point of a bee swarm.
To Crusaders, pure evil polluted the Levant.

Power fosters the denial of freedom.
Historian Suetonius was superstitious.
Virtual twins are Gouda and Edam.
All love at first sight is suppositious.

TRUISMS

A test of the body is a test of the soul.
Photography is not art but merely artifice.
About 250 million years old is all coal.
Only a *temporal* truce is an armistice.

Racetrack gamblers find taboo using $50 bills.
More mentions of Jesus are made in the Koran than Mohammed.
Nothing hates transplanting more than daffodils.
Exaggerated connoisseurship in a field is considered being mannered.

Everyone is revolted by eating a carp.
Asian women wear gloves while driving.
Precise tuning is impossible on a harp.
Vulgarity is synonymous with striving.

The Lebanese are besotted with anise.
Every Hitchcock's plot: kill my wife for me.
Force in any form is destructive of peace.
Eight feet is a standard jump for any flea.

Most organisms are essentially microbes.
No matter its coat color, Arabian horses have black skin.
Hollywood film acting is strictly wardrobes.
Sand acts as both water and soap to the laving Bedouin.

The liqueur Arak is pronounced "*ah-dut.*"
All donkeys bear a cross image on their backs.
Olykoek (oily cakes) is the original of donut.
Asians, unlike westerners, have dry earwax.

All humor springs from imperfection.
True prayer involves not asking but giving.
Success finds its roots in early rejection.
Nature in its cool disinterest is unforgiving.

Heroic failure is a cultic British delight.
The *colors* with which kids draw is revealing.
Shallower than a sound is an ocean bight.
Any children early abused are forever healing.

Every verb implies a state of being.
The only way to treasure Venice is on foot.
Political parties are dedicated to disagreeing.
A major carcinogen is the carbon in soot.

Foam will never form on pure fresh water.
The planet Earth turns from west to east.
Fascism is imprinted in every *imprimatur*.
Baking powder is a valid substitute for yeast.

Mr. Hyde yearns to revert to Dr. Jekyll.
The Sentinelese kill anyone in a uniform.
The only true American pear is the Seckel.
Neither language nor alphabet is cuneiform.

Kielbasa must be boiled for one hour.
German soldiers got no air support on D-Day.
Bees tend to overlook any red flower.
No beef is more flavorful than Charolais.

TRUISMS

All earthly pleasure's at bottom merely relief.
Defeat is more real to conquerors than victory.
Anglicanism has no original religious belief.
Human emotions exist to be contradictory.

A demagogue's best friend is always a mob.
Any child taught confidence owns the world.
Insecurity's the face behind the mask of a snob.
The art of treen thrives on wood that's burled.

False teeth flatten the taste of good wine.
Evelyn Waugh hated Sir Winston Churchill.
Without support, no plant becomes a vine.
The only closed curve on earth is a circle.

Pike is the standard fish for *quenelles*.
No daydream is ever a legitimate dream.
One must not blow out Shabbat candles.
The lackey mind depends on the meme.

Persimmons ripen from the inside out.
A fief must be lawfully owned to be a vassal.
Trout for food notoriously eat other trout.
Uruses are the ancestors of domestic castle.

Fresh urine has no bacteria in it.
All living things must reproduce.
Technology changes by the minute.
Many children cause child abuse.

ALEXANDER THEROUX

Exotic football snap-counts lead to offsides.
Romanians slice mamaliga with a thread.
There is nothing at all organic in fluorides.
The main delicacy in Malta is their bread.

The basil plant to Hindus is a goddess.
Iranians are especially mistrusted in Israel.
People shrink from anything apodous.
The linear refers to ancestry, never the lineal.

German mayors are invariably stout.
King David's grandmother was a Gentile.
No true person of faith scorns doubt.
Developed nations are the most infertile.

The French rarely use a knife on a crust.
A college fraternity by definition is a clique.
The major human addiction is simple lust.
Singh is the last name of every male Sikh.

Every last birth is a sentence of death.
Both Koreas would join to fight Japan.
"The Scottish Play" is euphemism for *Macbeth*.
Both men and women may wear a caftan.

Political contributions are an utter folly.
Charles Dickens' novels were all serialized.
Drupes, not berries, are the fruit of holly.
H.L. Mencken said Okies should be sterilized.

TRUISMS

Flirtatious people are strangely undersexed.
A cross is never seen in a Mormon building.
Modification's the sole role of the circumflex.
All wood in ancient Egypt demanded gilding.

Military men are very rarely intellectuals.
Theology plays no part in the Hebrew Bible.
The greater the truth, the greater the libel.
Gender fluidity confounds even transsexuals.

Rain consistently falls in round drops.
Constable and Turner were never friends.
No town is not sterile without bookshops.
Binoculars always employ a convex lens.

France had no equivalent to Victorianism.
Oxygen atoms are heavier than hydrogen atoms.
Hands are the first part eaten in cannibalism.
Perfume is the *sine qua non* of all pomatums

A tyrant rules only unwilling subjects.
Sexual provocation is behind all ballet.
Languages are constituted as dialects.
Woman may propose to men on leap day.

Sour cream enhances the taste of pizza dough.
St. Thomas More was an extreme communist.
Funerals are actually celebrated by the crow.
Lake Baikal in Siberia is virtually bottomless.

Reformation, as such, is always a paradigm.
There are no verified reports of xenoglossia.
A lemon has twice the vitamin C of a lime.
The north side of any forest thing is mossier.

Only Muslims expect intercourse in heaven.
Courtship has disappeared from the world.
The most sacred Scriptural number is seven.
Aromas are released in wine while swirled.

Any cloth stretches best along a diagonal.
Schooling fish lose their compact structure at night.
Every culm in cross-section shows triagonal.
Light, which is invisible, should not be called white.

Freedom is wildness in the American dream.
Joseph Smith nullified OT and NT differences.
Grazing animals, worldwide, relish phleum.
Holidays tend to offend Jehovah's Witnesses.

Bonsai thrive best in pure volcanic soul.
Flossing teeth is more important than brushing.
The dog of potluck dinners is the casserole.
Good etiquette militates against all rushing.

Any fish spoils faster than any piece of meat.
There are no hurricanes in the South Atlantic.
Every nose on a human being is a knife pleat.
No candidate in a primary is not sycophantic.

TRUISMS

Hope that is ascertained is never hope.
Platinum jewelry never fails to be marked.
A knot alone gives meaning to a rope.
Commands in the Army are always barked.

The United Nations agrees on nothing.
No truly major black novelist exists.
Insincerity positively thrives on gushing.
Sexiness resides in the motion of wrists.

Young people loathe brown furniture.
Influenza viruses are constantly evolving.
Inverse length is the unit of curvature.
Of the Trinity, there is never any solving.

Spoken Flemish, unlike Dutch, sounds French.
The southern is the only ocean that circles the Earth.
Every billionaire, even polished, bears a stench.
Cooking failures are always a source of mirth.

Vinegar should never be combined with peroxide.
The art of navigation owes everything to astronomy.
Forests and soil store up tons of carbon dioxide.
No conservative doesn't loathe a managed economy.

Yearbook photos tend to appear somber.
Not one personal letter of Shakespeare exists.
Lewdness attaches to hair tinted ombre.
The Swedish word for ankle is, oddly, *vrist*.

No country is the same in habits of breakfast.
Cyclones concentrate in western parts of oceans.
An atheist cannot hold political office in Texas.
Insults with the feet greatly offend all Laotians.

A competitive swimmer over age 20 is old.
The French lay soup spoons mouth side down.
Buried underground is 80% of world gold.
An adjective may well function as a noun.

Iago always speaks is in prose, Othello poetry.
White wine will actually erase a red wine stain.
Alfred Hitchcock's color movies are bad TV.
Omega-3 makes up most of the fat in our brain.

Naturally antibacterial is the nature of bamboo.
No Shakespeare play uses contemporary settings.
Only Gruyère should be properly used in fondue.
Peas, not rice, are tossed out at Czech weddings.

Wine is a living thing; traveling exhausts it.
The first word spoken on the moon was *Houston*.
The English customarily pamper one with possets.
No aquatic habitat is ever wanting in neuston.

Raw *foie gras* cannot be obtained in America.
Chubby women are found sexy in Mauretania.
Low woody evergreens comprise *genus* erica.
Air routes over communities foster hemicrania.

TRUISMS

Signature placement can destroy a painting.
Amazon pays not a penny in United States taxes.
Blue/lapis did not adhere in wet fresco painting.
Preoccupation is the major cause of parapraxes.

A travel writer taking trains is laughable.
Happiness is missing in all pages of history.
Philadelphia sports fans are never affable.
No interpretive answer ever solves a mystery.

No solid stone doesn't mime a setting hen.
Very few Jews have bothered to live in Japan.
Pastry chefs tend to be effeminate men.
No schoolmaster's cane hurt more than rattan.

Sugar found in sap is of no use to the tree.
Good luck is assigned at birth to a baby's caul.
All self-portraits are fake autobiography.
The larch, though a conifer, sheds its leaves in fall.

To a dry alcoholic, addiction elsewhere beckons.
Changing daylight (not weather) explains dying leaves.
An unpinned grenade explodes in seven seconds.
Every magician finds himself naked without sleeves.

A pointed nose in Asia is considered cool.
No car mechanic looks you in the eye.
Tastelessness in Branson, Mo. is the rule.
Dryness is always abhorrent in a pie.

ALEXANDER THEROUX

All U.S. Olympic coverage is jingoistic.
Nobody on earth enjoys a cheese ball.
Written history is strictly impressionistic.
You will never see a ballerina sprawl.

Time moves solely in one direction.
Blindness is virtually a given in Nepal.
Two knees are not used in a genuflection.
Disdain is the proclamation of a wall.

Colors in Rembrandt's oils rarely print well.
Policeman's clubs are made from Osage orange.
An aperture to the left is very rare in a seashell.
A plagiarist's plea is that he's offering homage.

Granite is actually composed of 50% oxygen.
South Carolina grows triple the peaches of Georgia.
Skin turns ashen and lips blue as shock begins.
Modern drugs have largely replaced chirurgia.

Earthworms cannot bear to live in acid soil.
Sodium is inert combined in water with chlorine.
Waterspouts are functions of the French gargoyle.
New mown hay smells like poisonous phosgene.

Scorpions under a night light all fluoresce.
Fish was a food despised in the Homeric age.
Rocks in a triangle serve to symbolize distress.
Ancient drama showed no violence on stage.

TRUISMS

Gunstocks are best made with black walnut.
Apple and Google bank profits in foreign countries.
St. Paul preferred young males to remain uncut.
Any small items *kept apart* are technically "sundries."

Prevailing winds never blow north/south.
It is safer to choose a credit card over a debit card.
Midwesterners pronounce drought *drough*.
The Iraq war, as Vietnam, was based on a canard.

The golden eagle glides but never hovers.
God in the Old Testament speaks only to men.
First editions are worthless without their covers.
A burrow is a hole, but one shelters in a den.

A narwhal's favorite food is halibut.
Twice a day a broken clock is correct.
Chastity alone dignifies the celibate.
Nothing reverses the abuse of child neglect.

The planet Mars is half the size of Earth.
A squirrel without moving can see in all directions.
Condescension is involved in all mirth.
An elephant's penis is S-shaped during erections.

A skunk's the primary eater of common toads.
Terroir is to wine what *merroir* is to oysters.
Giethoorn, Holland, functions without roads.
Seclusion, not beauty, is the point of cloisters.

Any wine decanted suffers certain trauma.
Horatio Alger boys all dreamt a similar dream.
Nothing can budge an overloaded llama.
The robe that Jesus Christ wore bore no seam.

Bananas cannot naturally reproduce.
A poet of lyric brevity cherishes white space.
Pleasure is lessened by a cut prepuce.
There's no shape or dimension to cyberspace.

It is fully impossible to tickle oneself.
The New Yorker cartoons leave one forsaken.
1% owns 45% of the world's entire wealth.
Popular judgment is consistently mistaken.

A person's age should include nine months gestation.
Compost piles need balanced nitrogen and oxygen.
As to ancestry, the Bible recognizes only agnation.
Hollywood actresses are virtually built of collagen.

Canny Wall Street traders buy at the bottom.
The fiercest toxic creature is the Irukandji jellyfish.
All things microscopic apply to quantum.
Braziers are the ancient parents of the chafing dish.

Surgical masks do not prevent disease.
It is illegal to peddle one's own bone marrow.
Foot odor has the odor of blue cheese.
Achilles healed his wounded men with yarrow.

TRUISMS

Every church gargoyle is merely a throat.
Flamingos eat with their heads upside down.
Nothing explains why Jesus never wrote.
There are no plural options for a mass noun.

The first toilet in public stalls is rarely used.
Dandified fastidiousness in novels is always gnomic.
Earnest people cannot bear to be confused.
Government expenditures are never economic.

No single ant ever lives alone.
Many Jews believe Enoch was the Messiah.
Mozart in opera favored solos by a baritone.
Every child molester is the prison pariah.

Salt is the only rock eaten by a human.
String theory posits as many as ten dimensions.
Panic is the death knell of any acumen.
Prostitution thrives in business at conventions.

The heat of sun arouses every bird's libido.
Emily Dickinson, punctuating, overused the dash.
Redirecting an attack is the secret of aikido.
Bird seed sold blindly in opaque bags are trash.

Rules never apply to any genius.
No bests exist—Academy Awards are a joke.
No description exists of Jesus.
Egg tempera painting relies strictly on the yolk.

Raspberries bear fruit only on second-year canes.
Keyboards breed more germs than toilet seats.
Jaywalking is considered anathema by Danes.
Carbon monoxide puts the red in all sold meats.

Movie credits never declare the film's date.
Protestants, to a one, hate Catholic Marianism.
All single-roomed gazebos have sides of eight.
War is the extreme voice of all nationalism.

No revolution will ever abolish poverty.
Romans are always beardless at Oberammergau.
Every state's idiot tax is called the lottery.
The densest population on the planet is in Macau.

The hottest pepper on earth is Bhut Jolokia.
Thirty percent of the worlds eat with chopsticks.
Sound becomes hearing solely by the cochlea.
Vampires actually do exist—they are ticks.

Satin slippers make a woman's feet look smaller.
No record exists of anyone meeting Shakespeare.
Along avenues of poplar trees, rarely is one taller.
Parents with their children always hold one dear.

Bowls of candy and mixed nuts breed germs.
Black truffles do not grow in north America.
The Versailles Treaty meted out revenge, not terms.
Ku Klux Klan lingo is strictly faux esoterica.

TRUISMS

Red-haired women should never wear brown.
Cormac McCarthy never uses quotation marks.
No church gargoyle does not wear a frown.
Most pedophiles like to congregate in parks.

TV remotes in hotel rooms are pestilential.
We are always servants to the rules we set.
Every tenet in the Koran is consequential.
Slight burgundy is found in every brunette.

Reforestation is a slave to geometry.
Eton allows no more than seventy "collegers."
Racism relies much on anthropometry.
Faults a politician never knowledges.

There is no greater hate than lost love.
At 160 degrees, bacteria are destroyed.
Beauty most New Guineans are void of.
A rotating ellipse is always a spheroid.

Nelly Dean is the true villain of *Wuthering Heights*.
Mel Miller is the true villain of *A Face in the Crowd*.
The Mahdi has been born according to the Shiites
—*no, not yet born* declare the Sunnis, just as loud.

Pigs are unable to look up at the sky.
Professional soldiers hate civil wars.
Zen Buddhism is the foundation of bonsai.
Dreams most commonly feature doors.

ALEXANDER THEROUX

Every phrase in a truly great poem is a title.
Guilt is increased by the nature of whispers.
Self-denial in the matter of penance is vital.
Brothers are said to be humanized by sisters.

All the world's spiders have eight legs.
Cruise ships are forever prone to disasters.
Unverified is the value of mustard plasters.
Bigger breeds of chicken lay brown eggs.

Deli meats are a notorious cause of cellulite.
Emerald green is regulation color for redheads.
No printed Congressional study is not recondite.
English football is what gave birth to skinheads.

Identical twins are always the same sex.
Repeated stirring is the key to good risotto.
Vulnerability arouses the fetish of necks
Applause by every standard is staccato.

Asians very rarely converse at meals.
Blacks suffer the most kidney complaints.
Silence is the way a coward squeals.
Feistiness is a common trait of saints.

In films, Gene Autry always played himself.
Mow a field before goldenrod goes to seed.
Fertility is strong in any continental shelf.
Neither of Shakespeare's parents could read.

TRUISMS

Red maple leaves, all serrated and toothed,
bear a red stem and have smooth grey bark.
Sugar maple leaves are rounded, smoothed,
with a green stem and grey bark that is stark.

No war is righteous other than that of defense.
US doctors are overrated, UK doctors under.
Good manners mask bad by accepted pretense.
To Aristotle, cloud collisions caused thunder.

An older face should avoid a trimmer bonnet.
Refrigerating plastic wrap prevents undue cling.
Never drape a U.S. flag or place anything on it.
Every Estonian looks for an occasion to sing.

Stainless steel knives never keep an edge.
Cognac is brandy, but not all brandy cognac.
The oldest human tool is probably the wedge.
Herpes B virus is carried by every macaque.

Prune is, oddly, the French word for plum.
All James Bond movies end in water or near it.
Want of devotion in fasting turns it glum.
An intelligent vessel makes the river steer it.

The sun which goes down never really sets.
Brits prefer marmalade to jelly in a dish.
Blacks who smoke prefer menthol cigarettes.
Singer Elvis Presley never once ate a fish.

There was no moon when the *Titanic* sank.
No Bogart bow-tied played a bad character.
Privilege is perpetually conferred by rank.
Joseph Haydn at age five was a chorister.

Bankers in the Middle Ages mainly wore red.
The flags of Romania and Chad are identical.
The population in Wales is factually inbred.
Secret sects all thrive on a covert conventicle.

In all double acts, one is a perfect fool.
Satiety from over-abundance springs.
Rotation is the pavane of every spool.
Switzerland has never allowed kings.

A novelist's second book invariably fails.
Africans are puzzled by American blacks.
No small talent involves memorizing sails.
Most authors using three names are hacks.

The Polish and Indonesian flags are the same.
90% fish are caught in the northern hemisphere.
Only by deriding can one properly declaim.
Praise in show business is always insincere.

Nothing's viler than an overindulged pet.
Poets portray heaven by way of jewels.
No cat is never happy when that cat is wet.
The most mediocre painters follow rules.

TRUISMS

British gun holsters are thin; U.S. thick.
Sound in *noir* films is a brooding saxophone.
Immaturity alone delights in slapstick.
All Savoy Opera's comics were a baritone.

Tsunamis travel faster in water that is deep.
One does not wear diamonds in daytime.
An attempt at full life is curtailed by sleep.
Extremes of pH will destroy an enzyme.

Elm is generally avoided as sawmill timber.
Celery as a plant is very high in sodium.
Fast reactions require a person being limber.
Ethnic hatred engenders the deepest odium.

Mad love affairs are fatal to ambition.
Polyester as a fabric does not breathe.
Nursing is not a trade but a mission.
Smell best unlocks memory's sheath.

Newport mansions disdained swimming pools.
No human talent compares with self-sufficiency.
Donkey fathers are less intelligent than mules.
Iraq rates lowest in English language proficiency.

Only an ignoramus never planted a tree.
Austerity and hedonism are oddly symbiotic.
Oak is never used fermenting Chablis.
Pomegranate juice is naturally antibiotic.

Somewhere is an edge to the universe.
Contempt of wealth is the highest wealth.
Back windows do not exist on a hearse.
Violence festers in missing love of self.

Crows are virtually never seen dead.
The flute is always held by opposing hands.
Old memories actual crowd the human head.
Valuable aluminum exists in beverage cans

Action alone overcomes melancholy.
Character in a person is the power to refrain.
Philistines all prefer to say "I" rather than "me."
Geosmin creates a smell in falling rain.

It is a mistake to eat any wild fungi raw.
Bracelets make a woman's arm look plump.
Most abstract impressionists could not draw.
The exerted muscles of a cow are in the rump.

Canadian haute cuisine does not exist.
All ocean waves, specifically, are tidals.
Nothing's more sexless than the wrist.
Asians are virtually never matinee idols.

Marx Brothers films are for eight-year-olds.
Guilt is the legacy of the selfish who know it.
Mantegna is the master of drapery and folds.
Rare is Wasabi, as it's impossible to grow it.

TRUISMS

Superstition involves an excess of faith.
All flamenco dancers look like Gilbert Roland.
The mother of machine tools in the lathe.
There was not one Nazi collaborator in Poland.

Poplars grow well in burned over areas.
Aspen, ash, and hollies separate each sex.
Sadness adhibits symbolically to wisterias.
The probing part of the tongue is its apex.

Rhyme is never used in Eskimo songs.
Napoleon always wore cologne in battle.
In Africa there can be found no swans.
Grass is not bitten but ripped by cattle.

The first Book of Mormon was unpunctuated.
No deadly virus disease has ever been cured.
Capitalists thrive on everything unregulated.
Open space is always one fourth of a fjord.

Onions never flourish next to beans.
Rock mates white country with black blues.
A committee succeeds that hastily convenes.
Nothing depressing is ever truly news.

A self cannot be saved by a self not seen.
Picasso's *Guernica* is ruled by the color gray.
No triathlon includes the number thirteen.
Empty spaces are discouraging in a résumé.

ALEXANDER THEROUX

Few Spanish place names exist in Oklahoma.
Shakespeare renounced his art to retire at fifty-eight.
Black folks are highly susceptible to glaucoma.
The average segments of an umbrella are eight.

Tragic is the country that needs a hero.
Prejudices are enthusiasms we disagree with.
Considered "even" is the numeral zero.
The eighth day is law for having Jewish *brith*.

Firefighters often willfully start fires.
Indians are never comfortable in schools.
A Cereus blooms one night, then expires
All haggling pivots on arbitrary rules.

Scammers perennially follow the headlines.
In Henry James novels, the dialogue is action.
Creativity often soars in the face of deadlines.
The planet Earth is racing toward calefaction.

Royalists and Republicans are ever at odds.
Parvenus prefer saying "closure" to "closing."
The French nearly beheaded Madame Tussaud.
Wagner loved wearing pink while composing.

World crime is led by human trafficking.
Judy Garland never appeared in a Broadway musical.
Any moral boost in the UK recalls Mafeking.
It is the spite of a virus to be shockingly mutable.

TRUISMS

Chaplin was a bore compared to Keaton.
Mountains all range from north to south.
No worthwhile biscuit is ever overbeaten.
Bad teeth always slubber a pretty mouth.

Vladimir Nabokov reviled Saul Bellow.
The Afghanistan War cost the U.S. a trillion dollars.
Eaters respond happiest to the color yellow.
Agnosticism is common among Biblical scholars.

Treason is the extreme form of dissent.
Britain ever fancied countries with good horseman.
There are no Black people in Tashkent.
"Vikings" was never a term used by Norsemen.

Political change comes from below, not above.
A pigeon need not lift its head to swallow water.
The mitten is the ugly stepsister of the glove.
Anything compulsive is a personality disorder.

Clearwater, Fla., is the hub of Scientology.
A parricide was the painter Richard Dadd.
No gourmand is not fascinated with enology.
All religions but Islam are banned in Riyadh.

A splice is stronger than a knot.
To believing Muslims, all the world's Kafiristan.
The fairer the paper, the fouler the blot.
Timid tourists like hotels with the American plan.

Travel, for amateurs, is mere accumulation.
Whoever prefers "Romish" to Catholic hates.
A satirist needs vocabulary and vituperation.
Pious Muslims end Ramadan by eating dates.

Vagrancy is not going to but escaping from.
Plagues begin by animal/human contact.
All Scottish literature's predominantly glum.
Expressionism is in its inefficiency abstract.

Nobody ever thoroughly reads a handbook.
57,318 people inhabit Baum's Emerald City.
When cooking, remove the vile skin of snook.
Slowness by a remitter plagues the remittee.

No seller can't squeeze a buyer by insouciance,
Speech was given man to conceal his thoughts.
The more color in vegetables, the more nutrients.
Any given rope is actually *weakened* by knots.

Penance is the gateway to peace of mind.
Abuse of a thing is no argument against its use.
Every country on earth is artificially designed.
No commercial or advertisement isn't a ruse.

Tuberculars tend to be compulsively optimistic.
The third brother in fairy tales has all the virtue.
The people of Fiji lead the world as albinistic.
Juvenile crime occasions the standard curfew.

TRUISMS

Only two Northern white rhinos are still alive.
Children almost never appear in *noir* movies.
No swallow cooped up in any way can thrive.
There are flaws and imperfections in all rubies.

Most viruses do not make humans ill.
Rain always complicates flash photography.
The oldest language on the planet is Tamil.
Deodorants interfere with a mammography.

Use turbinado sugar to torch *crème brûlée*.
Every perennial garden is a Brigadoon.
No fidgety woman doesn't avidly crochet.
Lightning strikes vocalize every monsoon.

Only ten letters are used on any eye chart.
Chicago does not have a single gun store.
Completely penniless at death was Mozart.
Marines alone can call the "crotch" the corps.

No child is ever born with a single freckle.
All great voyages have gone not east but west.
Weirdly, Jekyll created Hyde, not Hyde Jekyll.
No host should ever plan his day for a guest.

Freckles on the body are never cancerous.
Anton Bruckner suffered from numeromania.
All opinions that are biased are slanderous.
Sexual disturbance lies behind pyromania.

ALEXANDER THEROUX

No extreme right-winger doesn't border on lunacy.
A fireman never leaves the station without his boots.
A struggle for true contemplatives is community.
Physicians and insurance companies are in cahoots.

Brown trout are particularly avaricious.
Cymbeline is rarely performed Shakespeare.
Falling in love is always adventitious.
Currency in days of pharaonic Egypt was beer.

The CIA cannot operate in the United States.
All boys' adventure tales have a missing father.
A pretty girl looks even prettier on skates.
A brother not a companion is always a bother.

Pregnant women should avoid eating sushi.
The more reliable the source, the more likely the spy.
Hutu are Esau, and privileged Jacob the Tutsi.
It is quite unscientific to use the plural of sky.

Each human tongue has its own unique print.
The strongest human muscle is that of the jaw.
Car thieves are often thwarted by window tint.
Sitting on sidewalks goes against Nevada law.

Economics is the motor of human history.
No biscuit is fully immune to a weevil.
Drugs and meds have replaced the bistoury.
Unbridled capitalism is the essence of evil.

TRUISMS

A Twinkie's center is not cream but Crisco.
The English Civil War to Marxists was a Revolution.
Pirates legendarily are thought to be Morisco.
Russian loanwords figure highly in spoken Aleutian.

Suspicion weirdly partners with credulity.
Sycamores are the most ancient of hardwoods.
Depression in old age often shown by garrulity.
Old country stores mainly sold yard goods.

Karl Marx never prophesied the rise of fascism.
Lupins are the Karner butterfly's obligate plant.
Ritual and repetition are flagrant signs of autism.
Scientology's crypto language is classic cant.

Tearing wrapping paper in Japan is held as rude.
Strong opinions to the bourgeois are insubordinate.
Rare is the Polynesian/Melanesian who's a prude.
An axis is needed to find position for a coordinate.

Julia Child approved of instant pie crust mix.
Burdock is nature's opportunistic hitchhiker.
Hung on an eastern wall is the usual Crucifix.
Most deaths are passengers *behind* a biker.

Primogeniture interferes with natural selection.
Bread can be made from toxic-removed acorns.
A spy is suspected on both sides in a defection.
Awoken is grammatically preferred to *awakens*.

ALEXANDER THEROUX

Over two-thirds of Utah is owned by the U.S. government.
The English upper classes love hyphenated surnames.
All Biblical story lines are grounded on covenant.
Gun violence is traceable to the use of video games.

Sparrows always flourish in bracing climates.
Dartmouth requires every graduate pass a swim test.
An immune system owes all to the thymus.
A northwest wind blows *from, not to*, the northwest

Japanese women of old blackened their teeth.
It is strictly capillary action that grows plants.
All mystery turns on what's hidden or underneath.
Both lungs and ears are missing in all ants.

Jesus was transfigured but never enraptured.
Fruits all ripen, but vegetables do not.
All public fads are hideously manufactured.
Creativity, as such, can never be taught.

No migration is not also transmigration.
R.L. Stevenson never delineated a convincing woman.
Joy is connotated by carbonation.
Ashkenazic Jews during Passover refuse to eat cumin.

Stock markets operate between greed and fear.
Saharan Ténéré is the most sunlit place on Earth.
No quack isn't also an aggressive pamphleteer.
The only organ that expels itself is afterbirth.

TRUISMS

In Japan the belly centers emotions and thoughts.
Plants deprived of animal partners become extinct.
Margarine in any form is, to real butter, ersatz.
All liabilities in one's lover are always indistinct.

The cliché movie newspaper is *The Sentinel*.
Early friendships are erased as awkward obligations.
The predominant veterinary anesthetic is fentanyl.
Catholic monastic life revolves around abnegations.

Every trumpet plant is an insect killer.
The cellulose of plants is fully indigestible.
No bought sausage is not mostly filler.
The shrew's movements are bidirectional.

Karl Marx, big-hearted, was a humanitarian.
Bracken loves—grows next to—stinging nettle.
Loud rallies give life blood to a totalitarian.
Oral cancer is connected to the chewing of betel.

Bureaucrats depend on feeble euphemisms.
March weather makes apologists of weathermen.
Mexico leads all the world in exorcisms.
Only Anglican prelates can be called clergymen.

Inbreeding constantly weakens any race.
The 2nd Amendment has nothing to do with hunting,
No spy can maintain his original face.
Crossbreeding strengthens a race in its welcoming.

Drunks among Mormons are non-existent.
Kings are required when writing of realms.
The flavor of anise is decidedly persistent.
Fungoid killers cling irrationally to elms.

Giraffes are missing any vocal cords.
Red print on eco-labels is meaningless.
Haitians for coinage once used gourds.
Fearing "God bless *you*," ferblets say "God bless."

No hummingbird ever walks on its feet.
Seafloor under the Arctic Ocean is unknown.
Enjoyed eaten raw is any young sugar beet.
The hand of a human body has the most bone.

No invader will ever conquer Afghanistan.
Psychotics habitually wear too much clothing.
No large islands exist in the Sea of Japan.
The Chinese look at Tibetans with loathing.

A narrator's voice is always an invention.
The surname Dvorak is pronounced *vor'shack*.
The Laotian language has no declension.
A messy image is elemental to a Rorschach.

Shakespeare left behind not one private book.
Roman togas had a pocket, located on the left side.
Sounds are magnified by winds of a chinook.
American Congressman to lobbyists are fully tied.

TRUISMS

All children without books grow up abused.
Pythons do not exist in South America.
The first toilet cubicle in a row is the least used.
Hexagrams in all instances are occult esoterica.

Elephants do not drink through their trunk.
A good spy always avoids consistent behavior.
The prime predator of honeybees is the skunk.
Martyrdom defines the concept of the Savior.

A loaded bee cannot fly upside down.
Every war movie has a soldier named Kowalski.
Only self-ridicule is a commandment of a clown.
Only permanent revolution would please Trotsky.

A person never stops to admire a hedgerow.
Continuous movement is accepted as stillness.
Meat's flavored if animals browse on oregano.
Anxiety in excess is a sign of mental illness.

Nothing has more hideous shape than teeth.
Moths emerge from cocoons, butterflies chrysalises.
No boundary marker in Scotland isn't a meith.
Every large company depends on factor analyses.

No earthly menu offers more than for the ant.
Fado music most approximates the human sob.
Trees in the Orkneys are scandalously scant.
It is always a single mind that constitutes a mob.

Conspiracy theories are always retrospective.
Animals always turn around before lying down.
No worker finds much incentive in a collective.
Grey in fashion rarely goes well with brown.

To Muslims, imperfection adds to a work of art.
Audubon boasted of drawing every bird life-size.
No true scientists ever use or rely on a pie chart.
What's best for catching trout is to use dry flies.

Sherry goes down best on a blustery, rainy day.
Rural U.S. voters mistrust all government facts.
The sky for unerring consolation is too far away.
Men dislike the slackness of women in slacks.

In the city of Dubai, no one *walks* anywhere.
Human feces are mostly bacteria, not old food.
Mist most characterizes the month of Brumaire.
Neither croc nor alligator food is ever chewed.

No one has ever seen eels or congers mate.
UK telephone pole cross-arms all face London.
The best of all survival foods is the pitted date.
There is no one right answer to a conundrum.

Great fortunes are built on forgotten crimes.
The Tempest, alone, gives us Shakespeare the man.
A fish appears cooked if sprinkled with limes.
Only one woman, Maryam, is named in the Koran.

TRUISMS

No Beau Brummell can abide the Establishment.
Mushrooms with white gills are usually toxic.
Revenge is inherent in the matter of punishment.
Every magician is naked without his pockets.

Mary Baker Eddy found pure evil in being mesmerized.
It was railroads that exterminated Native Americans.
No justifiable health benefit exists for being circumcised.
A pouch is used for capture, not storing, in pelicans.

Eating alone is a reason someone overeats.
A steady hum is the equivalent of silence.
Spontaneity was worshipped by the Beats.
Tardiness is always an expression of defiance.

A whale, a mammal, will never drink salt water.
Edward Lear never used the word *limerick*.
1.2 million killed at the Somme—pure slaughter
All the ocean floors are specifically basaltic.

No rivalry exceeds Sooners and Longhorns.
The world's costliest gas is found in Norway.
For security hedges, nothing beats hawthorns.
Australian brides say "submit," but no longer "obey."

Of Shakespeare's juvenilia, we have nothing.
Sacraments, not contracts, are real weddings.
Provocation is the overt resolve of strutting.
A Mansfield bar on trucks prevents beheadings.

In Greek epics, women always begin the tragedy.
Permanence can be snatched only out of flux.
A satellite is traveling the slowest at its apogee.
Huge world pollution is traced to plastic cups.

R. L. Stevenson feared and detested dogs.
No Frenchman goes without his *couteau de poche*.
The best chowder clams are ocean quahogs.
Every color can be seen in an ocean swash.

The city of Chicago has banned all handguns.
"Amalgamated" is the go-to business in movies.
A hard lot in novels is always had by stepsons.
Sweet wine enhances the taste of blue cheese.

Anarchist attitudes all age very badly.
Actors can't wear make-up in Oberammergau.
Beauteous music comes across as sadly.
All geniuses are portrayed with a heavy brow.

An actor's upstage is toward the back.
No waterfall truly exists without its ouzel.
No lent book is ever returned intact.
Almost all sitting judges warrant self-recusal.

A flamingo can only hunt when it is wading.
In Pre-Raphaelite portraits something's always a bit off.
African slaves expressed revolt by hair braiding.
Maria, the czar's third daughter, was the prettiest Romanov.

TRUISMS

A book collector's wife considers him a fool.
Beavers' favorite tree is the quivering aspen.
No such thing exists as an exception to a rule.
Only something without intention can happen.

The wood of the Viburnum bush is best for arrows.
Every heretic Arius has his heretical Athanasius.
There is a total absence of trees in the Faroes.
All variations of natural wild rice are monoecious.

An actor's stage right is the audience's left.
No one knows how "Yahweh" was pronounced.
Major museum holdings are the result of theft.
No Israeli crime by U.S. Congress is denounced.

Illness often renders a victim's hair thready.
It's the world's children who mainly suffer hunger.
Water must circle to be called an eddy.
No one eats more organically than a game hunter.

An actor's downstage is toward the front.
The only true prairie tree is the cottonwood.
Publicity of any kind is a manufactured stunt.
Cleopatra means the "key to fatherhood."

Loyalty, like guilt, can oddly kill.
Cowboy sidekicks are naturally zany.
The wish is always father to the will.
Few are chosen, called are many.

Authority is always the mask of violence.
Tongans prefer women fatter than thinner.
Trappists find prayer in a state of silence
The noon meal in Maine is called "dinner."

Every single part of a beet is edible.
To Ethiopians, the exonym Abyssinia's pejorative.
A true Wiccan's palm reveals a pentacle.
Duty to Kant stands as the categorical imperative.

Shagbark hickory is best for bow staves.
An actor's stage left is the audience's right.
Senegal exported the most African slaves.
Light, which is invisible, is not at all white.

All whores eventually become bow-legged.
Brooms are taboo on a Chinese New Year.
Early English antique furniture is pegged.
Eggs make virtually every mixture cohere.

No altruist ever remains in law school.
A mountain's not a mountain if there's nothing below.
Every problem solved constitutes a rule.
Perfect insulation, being mostly trapped air, is snow.

Overfamiliarity in any servant is a vice.
Few Asians are ever found as redheads.
Grass is the proper term for all wild rice.
January 1st is the birthday of all thoroughbreds.

TRUISMS

Safety is always the reckless move in chess.
There are no maple trees in Hungary.
Belts should not be worn with morning dress,
All British puddings are basically flummery.

A logical antimony is that a liar was a Cretan.
A Chinese garden always includes stones (mountains).
No valuable rug from the front is ever beaten.
Rome is unsurpassed for the most beautiful fountains.

Clambake smoke drifts toward the handsomest.
Drug names have three syllables, usually a dactyl.
Grace alone can save us, asserts the Jansenist.
Classical geometry cannot represent a fractal.

Melanism does not exist in humans.
Each tree has its very own sound and song.
One never finds a hornwort blooming.
No true native requires a tie for a sarong.

The Netherlands has the world's tallest men.
Much Ado is least worthy of Shakespeare's plays.
Tarantula kebabs are popular in Phnom Penh.
Old French fortifications for defense wore a *fraise*.

A rotating E eyechart exists for the illiterate.
Handphones have more bacteria than toilet handles.
Effort is always required in anything deliberate.
A paranoid house is always a circus of panels.

Abstraction is the natural enemy of actuality.
The color of the glass affects a coffee's taste.
In Norse sagas, women ever begin the tragedy.
It is seaweed that adds stability to toothpaste.

No intrusive waiter should ever be tipped.
Less than 10% of the world's money exists in cash.
Gables are impossible in a roof that is hipped.
The upper is double the number of a lower eyelash.

Withhold due praise and you besmirch.
No mind of a true ideologue is ever limber.
No practicing Quaker kneels in a church,
Nor in his meeting house made of timber.

No community life is not a living hell.
Sports fans are a confraternity of fools.
Urine best reveals that one is not well.
By definition, ardor invariably cools.

Lending people money makes them hate you.
Cops always hold their flashlights overhand.
For canoe paddles, choose for wood the yew.
Olives, brined, always taste better canned.

Hare Krishnas offer prayer chanting hymns.
There are no natural groves purely of elms.
Korea names are mainly Parks, Lees, Kims.
Hotel room carpets suffer the same smells.

TRUISMS

The merits of rival causes are never absolute.
The largest mountain range on Earth is undersea.
Nucleation is the virtue of a champagne flute.
Khat is the most preferred drug in Djibouti.

Use persimmon wood for golf club heads.
Silkworms only eat fresh mulberry leaves.
Shredded hard butter on toast best spreads.
Experience rests solely on what one perceives.

Wilderness always looks larger through a window.
No Roman Catholics appear in Joseph Lincoln novels.
Unexplained still is the one-foot stance of a flamingo.
True humility, which never is abject, also never grovels.

Red in a mushroom indicates toxicity.
Every obituary is an essay on omissions.
Humiliation characterizes most publicity.
The cowardly take refuge in coalitions.

No water ouzel doesn't love a waterfall.
Air Force One charges all reporters to fly.
A circle is ever the shape of an African krall.
Guilt is the main reason people fear to fly.

Wills are less about money than of love.
Moose cannot be tamed and will die in a zoo.
Asymmetry defines every baseball glove.
What survived Hiroshima was alone bamboo.

A condor never attacks a living animal.
Torpor works at a every conveyor belt.
Palms are the gourmet cut for a cannibal.
Condolences are virtually never heartfelt.

No American waterways run westward.
Vaunted short cuts are usually rumors.
No one in the Bible is named Edward.
Fashion fabricates its own consumers.

The only true prairie trees are cottonwoods.
In Marxist terms, nationalism is reactionary.
Filipino cuisine is an utter mélange of foods.
Abridgement is debridement in a dictionary.

Cal*a*fornia was initially the correct state spelling.
A squirrel's main enemy is the pine marten.
Tasting food is inconceivable without smelling.
Plaid has never been the synonym of tartan.

Peruvian wine is the worst in the world.
No animal can dig faster than a badger.
Vertigo is promised in anything whirled.
Water reed is best material for a thatcher.

No wild moose has any natural enemies.
Pastry-making is the *summum bonum* of cookery.
Voodoo is common among the Beninese.
An archaeologist's dream is of broken crockery.

TRUISMS

Fourteen is listed as the riskiest age in a teenager.
Helen Keller tried to keep the sun in her face.
The greatest symphony is Mozart's No. 41 in C Major.
Ten is the standard step a duelist had to pace.

The Atacama Desert gets not a drop of rain.
Every wooden barn at some point sags.
Bullfight aficionados rejoice at animal pain.
Auto dealers hawk cars by waving flags.

Broccoli is a vegetable rarely eaten in France.
Virgil read only *Aeneid* books 2, 4, and 6 to Augustus.
Elizabeth Smith Miller was the first woman in pants.
Congressional lobbying is an evil form of injustice.

Without preserved goose, no cassoulet is true.
Hippopotamuses can neither swim nor float.
Nothing's less useful than the runway *behind* you.
Every good hunter is a ventriloquist of troat.

Decadent societies have high suicide rates.
Austrians (cf. Dr. Dr. Schultz) repeat titles for each degree.
Scripture makes fifty (50) references to dates.
The tea that most retains its flavor is consistently black tea.

Pony Express stations stood every ten miles.
Julia Child despised the use of pressure cookers.
The chronically anxious like seats on the aisles.
John Calhoun was patron saint of "statehooders"

Redwood shingles are all decay-proof.
Israel does not have a written constitution.
The tongue is a floor to the mouth's roof.
Reform emasculates every revolution.

Scholar Hannah Arendt was on an Irgun hit list.
Pizza was invented by Aeneas (*Aeneid* 7.116).
No innovation in music was not initially hissed.
Venison cooked without some fat is too lean.

Pedants who inhabit record-shops are losers.
An artist's never someone who can't draw.
Finns, like Indians, are inveterate boozers.
A permissive mother is her daughter's flaw.

A raging ocean loses never a single battle.
Greek tragedies always began at dawn.
No shape is as fetching to babies as its rattle.
Khrushchev force-fed his nation corn.

Tanzania is the primary country of lions.
There are no basements in Las Vegas.
Masks were the visages of the Mayans.
Awkwardness defines *les femmes* Degas.

Blacksmiths were always given the finest bread.
No American colonial battle was fought under Old Glory.
The color brown demands investment in brick-red.
Plain didacticism is a boring imitation in every allegory.

TRUISMS

Copper beeches grow very, very slowly.
The older you are, the more you're talked down to.
Failure accepted makes a person holy.
From whom we take money, we're inevitably bound to.

Light griefs speak, heavier ones are silent.
Weight a cooking skate to prevent it curling.
No importunate person is not an assailant.
92.5% silver is officially required of sterling.

An obsequious teacher is always a high grader.
The first rule of deep diving is *not* to hold your breath.
FDR's Henry Morgenthau never attended a seder.
Life imprisonment is literally held a "civil death."

There is no word for "privacy" in Russian.
A tablecloth must always have straight creases.
Every lifeguard must be expert in succession.
High school boys were either jocks or greasers.

Rawhide is a cowboy's essential tool.
Tuaregs consider everyone their inferior.
A donkey is less stubborn than a mule.
Having its special tide is Lake Superior.

It is never done to lick or bite a chopstick.
Brits have no response to an expression of thanks.
Consumed by habit is much women's lipstick.
Religion, more than any other field, breeds cranks.

ALEXANDER THEROUX

Every last substance is transparent.
if the cutting is made thin enough.
No child ever has the same parent
in the same family, which is tough.

The first *blin* made is always lumpy.
Protection defines every flower's sepal.
Pioneer dresses invariably look frumpy.
Officiousness defined a Dickens beadle.

The happiest women have no history.
African fathers eat alone out of respect.
Prestige cannot exist without mystery.
Compulsive travelers: men henpecked.

No Frenchman prepares salad with a knife.
Slavery was the essence of Saharan caravans.
Deliberation and action are always at strife.
Surgery proves most delicate on human hands.

Colonialism is the extreme of nationalism.
Sitting facing east is to have the seat of honor.
Rationality is the victim of all chauvinism.
The youngest official language is Afrikaner.

Huck Finn and Tom Sawyer's ages are not given.
Angle of incidence is equal to angle of reflection.
Old Testament garments are never torn, but riven.
Only the truly passionate kiss involves advection.

TRUISMS

Add a wine cork to tenderize cooking octopus.
Touching a Chinese gambler's shoulders is taboo.
Neither teeth nor stomachs have the platypus.
Distilled white vinegar will eradicate bamboo.

Horses and cattle are not native to the USA.
Without dates, no one could live in the desert.
Underestimated is the insulation factor of hay.
A woman's figure upgrades in a hobble skirt.

Cheese as a food is much older than bread.
St. Paul was less than five feet tall.
The Golden Gate Bridge is in fact rust-red.
Mating sound in nature is a *wrawl*.

It is impossible to find an Amish physician.
Sunlight is, of all, the greatest disinfectant.
Women hate the *sex a tergo* sexual position.
Symbolism favors any lines intersectant.

All Portuguese wines are far too fruity.
Suspicion is driven to collect its own evidence.
Love as a motive outweighs that of duty.
Reason is often perverted by eloquence.

The Incas had no knowledge of the arch.
No active Pope has been known to go swimming.
Leaves are oddly shed by the coniferous larch.
Drawing an object's *outline* alone defines limning.

ALEXANDER THEROUX

No one beats an Asian woman for shrill.
Bad film directors always cut defensively.
Sixty uncontacted tribes still live in Brazil.
Never approach a tiger unapprehensively.

Gondoliers have always been notably open to sex.
One side of the moon constantly faces the Earth.
Biblical wholeness is expressed by use of triplex.
Caesarean section reduces risk in a breech birth.

Scholars delight in anything occurring twice.
The most ancient textile in all history is linen
Lust is a crime which should be seen as a vice.
The Chinese think cold drinks bad for women.

Bulls are completely unaware of color.
No carrier should launch an airstrike under attack.
Crane & Co. has patented the blend in the dollar.
Renoir believed the queen of all colors was black.

The face of the *Mona Lisa* has no eyebrows.
Radiation cannot penetrate Earth's Van Allen belt.
Drink alone technically defines a carouse.
The only *unexploited* world fish is the rainbow smelt.

All of the plots in classical ballet are inane.
Revenge is the soul of Jacobean tragedy.
The tarot [ack in fact originated as a game.
Most Italian American dishes are from *southern* Italy.

TRUISMS

Salt is not and never was a spice.
Adolf Hitler never saw a bombed-out German city.
All white rice came from brown rice.
The dumber the discussion, the larger the committee.

A lobster chews food with its stomach.
Always measure ten times and cut only once.
No archaeologist isn't thrilled by a hummock.
The names of full moons alter by months.

Never trim the fat off fresh prosciutto.
A Comanche *tipi* faced the rising sun.
To hold a piano note, use pedal *sostenuto*.
Wearing mufti always trivializes a nun.

In Italy, meatballs are never eaten with pasta.
A New York City block equals a rural village.
A peculiar Franco-Italian is spoken in Aosta.
State officials keep a weather eye for pillage.

Every bullfighter is essentially a coward.
The key to crunchy breadcrumbs is high heat.
By the jangle of keys, janitors are empowered.
Never to advance in the military is to retreat.

The pressing of garlic is a true abomination.
The nature of every serpent is to convolve.
Wheezing is the applause of carbonation.
Elizabethan rhyming couplets indicate resolve.

Pointe shoes are all made by hand in ballet.
Monday's fish in restaurants is never fresh.
Hollywood's a metaphor, like Broadway.
When speaking of sin, you speak of the flesh.

Brunch is only served on weekends.
Masons and the U.S. government are weirdly connected.
A miser's only delight is his dividends.
Firm resistance is the sole anodyne for being rejected.

Masons do not solicit memberships.
British snobs stir tea with only half a swirl.
A woman can fire out rays from fingertips.
Reason never, ever mastered a teenage girl.

Woman is the subject/center of every ballet.
It was persimmon trees that inspired Christmas trees.
Solemnity undermines the nature of coquet.
Amputations should always be made *below* the knees.

Composite dishes are not eaten in Italy.
Political concession speeches are always maudlin.
Any concession speech is given bitterly.
Boiling hard is the justification of a cauldron.

Charles Darwin never visited North America.
A great line cook needs unvarying *mise-en-place*.
No religious rites or rules are free of esoterica.
Plagiarism discovers a happy quarry all templates.

TRUISMS

France does and will not extradite its citizens.
Asters and goldenrod madly attract each other.
Barbecuing is a hazard regarding carcinogens.
No one laughs at everything like a grandmother.

All civilizations have been built by menials.
To roast duck, always begin with a *cold* oven.
Mascots subversively endorse breakfast cereals.
Psychiatrists detect mental illness in a glutton.

Attention is the doorway to gratitude.
Restaurants never make hollandaise to order.
No success quotation is not a platitude.
Every badly deprived child grows up a hoarder.

Abraham Lincoln was never a churchgoer.
Meals served in a sloppy kitchen taste like swill.
No reward is too small for a whistleblower.
Toxicity is the by-product of every paper mill.

Walnut, absorbing recoil, is best for rifle stocks.
Japanese never say *emperor* but "O-Tenshi-Sama."
No chemist is not titillated upon seeing a redox.
No teeth are found on the top mouth of a llama.

Beauty matched with depravity is twice as sexy.
Animals are the first things humans ever drew.
Owlishness is seen to be a virtue in any prexy.
In India, bad luck is associated with the color blue.

Shallots are rarely used in American homes.
After LBJ's Civil Rights Bill, presidents lost the white vote.
Trylons are symbols for males, females domes.
It is the nature of every minority to become a scapegoat.

Hollandaise sauce is a Petri dish of biohazards.
Visuals on a pie chart always go clockwise.
Peremptory demands are the slang of placards.
Atheism is not at all uncommon among rabbis.

Liberty without law always leads to chaos.
Commercial chickens are full of salmonella.
Persuasion is the hidden ambition of pathos.
Any form at all in a circle can be a *mandala*.

All L.L. Bean catalogue models are wholesome.
Restaurant failure-rates are about 60%.
Any intemperate extreme is truly loathsome.
The earnest into the maudlin always ferment.

Virgil's was the great age of road building.
Geese in France are raised mainly for their livers.
The top thrill in love is of a partner yielding.
Poor folk, unlike the wealthy, are greater givers.

Use "00" flour for making homemade pasta.
Give power to any man, and he will abuse it.
There is no vegetation at all in Antofagasta.
A Bible meaning is by whoever construes it.

TRUISMS

A cube has equal, square-shaped sides of six.
Italians avoid preserved lemons when cooking.
One may stare with impunity at a lunar eclipse.
Any and all desserts in Britain are a pudding.

Strictly avoid ever frosting a warm cake.
Dhaka, throughout, is a sea of air pollution.
Courtesies all depend on custom's sake.
There is no such thing as moral evolution.

A mobster, harboring secrets, disappears.
Not receiving mail is in fact a daily blessing.
Variability defines all modern airplane fares.
Russians have a penchant for confessing.

Satiety in lust forthwith ends it.
Fascism is lawlessness in the name of law.
Steaming any wood best bends it.
Asians are mad to purchase a bear's paw.

What an actor earns is never realistic.
Dante in hell gives pedophiles no storey.
Clutch-hitting in baseball as a statistic
has never proven to be a valid category.

Time is the puppeteer of all existence.
Behavior is found as repetition in a race.
Vulgarity is the main fuel of persistence.
The best paprikas are never hot to taste.

ALEXANDER THEROUX

Each group is safe only among its members
is the immigrant's paranoid misassumption.
A forest fire proliferates by flying embers.
Any spiral shape slows down as a function.

Coyness is ever the superficies of lust.
Viruses need a cell to inhabit to multiply.
A breast is merely part of a woman's bust.
The truest Hawaiians live on Molokai.

Political correctness is a function of time.
Conspiracy theories strangle information space.
There is loss of sincerity in all poetic rhyme.
Random height enhances the steps of a staircase.

Torture exacts compliance, not cooperation.
The Kikuyu in Africa consider twins taboo.
No ballet is a match for floral aestivation.
Cretan hieroglyphics no one can construe.

Extremely loud noises are inveterately toxic.
Diaries, being biased, are never truly honest.
Every high altitude is potentially hypoxic.
Parsimony craves what has been promised.

The Rongorongo script has yet to be deciphered.
Americans worship their flag as a sacred object.
For the ceramic flush-toilet, *ta* to Tom Twyford.
Persian rugs are woven with a deliberate defect.

TRUISMS

Sea salt has more nutrients than kosher salt.
No Horatio Alger hero ever worked in a factory.
Lava rocks are composed mainly of basalt
Black is the required color of every phylactery.

No social refinement does not verge on the effete.
90% of worldwide trade travels by sea.
Best-selling books always hale from Grub Street.
A flaw is never missing in a dead absentee.

The Beatles were unable to read (or score) music.
Revolutions are all created by an excess profits tax.
The ancient Carthaginian tongue was actually Punic.
Chewing gum is made of resin and food-grade wax.

The French don't make French bread at home.
Augustus found Rome brick and left it marble.
Aspiration is the sole symbolism of the dome.
Spoken Cantonese sounds exactly like garble.

The telephone was initially regarded as a toy.
Property-owning ever fosters class warfare.
No political promise in a primary isn't a ploy.
Acute self-awareness often breeds despair.

Greeting cards only celebrate abstract nouns.
A tornado usually travels southwest to northwest.
A bay opens once—many inlets form sounds.
At age twenty-one, a human face and figure's at its best.

Sheep outnumber people by three Down Under.
Javanese cuisine has only seventeen rigidly defined courses.
Tororo, Uganda is ground zero for thunder.
No British reporter has to reveal his or her sources.

No kiss without a taste of sin is sweet.
Ticking clocks in films document fake drama.
A mother and daughter repeatedly compete.
Blunt-cutting hair in films indicates mad trauma.

Rednecks take pride in being unscholarly.
Iron ever sharpens iron; scholars, a scholar.
Staring, always rude, is done improperly.
Paper is not used in making a U.S. dollar.

A tick is not an insect but an arachnid.
Children's sing-song taunts are universal.
Time passing on Sundays is ever flaccid.
Perfection is always lost without rehearsal.

Warm water transmits sound faster than cold.
Furniture movers in fiction are all portrayed as comic.
People in Nepal duly reverenced the marigold.
The Hollywood template is solely anatomic.

Fruits not quite ripe make the best jellies.
Metaphors are always equally analogues.
Dying fish fall upward with their bellies.
Shakespeare had a great dislike of dogs.

TRUISMS

A country's port cities breed revolutionary ideas.
A camera tracking action is often best handheld
Harmony means weakness to the two Koreas.
Passion with the English is reservedly withheld.

Adolf Hitler felt vain about his eyes of blue.
Stuttering is the only handicap people still mock.
In Australia, Darwin never saw a kangaroo.
Less than 4,000 speakers now can speak Mohawk.

A nun is always more than half neurotic.
The gambler's natural state is in arrears.
Love by its arbitrariness is ever episodic.
An evangelist's blustering is in his prayers..

No woman may give evidence in Hindi courts.
As water evaporates, it takes more water with it.
Pimps to find their prey habitually troll airports.
Guests like fish all stink after a three-day visit.

All obscenity is founded on personal aversion.
The Hurons were historic allies of the French.
No one's faith is as deep as after a conversion.
A true diabetic's thirst is impossible to quench.

No royal wills are ever publicly revealed.
Frenchmen never kiss the hand of a young girl.
Mormon wives, creepily, are eternally "*sealed.*"
No manufacturing luthier does not love a burl.

ALEXANDER THEROUX

Olmec writing remains impossible to read.
Lack of security in mailboxes is primitive.
Second-cut hay, nutritious, is best horse feed.
The Japanese language features no infinitive.

What divides, keeps dividing forever.
A battered, dented look is macho in canoes.
Muslim unity is a hopeless endeavor.
Lyrics repeated in music drives the blues.

Legislation succeeds only by balancing contrasts.
Fixed white lights are disastrous to migrating birds.
Aquariums are healthfully aerated by hair grass.
Dried herbs have stronger flavors than fresh herbs.

Tomato dishes clash with champagne.
Uncontrolled inflation poisons everything.
No solitary, confined, is ever quite sane.
A revulsion adheres to lovers that cling.

No dying fish can retain its colors.
Thin bottomed saucepans are useless for anything.
Snipers rely completely on covers.
Stealth-shunning is a teenage form of banishing.

There is never any white meat on a goose,
A broomstick on a mast is naval praise.
A child enuretic heaps on himself abuse.
Fully uncover any meat during a braise.

TRUISMS

Cream, with its fat and oil, is lighter than milk.
The famed circus name was Rungeling, not Ringling.
No strength in a metal can match a rope of silk.
Purity is always compromised by commingling.

Supreme Court justices can accept unlimited gifts.
The Chinese believe that cold drinks hurt a woman.
All the greatest novels incorporate the use of lists.
Ashkenazic Jews during Passover never eat cumin.

One's nemesis is invariably born of retributive justice.
Mme. Pompadour is the model for all female careerists.
The title of Emperor was flatly refused by Augustus.
No shallower idiots exist than Hollywood premierists.

South Africa only got television in 1976.
In the 40s, comic book sales outpaced fiction.
Mortar is forever the girl cousin of bricks.
No Southern Congressman has good diction.

October is the leading month for bird migration.
Gertrude Stein was an avid fan of comic books.
Scriptural pedigrees follow the rule of agnation.
Eating is passion required for all good cooks.

Israel has US-sponsored rights to expansion.
Vinegar kills the pain of box jellyfish toxin.
Lethal in football is every goalpost stanchion.
Four hours of sleep a night is enough for oxen.

ALEXANDER THEROUX

Savile Row long scorned Y-front underwear
and belted trousers as ruinously constricting.
Constantly growing is the human outer ear.
A spider and fly are perpetually conflicting.

Every pigeon has a longer tail than any dove.
A woman's hair is ruined left too long in plait.
The power to hate increases the power of love.
The power of love increases the power to hate.

A "dynasty trust" skips single generations.
No Irish cause ever won Samuel Beckett's allegiance.
Preventable are most diabetic amputations.
Every political position assumed is always a grievance.

A woodcock will never alight in trees.
Crystal does not break—it shatters.
HIV may be killed by the sting of bees.
Erethism is a plague suffered by hatters.

No cafeteria ever serves up fruitcake.
Dipping is the treat of all fondue.
No lovers splitting suffer equal heartache.
True denim jeans are always blue.

There are few chewing scenes in movies.
American Indians never sported beards.
Humor is anxiously avoided by all Sufis.
A description not a title is Scot for *lairds*.

TRUISMS

The true flow of electricity, whether minus
to plus or the reverse, has never been proved.
All hatless youths get troubled in the sinus.
The lover is more virtuous than the loved.

A cowboy feeds and waters his horse first.
Bavaria, not Prussia, was the seedbed of Nazism.
No high-sodium beverage ever quenches thirst.
Baptismal water is the "Jordan" in every baptism.

Every bird is basically a living dinosaur.
Despair feeds political totalitarianism.
Voting is officially mandatory in Ecuador.
There is no such thing as Jewish monasticism.

An eroticism adhibits to everything disguised.
Seven bells are never struck in the British navy.
Goat milk, germ-free, need not be pasteurized.
A gigolo's hair is always described as "wavy."

4,000 typos sullied *Ulysses* when first published.
"Originalist" Supreme Court justices all crusade.
Anything clustering around a mean is "established."
A dark image cast on ground is shadow, not shade.

Americans prefer drinking everything cold.
Salt hay eaten by cows spoils the taste of milk.
All penicillin develops and depends on mold.
A major status symbol in China is wearing silk.

ALEXANDER THEROUX

The faces on a totem pole should be startling.
Ivory-billed woodpeckers were Audubon's pet bird.
Tallulah Bankhead called every person "darling."
Barbaric insolence is stated by every woman furred.

Most movie actresses were of farm people.
Happiness is never as quality of obsession.
The dimmer the sect, the smaller the steeple.
Pride, beyond all else, refuses all concession.

Light selects the shortest path to reach its destination.
Mark Twain never delineated a desirable woman.
Wearing jewelry is by nature a pathetic affectation.
Hibernating bears convert protein from their urine.

Indians used larch root strings to sew canoes.
Russians never sit at a table wearing a hat.
Judaic law explicitly forbids sporting tattoos.
Frass is the scientific name for insect scat.

Flowing sap facilitates bark removal.
Shakespeare ceased writing at the top of his powers.
Teenagers only thrive by peer approval.
It takes bamboo a hundred years to sprout flowers.

Jesus was crucified, facing south, seeing Jerusalem.
All human beings originally had brown eyes.
Writing well should predominate every curriculum.
Snobbery is the face the insecure use in disguise.

TRUISMS

Camels never flinch climbing steepest grades.
No mattress beats a balsam-bough bedding.
Hearing loss is irreversible despite hearing aids.
A perfect murder is best arranged by sledding.

Friday is the day of congregation for Muslims.
The Samaritans were first to receive the Gospels.
Beagles are best detector dogs at U.S. customs.
Nothing non-organic can ever qualify as fossils.

No tradition of anti-Semitism exists in Edinburgh.
Dowsers cannot determine water depth or width.
Flashy uniforms are catnip to every generalissimo.
While kin are relatives, acquaintances are kith.

General Oliver Cromwell never lost a battle.
Conducting, Toscanini never "interpreted" composers.
To the new world, Cortés introduced cattle.
The liar feels full justification by delayed disclosures.

Shame is necessary to leading a moral life.
A bobolink thrives alone in damp meadows.
Wetlands are being choked by purple loosestrife.
Trampolines are a direct menace to elbows.

Men routinely hunt while women gather.
Dark Harbor dulse grows best in the dark.
For a diffident son thank a martinet father.
No bones exist in the body of a shark.

ALEXANDER THEROUX

No Trappist business can be a profit-making venture.
Native Americans were never given a state of their own.
To censor is to suppress, strong disapproval censure.
Kolsch beer cannot be brewed outside of Cologne.

Elizabethan playhouses had no front curtain.
Vidalia onions contain more water than others.
The outcome of any *mission* is never certain.
Older brothers are smarter than younger brothers.

All living things contort toward sunlight.
A church to Cape Codders is a "meeting-house."
"Glaire," or book shine, depends on egg white.
The smell of blood never leaves a slaughterhouse.

Sucking noodles in Japan is not bad manners.
No U.S. president has ever been charged with a crime.
The martial mind is forever partial to banners.
One, oddly, never encounters *Hamlet* for the first time.

A single-edged knife blade cuts much faster
and more cleanly than any double-edged one.
Only a thing irremediable constitutes disaster.
A humorless nincompoop alone savors a pun.

The briefer a lawyer's letter, the scarier.
Dulse, sun-drying, can be poisoned by rain.
A license is required in England to be a farrier.
Neither God nor gods is worshipped by a Jain.

TRUISMS

No Japanese meal includes a sweet dessert.
Clams are usually buried four inches in a seashore.
An actor is always *faking* the role of extrovert.
Sociology is the graveyard section of a bookstore.

Champagne does not improve by aging.
A poor acidic soil nutrifies the cranberry.
A Wagnerian opera needs major staging.
Andalusia is the only true source of sherry.

Rain always presages a change in weathers.
Public use of toothpicks in Japan is not offensive.
A bird's skeleton weights less than its feathers.
The act of awakening tends to the ascensive.

The pith of a chili is its hottest part.
Fission explains the saga of doubles.
No sorbet can ever be too tart.
Every true Soviet respected shovels.

Oysters love being paired with Muscadet.
The Ramones, embarrassed, hid in their hair.
Hoping to recoup is the hapless gambler's bet.
Every anarchist is a rabid pamphleteer.

New Englanders prefer houses painted white.
The sexiest women on earth are Brazilian.
Only unappeased people are driven to write.
No Congolese dictator is not also reptilian.

Drinking from bowls is Japan is accepted.
The sweetness of desserts closes the palate.
That drive is insane seeking the perfected.
Each seed of a tree cone is circumvallate.

Tavel is the premier rosé wine of France.
Revolutions always flourish with brief slogans.
Islamist law bans every form of dance.
Nihonto swords strictly belonged to *shoguns*.

Horsemeat has been sold in France since 1811.
The Gilded Age is Twain's most biographical book.
The Hebrew Bible finds corruption in leaven.
Plagiarism flourishes in the world of the cookbook.

No life can be lived without narrating itself.
No classifications exist for Rhône Valley wines.
A feathered hat identified Ghibelline from Guelph.
The most ancient trees on earth are nature's pines.

All boys tend to be happy in a pack.
Every culture has a Great Flood story.
The house edge is small in blackjack.
Rumors are inescapably derogatory.

The hands reveal a person's personality.
Increase your knowledge, increase your sorrow.
War turns on the fulcrum of nationality.
Portaging canoes is done best at a river's oxbow.

TRUISMS

English is in fact a dialect of German.
Lying, for children, is a form of fable.
Every daily sunrise is a sermon.
Claim adjusters cherish an actuarial table.

Swamp ash is the best wood for guitars.
Lincoln was a poor extemporaneous orator.
Green to yellow to brown colors all cigars.
Hawaii is much further south than Florida.

Only in bad fiction do people say, "Pshaw!"
The Scots like eating their porridge standing up.
Nothing positive is ever ascribed to Esau.
Men find attractive women's eyes slanting up.

No totalitarian does not love an armband.
January 6th is a significant part of Yuletide.
Frenchmen only kiss a married woman's hand,
and they do so only indoors, never outside.

A rasher of bacon is three slices and no more.
Up to 1870, the title *professor* was held in disrepute.
A parent's angst ever attends a baby's Apgar score.
Most patterns of seashells prove to be circumvolute.

Odd behavior produces estrangement in others.
Bringing bananas on any shipboard is a Jonah.
Beware a family where fathers temper mothers.
A teenager should play the role of Desdemona.

Fastenings in all forms are prehistoric.
The world's oldest ice is in Antarctica.
All sermonizers treasure the allegoric.
Pornography addicts despise erotica.

Shoes always stink when placed by a fire.
Never addresses the Queen before she speaks.
Poetry instead of a cowshed prefers "byre."
Animals show most markings on their cheeks.

Sails in the Navy do not flap, they "flag."
A fistful of arrows equaled Spartan drachmae.
Fertilizer ($Ca_3[PO_4]_2$) is usable from steel slag.
One's diet has nothing at all to do with acne.

Jesus' answers were always quick,
as if he knew what you were going to ask.
but they never involved realpolitik,
and he obviously saw through any mask.

Queen Victoria had a small mania for tartans.
Fog is worse than sun for melting ice.
Crimson colored clothing for male Spartans.
Healthy phytic acid exists in brown rice.

The Nile flows directly south to north.
Sarah Bernhardt claimed Hamlet was a woman.
Dimension is forever seeking a fourth.
No insincere or lying penitent is ever shriven.

TRUISMS

Classical ships never left the sight of land.
On all official parades Queen Elizabeth rides side saddle.
There exists a worldwide premium for sand.
Noiseless was the canoe when any Indian would paddle.

Sunlight in green glass bottles skunks beer.
The term "Ms." is not permitted in royal circles.
Fawns carry no scent, unlike all adult deer.
Chinese insults sharpen by allusions to turtles.

Civilizations in every case began on rivers.
Happiness in every instance involves a return.
Highest blessings go to anonymous givers.
No primitive society lacked a form of a quern.

Ancient Egyptians wrote down no vowels.
Robert Browning never met his severe father-in-law.
Ears are never found symmetrical on owls.
Hurricanes never occur in the country of Panama.

Handwriting ever betrays a state of mind.
The city of Dublin is alive with her dead.
None identify smells better than the blind.
A hunting Sioux had a non-existent tread.

Never fell a tree against the wind.
Avarice always feels desire after fulfillment.
Every Spanish Hapsburg had a monstrous chin.
Great poetry is the act of superb distillment.

ALEXANDER THEROUX

The old Christian year began on March 25.
Filipino cuisine is the most diverse in the world.
Hickory tree twigs have the hardest withe.
A flag should never be raised when it is furled.

The Northern Hemisphere contains the most land.
There are 800 different brands of beer in Brussels.
The index finger is least needed on the human hand.
The nature of all casino gambling is its "hustles."

No vaccine does not depend on egg white.
Hitler's military mistake was to divide authority.
Ice reflects as much as 90% sunlight.
Warm temperatures soften speech sonority.

All U.F.O. "experts" suffer from grandiosity.
During the war, UK miners were exempt from draft.
Anderson & Sheppard refuse photos, shun publicity.
The artist Yoko Ono notoriously rarely laughed.

Everybody misspells the word *Philippine.*
Gay soldiers often become chaplains' assistants.
19th-century corsets and says were all baleen.
Serbs and Croats despair of any coexistence.

Shunning a person is a form of bigotry.
Women meant nothing to A.E. Housman.
Gothic cathedral towers avoid symmetry.
Visual music is the nature of the fountain.

TRUISMS

A Zouave craze permeated the Civil War.
Lilac is considered a half-mourning color.
Red was a sign of Passover on a house door.
Cotton and linen, not paper, makes a dollar.

Every ceiling is honored more than any floor.
Waving with *both* hands is required in distress.
Cape Malays were used as slaves by the Boer.
Sex is often followed by psychic loss, *tristesse*.

Horror movies love the whole-tone scale.
No London existed before the Romans came.
All nerds in high school were always pale.
Pearls are jewels of choice for a *grande dame*.

Argentinians believe that they are Europeans.
No William, going by "Billy," wants to grow up.
Virtually no Muslims exist among Koreans.
Any tie-in to azidoazide azide will blow up.

Medieval churches always ran east and west,
with the altar at the east end, facing Jerusalem.
Who has the least to tell, always listens best.
Earth's most abundant metal is aluminum.

Everything is closed during August in Paris.
Puccini named his operas after lead soprano roles.
A cruel and exploited life awaits an heiress.
The intellect and will, both, compose our souls.

ALEXANDER THEROUX

All celebrated collaborations fell apart.
Acronyms fascinate the minds at NASA.
Fish never actually swim—they dart.
To overlook a woman is to harass her.

Elvis Presley never learned to swim.
Distillates, once bottled, can never improve.
Leafage of any sort provides a scrim.
Ain Ghazal is the oldest piece in the Louvre.

The Dakotas have no professional sports.
Norwegians enjoy eating the bones of fish.
The letter "X" is meaningless in airports.
Agar helps all cell growth in a Petri dish.

Shad never eat anything on a spawning run.
If women voted, Abe would have lost in 1864.
A punch line is the common work of a pun.
A bore is one who never knows he is a bore.

Every true explorer is thrilled at being lost.
Mazal is the word that closes diamond deals.
Best pick rose hips after the first light frost.
It's blood, not oil, that turns history's wheels.

Mosquitos cannot survive cold high elevations.
There are species on this planet we have never seen.
Life is cheap in the world's saturated populations.
For long centuries, all wedding gowns were green.

TRUISMS

Every human being starts out as an anus.
A gentleman's clothes has *handsewn* buttonholes.
Hair's black or white: spurious is *greyness*.
Olive oil lamp soot inked the Dead Sea Scrolls.

Almost all purees actually taste best when tinned.
The Lincoln family was never photographed together.
A good lapel, firm, must still flutter in the wind.
Of anywhere else, Mexico City has the best weather.

Taxation in all forms is legalized theft.
Two-foot-nine's the smallest space miners can work in.
A homburg should be worn tilted to the left.
Wood from any birch tree is, dendrologically, birken.

Shakespeare has it badly in for tailors.
A good confidante is always a bad confider.
Red sunrises greatly spooked all whalers.
Herefordshire Redstreaks make the best hard cider.

Lolita, in that novel, died on Christmas Day.
Celery never belongs in a good lobster roll.
A cheetah hunts its prey only during the day.
Always beat egg whites in a copper bowl.

Tailor shops infamously let in little light.
Potatoes have more chromosomes than a human.
Almost all sword fishing is done at night.
The world's second most popular spice is cumin.

ALEXANDER THEROUX

The sun is held together solely by gravity.
Refrigerating perfumes preserves their scent.
Visitors in Dostoevsky are always offered tea.
The ideal media broadcasters have no accent.

Cows have regional accents just like humans.
South America's most educated country is Uruguay.
What does not reflect light, nothing illumines.
No girl or woman looks unattractive wearing a beret.

No human being is a murderer at birth.
Excess in a recitation best describes a rhapsody.
Gravity is far from uniform on Earth.
Potatoes are not served at English "high tea."

Refrigerating potatoes adds sugary innutrition.
The UK issues stamps without it printed name.
Symmetry to Japanese apes artificial perfection.
To explain faith by way of reason is truly lame.

A classic violin matures well over decades.
New Zealand has the world's best trout fishing.
Tartarus is the place of punishment, not Hades.
Fulfillment is absent in the *act* of wishing.

Blues songs need a B7th to go with an E and A.
Decorations in Japanese homes are left off-center,
and no human figures are ever kept on display.
No child missing a mother is not a born dissenter.

TRUISMS

Scallops rarely live more than a single year.
Birds never taste the food that they eat.
For a painless hanging, knot behind the left ear.
No heart needs a body to tell it to beat.

Abe Lincoln never believed in *racial equality*.
An ounce of mother equals a pound of clergy.
The nature of etiquette are facts of frivolity.
Justice in law should never prevail over mercy.

An adult grizzly bear cannot climb a tree.
Bastardy is a canonical impediment to ordination.
The most complicated human joint is the knee.
The only legitimate tax is done by capitation.

Colors bees most love are violet and blue.
Waltz King Strauss never danced, did not know how.
Falciparum malaria will always kill you.
Michelangelo's *David* speaks mainly with his brow.

The enemy of any timepiece is friction.
No woman has ever entered an iconostasis.
Every border crossing is a malediction.
The stage on film becomes the actors' faces.

It is utter folly to give a child a choice.
Cummerbund pleats should open upward.
Othello on stage requires a bass voice.
The intuitive mind is fully unstructured.

Regimental stripes always go diagonally.
No one ever called Jesus the name "Jesus."
Stop signs are all constructed hexagonally.
Every thesis has its antithesis and synthesis.

The electric chair was invented by a dentist.
The whole-tone scale has an otherworldly aura.
Autarky is the goal of *journeyman* apprentice.
Hannukah is never mentioned in the Torah.

Herring milt is no different than shad semen.
Much of *Lolita* was written in a '52 Buick.
Spirits haunting Scrooge are all eudaemon.
Volume is always measured by the cubic.

Trash is never left on the curb in Nantucket.
Waste-to-Energy facilities are kept spotless.
Medieval sieges depended on the trebucket.
Ray Chandler's novel were chiefly plotless.

Every extreme attitude is a flight from the self.
Mein Kampf never slotted on the Vatican's *Index*.
A busty woman's breast constitutes a shelf.
Obese people's chins become part of their necks.

Milkmaids traditionally use a three-legged stool.
The grandiose mind suffers from low self-esteem.
Exceptions are what are forced to make a rule.
Tension separates Ashkenazim from Sephardim.

TRUISMS

Dominant mothers figure large in assassins' lives.
Bouquets to Japanese are a wanton waste of flowers.
Oxygen becomes toxic in high pressure dives.
Rice has its perfect substitute in cauliflowers.

Sicily's poor soil refuses to grow good food.
Singer Tom Jones never read the book *Tom Jones*.
No Cape Cod morning fails to be bedewed.
The human hand—fifty-four of them—has the most bones.

Orthodox churches have no pews or chairs.
Best views of London are to be had from the north.
Stairs is always plural—"There *are* stairs."
Tom-tom sounds always follow the perfect fourth.

A badly burnt *roux* can never be saved.
Pantyhose worn will repel jellyfish stings.
Every couturier has been proven depraved.
Sparta, the city-state, always had two kings.

Beech wood makes the best Windsor chairs.
Kerouac, of *On the Road*, never learned to drive.
To the Chinese, evil events happen in pairs.
Potatoes planted next to tomatoes never thrive.

Never climb up sandstone when it is wet.
Eugene O'Neill, fixated on it, never visited Ireland.
Most of Asia receives its water from Tibet.
No non-circular flower arrangement is a garland.

In the market, 10% is a correction, 20% a crash.
Eyes should always be kept forward at a urinal.
A horizon at sunset leaves a micro-green flash.
Climate figures in the width of the birth canal.

Prison inmates are required to wear long sleeves.
The fatter you are, the fatter is your tongue.
Italians wear red underwear on New Year's Eve.
Inhaling moldy hay spores causes farmer's lung.

No ruminant has teeth in the front upper jaw.
Italians customarily eat fish on New Year's Eve.
That country is barbarous that eats foie gras.
Anything that's woven constitutes an inweave.

The bisexual sea: *La mere* in French; *il mare* in Italian.
Anything complete negates the Buddhist idea of Becoming.
A sire is the name of stud once denominated a stallion.
"Highly qualified persons" is code in juries for *no women*.

A staircase to a child is an image of fear.
Every "ism" is an aspect of a daddy.
The air over Newark, N. J. is never clear.
Islam's highest honorific epithet is Mahdi.

Ice age glaciers never reached Africa.
Genius first involves denial of common sense.
Thyroid sufferers should never eat brassica.
Advent is a season, not of joy, but penitence.

TRUISMS

Japanese wear no jewelry at a tea ceremony.
Happiness is repugnant to every biographer.
The Chinese on their New Year eat abalone.
Adversarial drive animates a cryptographer.

Never take the kettle to the teapot—
always take the teapot to the kettle.
An arid summer prevents black rot.
Tin predominates in all bell metal.

All cooks are temperamental in Wodehouse stories.
Ancient Olympic Games were never held in Athens.
Weight—wet fish—increases stability in dories.
Outdatedness is the precondition of all fashions.

Willow tree wood is best for making baskets.
Horatio Alger wrote nothing of the American Indian.
No American state law requires the use of caskets.
Any happening at noon may be called a meridian.

Most Nazi books are unavailable to buy.
Danger feels diminished by numbers of people.
Bigger than the sun are all stars in the sky.
Eavesdropping in Oklahoma is officially illegal.

Carbon at its very densest is a diamond.
Any water that is carried is never enough.
A vagina is never covered by the hymen.
Worse than smoke is the nicotine of snuff.

Singer Elvis Presley never owned a passport.
To the Japanese, no Asian is an outsider (*gaigin*).
Armenia has access to no ocean or seaport.
The essential drink of the Pilgrims was cider.

Any group of political elite is anti-people.
No substance has ever supplanted paper.
To be masked in New York State is illegal.
Most skilled in fashion design is the draper.

Conspiricism is a type of mental malady.
The KKK spread more largely in the North.
Psychiatry's goal is that patients see reality.
Stateliness in music loves a perfect fourth.

"I've got to get the messages," is said
in the UK, never "I've got to go shopping."
Mantou (dough) in China replaces bread.
Gathering information by government is stalking.

No reverse gear can be found on a motorcycle.
Showing your teeth is a "tell" playing poker.
Revelation 12:7–9 identifies Jesus as St. Michael.
Britain's Queen Alexandra always wore a choker.

Farmers are extremely careful laughers.
Seating in fashion shows is very rigid.
Chat in society is mainly that of chaffers.
Polyamy, Russia is perpetually frigid.

TRUISMS

Cats lack the ability to taste sweetness.
America is never mentioned in Scripture.
Meekness, humility, is never weakness.
Obesity badly causes vascular stricture.

The pop stars of India are their gurus.
Ikon faces are made thin for asceticism.
The name of G-d is never used by Jews.
Confucianism thrives on the aphorism.

Gold Rush apples make the best apple cider.
It's a Greek custom to play poker on New Year's Eve.
A death noise is often the sound of stridor.
Experience allows the occasion to apperceive.

Curry is not and never was a spice.
Zebras are black with white stripes—not vice versa.
Love seeks the opportunity to sacrifice.
Thievery is an occasion of sin to every bursar.

Middle Eastern nations have the least alcoholics.
Film noir protagonists—men—are always weak.
Every tree in nature shows perfected hydraulics.
Twenty-five years must pass to make an antique.

Kissing is especially repulsive to a whore.
Our solar system all formed at the same time.
New Jersey voted not to re-elect Lincoln in 1864.
Prof. Moriarty is never linked to minor crime.

What can exist, therefore must exist.
For a first tree cut, less than one-half of the radius.
Three main joints stabilize the human wrist.
A cultural commonplace is Jewish love for an alias.

All armies prefer high ground to low.
Hummingbirds cannot walk on their feet.
Landscapers never plant a female ginko.
Salting any grapefruit makes it taste sweet.

Indians and Pakistanis never agree.
Yellow is a sacred color in Polynesia.
The way to say "fuck you" in Hollywood is "*trust me.*"
All parts are poison in the perennial artemisia.

All metamorphic rock shows schistosity.
The envious much prefer facts to ignorance.
Australia leads all nations in generosity.
No Prussian mind isn't given to belligerence.

There are no tigers on the continent of Africa.
Writers, oddly, capitalize Black but small-case white.
The book of Exodus informs the Haggadah.
The Nile crocodile has by far the strongest bite.

John Milton distinguished China from Cathay.
No secret is more poorly kept than a happy one.
Prince Charles in Scotland is the Duke of Rothesay.
Only a half-wit goes through life seeking fun.

TRUISMS

Clocks are a major taboo in gambling casinos.
You can tell regions of the U.S. by their fences.
New Mexico has the largest proportion of Latinos.
Everyone in Congress fudges operating expenses.

Women as species are closely related to cats.
A green hat in China indicates cuckoldry.
Modern people wear caps, virtually never hats.
Nassarius shells were humans' first jewelry.

The state of Florida does not tax income.
Doo-wop groups rarely came from the South.
The style of best-selling prose is humdrum.
10,000 taste buds exist in the human mouth.

Adolf Hitler never wore a wristwatch.
Israel is filled completely with outsiders.
Scotch-hopping was the original name of hopscotch.
Flying in the rain is hazardous to gliders.

In math, there is no largest prime number.
All science-fiction has a survivalist streak.
Connotations are mostly negative of *lumber*.
Homeric is easier to read than Attic Greek.

Anyone who refers to himself in the third person
is psychotic, hopelessly vain, or simply deluded.
Complete silence fosters prayer for a Cistercian.
In Oregon, Blacks have been historically excluded.

ALEXANDER THEROUX

Since all college football teams play different
opponents, no one can determine who is best.
The Hohenzollern mind is born belligerent.
No brown-headed cowbird ever builds a nest.

Dying was Sarah Bernhardt's dramatic specialty.
95% of Earth's fresh water is locked in Antarctic ice.
Sentiment is the literal opposite of sentimentality.
Shelf-life is brief with brown (but not white) rice.

It is impossible to trace a stolen fur.
There are no external nostrils in a gannet.
No spice has more uses than myrrh.
Rhodium's the most expensive metal on the planet.

Actors are refused listings in the *Social Register*.
Black is a foreboding color in Japanese culture.
Deprivation is the main intention of divestiture.
The voice box (*syrinx*) is missing in a vulture.

All eucalypti come from Australia.
Zebulon Pike never fully climbed Pike's Peak.
Bees make "mad honey" from toxic azalia.
Subtlety of patterns is the language of batik.

Snails have the most teeth of any animal.
One must never say of the flag "Stripes and Stars."
The word *flammable* is preferred to *inflammable*.
Objectivity is the first sacrifice in all memoirs.

TRUISMS

Argentina and Chile *both* own Tierra del Fuego.
Johnny Hodges let no one carry his alto sax.
Walking is the best, quickest cure for lumbago.
Being insoluble in water is the nature of wax.

Notoriety is more famous than fame.
BBQ in South Carolina uses only white oak.
Listed first is the Japanese family name.
Natural vitamin D exists in all egg yolk.

A Japanese tearoom is used for nothing else.
Northern Ireland never banned the fox hunt.
Even the very best of hairpieces look like pelts.
Craven is the word for M.L.B.'s sacrifice bunt.

Never shave in the deep jungle—sepsis!
Bonds do not do well in times of inflation.
Write no book without passionate cathexis.
Travel is always queered by a destination.

The Great Synagogue of Oran was once a mosque.
The best way to inspect is to imagine.
Skiers habitually click their poles together for luck.
No Chinese fable excludes a dragon.

Beware—kelp at sea always masks rocks.
Only "Yankees" put sugar on their cornbread.
Never make a quilt with thirteen blocks.
Blue in nature keeps secretly a touch of red.

Germans in Pushkin's stories are always evil.
Corn grows better than wheat in Appalachia.
Adolescence characterizes everything medieval.
All honeybees are passionate for echinacea.

Salt, sprinkled on grapefruit, makes it sweet.
"Interesting" is forever the coward's adjective.
Natural goodness is sullied by any additive.
Thoreau believed heaven lay under our feet.

Indonesians fear wearing green in the ocean.
Pasta should not be served with a meat dinner.
Being very short is the condition of a Laotian.
Of graphene, nothing on the planet is thinner.

God in 1 Thessalonians 4:16 sounds a shout!
Never fail to always cook morel mushrooms.
Dark skin indicates aggression in a trout.
500 preps for pregnancy are made in wombs.

One straight man is worth three comedians.
Pointing feet at someone in Samoa is bad form.
Beekeeping is the prime passion of Slovenians.
The country of Israel avoids anything cruciform.

A sloop never has more than one mast.
No jungle boarder can properly be guarded.
Hinduism deals in everything by caste.
Calumny is now assigned the word "retarded."

TRUISMS

Democracy is utter krypton to a czarist.
A violin bow should be rosined ten strokes.
Trivial details hallmark a first-rate diarist.
Truffles are incomprehensible without oaks.

Below 40 degrees south there is no law.
Below 50 degrees south there is no God.
No Arabian rug is woven without a flaw.
Everyone in a Japanese house goes unshod.

Dolphins always sleep with one eye open.
The fuller the refrigerator, the more energy efficient.
True coquetry always goes unspoken.
An overweight policeman is professionally deficient.

C minor is the key for musical solemnity.
Filipinos press hand to forehead in greeting.
Suspicions are raised in double indemnity.
Snobbery is involved in the art of seating.

Tolstoy and Dostoevsky, contemporaries, never met.
South Africa has two capitals: Pretoria and Cape Town.
The eyes of holoanencephalists are invariably close-set.
A sad wistfulness characterizes the European clown.

Retiring at age sixty-five is a waste of resources.
Borneonians believe Queen Elizabeth II a centaur.
Almost all white horses are actually grey horses.
A well-schooled mentee usually goes on to mentor.

ALEXANDER THEROUX

No ship ever rounds Cape Horn anymore.
The Bantu believe that pygmies are animals.
The bathtub gave inspiration to Christian Dior.
Hands, cut in strips, is first reach of cannibals.

Bowdlerization is always a totalitarian act.
True fame in England puts you on a biscuit tin.
An interpretation consistently throttles a fact.
The clitoris is also endowed with a foreskin.

What purports to be equal is rarely fair.
An Eagle Scout must earn twelve merit badges.
Mediterranean men most value a woman's derrière,
No gender segregation exists on Islamic hajjes.

No blowing wind on Earth is ever steady.
A horse always licks its lips when being trained.
Never is heard "speghetto," singular of spaghetti!
In the region of Antarctica, it has never rained.

Etonians always refer to Eton as "the School."
No single true, blue pigment exists in nature.
Every human brain can be called a bascule.
The U.S. openly plagiarized British legislature.

Time, distance, & situation determine "4th and 1."
Gorillas consider a stare an act of aggression.
The exact color of France's Eiffel Tower is dun.
An answer is already half made by its question.

TRUISMS

A delicious honey can be made from weeds.
Abraham Lincoln is in the wrestling hall of fame.
Direct eye contact is offensive to most Swedes.
Most of the streets in Japan do not have a name.

Winston Churchill never took a bus in his life.
Physically punishing children is a crime in Sweden.
Feminists in general despise the word *wife*.
Mormons believe Jackson County, Missouri was Eden.

The source of all evil is found in the human race.
Argentina and Chile despise and distrust each other.
Bacterium, protists, and worms are missing a face.
Boys (not girls) most nauseate a pregnant mother.

People who cry in novels never blow their noses.
There is no seasonal respite in Cape Horn anymore.
Bible flowers list only lilies, camphire (henna), and roses.
Old Rome's decline was due in part to toxic lead ore.

A coming always—significantly—involves a going,
Only six of Aeschylus ninety plays have been preserved.
Fish never feed off Cuba with a south wind blowing.
No public seat, when and wherever, should be reserved.

One day the sun will fully consume the Earth.
No activities on Sunday are allowed in Tonga.
Of all cities, none is more isolated than Perth.
Argentinians favor the tango *and* the milonga.

A casket should always be carried foot first.
The U.S. flag must be hoisted briskly, lowered slowly.
A woman receiving flowers is weirdly coerced.
Superstitions are compulsive with every hockey goalie.

Never buy your milk in clear containers.
Wind force is equal to the square of the velocity.
Losing is a kind of music to complainers.
A close-hauled ship gives way to one running free.

The human pain threshold is 200 decibels.
Gales at Cape Horn all blow east to west.
Winos by choice generally prefer muscatels.
Mythology fiction always fixes on the quest.

No produced mustard is ever inedible.
The otter is the enemy of the beaver.
The Mormon fable is at best incredible.
Reverence is toxic to a non-believer.

Ernest Hemingway always wrote standing up.
There is no mention of Jerusalem in the Koran.
Thank Fannie Farmer for the measuring cup.
Tobacco is banned in the country of Bhutan.

Italians abhor combining fish and cheese.
All analysis involves reasoning backward.
Number 8 is thought lucky among Chinese.
No paranoiac does not love a password.

TRUISMS

Every list compiled is always subjective.
Style never makes the mistake of arriving first.
An adjective, not a noun, is the word *detective*!
Cactus juice better than water conquers thirst.

You cannot hum if your nostrils are pinched.
A Basque always pulls his beret down straight.
Mississippi's the leading state of those lynched.
The handshake of an invert is always ornate.

Cameroon criminalizes homosexuality.
Water bagels are far superior to egg bagels.
The Indian Ocean includes the Arabian Sea.
A single year is the limit of home appraisals.

Every human fear is a fear of losses.
A biographer has not the right to imagine.
France has defined five mother sauces.
Industry never grew in the Appalachian.

Plato judged homosexuals to be extra virile.
Men kiss the hands of married women only.
The sermon centers all services Presbyteral.
Depressed individuals are, primarily, lonely.

Transcendentalists equated sloth with sitting down.
Only the best students fall in love with teachers.
A gerund can take an object; not so a verbal noun.
H. Thoreau termed "men of straw" all preachers.

Sigmund Freud had a morbid fear of trains.
Roulette wheel rotors are divided into octants.
In traffic circles, drivers forego their lanes.
Twenty years is the ceiling for valid patents.

Sharpening steel doesn't sharpen, merely hones.
Parsifal, a sacred opera, never mentions Christ.
The clavicle is the weakest of all human bones.
Nothing other than personal gifts are sacrificed.

Expurgation is always an act of cowardice.
A woman never comments on a gentleman's attire.
A U.S. vice president is virtually powerless.
The Homestead Act was braced by barbed wire.

The act of weeping makes one feel happier.
No boys in Alger books became millionaires.
Larger eggs, lighter in color, are top caviar.
Reductionism is the bane of questionnaires.

The Chinese have a compulsion to wager.
Hypochondria keeps most physicians in business.
Stress in any form is crippling to a teenager.
The Puritans banned the existence of Christmas.

Lamb solely used in meatloaf, soft, crumbles it.
No writer finishing a book doesn't suffer self-doubt.
The spider "balloons" its prey, that is, bundles it.
The left hand is used in handshakes by a Boy Scout.

TRUISMS

When riding a bike on a road, go with traffic.
Always use a timber hitch for diagonal lashing.
Decoration in a mosque is strictly calligraphic.
Cross-dressing is a commonplace at Fasching.

Southwest Ethiopia is the birthplace of coffee.
Turritopsis dohrnii jellyfish are biologically immortal.
Ending sentences with "but" is common to an Aussie.
Heaven is commonly understood as having a portal.

BBQ in Tennessee uses only hickory wood.
Churchill, piqued at him, skipped FDR's funeral.
Nothing innocent lies underneath a hood.
Every language invents its every single numeral.

Beeswax wood—never apply a varnish.
Saluting the quarter deck is a naval custom.
Contrast—don't add—flavor by a garnish.
No civil Roman period matched the Augustan.

W is a letter that the French never use.
Churchill was the weakest of the Big Three.
To appease a jealous God? Cut the prepuce.
At night, taxi fares are doubled in Djibouti.

No Italian ever sips cappuccino after a meal.
Surfers never use yellow surfboards in Africa.
For Tibetan monks, infinity is the color teal.
To a Ukrainan, all Russians are anathema.

ALEXANDER THEROUX

Baseball players avoid stepping on a foul line.
Grating Parmesan cheese over clams is barbaric.
Mystery writers overuse death by strychnine.
I. Berlin's holiday songs are only atmospheric.

Democracy is strictly a case of mathematics.
Hanukkah has sixteen different spellings in English.
Truth comes only from logic said the Eleatics.
Laughter will consistently passion extinguish.

The term "jiffy" is an actual unit of time.
"Jingle Bells" was written for Thanksgiving.
Blanks are pickled in pre-minting the U.S. dime.
A Corsican is notorious for being unforgiving.

Gilbert & Sullivan's names are never reversed.
Modernism as a term becomes immediately passé.
Women receiving gifts of flowers are coerced.
The perfect light for photography is a gray day.

A healthy cranberry alone will bounce and float.
The Constitution was writ to weaken the states.
Analysts find evasion in a wearer of a raincoat.
Only an electoral authority is allowed mandates.

Extreme shame is tantamount to annihilation.
There are no blood vessels in the feet of a duck.
The Russian mind greatly fears westernization.
Keys are normally dispensed with on a fire truck.

TRUISMS

Roosters in China are neither eaten nor killed;
they are considered protectors against a demon.
Stains are less evident in cloths that are twilled.
A British aristocrat finds romance in treason.

Coal is the world's major source for electricity.
Shakespeare never mentions the Avon by name.
Theft and need harbor a legitimate complicity.
Guilt constitutes the major ingredient of shame.

It is self-defeating to *try* to read an eye chart.
The Greek Parthenon has no straight lines.
A secretive life was necessary for Descartes.
No mugs without lids can be called steins.

The Indian measurement *kos* is never uniform!
Sauternes are too sweet to be drunk with food.
High quality in democracies is ever the norm.
"Jonquil" is the best seven-letter Scrabble word.

Film close-ups were avoided with Fred Astaire.
Condemned is a lawyer when the guilty is acquitted.
The discernible front arms are called legs on a bear.
On surveys, the true eunuchs are the uncommitted.

Reviving Broadway is like rouging a corpse.
No Pakistan ruler is elected by democratic means.
Painted plywood consistently bows and warps.
Phytohemagglutinins toxify uncooked kidney beans.

Vladimir Nabokov never owned a home.
Tahitians prefer swimming in fresh water to the ocean.
The dullard mind is attracted to chrome.
Coffee is mainly drunk from plastic bags by a Laotian.

Dancing on toes is strictly for women in ballet.
Tonga has never been controlled a foreign power.
Good writing, above all, is the enemy of cliché.
No architect's content until he designs a tower.

Figs are not fruit but flowers turned inside out.
Comedians Abbott and Costello never did smut.
A model's sexiness conveys petulance in a pout.
Union uniforms, boiled, made Confederate butternut.

No true Polynesian will touch a temple tiki.
Summer is America's high season for shooting.
Inconsistency is the default in anything streaky.
Motivation is the linchpin of sports recruiting.

All comedians secretly want to play drama.
Shameful to a Tongan is showing naked flesh.
Humming is the communing way of a llama.
France has banned the public Christmas crèche.

Ayn Rand never put a child in her novels.
A gallon of ice-cream must weigh 4½ pounds.
Personality is anathema in runway models.
Nazi minds gloried in many-colored browns.

TRUISMS

The world's favorite smell is vanilla.
Horsemeat tastes much sweeter than beef.
Tax cheats thrive on the island of Anguilla.
Fear constitutes a major part of grief.

Gaelic as a tongue has no words for *yes* and *no*.
A ship in storms *pitches* one way, *yaws* the next.
A paraphilia exists focusing on a woman's toe.
A written scroll is historically older than a codex.

Nothing is easier than a reunion fuck.
No one's more primitive than a litterer.
Men with good kidneys never drove a truck.
Than a child's death, nothing's bitterer.

Every automobile resembles a hippopotamus.
Palm trees in Tahiti are metal-banded against rats.
For seconds only does food stay in the esophagus.
Bareheaded, JFK ended the stylishness of hats.

Copra has a spontaneously combustive nature.
Unbearably bad is all Christian rock music.
Crass *bargaining* in Congress drives all legislature.
Most children could once easily identify a Buick.

Lepidoptery is not allowed in a nature preserve.
Off-the-record comments must be requested *beforehand*.
Conservatives, regarding the EPA, rarely conserve.
Russians protect a Motherland, Germany a Fatherland.

No private physicians can be found in Samoa—
all hospitals and pharmacies are government-operated.
For fetish wear, the top fashion is a feather boa.
On sixty-eight cruel occasions, Joan of Arc was interrogated.

Privacy, for bathing, in Samoa is unknown.
Old people have a passion for a wall calendar.
America's largest offensive was the Argonne.
The prime ingredient in all sachets is lavender.

Always sprinkle salt from a high hand.
Adolf Hitler both hated and feared the sea.
The last place settled on earth was Iceland.
Rhythm in children's verse is mainly the trochee.

White House workers can accept no tips.
Kangaroo rats die when they drink water.
That is nitrogen air in every bag of chips.
"Pettitoe" is haute cuisine for pig's trotter.

April is high season for bird migrations.
The French greatly dislike turnips—*navets*.
Pathogenic bacteria thrive in gas stations.
Overgrown teeth are common in rabbits.

Medical care in USA leads the world in cost.
Only fools and water go the way they're diverted.
Evergreen trees stop growing during a frost.
A church without a sermon is a church deserted.

TRUISMS

The sole fuel for migrating birds is fat.
Egyptians shake pepper on their melons.
Personality is the language of the hat.
In most Middle East countries, gays are felons.

Chunky: too large for one bite, too small for two.
In Dürer's *Melancholia* is a mysterious polyhedron.
Edison's first filament was carbonized bamboo.
All Jewish prayers are said to pass through Hebron.

Veal should be sautéed and never boiled.
Syracuse the city is rarely without snow.
Children after five years old are soiled.
Birds never face the same way in a row.

All forces are either a push or a pull.
Japanese hide their thumbs when passing a graveyard.
A baseball requires 150 yards of wool.
The habit of staring can be a lethal act in a jail yard.

Unhappiness is a physical affliction.
All anthologists include their own writing.
Every child's given kiss is a benediction.
Any ray-finned fish can be called *whiting*.

Stupid people always repeat things twice.
Isa (Jesus) is mentioned seventy-eight times in the Koran.
Mortar for China's Great Wall was sticky rice.
There are no parables in the Gospel of St. John.

Geography is the grandfather of history.
Any object not reflecting light is invisible.
No enchantment is possible without mystery.
Jesus was never seen to laugh, ride a horse, or get ill.

Jersey, the British island, is not part of the UK.
Monopole turbines in the U.S. kill 350,00 birds a year.
Cartoons were transfigured by the use of Benday.
Traditionally, religious festivals call for bock beer.

Asians are indifferent to eating bread.
Judgmental types are never merciful.
Heat is not absorbed nor released in lead.
Burning in any form is irreversible.

No belated rectification fully corrects.
A true sailor *puts in* a knot, never ties one.
Gothic cathedrals are romantic *for* defects.
A genius, missing any tool, devises one.

Oil wrestling is national sport of Turkey.
You never hear the phrase "beloved dentist."
Turtle tanks of glass are persistently murky.
Every weak waffler is a confirmed centrist.

Old women, when talking, love to whisper.
Of war, a politician serves only as witness.
Hauteur out of compulsion speaks crisper.
The U.S. Midwest is the realm of unfitness.

TRUISMS

Harvard grads once had to be able to swim.
Moods are affected by ceiling heights.
The most common Korean surname is Kim.
Bhutan functions without traffic lights.

Edmund was the first patron saint of England,
followed then by Edward, finally St. George.
Harvesting ginseng is forbidden in Finland.
The oldest skeleton was found in Cheddar Gorge.

The real Richard III was never crookbacked.
Chinese as a language has no verbs to conjugate.
A talentless painter finds refuge in the abstract.
North Americans are least likely to emigrate.

Everyone gullible is a serious voter.
Fake deodorants mask good smells.
A Jewish merchant has an extra motor.
A modern city is soulless without bells.

In most world cultures, a horse saddle is a rug.
No wind but Zephyr can enter Venus's garden.
Mary was conceived by her parents' simple hug.
Shakespeare's mother's maiden name was Arden.

Robert Lowell's poems are "grade-B Georgian."
The Pacific is milder than the wild Atlantic.
No pintle is ever complete without a gudgeon.
Arabic is indispensable in matters Koranic.

ALEXANDER THEROUX

No one's written memoir is not a boast.
The nighthawk has no song, only one note.
The Sargasso Sea exists without a coast.
Raging martinets always rule a sailboat.

Everything in life lives only to die.
Dry air is always denser than moist air.
Earth has an inadequate water supply.
Variation in looks renders life unfair.

Higher taxes eve impose higher costs.
No Jewish person dislikes a dill pickle.
Design is the quintessence of frosts.
New England weather is always fickle.

Self-hatred is the passive tense of murderer.
Mao Zedong presented wax mangoes as gifts.
A poacher in Britain had to elude a verderer.
A true romantic spends his life rehearsing ifs.

No mention in Scripture that Noah was mocked.
Pencils, stop signs, nuts and bolts are hexagonals.
No infusion proves effective unless it is decoct.
Every parallelepiped includes four space diagonals.

Bastards specialize in hating their fathers.
Vietnamese is all monosyllabic words.
Sex is declared by the height of garters.
As many animals, as many name for turds.

TRUISMS

Canada for identity is missing a face.
Doubt to all rigidified minds is treason.
Poverty to the affluent is disgrace.
No vaguer charge exists than "heathen."

Wilderness is freedom to an animal.
It helps in sports radio to have a low IQ.
New Hampshirites are notably unaffable.
Owls of all birds alone can see the color blue.

To think is, automatically, to condition.
The best bear meat is a dry young sow.
The ocean is a motherlode of detrition.
Not to milk her daily fully pains a cow.

Diffident people thrive on coteries.
Nice guys always finish anonymously.
Only a sloven doesn't bag his own groceries.
Hunger and despair run synonymously.

There has never been a Jesuit pope.
A fork is as only graceful as its tines.
Compressive strength is missing in a rope.
Wayward NFL stars are rarely given fines.

No word exists in Mandarin for *yes*.
Fungi long ruled our planet before any trees.
The first rule in hunting is quiesce.
Desalinization provides water to the Maltese.

The color of a polar bear's skin is a solid black.
Jib sails, triangular, kept a ship steady on course.
Good luck can be had touching a hunchback.
The horn of every unicorn is pointed antrorse.

Cupid and Psyche lived the classic doom of love.
No Mormon ship ever sank in an Atlantic crossing.
British dandies would wear only a kidskin glove.
Stocks pain was not restraint but public scoffing.

In April 1775, Paul Revere cried not, "The British
are coming!" but rather "The *Regulars* are coming."
Only Hasidic communities in Israel speak Yiddish.
In Area 51, Nevada is heard mysterious drumming.

Locust trees have a very shallow root system.
Kenyans are always victors in the Boston Marathon.
Owls in Renaissance art represent wisdom.
A diamond of 100 carats is referred to as a paragon.

On the far, far trail to Chimney Rock,
fur trappers, explorers, then pioneers,
the young virgin nation's hardiest stock,
crossed the plains in spite of all their fears.

Steamboats built St. Louis and Kansas City.
No rivalry surpasses Liverpool and Manchester United.
A vice that's never a virtue is that of pity.
Hillbrow in Johannesburg is the world's most blighted.

TRUISMS

Trump's Jan. 6 demagogic *autogolpe* (self-coup)
was a Latin American-like ploy to steal an election.
The blackbird mentality must compulsively aggroup.
Orgasms do not necessarily require an erection.

A straight man in comedy teams is billed first.
Woodpeckers never drill into live wood for insects.
Africa nations are plagued by the resource curse.
Being older is considered virtue among architects.

Much in admiration is frankly servile.
Lenin enjoyed having all priests shot.
Iran and Iraq will never reconcile.
Drivers prove worst in a parking lot.

The first 2.5% of gambling revenue generated
in casinos goes to gambling addiction programs!
Catholic saints aren't worshipped, but venerated.
Prizes won at midway games are whim-whams.

The most bombed place in the world is Laos.
Siena (olive) was Florence's (lily) arch enemy.
The etymology of the word *gas* is, aptly, chaos.
The goddess Demeter gave us Russian Dmitri.

There is a priapic strain in all evangelists.
Sailboats have right of way over motorboats.
A common foundling name is DeAngelis.
Salacious tales are often linked to overcoats.

The first mate is the prime minister of a ship.
The self-help section of a bookshop is the slum.
More sensitive than fingertips is the human lip.
Going a different direction is the aim of a thumb.

Every year products are made worse.
Gin is too fruitish when it fails to be dry.
Down East talk is intentionally terse.
All sophisticated wit is essentially wry.

Air pollution is the worst in Kanpur, India.
Radio's Rush Limbaugh, a cretin, had 18 million listeners.
Brainless is the flowering plant, forsythia.
Evangelistic television healers are all quack practitioners.

"Pink toes" is slang Black men use for white women.
Any renewable energy will need renewable storage.
Santa Fe is fragrant with the piney wood of pinon.
Edible are both the leaves and flowers of borage.

Drinking was never disallowed during Prohibition.
The Southern Poverty Law Center is anti-Muslim.
Newborns cry tears full weeks after parturition.
Every Presidential oath made is *formally* solemn.

Civil War soldiers rarely employed their bayonets.
Great happiness does not conduce to record itself.
Interior featurelessness is demanded in silhouettes.
Strong papal loyalty distinguished every Guelph.

TRUISMS

Change is terrifying to the timid mind.
Noah is an evil man in the Book of Mormon.
Sleep issues sorely bedevil the blind.
No one knows more secrets than a doorman.

Jumpy, Deafy, Dizzey, Hickey, Baldy, Wheezy,
Gabby, Nifty, Sniffy, Swift, Lazy, Puffy, Stuffy,
Burpy, Tubby, Blabby, Snoopy, Shorty, Breezy,
went unnamed as Disney dwarfs, as did Tuffy.

Circumcision, worldwide, is on the wane.
Dreaming is a mento-biological necessity.
None are more laconic than natives of Maine.
Vaingloriousness is the offspring of audacity.

Achilles was called "Pyrrha" due to his red hair.
Paddlewheels on steamboats replaced the screw propeller.
Amateur radio stations are the virtuosi of dead air.
Baleful in da Vinci's *Last Supper* is a spilt salt cellar.

Originality before all else requires self-permission.
After the 16th c. all ships were identified as feminine.
Francisco Franco banned the language of Galician.
His personal life is never discussed by a Bedouin.

No man ever drives a team of oxen without cursing.
Creative people physically see more of the world.
Sinatra, when filming, loathed repetitive rehearsing.
Cherry is by far the handsomest wood that's burled.

Italian riff-raff were always exiled to Pantellaria.
Gary Trudeau's cartoon ideas came during showers.
Tamales and *champurrado* are served on Candelaria.
Only after midnight, can time be called "small hours."

Never judge yourself with other people's eyes.
Hollywood, the machine, is about money, not art.
Their feet—sensors—provide taste for butterflies.
Never-endingly stuck is a nested shopping cart.

For progress to flow, never focus on the endgame.
Sherlock Holmes was a specialist on tattoo marks.
Under Thai law, no family can share a surname.
Love poems and a novel were written by Karl Marx.

Buffalo grass, fine in the blade, is best to fat up cattle.
All unsold tickets for any concert should be given away.
Pro football fans are, by far, the noisiest in Seattle.
Savonneries for centuries have flourished in Marseilles.

The Parthenon was originally a riot of color.
Skyquakes often sound off Catalina Island.
No bank is allowed to refuse a ¾-ripped dollar.
The overly suspicious always sit an aisle end.

The Bloods were red, the Crips wore blue.
The overwhelming desire of lust can execute good will.
Missing one meal can kill an active shrew.
Schizophrenia and autism are antipodes in the mentally ill.

TRUISMS

In classic love epics, there is never consummation.
The Holocaust is referred to in Yiddish as *Khurbn*.
Mob informants all live in an undisclosed location.
Being distilled in the U.S is law for making bourbon.

Thirty-one letters were added to the Deseret alphabet.
Leonard Cohen rhymes Hallelujah with "before I knew ya!"
There are too many holes and keys—seventeen—on a clarinet.
All klaxon automobile airhorns blare out "*Chattanooga.*"

The first book printed in English, by Caxton,
a translation, *Recueil des Histoires de Troye*,
a courtly romance in 1476 in Anglo-Saxon,
was printed in Belgium, a daunting redeploy.

A *matelot* is Middle French for a mariner or a sailor.
The deeper one peers into space, the further back in time.
Mary Miles Minter's mom killed William Desmond Taylor.
Decimus (1/10th) is etymology for the American dime.

Cryptocurrency involves strictly wildcat banking.
Love's drive is further pursuit for what we possess.
Most psychotics have been subject to spanking.
A sex change is anathema to most who cross-dress.

Heat is non-existent in an English country house.
Nietzsche said the universal means of value is power.
Hatred poisoned father and junior Johann Strauss.
Stems, leaves are edible (but ignored) in cauliflower.

Avoidance is a routine symptom of anxiety.
Guinea hens show a proclivity for eating ticks.
Mental is harder to master than physical sobriety.
The Army measures walking distances in clicks.

Electricity is perversely consumed as it is made.
Fasting always generates a certain illumination.
Pre-dawn is classic designated time for a raid.
Hollywood (cf. Mt. Lee) sadly needs identification.

Marilyn Monroe, the world's top glamor girl,
died on Saturday night, lonely, without a date.
A "countess" is the title for the wife of an earl.
Et can grammatically pass for past tense of *ate*.

Norwegian law requires harvested acres to be replanted.
At the Brown Derby the in-thing was to eat Cobb salad.
No champagne or sparkling wines should be decanted.
Many if not most lullabies are in the form of a ballad.

Men sporting bangs always appear slightly twee.
Basketball is all about the strategy of passing.
The Third Estate like piranhas feed on negativity.
Without a rope team, never try crevassing.

Recurrence in nature is its prime protector.
Sweetness is the natural sign of ripeness.
Self-reproach infects the mind of a defector
Burmese people are renowned for brightness.

TRUISMS

No American household owns a scone cutter.
Buildings contribute greatly to greenhouse gases.
Scrunchion is used in Labrador for drawn butter.
Elton John has collected of 250,000 eyeglasses.

Thanks to the ocean, most of our planet is dark.
The Deerslayer, white, grew up with Delaware Indians.
Animals as a last resort will happily eat bark.
A "thank you" letter comprises St. Paul's Philippians.

Fisher cat screams sound like a mad woman.
No egoist could match that of Frank Lloyd Wright.
Torture proves a human can become inhuman.
A refuge for any buccaneer was any coastal bight.

Without Andrea Palladio, we'd have no Inigo Jones.
A Mepps Aglia spinner, for trout, is the best lure.
Teeth—cementun, dentin, enamel—are not bones.
The Severn has freakish tides, with a treacherous bore.

Being biracial is to be both and also to be neither.
The biggest ocean waves are beneath its surface.
Iron causes orange in the teeth of every beaver.
4 p.m. for upper classes, 5 for others is tea service.

Joan Crawford's daily diet was soda crackers
with mustard, a coddled egg, no butter, no salt.
Leading a football defense are the linebackers.
Nothing not a 360° flip is officially a somersault.

Data is always nourished by numbers.
Switchtracking is standard tactic in a losing argument.
Sleeping naked fosters restful slumbers.
"Your English is great" is a backhanded compliment.

27,000 trees are daily cut down for toilet paper.
Chaplin got no Walk of Fame star until the 1970s!
Any "first hand" in fashion is the genius draper.
Three kisses involve a greeting to the Lebanese.

Lying is common for United States presidents.
Masai youth jump high to gain female attention.
Evaluation is the primary role of medical residents.
Authority to anarchy is a red flag of dissension.

Truth is the revelations of the morning after.
Cryptocurrency is a toxic form of gambling.
Melancholy is often earmarked by false laughter.
Walking with a goal kills the joy of rambling.

Norma Talmadge, William Haines, and Vilma Banky,
silent stars, failed in talkies by dint of their odd voices.
A colicky baby (gas in the abdomen) is always cranky.
What consistently spoils a child is offering it choices.

The *lingua franca* of anarchists is dynamite.
A hyperthymesiac recalls being in the womb.
Fashion designs are protected by no copyright.
Ferns, mosses, and liverworts will never bloom.

TRUISMS

Everyone is harsh who newly comes to power.
Praying out loud anticipates an answer from God.
The full wheat berry is used in graham flour.
A yellow dress was a medieval sign of a bawd.

The brain records in segments, not continuously.
William Randolph Hearst hated Charlie Chaplin.
A liberal's singular vice is funding promiscuously.
Polymers like Dacron are mainly made in Akron.

On rivers, moor your boat facing into the stream.
The largest world exporter of raspberries is Serbia.
Lard is the main ingredient of standard cold cream.
Jesus Christ could not abide the vice of *superbia*.

Hawks do not drink, but *bowse*.
African huts tend to be always round.
Only after calving do heifers become cows.
No honeymoon is not a proving ground.

A single trunk makes for a stronger tree.
Politicians offer style but never substance.
Water is weirdly anoxic in the Black Sea.
Sex is the supine metaphor of the dance.

Sleep is the mother of good digestion.
A bigot is glaringly never not a bully.
Finite the answer, infinite the question.
There is a downside to every pulley.

Soak lemons in water for more juice.
What an old man does is always right.
Every political promise is always a ruse.
Hares have red meat, rabbits white.

No one publishing his letters is not a nudist.
No cigar should be smoked more than halfway.
The frankest people are always the crudest.
Truth, unlike logic, offers no single pathway.

Pureed carrots are the most popular baby food.
No bullshitter ever exceeded Elbert Hubbard.
Unctuousness is the dark cousin of solicitude.
New Englanders call every cabinet a cupboard.

The chemist Chesebrough, inventor of Vaseline,
ate a spoonful of his product every day for health.
Landscape painters, defiantly, avoid using green.
All philanthropy should be distributed by stealth.

Vivisepulture was the nightmare of Edgar Poe.
No substance that is serous is not also viscid.
Fur in fashion is rarely warm when it is faux.
All bottled-in-bond ingredients must be listed.

Spam, due to nitrites, needs no refrigeration.
Gideon Bibles are always King James version.
Two miracles must be proven for canonization.
Only trips short and leisurely are an excursion.

TRUISMS

A good grocery bag should not only open
with one snap of the wrist but stand upright.
Every escarpment has a genius for sloping.
No color wheel includes the color white.

The hardest animal pelt to skin is a red deer.
The Gibson Girl, poised, was famously aloof.
Suicide is mentioned thirteen times in Shakespeare.
Repentance is best when not following reproof.

Teff is the smallest grain in the world.
Whistling indoors invites evil in Lithuania.
Everything that is curved is also curled.
Sexual neurosis explains most kleptomania.

Silence is the language of listening.
David Levine cross-hatched to highlight caricature.
Polytetrafluoroethylene coatings prevent sticking.
Turks and the Bulgarians have very little rapport.

All Harvey Girls had to wait a year to marry.
Carousel horses, large at the edge, are small at the hub.
Smog is, weirdly, both opaque yet hideously glary.
Only what's eaten with a spoon defines a true syllabub.

Russia offered Birobidzhan as a locale for Israel—
Great Britain proposed the country of Uganda.
Salt for its demoisturing quality is antibacterial.
War recruitment posters all rely on propaganda!

The phrase "post-traumatic stress disorder"
is but "shell shock" in iambic tetrameter.
Any decomposition can be garden fodder.
No good definition exists for parameter.

No interference in patterns can't be called a *moiré*.
When borrowing begins, instantly follows begging.
Gossip appropriates from truth to offer hearsay.
Nothing arouses like sheerness in a girl's legging.

An inverse is invariably a contrapositive.
In the Hebrew Bible, scorn's returned for scorn.
Determination should be undemonstrative.
No munching herbivore is daunted by a thorn.

A handful of hiss outweighs a thousand claps.
Zero is the result if extracting any number from itself.
Leonardo's brain is required re-folding maps.
Perception philosophically is not the "thing-in-itself."

Square roots of any prime number are irrational.
Actors need a playwright to give them identity.
Peru's Cotahuasi Canyon Road is close to impassable.
All the beatitudes of Jesus Christ call for lenity.

1961 was the greatest year for Bordeaux wine.
Smoking addiction is psychological, *not* physical.
Van Gogh was mesmerized by a pigment: lutein.
Happiness is never a message of the apocalyptical.

TRUISMS

The most beautiful flowers bloom in July.
Only cash, never checks, work in Dhaka.
A "coffin" was the original name for a pie.
"Huaxyacac" is correct word for Oaxaca.

No female in life has never been molested.
The anatomy of every plant seeks to climb.
Cornbread is never satisfactorily digested.
Black dionysianism is the soul of ragtime.

Of the many milks, yak milk is tastiest.
Paradisaical scenes animated 17th-c. *fijjnschilders*.
Czech Republic leads the world in atheists.
Holy Roman Empire coins were called guilders.

You cannot bemoan what you cannot gainsay.
Parabola parabola parabola ran the squirrel.
An official week begins, not ends, on a Sunday.
Scissors, pants, thanks: found always in the plural.

Only web-footed birds can take flight in water.
A typhoon is a cyclone is a tempest is a hurricane.
Its etymology by name links water with otter.
Every zoo and variation of it is not inhumane.

Ufology is a circus of credulous clowns.
What is necessary is not necessarily sufficient.
The UVa. campus is called the "grounds."
Any letter suffices as a variable coefficient.

Emily Dickinson wrote her poems for self-therapy,
essentially, with little or no interest to communicate.
Giving of oneself is the highest form of charity.
Roller coasters are mainly shaped like a figure eight.

Women have little patience for dreamers.
No job requires less talent than real-estate agent.
A whiff of the nefarious typifies schemers.
None owns the whole earth more than a vagrant.

John Updike never wrote a major novel.
Indonesians to say "look" point with a thumb.
Body shaming plagues the average model.
Singapore has banned the sale of chewing gum.

The Arctic sun doesn't so much shine as scorch.
Fear keeps us safe, as disgust encourages caution.
Cow parsnips flavored original Ukraine borscht.
Parts of British Columbia still speak Wakashan.

Genius is terrifying to ordinary people.
Cold air is an aid in making vision clear.
Godliness adhibits to a church's steeple.
No generalization is not also cavalier.

Irony is the fist, and satire is the glove.
Perfect beauty is unconscious of itself.
Oxytocin is the actual hormone of love.
Migratory birds love a continental shelf.

TRUISMS

The *NYRB* has an irksome, unholdable shape.
Chen Luwen, fourteen, was the concubine of Mao, sixty-eight.
Sunlight alone transforms a raisin from a grape.
On Noah's Ark the number of humans was eight.

Most Shoah victims died from chronic diarrhea.
American women leaders and heroines never nested.
Babies born are already one year old in Korea.
The weak-shouldered should opt for double-breasted.

Tyrant schoolmasters favored a malacca rattan.
Edmund Wilson termed *Lord of the Rings* "balderdash."
WW II liberated all suppressed women in Japan.
Jimmy Durante never once identified Mrs. Calabash.

All experience is interpreted experience.
No one can truly get close to a drunk.
The greatest chefs intuit their ingredients.
Televangelists fully depend on bunk.

Taqwa, fear of God, bonds a Muslim to the Divine.
No one had harsh words for Claudius, but Hamlet.
Whores, murderers, cheats were in Jesus' bloodline.
No wear was more durable than a herdsman's camlet.

Military cadets are schooled to abandon their will.
Al-Qurtubi, Al-Tabari, Ibn Kathir: greatest Koranic scholars.
Each American yearly adds 60 tons to a landfill.
Six years is the average lifespan of American paper dollars.

ALEXANDER THEROUX

Pick fiddleheads when they are still unfurled.
Simone Weil never commented on the Holocaust.
Diamond patterns are the designs most knurled.
Jewish Shavuot became the Christian Pentecost.

The Pygmy diet in the Congo is limited to yams.
No great conversationalist is not an astute listener.
Epileptics need to heed electroencephalograms.
Any lump has hope, if a ladies' man was Kissinger.

Every automobile bumper sticker brags.
No shoemaker's best friend isn't his awl.
All imperialists are worshippers of flags.
Thorn bushes is the halo of a Zulu kraal.

The author of *Cheaper by the Dozen* died at fifty-six.
Rolls-Royce's interiors are made of bull leather.
No cross without the body of Jesus is a Crucifix.
Climate is of a place long-term average of weather.

What's easy to play on the violin? Playing badly.
Napoleon decreed in 1808 all Jews adopt a surname.
Hearing beautiful music is, weirdly, received sadly.
Imprisonment is the legacy of truly worldwide fame.

The favorite music for Pygmies is water drumming.
Thoreau thought blackflies to be fiercer than wolves.
Self-applause is the subtext of a busy man humming.
Theory offers it is generally safer to push than to pull.

TRUISMS

Impartiality is not a virtue with a serious writer.
Rape as an atrocity is a standard conquest in war.
At first a human, no instrument, was a typewriter.
Caesar equals tsar *and* tsesari *and* kaiser *and* czar.

Only Cuba and North Korea sell no Coca-Cola.
Marriage with the Bambuti is by sister exchange.
Eating tainted water plants can cause fasciola.
Mainly reserved for the ill is bland blancmange.

Lottery tickets are a form of secular prayer.
National Geographic overdoes it with chimpanzees.
Mere formatting skews every questionnaire.
25% sweeter than table sugar is honey of honeybees.

No original writer is not infuriatingly certain.
West Point turns out computer punch cards.
Rooms seem higher with a vertically striped curtain.
A cemetery must adjoin a church to be a graveyard.

Luddites, unable to feel microwave oven heat, panic.
Most slaves came from Senegambia and Angola.
The classic staple of all survival food is the bannock.
Iranian Sunni and Lebanon Shia have no ayatollah.

Chechen honor is "vested" in women of the clan.
FDR allowed no note-taking at a personal meeting.
Ukraine men meeting a woman will kiss her hand.
Bedouin people rub noses as a means of greeting.

A royal wedding always involves myrtle.
Goats in Scripture are shunted to the left.
No true Scottish house is wanting a spurtle.
Any truly wealthy widow is rarely bereft.

Rivalry in friendship is a given.
Old Testament prophets loved complaints.
Consider any goaded ox as driven.
Eccentricity explains the Catholic saints.

Collectors are dominated by sheer appetite.
The urge for political power is for sexual mastery.
Brazilian wandering spiders have a lethal bite.
Mormon "prairie dresses" (pastel) subtext chastity.

Soap operas float on overwrought organ music.
Jewish cadets at West Point must worship on Sundays.
There is no written tradition in Manchurian Tungusic.
Male and female look exactly the same with blue jays.

Afternoon tea in Britain begins at exactly 4 p.m.
Few Alaska rivers or ponds aren't called the Salmon.
Israeli checkpoints and roadblocks sully Bethlehem.
White barbecue sauce is preferred by an Alabaman.

Studying the inside of the outside fixes all form.
An English scone needs butter and jam to shine.
The military mind/brain is fashioned to conform
Chinese *xin* means both the "heart" *and* "mind."

TRUISMS

Trust only those who are trying to seek the truth,
not those who jactitiously claim to have found it.
Virtually a spice rack are the contents of vermouth.
A form of art was pigments by those who ground it.

Each Murphy family has a spud, every O'Neill a Tip,
every Rhodes a Dusty, every Kerry family a Corky.
Fake funnels show the shallowness of a cruise ship.
Alexei Peshkov, bitter, adopted the like name Gorky.

No bird out-sings the meadowlark: "*Spring is here!*"
Old painters used green earth to underpaint flesh tones.
Budweiser, sheer piss, is the world's most famous beer.
The Honeymooners were plagiarized by *The Flintstones*.

Hippos, plowing depression beds, can make a pond.
LDS ladies weird helmet hair is a face-framing thing.
Only 2% of the American public is naturally blonde.
Silicon is now used for a watch's crucial hairspring.

The foot of every bird is a fork.
Always poke a cooking popover twice.
Loins are always the leanest cuts of pork.
A back wall must be hit in casino dice.

Voting is by law compulsory in Australia.
TV food mavens cheer whenever garlic's added.
A death threat is a black vase holding an azalea.
Vapid is, weirdly, the antonym of *sapid*.

ALEXANDER THEROUX

Chewing a grayling fish fin cures a toothache.
Balthus' *The Guitar Lesson* mocks a *Pietà*.
No medieval witchcraft excludes a mandrake.
Adam's finger mirrors Michelangelo's Creator.

Ralph Ellison hated Charlie "Bird" Parker,
calling him "a poster boy for white bohemians."
Mark Twain's view of man grew ever darker.
St. Paul made few converts among Athenians.

Almost all the Russian oligarchs are Jews.
Our life is spent needing to prove our birth.
Only the *upper* lips of hounds are flews.
El Azizia, Libya is the hottest spot on Earth.

Apples are originally from Kazakhistan.
Sugar fructose is the fuel of speeding sperm.
A Kligrapp is secretary in the Ku Klux Klan.
Cut moisture in a house by a sloping berm.

Average playing time in the NFL is 3.3 years.
In China, becoming takes precedence over being.
Scientists can't explain the earlobes of the ears.
The blind dream in visual images, so are seeing.

Men of law are absent from Proust's gallery.
No love beats a mourning dove for its mate.
Hookahs in India are flavored with jaggery.
Bites—*and holds on!*—does the toxic krait.

TRUISMS

"God bless America" is a chauvinist prayer.
David Attenborough dislikes rats and spiders.
As a polygon, there are no faces to a square.
Spitter apples make the very best of ciders.

Jews cannot flush the toilet on the Shabbat.
Salvation of souls is the supreme law of the church.
Ale partners cheese in a true Welsh rabbit.
The dry fruit "samara" is the winged voice of birch.

Stars always twinkle, but planets do not.
Live oak wood is the best for ships.
When acting, gesture only to the thought.
Revenge patience strategically equips.

The *Roman Martyrology* is the roll of sanctity.
A sapphire is the stone for a Cardinal's ring
Detachment from reality is a sign of insanity.
A unique dialect is spoken alone in Beijing.

Form comes not from what a poet gives but *receives*.
No one reads Shakespeare's *Edward the Third*.
Water, sealed in, is what causes fall of autumn leaves.
Immunity from plagues needs a vaccinated herd.

No one knows who invented fire hydrants.
Pedophiles always treat children like adults.
Absolute rule is the mainspring of tyrants.
Street games often involve chanting insults.

One emotion that M. Proust never explored
at all was that of a man becoming a father.
The oldest of cultivated plants is the gourd.
On Rosh Hashana 100 times sounds a shofar.

The law is not a field where genius exists.
A tufted titmouse's whistle is a tugboat's.
Fly fishing is, predominantly, about wrists.
The quaver, a half beat, is an eighth note.

No bird has a harsher call-note than a shrike.
French statesmen are also always "men of letters."
Smoking was disparaged by the Third Reich.
Sex in the 1940s was seeing girls in sweaters.

Chocolates for solidity and gloss are waxed.
A Pigouvian tax should be levied on emissions.
Incomes are all increased with tariffs relaxed.
Big Pharma cozies up to American physicians.

Every gravestone cries out "*Eram! Eram!*"
The *hold* is not an official MLB statistic.
Jesus excoriated the tepid and "lukewarm."
To claim war is fought for peace is sadistic.

Faith, unlike reason, never shifts.
Venomics is crucial to evolving pharmacopoeia.
Ten years is the limit for facelifts.
Colon cleansing can badly exacerbate diarrhea.

TRUISMS

Jesus said not a word to Tetrarch Herod Antipas.
In order to be the man, you have to beat the man.
Every Greek youth yearns to imitate Leonidas.
Shakespeare praises no character named Anne.

Reasons given by losers are feeble excuses.
Selling comes natural to Chichicastenangos.
Fiber is often sacrificed in squeezing juices.
Hungary and Romania both claim the Csángós.

Gung ho in China simple means, "Work together."
Licorice candy contains anise oil—no real licorice.
Solar wind in the magnetosphere creates space weather.
Spoken Chalcatongo Mixtec is close to gibberish.

Abortion is health care; abortion is murder, both.
Saints omit; villains commit—actors seek the latter.
All trees in the United States are second growth.
Rubes, boasters, and sophomores all talk smatter.

Csángós are the lineal heirs of Attila the Hun.
Every nation capitalizes on its defining moment.
Hyenas kill, crunch bones, eat fast, excrete calcium.
Lawyers become snide to intimidate a deponent.

When interest rates are high, there is a credit crunch.
An unaltered U.S. forest can be seen on Cape Cod.
Pancakes in the U.S. is the standard meal for brunch.
Round haircuts (Lev. 19:27) in Scripture are outlawed.

Theory, for indefiniteness, is an opaque gray.
Pule—of donkey milk—is a very expensive cheese.
Asia's largest slum is in Dharavi, Mumbai.
Cutting noodles is considered bad luck by Chinese.

The Maasai people deeply despise Kikuyu.
Xeriscapes, lovely as lawns, also save water.
Yellow is hardest color to remove in a tattoo.
Storing food under its armpit helps the sea otter.

Chocolate has phenylethylamine, a mood enhancer.
Maasai believe God gave them all the cattle on earth.
Overweight Isadora Duncan was a clumsy dancer.
Latter Day Saints theology denies the Virgin birth.

Icing a brownie is disturbing and unnecessary.
At Alaska's North Slope begins bird migration.
Bone dry—meant for food—is a perfect sherry.
Scripture, exclusively, recognizes only agnation.

Damon Runyon called his dolls "tomatoes."
Rastafarians, not Christians, believe in Jah.
Just *prior* to cooking them, wash potatoes.
Spots within spots are rosettes on a jaguar.

White chocolate contains no actual cacao.
It is illegal in Germany to name a child Judas.
Elephants, when edgy, rock a foreleg to and fro.
Afro-American women are main victims of lupus.

TRUISMS

Overbeating batter incorporates too much air:
if you insist on cakey brownies, bake a cake!
Frenchmen highly prize a woman's derrière.
Scents are made from the fragrant huisache.

When traveling, elephants walk in single file.
The U.S. marks Cinco de Mayo more than Mexico.
Hashish is sweeter smoked through a narghile.
Stouter than chintz, all cretonne resembles calico.

The stripes on each and every zebra differ.
Chocolate causes no cavities, added sugar does.
Every single living vertebrate has a liver.
All lefties use "right-handed" baseball gloves.

A Boston butt has a bone in; never a *pork* butt.
Shin Upagutta, an arahant, was once a non-believer.
Commodore Vanderbilt's wallet was forever shut.
No known vaccine can prevent dengue fever.

No horses, cattle, sheep, goats, or chickens
existed in pre-Columbian North America.
Only those of native origin can be Britons.
No medical diagnosis attends to hysterica.

Scientology is the doctrine of the uneducated.
Sharp cheese snacks go begging for a martini.
A bromide of faith: praying hands, carinated.
Flowers are edible in the *fruit* called zucchini.

The Samaritan Woman perceives Christ in order,
calling him "Jew," "Sir," "Prophet," "Messiah."
A piece of India within the Bangladesh border
is within India yet in Bangladesh, an utter mire.

Genealogy obsessives are desperate for inclusion.
Steak and mushroom pie must include brown ale.
Consciousness is impossible without seclusion.
Illegal it is to export the tusk (tooth) of a narwhal.

MGM musicals could contain no minor chord.
Frank Sinatra's favorite song was "Laura."
Vale do Javari in Brazil is still not explored
All drive-in theaters prefer films of horror.

Civil rights groups, generating mass addiction,
grew reliant on corrupt tobacco industry support.
Zany plots are the black hole of science fiction.
Disease, not fighting, killed most at Agincourt.

Cutting liver meat is an imperfect art.
Elevators are fully scorned in Venice.
Pascal constantly argued with Descartes.
Running—*effort!*—is the key to good tennis.

Mars has 37% less gravity than planet Earth.
American eugenicists inspired Nazi race laws.
Biblical havoc always fixed on famine, dearth.
Singer Al Jolson felt he alone deserved applause.

TRUISMS

Women hosts on sports shows need re-examination.
No crosses or images exist in Church of Scotland.
Charities lead the world in financial peculation.
The month of July is by far the coldest in Auckland.

Fatherless women fall for domineering men.
Turkey is the primary source of illicit opium.
Stone walls always marked an Irish demesne.
Part of awards glory is the height of a podium.

An Elizabethan penny today would be $1.66.
Philip Roth, a Jew, loved Céline, an anti-Semite.
Japanese prefer a shorter, pointed chopsticks.
While *fortnight* is modern, archaic is *sennight*.

No overly solicitous lover isn't dumptrucked.
Film actors, mostly morons, are talk show favorites.
The obese love the fashion of the shirt untucked.
Hundreds are killed every year by falling coconuts.

Survivor types are heedless, merciless egotists.
John Wilkes Booth never played the role of Hamlet.
Sororal polygyny is choice by most polygamists.
Thermostatic properties best insulate a camlet.

Abstract Expressionism as art is incompetent excuse.
Lord Chesterfield called women children grown large.
Indirection is the magician's timeworn secret ruse.
Cations are listed before anions in matters of charge.

Buddha found himself—an *arhat* needs a teacher.
An actress' descent: mothers, aunts, spinsters, crones.
1930 box-office slumps initiated the double feature.
Accidia struck monks, mainly, at the hour of *nones*.

A toilet contains less bacteria than a kitchen sink.
No Monégasques can enter the Monte Carlo Casino.
People always skate counterclockwise in an ice rink.
The capital of trailer parks is Nevada, namely Reno.

More mediocre the product, more rabid its advertising.
Lennon stood always on the right, McCartney to the left.
No billionaire doesn't elicits connoisseurs of patronizing.
No American product from the 1930s was lacking in heft.

Emily Dickinson's dashes were part of the work,
as aural notations, pauses, the slowing of tempo.
A Norse warrior was braver when going berserk.
All four toes have more bones than the "big toe."

If neither a seer nor *vates*, that person is no poet.
The oldest cuisine on earth is from Mesopotamia.
Charity is dampened by an equal need to show it.
Water is pronounced "*wooter*" in Pennsylvania.

Imagination is the supreme cognitive faculty.
R. Nixon's black jaw reflected his dark soul.
Light can be warped and curved by gravity.
Very few moved East during the Dust Bowl.

TRUISMS

Lear, Polonius, Prospero, Shylock, and Duncan
were all strange because all had missing mothers.
All of Pieter Bruegel's peasants appear *lumpen*.
A visiting neighbor, even of good will, smothers.

No judgment is not a subjective judgment.
There has never been a three-pitch inning in baseball.
Anecdotal evidence in courts is repugnant.
No one was more gifted than Norse hero Heimdall.

Elizabethans loved houses beamed and pargetted.
Carolina Chocolate Drops used bones as instruments.
Paranoia conceives itself as being ever targeted.
Shakespeare said the "curse of God" was ignorance.

Jesus folded his burial cloth (John 20:7) neatly
to assure us, after three days, He would return.
A wadded napkin told his servant indiscreetly,
a Hebrew custom, the master would adjourn.

A big concert hall swallows consonants.
The uglier the tomato, the better it tastes.
Knowledge allows the greatest cognizance.
Women in Nauru all are missing waists.

In Haiti there are virtually no doctors.
You will rarely see a Jewish jockey.
Suspicion is the living faith of proctors.
The ultimate quinary color is khaki.

The jury never looks at those it sentenced to death.
A bialy needs slow-cooked onion and poppyseed.
No dialect, idiom, or patois is not also a shibboleth.
There is no antidote for poisoning by jimsonweed.

Bearded men are unkempt to South Koreans.
Having a foe is absolute terror to a coward.
By their mosaics, the Byzantines sang paeans.
Jewish parents love the name of Howard.

Female animals are also prohibited on Mt. Athos.
All Hebrew and Greek letter names are agrophonic.
Calm emotions elicit *ethos*—violent ones *pathos*.
Plants actually grow faster by methods hydroponic.

Charles Atlas in real life was Angelo Siciliano.
Adriana Caselotti was Snow White's singing voice.
Supporting, "trouser" roles go to a mezzo-soprano.
Only royals can receive a Phantom IV Rolls-Royce.

The drive for power is born of weakness.
Schubert specialized in miniature pieces.
Nowhere exceeds Burundi for bleakness.
With severe inflation, investing increases.

Proto-Sinaitic consists only of consonants.
Actor Robert Redford took only heroic roles.
There is partly an urge to kill in dominance.
A mystery is who wrote the Dead Sea Scrolls.

TRUISMS

A 6/3 depth makes perfect tire treads.
The plant rhubarb abominates wet feet.
Left-handedness adhibits to redheads.
Rabbits actually eat what they excrete.

The Chief Priests arrested Jesus, not the Romans.
Noah never speaks, merely listens to God and acts.
Human intuition is what the credulous call omens.
The state of Hawaii charges the lowest property tax.

Noah's daughters-in-law are never named.
A *billion* world children live in poverty.
Servility to power makes us all ashamed.
Excise taxes are merely legalized robbery.

1 Thessalonians 2:14–16 is openly anti-Semitic.
Beijing is source of the world's acid rain.
Rhythm in Homeric epics relies on the enclitic.
Bacteria, even, has a soul to a believing Jain.

For a garden's shady corner, plant hellebore:
it looks up with faces like a concert audience.
At 6 o'clock the sun rises and sets in Ecuador
all year round, an unwavering convenience.

Oxen simply cannot be taught to back up.
Cloud beauty has no translational symmetry.
Morbid withdrawal can indicate a crack-up.
Jehovah's Witnesses abominate the Trinity.

Third-shift workers rarely see their children.
Oxygen is the molecule that made the world.
Artful asymmetry is the glory of a building.
A prime minister usually becomes an earl.

No one knows how long albatross can live.
James, Jesus' brother, was never of the Twelve.
St. Paul, quoting Jesus, as to whom to forgive,
declares, "Nothing is unclean in and of itself."

A runway model never smiles on a catwalk.
Haiti is transshipment central for drugs to the U.S.
For the U.S. Constitution, thank John Locke.
Absolution is denied to those who don't confess.

No excursion in fashion is not calculated to entice.
MacArthur called Japan "a nation of twelve year olds."
Thomas Jefferson believed St. Paul corrupted Christ.
Mold cheeses vary but there is no variation of molds.

Soapwort, invasive, runs wild in every garden.
Film noir was the Jacobean drama of the 1940s.
Steel heated, then quenched, will further harden.
World War I lost *platoons* by feckless sorties.

America has no shared language, ethnicity,
religion, culture. Queerly exalting variety:
its highest value remains merely diversity,
which destabilizes, not affirms, its society.

TRUISMS

War presidents are always considered the greatest.
A coconut is clothing, meat, trencher, drink, and can.
It takes a lifetime of abuse to create a true sadist.
Want to lose a finger? Try cutting open a rambutan.

Crippled is any society that breeds graffiti.
The turbot fish has only eye, on the left side.
Wild oysters, exploited, are now less meaty.
No State House appointee is overqualified.

Malcolm X *opposed* all racial integration.
No crowded room isn't filled with carbon dioxide.
Calculated neglect is a form of flirtation.
An object in a sculptor's stone is already clarified.

It costs more to store electricity than to make it.
The risqué always spiced up a Cole Porter song.
Fasts, eggs, glow sticks: better when you break it.
A crowd, *pressing together*, constitutes a throng.

Snapdragons do poorly by replanting disturbance.
French rustics love cornichons with pork rillettes.
It was perfectly legal to beat Victorian servants.
Correction is the missing boat of human regrets.

The world murder rate is highest in Venezuela.
R.C. Mounties spend *a day* to shine their boots.
Flowing south to north goes the Monongahela.
Goldman Sachs, the fattest cat, sneers at lawsuits.

French kissing is a form of capillarity.
Astrology hasn't the slightest scientific basis.
Humans cannot synthesize vitamin C.
No living human can maintain homeostasis.

All pet owners on YouTube are truly certifiable.
Victorian women never wore pink or red clothes.
The Divine in nature is copiously exemplifiable.
Fraud is the quintessence of every fashion pose.

Ferns have vascular tissues, mosses do not.
Giorgio, James Joyce's son, spoke English poorly!
The worse the team, the dopier the mascot.
Failure is optimized by concluding prematurely.

Julius Caesar was not born by Caesarean section.
Van Nuys, California is capital of pornography.
The *right* knee is used in a Catholic genuflection,
whereas to a church dignitary it is the *left* knee.

Tattoo parlors are illegal in South Korea.
Convection boils water, conduction does not.
The Bible (book aside) never mentions Hosea.
Bus drivers are thanked by deboarding Scots.

All matadors, toreadors, picadors are torturers.
Hannukah is born of Jewish envy of Christmas.
Poets scroll their minds in the way of sorcerers.
Government is the mistress of all big business.

TRUISMS

"The Star-Spangled Banner" is all questions.
German bases are still named for General Rommel.
Liberals see the Constitution as "suggestions."
Most medieval fermented drams were hydromel.

Charlie Chaplin, a priap, married three teenage girls.
Thanks to dinosaur extinction, mammals survived.
Perfect roundness is very rarely found in pearls.
Legalized lying applies to most things advertised.

Viruses cannot be killed by antibiotics.
No butler kills anyone in an Agatha Christie book.
Fruit, weirdly, is avoided by macrobiotics.
For saltwater fishing use an O'Shaugnessy hook.

Language, while it shapes, disguises our thoughts.
The Deuteronomistic historians loved folk tales.
Gambling in Scripture can be seen in casting lots.
The Union Jack flag does not include Wales.

The Japanese are rabid fans of canned foods.
Every Ehud has his Eglon, every Eglon his Ehud.
Being spread is a requirement of bad moods.
Spying is a pastime in the average neighborhood.

Deductibles are a legalized form of thievery.
AIPAC has the U.S. Congress in its pocket.
All movie stars are predominantly scenery.
Victorian architecture thrived on the crocket.

ALEXANDER THEROUX

No *Wizard of Oz* character has a traditional family.
The passive voice allows a narrator to avoid "I."
Viruses, parasites, can't reproduce independently.
Caning is the punishment for all crimes in Brunei.

Envy is actually an aspect of idealization.
Amish dolls are faceless, to prevent vanity.
A martial mind came natural to a Thracian.
An apt reflex to modern life may be insanity.

Every half-truth involves a whole lie.
Japanese women rarely wear perfume.
Always prune tightly a Chinese *pensai*.
Pretentiousness is never not a costume.

No plant can grow or thrive without boron.
On the Sistine ceiling is not one Christian image.
"Hollywood Royalty:" a laughable oxymoron.
No divorce, after its scrums, isn't a scrimmage.

Never wash or clean any collectible coin.
No one disfigures books more than librarians.
Ulsterman all vaunt the Battle of the Boyne.
No one day is consistent with sabbatarians.

Balthus's adolescent girls are a construct
of his own pervertedly enigmatic profile,
and it is he himself who's the priapic object
his atrocious paint brush proceeds to defile.

TRUISMS

The mark of Cain signified God's protection
and not, as commonly believed, to be a curse.
It is typical to hide, not show, a predilection.
A coin's most prominent side is the obverse.

Orphans with parents are most WASP children.
Obsessive vision is born of furious virtuosity.
Concrete is man's oldest material for building.
Disinterestedness benefits intellectual curiosity.

Adele Astaire had more talent than Fred.
Two Talmuds exist, Jerusalem and Babylonian.
Creativity always expires on luxury's bed.
Spirit trumps matter for a strict Emersonian.

Quilting a "Lone Star" pattern brings bad luck.
Sweden broke the Chernobyl disaster, not Russia.
Hunting mavens crave the horns of a waterbuck.
Northern Poland was really the state of Prussia.

Anyone becomes a confidant on a yacht.
Gertrude Stein's three geniuses: Christ, Spinoza, herself.
A man chases a woman until he is caught.
Heiresses disdained any clothes purchased off-the-shelf.

Virtuosa, the feminine of virtuoso, is never used.
Never launder silks, velvets, or hand-dyed fabrics.
Crispness in taste is lost when a cocktail's bruised.
The largest charitable body is American Catholics.

Tulips on quilts signify romantic love.
No cruelty can surpass teenage cruelty.
Of a new lover, no one knows thereof,
touching the nature of his or her tenuity.

Most Biblical ideas of God involve the sun.
Improvisation defines swinging at a piñata.
Overdrafts can easily precipitate a bank run.
Women exceed men in avowing a stigmata.

A good journalist is always the first to arrive.
"Expedition" was Sam Clemens' word for sex.
The heiress curse is lack of focus and drive.
Cliché names for dogs: Rover, Spot, and Rex.

An older woman's blue jeans never fit.
Hostility animates every reform movement.
Short men prefer by far to stand than sit.
Assistance always impedes improvement.

Décor at Capote's B &W ball was mere balloons.
UK upper classes love the names Electra and Giles.
One flue penetrated better than two-flue harpoons.
The fabric of flax is the most ancient of textiles.

Gardening snobs detest impatiens plants.
Lee Radziwill called Jackie "my sister," never by name.
No sting is more painful than a bullet ant's.
To play was the essential message of Jakob Boehme.

TRUISMS

Dior's H-line deliberately flattened the bosom.
The anti-royal U.S. Constitution bans inherited titles.
No Secretary of Defense has ever been a woman.
Memorize the music—avoid reading scores at recitals.

Soup, for digestion, is the *last* course in China.
Far too chewy to be eaten raw is the quahaug.
Merely a symptom and not a disease is angina.
British upper classes own some form of a gundog.

Behind every chair stands a waiting footman
defines true wealth, as at 1920s Mar-a-Lago.
Tribal frontiers are strict with Kalahari bushmen.
Pushing rather than pulling defines a Dutch hoe.

No consummate servant has a footfall
Al-Quds—Jerusalem—is sacred to the Arabs.
Dignity is always undermined by a drawl.
Aquinas says knowledge is the gift of cherubs.

Every chicken sits on death row.
France is the motherland of perfect bread.
Wily boxers let opponents set the tempo.
The mark of Cain was on the forehead.

Scientology demands no belief in a god.
Mexican worship is fascinated with skulls.
No found natural diamond is not flawed.
Nova Scotia perfected a vessel's hulls.

No crowd hasn't a lower-than-average mind.
Frogs are wet and smooth, toads dry and warty.
Schizophrenia is found in no one born blind.
The standard days for any quarantine are forty.

Repeated stupidity makes comedy of history.
"Amen" alone can be said in prayers mentioning God.
Subtract curiosity and you have no mystery.
America's largest historic districts are on Cape Cod.

Norway has two languages, Bokmål and Nynorsk.
Abalone dislodges with the side blow of a chisel.
Mentioned in the Koran is the Al-Aqsa mosque.
Obdurate, hard to grow, choose rugs made of sisal.

A giant whale's favorite food is pteropods.
Never relinquish the sense of things to be feared.
Only seashore walks may be called "esplanades."
Women find men sexy with a light stubble beard.

South Sea chiefs exclusively wore golden cowries.
A bull's bravery in the ring is answered by butchery.
Sons are preferred but daughters hated as to dowries.
Dante selected the lowest hell, the ninth, for treachery.

Jean Genet found a "sunken beauty" in killers.
Nothing thrives in Odessa more than violinists.
Lusty was the reputation of medieval millers.
Taste and flavor are lost in imported Guinness.

TRUISMS

Biophysics still cannot explain protein structure.
There were 4,742 U.S. lynchings from 1882 to 1968.
The target of poetry on the spirit is to rupture.
No wave or roller isn't ferocious in the Bering Strait.

A Coke bottle shape mimes a cocoa bean pod.
Earrings mainly fall off on rollercoaster rides.
Andamnum fatale is in legalese an act of God.
24 hours *and 50 minutes* is the cycle of tides.

Hurt people unfailingly hurt people.
A priest may say three masses only on Christmas.
Great Britain at one time *mined* treacle.
El Greco's canvases were skewed by his strabismus.

No serial killer has not a parent problem.
Any guest of honor must be first to leave.
Basically, hygienic is the human rectum.
Cop killers are never granted a reprieve.

Mascara on the lower lashes hardens one's gaze.
Band leaders judge what to play by looking at women's shoes.
Queen Elizabeth I is never seen without a fraise.
Neither an airport nor a railway station can be found in Vaduz.

Husbands is the key topic of ladies-who-lunch.
Never state a telephone number on a formal invitation.
High interest rates give birth to a credit crunch.
The *Social Register*, oddly, reveals private information.

Every tall girl maintains a short best friend.
The suicide option to many is a comforting pillow.
Pedophiles, major recidivists, never amend.
Aspirin (salicin) is made from the bark of a willow.

The media adores you until they hate you.
Badly bullied were most school shooting gunmen.
Inedible until fully roasted is the cashew.
No repulsive taste exceeds that of a coot or mudhen.

South Vietnam began invading North Vietnam first.
Actor Richard Burton never watched—*any!*—films.
Any pieces stolen from the Uluru Rock are cursed.
No ceramic doesn't have pedigree in thermal kilns.

All male rulers in Baum's *Oz* books are wicked.
Parisian women never wear coordinated outfits.
Status was once conveyed by all beer steins *lidded*.
Black beaches alternate with white on St. Kitts.

Guns have more rights in the U.S. than citizens.
Miners feel themselves kings of the working class.
Stinging nettle weeds are natural antihistamines.
Copper-zinc alloy accounts for all cartridge brass.

Bullied children are already half-armed with weapons.
A sapling bent low stores energy for violent backswing.
1 Thessalonians 4:14–18 pledges reunion in the Heavens.
Wasteful social programs are a legacy of the left-wing.

TRUISMS

All "Thank-you" notes should be sent right away.
Be thrifty was Benjamin Franklin's main apothegm.
In medieval times, Easter was called Egg Sunday.
Micah prophesied Christ to be born in Bethlehem.

J. Edgar Hoover banned women from the FBI.
Never wear a necklace and earrings at the same time.
Older-looking growth is preferred to young in bonsai.
Robert Frost preferred that all poetry should rhyme.

A debutante's ball gown is always pure white.
Café de l'Homme gives best view of the Eiffel Tower.
Shakespeare defined love as love at first sight.
Much probiotic value is found in green banana flour.

All ornamental sweet peas plants are toxic.
No woman should wear high heels with a pencil skirt.
A rocket's loud noise can destroy a rocket.
Jesus was explicitly whipped with a lead-tipped quirt.

Success is the arch foe of worthwhile creativity.
Books sell very poorly at flea markets.
Scripture mentions no animals at Christ's nativity.
Immigrants have always been FBI targets.

Orthodoxies give rise to their own heretics.
North Korean leaders always wear a jumpsuit.
A hit for six in cricket's a "Dorothy Dix."
A main staple for early slaves was breadfruit.

No manuscript of Shakespeare has survived,
except, perhaps, three pages found of his hand
from the tragedy of *Sir Thomas More*, devised
in 1593 and, but for his additions, rather bland.

St. Paul roundly repudiated circumcision.
A quirk of Frank Sinatra was he *never* danced.
A direct antagonist of reading is television.
Value, artless, is what makes jewels enhanced.

Obfuscation in any poem or novel is obscene.
St. John was the most Hellenized of Evangelists.
Kheer—400 B.C.—is by far the oldest cuisine.
Coroner's offices have *gift shops* in Los Angeles.

Persistence is the essential virtue of all novelists.
Churchill's favorite pour was Johnnie Walker Red.
Inexactitude can prove fatal with anesthesiologists.
No country has not a version of its own flatbread.

In 1619, Compositor B mangled Shakespeare's plays.
Gone with the Wind is a favorite novel in North Korea.
Any and all translation fails that's driven to rephrase.
Scolding Israel's idolatry was the mission of Hosea.

There is small prestige in being a podiatrist.
600,000 Israelis now live beyond 1967 borders.
Violence can accrue in waking a somnambulist.
Anxiety disorder is the main malady of hoarders.

TRUISMS

Hitler never renounced Roman Catholicism.
John Paul Jones throughout his life craved flag rank.
Sub-Saharan Africa suffers the most albinism.
Slow-cook to tenderize all muscled shin or shank.

A fortress is useless for reasons it is built for.
Physicians heal best and quickest foregoing a bill.
Scots find formal occasions best at wearing a kilt for.
Both birth and death deny the validity of free will.

The weakest of all ocean tides are neaps.
Football has action for but eleven minutes a game.
Vertical pupils give everyone the creeps.
No loss of identity's worse than changing your name.

A potato plant's *real* fruit are small blobs on top!
The dead Confederacy was the grave of Calhoun.
No *replicas* of anything are taken in a pawnshop.
With no atmosphere, meteorites pepper the moon.

Gandhi, who was influenced by Christian ethics,
was in a way the least Indian of all Indian leaders.
Leicester was Queen Elizabeth's love, not Essex.
No doltish people alive are dumber than anti-readers.

J.S. Bach, a staunch Lutheran, wrote the eminent
Catholic mass—the stupendous *Mass in B minor*,
a composition that figuratively seems heaven-sent,
formatted as a Neapolitan *missa*, but nothing finer.

Joggers, to impress onlookers, check their watches.
Golda Meir flatly denied Palestinians ever existed.
No filling goes awry in the creation of kolaches.
Defects in real estate offerings are never listed.

Claudius is a greater rhetorician than Hamlet.
Stonewall Jackson never read a letter on the Sabbath.
Valuable is any garment woven of true camlet.
Cave paintings were mostly of the woolly mammoth.

Prejudices cannot be denied as being principles.
Scientists have concluded there is no end to space.
Revolutionaries love calling themselves "Invincibles."
Nothing can match for beauty a Botticellian face.

In 1849, Zach Taylor's inaugural speech was short,
negative, generalized, obvious, and poorly delivered.
Wine of the Douro region can alone be called port.
Javanese love "*biawak*," meat of the monitor lizard.

V. Lenin never held a job in his entire life.
The American realistic novel is all yearning unfortunates.
The pull of a mother is the push of a wife.
Laws and regulations to religious customs are subordinates.

The human voice dominates in all Italian opera;
but in Wagner's music dramas the orchestra does.
One quarter of Israel's population is not sabra.
No rebuke is worse than a *smattering* of applause.

TRUISMS

A servile bride handcuffs the established wife.
An American IOM bag to a refugee is salvation.
Florida, alone, reports no invasive loosestrife.
No entity in life is not weakened by bifurcation.

Astrology weirdly repurposes astronomy.
A prejudice held is no less a principle taken.
Moses' farewells constitute Deuteronomy.
The first astronaut meal on the moon was bacon.

Crustaceans are not covered by animal welfare law.
Rodeo riders avoid wearing yellow as bad luck.
Needless provocation of an enemy's the cause of war.
Dalmations ran *ahead* of a horse-led fire truck.

The British never drink sherry before the evening.
Ground pearls are taken medicinally in Singapore.
Psychiatrists must first cure illogical unreasoning.
Lesbianism is commonplace in the life of whore.

Mock turtle soup is made of boiled calf's head.
NHL players never touch the Stanley Cup until they win it.
No order to kill in the Mafia is ever openly said.
Small covers both minute (minOOT) and minute (MINit).

Apéritifs are served before meals, digestifs after.
Cowboys believe stepping in dung brings good luck.
Scorn is always present in the matter of laughter.
There are eight ounces of acid and bile in the stomach.

Snobbery, betraying weakness, is always a shallow act.
November is traditional time in Korea to make kimchi.
Stigmatized as menacing in fables was every hunchback.
Tantric esoteric rituals have never been done simply.

A brisket should always be cut against the grain.
In high society, friendships are ephemeral.
No confession is reliable when extracted by pain.
Pastoral poems are consistently nemoral.

Jesus Christ knew no vino other than red wine.
Emily Dickinson decorated gingerbread with pansies.
A movie star doing commercials is on the back nine.
Humans share almost 98% DNA with chimpanzees.

Advent, *pace* Christmas, is a penitential season.
The depiction of eyes has long plagues sculptors.
A non-reader in life commits intellectual treason.
Kimchi helps prevent rather than causes ulcers.

Sports figures love to go unshaven in a playoff.
Guangzhou, China is the world capital for eating dog.
Horse-betting software proves never to pay off.
Sleeping nose-to-nose comes perfectly natural to a hog.

"Want me to be honest?" is an enemy's question.
Maasai fare, cattle blood and milk, is a Jewish nightmare.
A meter running defines every psychiatrist's session.
No game's not robbery at an amusement park or funfair.

TRUISMS

Air-kisses, filing dislike, is the ultimate pose.
To keep brown sugar moist, add old bread to the bag.
Attitude expresses itself in physiognomy of clothes.
Nothing even close to benevolent flies a black flag.

The country Bulgaria has never been colonized.
The road into Gibraltar is also the plane's runway.
As love opens its heart, it also closes its eyes.
Aroma states grape variety, aging gives bouquet.

Butter the bottom *and top* of an egg coddler.
There are clandestine pleasures in forcing bulbs.
Hearing in adults is surpassed by a toddler.
Classic blue of all colors doesn't exist in tulps.

Vladimir Nabokov wrote his books on index cards.
New Hampshire, the cheapskate state, leaves its rich tax free.
Rochus Misch, a Jew, was one of Hitler's bodyguards,
a Holocaust denier, and a member of the SS with high esprit.

Materialistic people have a horror of death.
Pansies grow in cold weather, languish in hot.
No Ephraimite could pronounce "Shibboleth."
A dancing "quickstep" prefigured the foxtrot.

Morons believe road speed indicates intelligence.
Emily Dickinson planted *only* perennial flowers.
In math equations, simplicity alone proves elegance.
Malic acid is the acrid coating in candy that sours.

No substitute for butter duplicates its flavor.
Playbills lists actors: "In order of appearance."
All rich people's wealth is a product of labor.
E. Pound's *Cantos* are a fund of incoherence.

Fiction is fact recapitulated into truth.
When an actor is bad, applause makes him worse.
The hardest substance in body is a tooth.
A dead body freezer box is required by a hearse.

Elvis Presley always wore lifts in his shoes.
Levittown houses—"pods"— had no basements.
Corn through the body is quickest to suffuse.
El trains are prime canvases for urban defacements.

Jews, using a *yad*, never touch the Torah.
A person can get a hernia opening blister packs.
Same-sex was the sin of Sodom and Gomorrah.
Being prolific is a passion of literary hacks.

Australia leads the world in female serial killers.
Formaldehyde, carcinogenic, pollutes cemeteries.
Bad songwriters are given to weak verbal fillers.
No city had more bookstores than Buenos Aires.

Ticks do not drown in water.
The French all spoon soup *toward* the self.
War is only won by slaughter.
The truest humility is not deceiving oneself.

TRUISMS

Brown rice, unlike white, quickly goes bad.
Ninotchka looked sexier as a Soviet than styled.
Explosive bolts hold rockets to a launch pad.
All western Europe Fyodor Dostoevsky reviled.

Anthony Comstock, so prudish a puritanical scourge,
banned contraceptive matters from mailings, in spite,
and sought to proscribe in his fundamentalist purge
all shop owners for leaving naked dummies in sight!

Marx is shamelessly materialistic and empty of faith.
The French, dining, keep their napkins out of sight.
Wild boar's head was choicest food of Henry the Eighth.
In computing, there are eight bits in a 64-bit byte.

Paul Revere's first stop was in Medford, Mass.
The French prefer to fold rather to cut lettuce.
Cattle can die fed a hay of sweet vernal grass.
Actirasty—sun arousal—is a beachgoer's fetish.

Robins advance in anapests: *run run stop*.
The killers of prophet Joseph Smith got away with it.
Kwanza and Juneteenth are pandering sops.
Staying more than three days oversteps every visit.

Tradition has twelve horses in a merry-go-round.
VP Dick Cheney championed the torture program.
A calumny is calling Muhammad "Mahound."
J. Edgar Hoover, phobic, feared germs and women.

A squirrel's dray is always more than twenty feet high.
Americans now try to make every Mondays a holiday.
One may wear white tie at events calling for black tie.
"*La Fête Nationale*" in France we call Bastille Day.

Frenchmen use bread scooping food onto a spoon.
Ray Charles gauged a woman's looks by holding her wrist.
A horse can more easily feed with a sliding bridoon.
Few 19th-century English novels exclude the game of whist.

Lizzie Borden, caught naked with her maid
in a lesbian act by her stepmother upstairs,
brutally bashed her, and then, deeply afraid,
had to kill her father to cover up her affairs.

Straw sandals are associated with death in China.
Logic is proven false by the "crocodile's dilemma."
Non-Muslims can never enter the center of Medina.
Elizabeth shares hubris with Jane Austen's Emma.

Fish is the Passover meal in da Vinci's *Last Supper.*
Neurotics profess guilt to claim credit for sin to be absolved!
All climate change plan right-wingers look to scupper.
Darwin never *once* claimed from monkeys humans evolved.

30,000 Mormon polygamists still live in the west.
Democrats claim we can save money by spending it.
Alchemists have sought the magic solvent, *alkahest.*
A frail heart can spare itself romance by forfending it.

TRUISMS

There has never been an *English* Royal House.
A walrus's teeth can break through eight inches of ice.
Southern Confederate statues all stand facing south.
A slave's main meals were generally beans and rice.

A baby llama is endearingly called a cria.
Tokyo was once a small fishing village named Edo.
Dulia is worship of saints, of God *latria*.
Suspenders are recommended for wearing a tuxedo.

Revenge is a perverted form of repentance.
Pusillanimous men are jealous of NFL's Tom Brady.
There are 35 million *Mayflower* descendants.
Ghost hunting as trade or enterprise is beyond shady.

Boys in the 1930s all wore horizontal striped T-shirts.
Jesus is a *warrior* in *The Dream of the Rood*.
Curvaceous women alone look good in pencil skirts.
An orca only gulps but never chews its food.

No one has ever seen a giant squid eating.
Serious lack of vitamin D can lead to dementia.
The Greenland Inuit sniff faces when greeting.
Comorbid disorders always partner anorexia.

Vultures urinate on their legs to keep cool.
The Wall Street emotions are fear and greed.
Probability inequalities were proven by George Boole.
Marcy's basic plea is, "Reason not the need."

Bread is banned to astronauts as crumbs can impair sight.
It is *fear facing loss*, primarily, that greaves.
Americans are clueless as to both Vegemite and Marmite.
A giraffe's pet food is feathery acacia leaves.

A tuna's eyes are the size of baseball bats.
Television is distorting, corrupt, profane, mercantile.
In the Peruvian highlands, dignity means hats.
Adolf Hitler was deep down always an Anglophile.

Southern girls often use vanilla as perfume.
A young hare (up to a year) is called a leveret.
A cataclysmic bust follows a Wall Street boom.
Every self-made egotist is given to asseverate.

Whoever tortures a human is going straight to Hell.
Ayn Rand, who worshipped it, considered money a virtue.
The medieval world held sacred the sound of a bell.
Pinching food with its downcurved bill hunts the curlew.

Astronauts drink a filtered mix of urine and sweat.
Groups of giraffes are officially called a tower.
The French do not slice it, they tear a baguette.
For centuries, green bananas have made a flour.

Stalin never forgave the world for his smallpox scars.
Paranormal loonies use REM Pods looking for ghosts!
Boxcars in dice (two sixes) mimic a railroad's boxcars.
No one is more bird-brained than game show hosts.

TRUISMS

Jazz became undanceable music after the 1940s.
Trespassers into Area 51 in Nevada are shot dead.
The U.S.A. is a metaphor for *no* political parties.
It is utterly disrespectful to touch a Thai's head.

No parent early losing a child does not take to drink.
Political conventions are now but merely coronations.
Never marry a woman who leaves dishes in the sink.
Doctors, ethically bound, may not inject at executions.

The *NYRB* is a basically Jewish periodical.
Xiaolongbao in China are traditionally eaten for breakfast.
Blacksmith blows were steady, never spasmodical.
Women with short, wide necks: avoid wearing a necklace.

Ethiopia and Eritrea live in perpetual acrimony.
Scares of MSG, safe as salt, are anti-Chinese racism.
Settling who cedes mastery structures matrimony.
Priestly pedophilia is the best argument for laicism.

Chains dampen the vibration of an anvil.
Shakespeare's personality? He gave it all away.
Snuff the flame—never blow out a candle.
A tree crotch is the favorite for a squirrel's drey

On the subject of abortion, both sides are right.
On the subject of abortions, both sides are wrong.
A child's first dream of imagination is flying a kite.
Sibilants should be muted in chanting plainsong.

The Lord's Prayer, for Protestants, asks God to forgive
us our *debts*; for Catholics, "Forgive us our *trespasses*."
Morbidity is the connotation in all behavior ruminative.
An artery, not a veins, determines arterial blood gases.

Only the father is involved in the Scriptural "beget."
Freud, indiscreet, ever shared secrets of his patients.
Budget restraints slow growth, shrink demands increase debt.
Accepting old age is the beginning of complacence.

B.B. King could not sing and play guitar simultaneously.
Brain abnormality is predominantly the cause of SIDS.
The Beatniks most valued poems done extemporaneously.
The French, unlike Americans, have lives away from their kids.

Anywhere love resides, duty is always below it.
No Japanese ships countenance alcohol on board.
A mule can work a steer into the ground, and not know it.
Tiffany goldsmiths create gems they can't afford.

A perfect poem is John Keats' "St. Agnes' Eve."
Diana Arbus was the true subject of her photographs.
Women seem to float in a Dolman—bat-wing—sleeve.
Greta Garbo burnt her mail and never gave autographs.

It is aeration that gives saltwater taffy its chew.
George Washington never signed the Declaration of
    Independence.
Dr. Watson never spotted a Sherlock Holmes clue.
Whipping was one Puritan punishment for Sabbath
    nonattendance.

TRUISMS

Neither calla lilies nor sunflowers have any smell.
Biblical movies, to a one, are fully unwatchable.
A lymphocyte for humoral immunity is the B cell.
Florida's water hyacinth invasion is unstoppable.

Trees in Australia shed their bark but not their leaves.
In 2 Kings, Manasseh is evil, in 2 Chronicles he is good.
Only the empty hand most deserves what it receives.
To help lighten the skin, many Africans use camwood.

No high-level executives were ever prosecuted
for the 2009 mortgage-back securities fraud,
simply because the U.S. *government*, deep-rooted,
was involved, as filthy, corrupt, and slipshod.

How much is enough asks always too little.
Liquidation of oneself by oneself is Chinese torture.
Contextualization—the magic wand for forgiving evil.
Look to the fourth line for a team's hockey enforcer.

Synthetic fertilizers are killing the earth's chromosomes,
wasting water and polluting runoff with toxic extensions.
Living soil needs *nutrients* in the same way microbiomes
colonize our colons and shepherd health to our intestines.

No one knows what the Colossian Heresy was.
No b & w jazz musicians played together in 1920s.
The Civil War to Southerners is the "Lost Cause."
Twenty-five years constitutes the normal life of U.S. pennies.

No original writings found in Scripture exist.
There are eight separate culinary cuisines in China.
High Noon (1952) was a parable for the blacklist
in Hollywood. But Gary Cooper? A HUAC aligner!

Beer can actually be brewed to ferment in a bottle.
Sadducees, unlike Pharisees, rejected an afterlife.
No field of knowledge was neglected by Aristotle.
Van Gogh mainly painted with his palette knife.

Emerson was infamously against charitable giving
"alms to sots, and the thousandfold Relief Societies"
and he included the poor, fools, those in idle living:
"Thy love afar is spite at home!" Fatuous *pieties*!

Hamlet's feigned madness in Shakespeare's play,
regarding the plot, is not at all coherently tactical.
Americans write gray, but the English prefer *grey*.
No kisses so thrill as one given on the clavicle.

Only the lame live sitting astride convenient fences.
The Chinese chop bones to splinters for the marrow.
J. Hendrix was never a draw with Black audiences.
English "whodunits" often feature death by harrow.

Owen Wister, Zane Grey, William S. Hart, Roy Rogers,
Frederic Remington, and Tom Mix were all Easterners.
Brooklyn Dodgers were first called the "Trolley Dodgers."
Protectionism in its every phase is a rebuke to foreigners

TRUISMS

Sex rewires the brain at the onset of puberty.
No gourmand dines more joyously than a goat crunching hay.
It is easiest on a full moon to catch an anchovy.
Men—"*ballerinos*" in Italy—were the first dancers in ballet.

Dante, at each chance for beatitude, always settled a score.
Yale, founded by Puritans, felt Harvard theologically soft.
Ethiopia is lowest choice for volunteers in the Peace Corps.
A pigeon by sound and sun knows the "roads" to its loft.

Hollywood westerns are all the same film.
The Irish harbor a psychotic need to blight a friendship.
The number 13 proliferates on the dollar bill.
China's Qamdo Bamda Airport has the longest airstrip.

Frontal lobe damage causes impairments in inhibition.
"Native Americans" is a nicety political correctness demands.
Pregnancy is thirty times more dangerous than abortion.
Henry James' *What Maisie Knew* is a novel all about hands.

Over-percussiveness is common in piano virtuosi.
St. Paul thought women should be forbidden to teach men.
Males more than females develop the amyotrophy.
Jesus warned even pious Nicodemus he wasn't "born again."

Global temperatures must never exceed 2 degrees Celsius
Rachmaninoff came to loathe his own Prelude in C-sharp minor.
The Desert Fathers (1) did penance and (2) were abstemious.
Cornmeal, sugar, water, yeast are the wants of a "moonshiner."

Nature in its every form is loveliest when pied.
True elegance is interested, not in fashion, but in form.
There are innumerable ways that a sari can be tied.
A murmuration is the proper term for a bird swarm.

A human's organs are the most nutritious for cannibals.
Summer in the Andes come like clockwork on November 15.
The Indian Constitution enshrines protection of all animals.
Van Gogh compulsively contrasted the colors red and green.

Piranesi fathered the visual calculus of M.C. Escher.
Lack of vitamin A causes blindness in rice-producing regions.
Prisoners agree that prison noise is the worst stressor.
Sprinkling oatmeal on their ale is a habit of Glaswegians.

Porky's Revenge did better box office than *Casablanca*.
Albert Camus, an Algerian, loved Algiers, disliked Oran.
Argentinians are obsessed with the bitters Fernet-Branca.
Africa, the great region of animals, has not a single swan.

Creeps, like clams, live in the mud of classified ads.
Africa's fifteen landlocked nations are all impoverished.
Huge shoals of fish in Britain gave us the word *scads*.
Kids of Hollywood stars are largely unaccomplished.

Jesus deals with capital punishment in that venue
when in John 8: 3–11, halting a woman's execution
for adultery—saying "Neither do I condemn you"—
for the accusers' own sins rob them of jurisdiction.

TRUISMS

It costs ten times more to ship cargo by land than sea.
Rafflesia, of a fetid stink, has no roots, stems, or leaves.
Growth is from the top, not from the bottom of a tree.
Cruelty adhibits to those who in a cruel God believes.

You can hear growing rhubarb squeak and pop.
One cannot see, taste, or smell toxic botulin.
Diamonds are rarely accepted by a pawn shop.
Cape Codders enjoy blue fish cooked in gin

Central Park is New York City's front yard.
The rich in past centuries were kinder to the poor.
A ten-year residence is allowed by a green card.
Mardi Gras crowds are seventh heaven for a frotteur.

The fabled Beauty marries beauty, the Beast's discarded.
No attributions to elder Pieter Bruegel can be made with
 certainty.
Job performances are high among the mentally retarded.
Space offers us an endless mystery to ponder the enigma of
 eternity.

A '20s straw hat "boater" needed a grosgrain hatband for style.
Deforested nations—Haiti, Rwanda, Burundi, Nepal—are all poor.
An angry, video game-playing white male teen is called a "Kyle."
A rooster tail spinner to catch brook trout is by far the best lure.

For a Northwest Passage, head to Greenland,
And then, as you sail, simply keep on turning left.
Oysters fried unfloured taste pallid, slightly bland.
Leviticus bans eating a beast whose hoof is cleft.

ALEXANDER THEROUX

To seek perfection, change is constantly required.
Pollyannas prefer saying *homes* instead of *houses*.
Television is the lost region of the totally uninspired
Computer hackers much prefer old web browsers.

Pre-dawn is the best time to begin climbing mountains.
The hippocampus in our brain records long-term memories.
Farewell "bubblers," Boston for public drinking fountains.
Weft-faced weaving alone is done on threaded tapestries.

Blake's "Jerusalem," though a hymn, is a Luddite poem.
New England's snow Feb. 6, 1978, shut the old men up.
No professional garden show countenances use of a gnome.
Little happens in the Chukchi Sea until ice is broken up.

In Jefferson's legal codes, slaves could not testify
against whites, but whites could do so against blacks.
But cut from the Declaration as a vileness to decry,
was his passage against slavery, immediately axed.

The fashionable always stands for conformity,
To snobs, true New York is only the lower two-thirds of
    Manhattan.
Affectation in behavior is an actual deformity.
Spoken Yiddish has a fascination with hyperbaton.

Striped bass normally feed throughout the night.
The emperor of China, enthroned, always faced south.
Roosters are always mutilated before a cockfight.
Taste requires the full need of saliva in the mouth.

TRUISMS

The painted edge between two colors fosters romance.
Elvis Presley films are only about respect and courtesy.
The Curé of Ars, surmising sex, prohibited all dance.
Indiscriminateness is a distinct hazard in all diversity.

Only the mad could live in Escher architecture.
Newton spent years deciphering the prophecies of Daniel.
Class distinctions exist solely and purely as conjecture.
A good nose and soft mouth most befit a hunting spaniel.

Joan of Arc, while at the stake being burnt alive,
wore fool's cap with her four crimes printed on it,
while the English in Normandy sought to connive
that she be comically aped in her pointed bonnet.

There are no fire escapes in any Dakota apartment.
Daughters, in medieval France, took their mothers' surnames.
Cookie sheets are improved by using parchment.
The Nobel Prize, oddly, was never awarded to Henry James.

T. Jefferson *hated all clergy* as "despots against liberty."
Paperwhite blossoms, from indole, exude the stench of urine.
A New England lobster roll is hopeless without celery.
A bride sewing her wedding dress is taboo to a Honduran.

Richard III's "Winter of our discontent,"
never forget, is "made glorious summer."
Pitch, not loudness, creates a tonic accent.
A Nixon burglar was called a "plumber."

Fish taste better steam-grilled on a cedar plank.
A debt that goes unpaid is a flinty pain increased.
Short men are unacceptable at any sperm bank.
Nothing evokes regret as disdain by the deceased.

Jesus condemned sins of the flesh less than sins of pride.
Only certain hairstyles are approved in North Korea.
There is no sense of neighborhood on NYC's East Side.
Being a barbaric foreigner to the Greeks doomed Medea.

Movies are now made for zany, wacky clothes-wearing,
disparaging, hair-dyed, tatted, out-of-step California teens.
Nothing can explain the oddity of human couples pairing.
The small watch pocket is inexplicable in standard jeans.

In his comedies, Shakespeare finds the women
greater than their mates: Portia, Viola, Imogen,
Beatrice, Hermione, Portia, Helena, Rosalind,
and Adriana, all infinitely superior to their men.

Although Christmas is proscribed in North Korea,
December 24th celebrates Kim Jong-Il's mother!
The Galilean Aramaic of Jesus was mocked in Judea.
No one ever makes use of the word *foremother*.

It is illegal to play radios in all of London's royal parks.
No sculpture can be attributed to Leonardo da Vinci.
Physicists speak of "flavors"—differences—in quarks:
up, down, strange, charm, bottom, top, and carefree.

TRUISMS

Bicycles in North Korea have license plates.
Preservationist hotels in Maine use no air-conditioners.
There is no official language in the United States.
Beneficiaries in immigration seek corrupt petitioners.

Oceans are 30% more acidic than thirty years ago.
It's illegal for Palestinians to gather on the West Bank.
Crofters greatly value —"white gold"—seabird guano.
Braising is a must for meat cuts from the foreshank.

Anchovies and jellyfish, rivals, compete for food.
East Siders in Manhattan look down on the West Side.
A masticating cow's edibles are quadruple chewed.
Snobs hold it demeaning to live in a "double-wide."

Time is burying us by the shovelful every minute.
New York's Harlem is anywhere north of 85th Street.
Shape and styles of a novel as a genre has no limit.
The Chinese consider jellyfish as an aphrodisiacal treat.

The Nazis, leader mad, all loved *Coriolanus*.
The Tudors disparaged the Plantagenets.
To charge a starving man for theft is heinous.
French law has rules for traditional baguettes.

Holy Scripture constantly rails against an east wind.
Sassafras was the first export from the New World.
Kith indicates a person's country, family one's *kin*.
Pitching in baseball is not merely to fling or to hurl.

ALEXANDER THEROUX

The American flag has had as many as twenty-seven versions.
Waterfront cities in the USA alone take pride of place.
Mark Twain called all sexual dalliances "excursions."
A singer's range distinguishes a baritone from a bass.

Deluxe restaurant menus never feature bluefish,
simply because its flesh is an unappetizing brown;
the same with wild Baldwin apples, not swish,
too ugly for supermarkets to sell or have around.

Christ never said he was "Son of Solomon,"
or "Son of Abraham," only "Son of David."
Fish all live and breath on dissolved oxygen.
Lower exports and inflation are interrelated.

Claudius in the play *Hamlet* is never named,
simply given the speech prefix "King."
Carried flat, an American flag is profaned.
No Sikh wedding doesn't involve a nose ring.

The hexagon is the strongest shape known.
Silence is always interpreted as agreement.
Adularescent light enhances a moonstone.
Weak causes make speakers more vehement.

Actors crave to play phantasmatic villains.
A need for law implies violation of a law.
Males are props at all debutante cotillions.
Broccoli is healthier when it is eaten raw.

TRUISMS

Changing your posture wins hot dog eating contests.
A 2-to-1 crew-passenger ratio ran the old *Queen Mary*.
Lady Diana Spencer made fashionable the coatdress.
WWI's official song: "It's a Long Way to Tipperary."

Most people learn to see what they expect.
No true Scot wants "Betty Windsor" as his queen.
Public clocks have given names in Utrecht.
Plants don't absorb but *reflect* light that's green.

Fear is a major component of battlefield bravery.
A "plain man" in Shakespeare always dissimulates.
Child beauty pageants smack of the unsavory.
126 pounds is the maximum limit of featherweights.

Genius is the sole rationale for artistic complexity.
Inhospitality—*xenia*—was the vile crime of Sisyphus.
The purpose of any maze is contrived perplexity.
Adolescent flirtation involves being mischievous.

Three angels, only, are mentioned in the Bible:
Michael, Gabriel, and evil Abaddon—Lucifer!
Adaptability is the main ingredient of survival.
Considered an actual speech organ is the uvula.

Andy Warhol's goal was to become a machine.
The English heart beats faster on St. Crispin's day.
No crop has fed the planet more than the broad bean.
When water is in your diet, a likely drink is whey.

Agincourt was won by the Welsh longbow.
Removing eyeglasses means candor in movies.
The push of the foot depends on the big toe.
The most counterfeited currency on earth is rupees.

German polysyllabic words conjoin like sticklebricks.
Women's painted eyebrows look surprised—or menacing.
Consecotaleophobia is a pathological fear of chopsticks.
Presumption is also ironic despair in the act of censoring.

Every suicide has seen absolutely no alternative.
Both Emerson and Thoreau held the South in contempt.
Conservation is a *bête noire* of ultra conservative.
Buying pet food in the United States is fully tax exempt.

Schiller always wrote with his feet in warm water.
In America, democracy and conformity are confused.
Permission, not endorsement, makes an *imprimatur*.
Teeth point toward the apex in anything saw-toothed.

Most great collectors suffered early as children
from neglect or crucial absence of their parents,
so, find affirmation and security in the building
of that grasping passion, permanent assurance.

No reading of the Book of Revelations is definitive.
Darwin termed his *Origins* the "devil's theology."
Neither Arabic nor Modern Greek uses an infinitive.
For many Japanese, suicide constitutes an apology.

TRUISMS

Stability of any kind is defenseless against time.
To make mayo, use *room temperature* ingredients.
To remain only in your head is to lose your mind.
Mercy flies in the face of any and all expedience.

Dostoevsky loathed the city of London—"Baal,"
he named it, as Maxim Gorky hated New York,
referring to it as "The City of the Yellow Devil,"
where gold is worshipped as a pagan bulwark.

Philistines have a penchant for comma splicing.
Buddhism has never been antagonistic to other faiths.
Dubious are the capacious gaps in wine-pricing.
Narcissism remains the strongest pull in lifting weights.

Never cut from a living tree any wood that's burled.
Robert Frost held that Nature is indifferent to all.
"Thy Kingdom come" is a plea for the end of the world.
To an Irish bride-to-be is tendered a Galway shawl.

A mind must extricate itself from ties of the will.
Czesław Miłosz claims Polish men dislike themselves.
Medical properties hale from the toxic flower squill.
Mystic symbolism is attached to all number twelves.

After death, you exist with your own legions,
for in all eternity what you are is how you see;
you share your fate precisely in those regions
where in your life, being you, you chose to be.

No Americans revere Edgar A. Poe like the French.
Dante and Beatrice prove a remote worship is best.
All waters are home to the voracious, invasive tench.
A discolored comb always indicates viral fowl pest.

Swedenborg thought angels formerly human beings.
A handful of many lifetimes cannot exculpate Judas.
Emotional impact is linked to the height of ceilings.
Still unknown and unknowable is the cause of lupus.

Attending church is not for the elect, but sinners.
Redwood forests, gloomy, all grow in perpetual fog.
Adolf Hitler felt ill-at-ease with native Berliners.
Camouflage by self-anointing protects a hedgehog.

Lithuanians consider a taboo to spit on a fire
or to place a bread loaf on a table upside down.
Sopranos commonly sing the melody in a choir.
Pigments on the Lascaux cave were reddish brown.

Basketball is the only original U. S. sport.
One tablespoon of vinegar gives great mileage.
Loud yawning has been ruled "contempt of court."
Clematis and wisteria need support by treillage.

The Chinese use ginger to disguise overripe meat.
Citizen Kane initially failed as a box-office success.
Most of the soil carbon on Earth is stored by peat.
Opening and closing a hand is a signal for distress.

TRUISMS

Stouts greatly predominate the Irish beer market.
The Salem witch trials were held in what is now Danvers.
The Minangkabau of Sumatra are a matriarchate.
Confucius denied swords to anyone incapable of dances.

No cast iron pan should be washed with soap.
Composer Olivier Messiaen said birds alone are great artists.
81 canonizations have been extended to a Pope.
Only the first four fingers of each hand are used by harpists.

Aardvarks, suspicious, only come out, early, at night.
While words are always written right to left in Arabic,
numbers in that language are written from left to right.
Maimonides cursed Jesus Christ as a detestable heretic.

Otto Klemperer conducted orchestras sitting down.
Pacific scallops are tough, dingy; Atlantic tender, translucent.
Cornwallis never personally surrendered at Yorktown.
It is ice crystals that make those high polar clouds noctilucent.

Indifference to injustice makes one its accomplice.
Electronic fishing (by any use of battery) is illegal.
The AIPIC lobby virtually owns the U.S. Congress.
A female is curiously larger than a male bald eagle.

Visionaries believe that they pray better outdoors.
O represents outside the nine in horse racing results.
Green wine—*vinho verde*—is drunk in the Azores.
C. Hitchens called Christ "Santa Claus for Adults."

Elvis broke Las Vegas rules by singing Gospel hymns.
Sambuca is an *ammazzacaffè*, a killer of coffee taste.
Crocodile is the most sought-after of all animal skins.
Packaging material makes up most American waste.

Slurp noodles in China—a taboo is to cut them.
1,800 souls have jumped off the Golden Gate Bridge.
Stock prices are said to dictate length in a hem.
Indians' favorite teeth-cleaning twig was the pepperidge.

"Grocery" was the old frontier term for a saloon.
Ferdinand Porsche developed and designed the Volkswagen.
For pathos, nothing matches mournful cry of a loon.
Some restaurants garnish plates with the (edible) snapdragon.

Zinc phosphide in any form will kill a rodent.
Lincoln insisted all photographs of him appear sober.
Oxygen on moist iron is the ultimate corrodent.
The eighth calendar month should literally be October.

Civil War uniforms consistently varied.
Iceland is considered the safest county in Europe.
In Shakespearean comedy, heroines married
often to avoid convent life, in a feisty flare-up.

Most U.S. chickens are fattened with estrogen.
Women-only communes all favor leftist pedigrees.
CAD-CAM and robots now assist a brain surgeon.
What has disappeared, ironically, makes memories.

TRUISMS

There is very little crime in the Netherlands.
Mega-yachts are typically over 260 feet (80 meters).
Only a status symbol (and pointless) are cigar bands.
Amateur journalism is the ugly spawn of tweeters.

Baseball players should be paid by performance.
Shell money is still currency in New Guinea.
Brunei severely punishes gender nonconformance.
Iblis is by far the worst among Muslim jinni.

Every room is full of things that are not in it
is a theory philosophers may affirm or deny,
but, out of logical necessity, to look within it
is what, regarding perception, one must try.

Opera fanatics never use a diva's first name.
Jean Rhys's novels are utterly depressing.
Every calumny is calculated to try to maim.
Mere arousal is given rise by cross-dressing.

No plot is more complex than *Il Trovatore*.
Wild rivals, Callas and Tebaldi never got along.
The perfect varnish comes from resin of a kauri.
A mainstay cultural dress is the Filipino barong.

Soprano Nellie Melba would brook no rivals.
Norwegians tolerate no slur against their king.
No drama can exceed normal airport "arrivals."
Infant gums are hurt by a frozen teething ring.

Bigleaf maple wood grain is visually psychedelic.
The discipline of listening is an endangered skill.
Idolatry must be avoided in veneration of a relic.
The mound insures the temperature of an anthill.

Jesus, oddly, once healed a woman with his cloak.
Prior to the 1920s, all U.S. stop signs were yellow
The best of a true limerick constitutes a dirty joke.
Tuned in perfect fifths are the four strings of a cello.

Eye contact in conversation is a must in Paraguay.
Faulkner's *Absalom, Absalom!* is bereft of paragraphs.
The most planted grape on earth is sauvignon cabernet.
Indians signaled by using shiny knives as heliographs.

Diana Kennedy hated all Tex-Mex food variations.
Wearing a baseball cap backwards bespeaks duncery.
Jehovah's Witnesses excoriate the United Nations.
Waste is the primary objection to disposable cutlery.

Plot holes in James Bond books are sky wide.
The way boats sail and the way to steer a boat are the same.
Synthesized urine used in fertilizer is carbamide.
After an issued hurricane watch, forget an insurance claim.

The CIA poison used to try to kill Castro was trillium.
A typhus patient gives off an intolerable stench.
A wife, no mere mistress, was the prayer of Pygmalion.
Michif links indigenous language with Canadian French.

TRUISMS

"Inclusions" in the diamond industry mean flaws;
a "strop" is a bad buy, a gemstone that won't sell,
also called a "pancake", a "fisheye," "ugly hawse,"
which, not selling, brings no luck or Yiddish *mazl*.

Sir Robert Peel hated, and was despised by, the Irish.
Movies based on comic books are louder with brighter colors.
Wearing socks with sandals is the definition of unstylish.
Wisdom teeth, erupting at 17, are the rearmost of your molars.

Mini health robots to travel in the body are in the works.
To Ian Fleming, James Bond resembled Hoagy Carmichael.
Oaths of a Scottish Highlander were always sworn on dirks.
Seventh-day Adventists believe that Jesus was St. Michael.

A diamond burned would give off carbon dioxide gas.
Every James Bond villain lives secluded in a secret lair.
Mere wealth, not pedigree, systemizes American class.
Gender in forensic crime labs cannot be identified by hair.

The Pilgrims forewent bathing; good clothing sufficed;
cleanliness at the time was never associated with water.
Ruling world economy (Rev. 13: 16–17) signals the Antichrist.
The oldest professional is not a prostitute but a potter.

Ricin poison, from castor oil plants, has no antidotes.
In Chinese restaurants, tables are wiped with aromatic tea.
Disagreement in writing is rendered by double quotes.
The Campbells and Macdonalds clans could never agree

ALEXANDER THEROUX

Thomas Edison and Nikola Tesla were constantly at odds.
Jewelers, due to shoplifters. show only two pieces at a time.
People believe (wrongly) that lightning *seeks* lighting rods.
Jollof rice and plantains comprises a Nigerian lunchtime.

One ton of recycled paper spares seventeen trees.
Thoreau ever walked westward, the nation's destiny.
More than four inches is illegal for golf tees.
From heartwood only comes the blackwood ebony.

R.W. Emerson thought Dickens a superficial writer.
Eleanor Roosevelt adored the music of Cole Porter.
Bug-collecting was a side-line of every lamplighter.
The best cuts of meat are from the beef front quarter.

Quaker George Fox prayed in holes of hollow trees.
Henry Miller declared that thought was a narcotic.
Asking no questions is an offense in interviewees.
Cod liver oil is held to be a natural antipsychotic.

Candy canes model on the shepherd's crook.
April is the best month for the Dow.
To be flowing is the characteristic of brooks.
With God omitted, there is no vow.

Tibet's Mount Kailash has never been summitted.
No high's as heady as glue-sniffing rubber cement.
Self-repudiation is involved in anything coveted.
A truism's an assertion that seeks common assent.

Fortiter Feliciter Fideliter

www.ingramcontent.com/pod-product-compliance
Lightning Source LLC
La Vergne TN
LVHW012244070526
838201LV00090B/117